OUR CHILDREN'S SONGS

OUR CHILDREN'S SONGS

Teaching the Gospel with the Children's Songbook

VIRGINIA B. CANNON

Deseret Book Company
Salt Lake City, Utah

Library of Congress Cataloging-in-Publication Data

Cannon, Virginia B.
  Our children's songs: teaching the gospel with the children's songbook /
    Virginia B. Cannon.
      p.   cm.
    Includes index.
    ISBN 0-87579-583-8
    1. Sunday schools—Hymns—History and criticism.   2. Sunday
schools—Hymns—Instruction and study.   3. Children's songs—History
and criticism.   4. Children's songs—Instruction and study.
5. Church of Jesus Christ of Latter-day Saints—Hymns—Juvenile—
History and criticism.   6. Church of Jesus Christ of Latter-day
Saints—Hymns—Juvenile—Instruction and study.   I. Children's
songbook of the Church of Jesus Christ of Latter-day Saints.
II. Title.
M2193.C538   1989 Suppl.   92-24975
                                                                  CIP
                                                               AC MN

Printed in the United States of America

10   9   8   7   6   5   4   3   2

Contents

Preface

I have prepared *Our Children's Songs* to help music leaders, teachers, and families teach from the *Children's Songbook* in such a way that children will grow to love the songs and their messages. Included in the book are brief stories of how some of the songs came to be, a short analysis of the message and musical qualities of each one, teaching suggestions, biographies of authors and composers, and facts about the history of children's music in the Church. It was not possible to include the extensive historic data for each song which a researcher might desire; however, I hope the information will provide interesting ideas and feelings that will keep children more involved in the songs and the significance of their teachings.

The *Children's Songbook* is a wonderful achievement. It provides a collection of songs that are interesting for children, that are fun for them to sing, and that teach them the gospel of Jesus Christ. It was a privilege to be part of the team that planned and prepared this notable publication. Not long after I was called to be a counselor to Dwan J. Young in the general Primary presidency in 1980, we talked of the need to combine the Primary music resources into one volume. *Sing with Me* had been produced in 1969; this was followed by *Activity Songs and Verses, More Songs for Children,* and the *Supplement to More Songs for Children.* Other fine children's songs had been published in the *Friend* magazine. Music leaders found it difficult to juggle the music from all these sources. We were excited to be able to proceed with the project of preparing a consolidated children's songbook.

As first counselor in the Primary, I was assigned to oversee this assignment. With the combined efforts of a capable Primary music committee, the General Music Committee of the Church, and the Church publication services, the task went forward. I am particularly thankful for those who happened to be in vital positions at the right time, for their talent and suitability to the task were remarkable. However, I firmly believe that the *Children's Songbook* came about because the Lord knew the children of the latter days needed this gift of music to help them understand the gospel and to solidify principles by which they should live. If these particular people had not been available, others would have been raised up to accomplish this important task.

The *Children's Songbook* not only presents fine music for the children of the LDS Church, but its appearance and presentation are excellent. The *Children's Songbook* received an award of excellence in book design from the Art Directors of Salt Lake City.

Worthy of special mention are four talented artists who were commissioned to create pictures for the *Children's Songbook* that would have a soft, sweet look to illustrate the themes of the songs. Their work has given the book a wonderful feeling of beauty and warmth to accompany the messages of the music. Richard Hull did the art for the Home and Family, Fun and Activity, and Preludes sections. Phyllis Luch created the illustration on the cover, the two-page art pieces that introduce each section, and a few of the drawings in the first three sections. Virginia Sargent's contributions are the fourteen pieces in the Nature and Seasons section. Beth Whittaker prepared all the small art pieces in the Heritage section and some of the pictures in the first three sections.

I have become aware of the momentous contributions of the composers and authors of the children's songs. Most gave their talents without remuneration so that the children could be blessed. Of significance is the inheritance of dedicated members of the Primary General Board. Since the earliest days of the Primary, board members have written words and music for Primary conferences, for special programs, or as they became aware of particular needs of the children of the Church. Twenty-three of these women wrote words or music for songs now contained in the *Children's Songbook.* Some of the songs in the book date back to pioneer times, when the first book of songs for children was compiled by Eliza R. Snow in 1880. Since that time noted LDS composers and writers have unselfishly added to the children's musical heritage, as have many writers who do not belong to the Church. To each of these I express my deepest gratitude.

I am appreciative of those who have offered their support of my efforts in compiling the information contained within this volume. My dear friends of the present general Primary presidency have given me encouragement. The authors and composers have willingly told me of their experiences in writing the songs and have supplied biographical information. Laurel Rohlfing, a former member of the Primary General Board and the chairman of the Primary music committee at the time the *Children's Songbook* was introduced, suggested some of the teaching ideas that are included with the songs. My family has also been most cooperative and supportive.

Lastly, I express my love to the children — my own twenty-four dear grandchildren; the children in the Monument Park 10th Ward with whom I have the blessing to be working at the present time; and children all over the world, many of whom I have had the privilege of meeting personally. For each of them I feel a deep love and admiration and a desire that they will live the principles of truth that they sing about in the songs from the *Children's Songbook.*

Introduction

On a warm summer evening in Israel, a group of students from the Brigham Young University Jerusalem Center gathered on the hillside of the Mount of Olives in the Orson Hyde Memorial Garden. After four and a half months of study at the Center, the young people were given the choice of spending their last evening in Israel anywhere in the area that would be most memorable for them. One by one and two by two the students began arriving here — the place where during the last months they had assembled for sacrament and testimony meetings. There was little conversation, but soon their voices spontaneously sang out softly and clearly with songs from their childhood: "I Know My Father Lives," "Jesus Once Was a Little Child," "Tell Me the Stories of Jesus," and, of course, "I Am a Child of God." At this time of thoughtful meditation and remembrance of special experiences, it was the songs of their childhood, the Primary songs, that became a means of expressing their deep feelings.

Ten-year-old Joshua was lost deep in a mine for five days. He had gone with his father and a group of Varsity Scouts to explore the mine. Through a miscue, Joshua became separated from the other boys and was soon hopelessly lost and alone, without food or water. He prayed, and his prayers were answered with a feeling of comfort and assurance. During the long hours when he was not sleeping, Joshua sang "I Am a Child of God" and a patriotic song he had learned in school. It was music that came to his mind to bring stability and peace. After Joshua had been safely rescued and was recovering from the trauma, a neighbor brought the boy a tape of Primary songs. Joshua felt secure as he went to sleep each night listening to and singing "A Child's Prayer." Music can be a healer for the troubled soul.

Katie was a sweet, sensitive child approaching her eighth birthday. She knew that when the bishop interviewed her for her baptism, he would ask her to repeat the fourth Article of Faith, as he had done with her best friend. Katie's mother worked with her, but she could not seem to learn the sequence of the words. Then her mother remembered that the Articles of Faith had been set to music, and she began teaching Katie the words and music to "The

1

Fourth Article of Faith." In no time Katie had learned the song, and when she had her interview with the bishop, she *sang* the fourth Article of Faith to him.

The power of music is immeasurable. It can influence lives and change behavior, for good or for bad. Many who have written songs for children have recognized the importance of music in teaching them gospel principles, in uniting them in commitment to a principle, and in sustaining them in troubled times.

Scriptures reinforce the importance of music. In Job 38:7 we read that when the Father told us about our opportunity to come to earth, we sang and shouted for joy. Music was a significant part of religious occasions and secular activities during Old Testament times. Angels sang at the birth of Jesus (Luke 2:13–14), and the apostles sang a hymn at the Last Supper (Matthew 26:30). In latter-day revelation the Lord told Emma Smith, through the Prophet Joseph, "And it shall be given thee, also, to make a selection of sacred hymns, as it shall be given thee, which is pleasing unto me, to be had in my church. For my soul delighteth in the song of the heart; yea, the song of the righteous is a prayer unto me, and it shall be answered with a blessing upon their heads." (D&C 25:11–12.)

This book has been prepared to help parents, leaders, and teachers present and teach the songs in the *Children's Songbook* more effectively, so that these songs will have a lasting impact in the lives of the children. The suggestions offered are intended to help music leaders develop their own presentations. Music leaders should study the Primary music resources and "Using the Songbook" from the *Children's Songbook*, pages 300–304, for further direction in presenting the songs to children.

Singing in Primary is a unifying activity that brings children and their leaders together in a oneness of purpose. Music sets the mood for learning, fortifies principles taught, and allows the children to experience the joy of singing.

Singing in the home, especially of the songs learned in Primary, reinforces gospel teachings and provides a joyful activity that binds family members together. Often parents can "sing a lesson," without preaching, at an appropriate teaching moment. Hearts can be touched as family members participate in music just for the fun of it. The *Children's Songbook* is a marvelous resource that provides the home with songs covering a wide variety of subjects and circumstances.

INTRODUCTION

The great desire of all who have been involved in the preparation and publication of the *Children's Songbook* is that children's lives will be enriched and blessed through the songs of the gospel — that they will be given strength to resist temptations and have a commitment to live the commandments of the Lord.

Teaching the Songs to Children

Children generally learn songs by the rote method — that is, by hearing the words and music and then imitating what they hear. The most effective teaching methods and aids are those that help the children listen carefully to the music, encourage them to sing the parts as they hear them, and reinforce the message of the words. In order to learn by the rote method, children need to hear the song sung several times, words and music together. As they listen, they should be actively involved, either by listening for some specific words or musical idea or by doing something with their hands, bodies, or with objects.

The leader can prepare to introduce a song to the children by:

1. *Studying the words.* Begin by determining the message the children can learn from the song. You may have personal experiences that you could relate to the message. Look for words that you might need to explain or to help children pronounce. Identify keywords or phrases that will help the children learn the song more quickly, including words that suggest teaching aids or actions.

2. *Studying the music.* Look for memorable characteristics of the melody and rhythm patterns that make the song interesting. Determine which words should be given musical emphasis (high or low notes, holding, slowing down, and so forth). Notice mood and tempo markings that add to the feeling of the song.

3. *Planning the song presentation.* Start with an attention-getter to draw the children into the music. Then involve the children in actively listening to the song, words and music together, at their level of understanding. Provide singing experiences, repeating phrases as needed for learning. Share your testimony of the principles taught.

4. *Practicing the presentation.*

5. *Preparing spiritually.*

Using Questions

It is an established fact that children will long remember songs that they have learned to sing from memory. Questioning is an important technique for encouraging children to actively listen so that they can learn a song quickly. The following steps can be used with the questioning method of teaching songs:

1. Ask the children a question that can be answered by some exact words of the song.

2. Invite the children to try to discover the answer as they listen to you sing the song.

3. Accept answers from the children. If there is any doubt about the correctness of the responses, sing the song again so the children can check the answer.

4. Invite the children to sing the phrase of the song that includes the answer to the question. (Sing the entire song and cue the children at the right time for them to join in singing this phrase of the song.)

5. Continue to ask questions, one at a time, each time singing the song for the children and inviting them to join in adding each new phrase that they learn, until they are able to sing the complete song with you.

Teaching Aids

Your enthusiasm, actions, and eye contact with the children provide the best teaching aids for music in Primary. However, pictures and other audiovisual materials can focus children's attention, stimulate interest in a song, and clarify the message. Teaching aids should teach correct gospel concepts. Children are easily confused about concepts that are misrepresented. For example, confusion may result if the gift of the Holy Ghost is illustrated as a wrapped present, or if Heavenly Father is represented by a picture of the Savior. Words should be represented accurately and not with sound-alike pictures. The word "I," for instance, should not be represented with a picture of a human eye.

Children enjoy singing time more when the songs are presented in a variety of ways. The following teaching aids and methods can add variety for the children:

1. *Words and pictures.* The children could:
   a. Arrange keywords or pictures in correct order.
   b. Identify rhyming words.
   c. Count the times a word or phrase is repeated.
   d. Answer the questions "who?" "what?" "where?" and "how?" of a song.
2. *Dramatizations, costumes, and props.* The children could:
   a. Pretend to be characters in a song. They could use simple props when appropriate.

    b. Draw pictures of characters or objects in a song.

    c. Make simple puppets from socks, paper sacks, or paper plates to represent characters in a song.

3. *Movement.* Movement is a powerful learning tool for young children, and older children respond to movement appropriate to their age. The children could:

    a. Use specific actions when suggested by the words in a song.

    b. Move to rhythms, melodies, and phrases of the music by clapping hands, tapping feet, nodding heads, or snapping fingers. They could also use their entire bodies to show the up-and-down direction of the melody.

    c. Use deaf sign language for words in a song. Teach a few keywords rather than a sign for every word.

4. *Visual aids.* Add variety to song presentations by using objects that children can see, touch, and manipulate. Examples:

    a. Clothesline on which to hang keywords or pictures.

    b. Flannelboard for pictures or word strips.

    c. Chalkboard on which to draw simple figures or shapes to illustrate a song.

    d. Objects on sticks — pictures or word strips — for children to hold.

    e. Roller box in which pictures (drawn by you or the children) can be displayed. Glue pictures on a roll of paper and rotate the roll so the pictures show through an opening in the box.

    f. Flip charts — pictures or word strips on cards, joined together by rings.

    g. Puzzles — large pictures cut into several pieces and put together as the song is sung.

    h. Letters to a keyword, to be unscrambled or hidden in the room.

    i. Objects that relate to the song, placed in a box or sack or hidden in the room.

5. *People resources.* An effective change of pace is to involve other people in teaching songs. Here are some ideas:

    a. Children in Primary are often the best visual aids for many of the songs.

    b. Invite a guest actor to represent a person mentioned in a song.

    c. Tell stories about the author or composer of a song, or, if possible, invite the actual composer or author to visit.

   d. Have a family, Primary leaders and teachers, a Primary class, or a soloist introduce a song to the children.

   e. Invite a guest to come in and bear testimony of a gospel concept taught in a song.

6. *Audiovisual equipment.*

   a. Use transparencies on an overhead projector to "build" a picture or write keywords from the song.

   b. A tape recorder can be used in several ways. You might play a recording of a song to help teach it, record the children's singing so they can listen to and evaluate themselves, or record sounds or clues to help the children identify an idea from a song.

Musical Ideas

You can illustrate the melody line of a song or a phrase of a song in several ways. For example, the first line from the song "Teach Me to Walk in the Light" could be illustrated in any of the ways shown in figure 1.

Show the melody picture to the children and hum the melody while tracing it with your hand. Ask the children:

1. To notice which words occur on various parts of the melody.

2. To listen to find another place in the song where the same melody occurs.

3. To trace the melody with you with their hands or move their bodies to show the up-and-down direction of the tune.

4. To discover what words come at the highest point or the lowest point of the phrase.

You could illustrate several phrases of the song and invite the children to place them in the correct order. Or draw the melody picture with figures relating to the song, such as stars or hearts. Using variations of these suggestions, you can capture the children's interest in the structure of the melody and encourage them to listen more carefully as they learn the song.

In a similar way, you can use the rhythmic pattern of a phrase and illustrate the long and short beats with dashes or with traditional notes. Invite the children to clap or tap the rhythm pattern several times and then identify where they hear that rhythm in the song. They could continue by counting how many times they hear the same rhythm pattern, or by playing it on simple percussion instruments or sticks when it occurs.

Line contour of melody

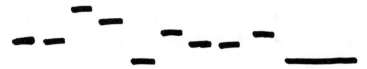

Short lines indicating the pitches of the notes

Representation of musical phrases

Traditional notes indicating the pitches of the notes

Exact representation of the melody on a staff

Figure 1

Reviewing the Songs

After the children have learned a new song, it is important for them to sing it frequently to implant it firmly in their memories. There are numerous creative ways you can review the songs with them. For example:

1. Show pictures or visual aids you used to teach the song and ask the children what song the pictures remind them of.

2. Allow the children to choose their favorite Primary songs.

3. Play "Name That Tune." (The pianist plays a few notes of the song to see if the children can guess what it is.)

4. Use a riddle to encourage the children to guess which song you are thinking of.

5. Add variety to the song by having different groups sing the verses or phrases: the girls, the boys, a class, the leaders and teachers. Try adding a descant, an alto part, or an instrumental accompaniment, or play a recording of the song.

6. Plan a "choose and review" time; select several songs and provide interesting ways for the children to choose which of these they will sing:

    a. Hide the titles of songs on a poster and let the children take turns finding them.

    b. Have the song titles written on slips of paper placed in a jar, a sack, or some other container from which children can draw.

    c. Place song titles around the room or under the children's chairs for them to discover.

    d. Make a tree (on a chart or from a real tree branch) and decorate it for each season or month with appropriate ornaments (for example, hearts for February, eggs for Easter, apples for fall, or snowflakes for winter) that contain the song titles. The children take turns removing one of the ornaments to find the name of a song they will sing.

Whatever methods you use, frequently provide the children an enjoyable experience in reviewing the songs so that their musical repertoire is constantly growing.

Helping Children to Sing Correctly

You should help the children sing clearly and with a natural, childlike tone quality. Do not encourage them to sing with a loud, forced, harsh tone that can cause vocal strain. The following vocal techniques will help children produce a lovely singing tone:

1. *Posture.* Good posture is the key to proper breathing and pleasing tone quality. Children should sit or stand erectly. If seated, they could move forward in their seats and sit with the upper body straight.

2. *Breathing.* Controlled breathing can help children develop beautiful tone quality, sustain musical phrases, and sing in tune.

3. *Tone quality.* Children should project a light, free, natural tone quality.

Help the children start and stop together, enunciate the words together, pronounce the words uniformly, sing the melody accurately, sing with expression, and watch and follow you.

There are two ways to conduct children's music: by pitch-level conducting or with standard beat patterns. There are some helpful directions regarding these conducting methods on pages 300–301 of the *Children's Songbook.*

Conclusion

As music leaders and parents sing and teach the songs from the *Children's Songbook* they should:

1. Be patient. Do not tire of repetition. Help the children understand and internalize the principles taught in the songs.

2. Demonstrate for the children the joy that comes in singing the songs of the gospel. Make singing fun and enjoyable.

3. Encourage excellence in musical expression. Help the children learn to appreciate the beauty in fine music. They will feel a sense of accomplishment in a good musical presentation.

May the children see the songs in the *Children's Songbook* as a representation of the truth and beauty of the gospel of Jesus Christ, and may they remember the words and melodies of these songs at important times in their lives.

The Songs

A Child's Prayer   12

Words and Music: Janice Kapp Perry
First Line: Heavenly Father, are you really there?
Topics Indexed: Prayer, Prayer Songs, Two-part Songs

This song helps children understand that Heavenly Father is real and that he gives help and comfort to his children. It is written in two parts: (1) a child's words to Heavenly Father, asking if he is really there to listen to and answer prayers, and (2) an answer to the child, giving assurance that Heavenly Father hears and that he loves and cares for every child. Each part is written to a different melody. The accompaniment does not contain the melody of either part, so it would probably not be used until the melodies have become familiar. The composer suggests that in performance the two parts should each be sung separately first, and then put together. The song lends itself to performance for special programs or meetings that emphasize the importance of teaching children.

The music includes an interesting variety of rhythm and melody patterns. Each phrase of the melody in the top staff begins with triplet pick-up notes or an eighth note and two sixteenth notes. Make sure these are not all sung as triplets.

Teaching Suggestions:

1. Introduce this song with the words of Matthew 19:14 printed on a poster or chalkboard. Ask the children to listen to the song to discover how the scripture is used in it.

2. Ask such questions as: "How do you feel when you pray?" "What do you ask Heavenly Father when you pray?" "Who listens to your prayers?" Sing the song and ask the children to listen for what the child in the song is asking Heavenly Father.

3. Have the children tap or clap the rhythm of the first melody, encouraging them to notice the difference between the upbeats of triplets and eighth/two-sixteenth notes.

4. Express your belief in the reality of our Heavenly Father and that he does truly listen to our prayers.

A Happy Family   198

Words and Music: Moiselle Renstrom
First Line: I love mother; she loves me
Topics Indexed: Fathers, Grandparents, Happiness, Mothers

This favorite song helps children express their love for their families. It has been changed in the *Children's Songbook* from 4/4 time to 2/4 time to help add lightness and energy. The accompaniment has been thinned by eliminating the left-hand chords, giving it a gentler feeling. The children in the younger age groups and even in the nursery love this song and seem to never tire of singing it. The melody flows naturally, mostly on even beats, and should be easy for children to learn. Alternate words, such as "grandpa" and "grandma" and names of the children, may be substituted for "mother," "father," "brother," and "sister."

Teaching Suggestions:

1. This song almost teaches itself as the children hear it sung. Use pictures of families to introduce it.

2. Have the children role-play the parts of mother, father, brother, and sister. Use simple props, such as an apron for mother, a tie for father, a ball for brother, and a doll for sister. Groups of children can take turns portraying the parts while the others sing the song.

3. Use stick puppets to represent the characters.

A Happy Helper   197

Words and Music: Moiselle Renstrom
First Line: Whenever I am good and kind and help someone I
  see
Topics Indexed: Cheerfulness, Happiness, Service

This song teaches that we are happy and kind when we give service to others. Little children could sing it as they are taught how to be helpful to parents, grandparents, and friends.

The song has a light, eight-measure melody with a mostly even rhythm of eighth notes. The second four measures imitate, with some variation, the first four measures.

Teaching Suggestions:

1. Teach verse two of the song first, since it is simpler and contains the complete message. Children will learn it quite easily by rote. Display pictures of children helping others.

2. Sing the song to the children and ask them how helping makes them feel. Then sing the entire song using a "follow-the-leader" technique — sing a phrase and ask them to repeat it without breaking the rhythm, then go on to the next phrase, and so on.

3. In the nursery, the leader could sing this song while encouraging the children to clean up. It can become a "theme song" to indicate that it is time to put the toys away or help in some other way.

A Prayer   22

Words and Music: Moiselle Renstrom
First Line: Father in Heaven, on this lovely day
Topics Indexed: Happiness, Honesty, Kindness, Prayer Songs,
*   Sharing, Talents*

The lyrics of this song are expressions that a child might offer to Heavenly Father in prayer. The words could help a child think of ways to be kind, honest, fair, and willing to share. The song can help children learn the meaning and language of prayer.

The rhythm of "A Prayer" is constant and even with mostly quarter notes through the sixteen measures. Each of the four musical phrases is different. The song should be sung smoothly, with connected tones.

Teaching Suggestions:

1. Ask the children to name some of the things that they ask Heavenly Father in their prayers. Ask them to listen as you "sing" a prayer to find five things you ask Heavenly Father. You may need to sing the song several times until they find them. As they respond, ask them to join you in singing the phrases that they discover.

2. Use pictures of a beautiful day and children playing happily while sharing with each other. (Do not use a picture of Jesus to illustrate prayer.)

A Smile Is like the Sunshine   267

Words: Anna Johnson
Music: Grietje Terburg Rowley
First Line: A smile is like the sunshine
Topics Indexed: Action Songs, Cheerfulness, Smiles

This is a song of happiness with a lilting melody. Its simple message and melody are appropriate for younger age groups, but older children will enjoy it, too.

Each of the four phrases has almost the same rhythm, with a

long-short, long-short beat pattern that produces a lilting effect. The 6/8 time contributes to the rhythmic swing. The tones move easily, with mostly skips. Two of these skips are rather large leaps of a sixth and seventh, which you will need to help the children sing accurately.

Teaching Suggestions:

1. Add variety to this song by encouraging the children to use actions.

2. Use simple visual aids such as a drawing of a smile, an eye, and a frown.

3. Invite the children to tap or clap the lilting rhythm.

A Song of Thanks 20

Words: Anonymous
Music: J. Battishill
First Line: Thank thee for the world so sweet
Topics Indexed: Gratitude, Prayer Songs

This song could be used as a prayer song or a song of thanksgiving for the many blessings we enjoy. It is intended for younger children.

The even rhythm of each of the four phrases is identical. The first and third musical phrases are the same except for the last two notes. In the *Children's Songbook* the song has been changed from G to F, a more comfortable key for the voice and pianist. The accompaniment has also been thinned to complement the simplicity of the melody.

Teaching Suggestions:

1. Ask the children to listen as you sing the song, to discover the things for which you are thanking our Heavenly Father. Use word strips or pictures to emphasize these points. The children could arrange these in the order in which they come in the song.

2. Sing one phrase at a time and, without breaking the rhythm, have the children repeat each phrase. They will learn this song quickly by rote.

A Special Gift Is Kindness 145

Words and Music: Sharon Steed
First Line: A special gift is kindness
Topics Indexed: Kindness

This simple song presents a clear message of the rewards that come from being kind to others. The use of the word "gift" helps children understand the blessing of kindness through a familiar metaphor. This is a happy song intended for younger children. It can be used to support many of the lessons that they are taught about being kind to others.

The two phrases of this song begin the same melodically and rhythmically. The tones move smoothly and evenly and seem to rise to a natural crescendo in the last two measures.

Teaching Suggestions:

1. Use a wrapped gift as a teaching aid for this song. Ask the children to guess what is in the package. Then sing the song so that they can discover what the gift contains. They can unwrap the gift to find the word "kindness" and pictures of children doing kind acts. Explain that kindness is like a special gift that brings happiness.

2. Ask the children: "What kind of a gift is kindness?" "What does kindness bring?" Sing the song and accept answers after each question; then invite them to sing the phrases as they learn them.

A Young Man Prepared 166

Words and Music: Daniel Lyman Carter
First Line: Though a boy I may appear
Topics Indexed: Commitment, Morality, Preparation, Priesthood,
   Primary Class Songs, Scriptures, Service

This song provides young men with a strong message of the importance of preparing to receive the priesthood. It was first published in the Blazer B Manual as the Blazer class song. The song as it appears in the *Children's Songbook* has a few word and music changes. In order to help the song appeal to all boys, the words in the last two phrases have been changed to, "I'll go forward a young man prepared," instead of the previous, "I'm a Blazer, a young man prepared." However, the original version should be used by the boys in the Blazer classes.

The rhythm of the song is energetic and full of many uneven, march-like beat patterns. You should help the boys feel and hear the irregular rhythm so they can learn it accurately. One of the unique features of the melody is the modern-sounding skip of a major seventh, from middle C up to B, which occurs four times.

Teaching Suggestions:

1. Use the word "prepare" as a key to teaching the song. Ask the group to discuss how they might prepare to go on a camping trip—what they would take for this adventure. Explain that the Lord has given them a greater challenge and blessing: the chance to hold the priesthood of God. Invite them to listen as you sing to discover what they must do to prepare to receive the priesthood.

2. Help the boys feel the strong rhythm pattern created by frequent use of a dotted-eighth note followed by a sixteenth note. These notes should be sung crisply and with emphasis. Invite them to clap or tap the rhythm.

3. Have the boys listen to the interval of a seventh as the accompanist plays it. Challenge them to discover how many times it occurs (four). Have them sing the two phrases where this interval occurs. ("If I prepare and live clean in ev'ry thought, word, and deed," and "Being armed with the truth, with the scriptures my guide.") These phrases contain the essence of what the boys must do to prepare to receive the priesthood.

4. The best visual aid for this song is the boys themselves, or a boy who has received the priesthood.

All Things Bright and Beautiful   231

Words: Cecil Frances Alexander
Music: Old English tune
First Line: All things bright and beautiful
Topics Indexed: Beautiful World, Creation, Summer

The words to this song enumerate some of the beautiful creations that the Lord has made for our enjoyment. It has been sung by Primary children since the early days of the Church. In the *Children's Songbook* some chords have been changed and the key has been moved from E to G.

The song has a refrain and four verses. The refrain appears at the beginning of the song so that this eight-measure melody will be sung at the first and again at the conclusion. One of the charms of the song is the variety of ways it can be sung: four verses with the refrain sung between each verse, one or more verses sung with the refrain at the beginning and end, or the refrain alone. The tune flows gently and smoothly throughout. However, there is a contrast in mood, with the refrain being rather exuberant and the verses more subdued.

Teaching Suggestions:

1. This song could be taught in connection with lessons about the creation of the heavens and the earth as recorded in Genesis 1. Ask a child to read parts of this scripture. Sing the song and ask the children to identify the creations mentioned in the lyrics. Use pictures or actual objects from nature named in the song as teaching aids.

2. Have the children build a scene of the world with its creations by adding pictures to a basic background of land, water, and sky.

3. Express your belief in the Lord as the creator of the earth and all the beauties that are here. Encourage the children to share their feelings about the beautiful world around them.

An Angel Came to Joseph Smith 86

Words: Anna Johnson
Music: A. Laurence Lyon
First Line: An angel came to Joseph Smith
Topics Indexed: Book of Mormon, Joseph Smith, Peace,
  Restoration of the Gospel

In four short verses this song gives a synopsis of the coming forth of and important messages in the Book of Mormon. These include the idea that the people of Book of Mormon times were blessed with peace when they obeyed the Lord, that children can read the Book of Mormon now, and that our Heavenly Father loves everyone in every land.

The words are set to a ballad-like melody that is almost haunting in its beauty and simplicity. The rhythm is unique and appealing in that twice there is a measure of 2/4 time inserted into the 3/4 meter song. The beat pattern in line one is the same as in line two, though the melody is different. The song flows smoothly and simply.

Teaching Suggestions:

1. Hold up a copy of the Book of Mormon and ask the children what story is contained in this book. Tell them that it is a holy book because it contains a sacred record. Tell them that you have four pictures, one to go with each verse of the song. As you sing the verses, challenge the children to place the pictures in the order in which they come. (Verse one: a picture of the angel giving the golden plates to Joseph Smith; verse two: a picture of Lehi and his family crossing the waters; verse three: a picture of the Nephites and Lamanites in the new land; verse four: a picture of a child reading the Book of Mormon.) Sing each verse and ask additional questions relating to the messages.

2. Have the children look up a scripture, read it aloud, and then listen to the words of the verse that describe that event. (Verse one: Joseph Smith — History 1:59; verse two: 1 Nephi 18:22–23; verse three: 4 Nephi 1:2–4; verse four: Moroni 10:3.) After each scripture is read, teach the words to the verse, asking questions and inviting the children to sing the phrases.

3. Have the children clap the notes of the melody to detect the changing meter that occurs in the third and seventh measures.

4. Bear testimony of the truthfulness of the Book of Mormon and challenge the children to read this sacred book.

Autumn Day   247

Words and Music: A. B. Ponsonby
First Line: Autumn day, autumn day, God gives richest gifts
*   today*
Topics Indexed: Autumn, Beautiful World, Gratitude

This cheerful song of gratitude has long been in the children's song resources of the LDS Church. In the *Children's Songbook* there have been minimal word changes and a transposition from the key of D to C.

The last phrase of the song, "Child, be glad with all that lives, but forget not God, who gives," provides the core of its message and is set apart by a distinct mood and a straightforward rhythm pattern. The meter of this last line is 4/4, a change from the 3/4 time of the first four lines. The other phrases include a catchy rhythmic pattern with dotted-eighth-note/sixteenth-note combinations.

Teaching Suggestions:

1. Show the children a basket or box filled with apples and other items from the harvest. Sing the song and invite them to explain why you brought the basket with its contents. Have them identify the season and what things happen during this time of year.

2. Teach the words of the song by asking a question, singing the song, accepting answers, and inviting the children to sing each phrase. Questions that you could ask are: "Whom should we not forget?" "What should we be glad for?" "What happens when the trees are loaded with apples?" "Six words describe the apples. What are they?" (Red, yellow, round, juicy, sweet, mellow.) "What do we see on every side?"

3. Encourage the children to sing the rhythm correctly by having them tap or clap the notes, draw illustrations of some of the beat patterns, or listen to the notes as they are played on the piano.

4. Help them understand the message of this song of gratitude by asking them what they should do when they receive gifts or kind acts from others. After they respond, sing the last line again and ask them how they can thank God for the many blessings they receive from him.

Away in a Manger 42

Words and Music: Anonymous
First Line: Away in a manger, no crib for his bed
Topics Indexed: Christmas, Lullabies, Two-part Songs

The version of this favorite carol chosen for the *Children's Songbook* has the "asleep, asleep" chorus and is the one most familiar to Primary children. The chorus can be sung in two parts, with one group singing the first "asleep" and holding the note while the other group sings the lower "asleep." The verse also makes a lovely duet when the harmony is added. The hymnbook contains another version of this well-known Christmas lullaby (hymn number 206).

Teaching Suggestions:

1. Ask the children to listen to a story about the birth of Jesus. Display pictures or cutouts as you sing the first two verses of the song.

2. Teach the song by rote, singing it, encouraging the children to listen to the various phrases, and inviting them to join in singing as they become familiar with the phrases. Have a child read the scriptures from Luke 2:1, 3–7, as the children hum the melody.

3. To teach the third verse, explain that this carol was written in Germany many years ago, and that children all over the world enjoy singing it at Christmastime. Place pictures or cutouts of children from other nations around the manger scene to illustrate this idea as you sing verse three.

4. Younger children can pretend to rock a baby while they sing or hum the song.

Baptism   100

Words: Mabel Jones Gabbott
Music: Crawford Gates
First Line: Jesus came to John the Baptist
Topics Indexed: Baptism, Faith, Jesus Christ — Baptism,
  Jesus Christ — Example, Obedience

This song describes the events of Jesus' baptism by immersion at the hands of John the Baptist. It points out his obedience to the Father and the fact that we are also obedient when we follow his example. Music leaders and parents will find it an effective tool for teaching the principle of baptism.

The accompaniment has been simplified for the *Children's Songbook* by condensing the three staffs to two and thinning the notation and chording. The key has been changed from E to E flat. The climax of the song is reached in the next-to-last line on the highest tones ("and was baptized . . . "). According to the 12/8 time signature, the eighth notes receive one count and the dotted-quarter notes receive three counts. However, to facilitate a smooth, flowing pattern, the leader should conduct four beats to a measure. The most difficult rhythm occurs in the third-to-last measure, where two eighth notes, marked "2," are given the same note value as a dotted-quarter note.

Teaching Suggestions:
1. Introduce this song by using the fourth Article of Faith (the song or scripture); ask the children to identify the first four principles and ordinances of the gospel. Sing the song and ask them to discover which ordinance it teaches.

24

2. Have the children find the scripture in Matthew 3:13–16 and read the events that took place at Jesus' baptism. Sing the song and, through questions, encourage the children to compare the words of the scripture with the song.

3. Continue to sing and teach the song by asking the children to detect the *who?* (Jesus and John the Baptist), *where?* (in Judea), *when?* (long ago), *what happened?* (Jesus was baptized), *how?* (by immersion), and *where?* (in the River Jordan's flow). Print these question words on cards and show a picture of Jesus' baptism.

4. Have the children listen for the "rippling" sounds of the River Jordan's flow in the accompaniment. Allow them to express their feelings about what the music reminds them of.

5. Have the children compare their baptisms with that of Jesus. A child who has been baptized recently could briefly tell of his or her experience.

Be Happy! 265

Words: Alice Jean Cleator
Music: Arthur Wilton
First Line: Be happy like the little bird
Topics Indexed: Cheerfulness, Happiness

This song of joy and happiness is one that younger children especially enjoy. It was printed in the *Primary Songbook* beginning in 1920. Each of the musical phrases is different, yet the melody of the first and second lines begins the same. The rhythm of every measure is the same (except at the end of the phrases), with a quarter note, eighth note, quarter note, eighth note. This produces the lilting beat felt throughout.

Teaching Suggestions:

1. Have the children "pass a smile along" by having one child smile at the child sitting next to him or her. This child then smiles at the next, and so on until all of the children are smiling. Tell them that when we are happy, others "catch" this happiness and feel happy, too. Ask them to listen to you sing a song about being happy.

2. Simple pictures of a smile, children playing happily together, a bird in a tree, a heart, and a little stream of water will help you teach the words.

3. Ask a question, sing the song, accept answers to the question,

and then invite the children to sing that part of the song with you, until they have learned all the words.

4. Invite the children to clap the rhythm with you as they sing or hum.

Beautiful Savior (Crusader's Hymn)   62

Words: Anonymous (twelfth century)
Music: Silesian folk song, arranged by Darwin Wolford
First Line: Fair is the sunshine
Topics Indexed: Descants, Jesus Christ — Example, Jesus Christ — Son of God, Praise

Many musicians, including several LDS composers, have created arrangements for this song of praise to the Savior. For the *Children's Songbook* Darwin Wolford has provided an arrangement that is well suited to performances by children. It is compact and easy to play and to sing. The melody of the song is carried throughout the accompaniment.

In teaching this hymn, you should discuss its message with the children so that they can communicate it to the listeners. The idea that Jesus is fairer and purer than all God's creations instills a desire to praise and honor him.

The song builds gradually in strength through the three verses to a climax in the last verse, maintaining a majestic feeling to the end. The melody moves smoothly and easily on even beats. Children can experience a feeling of accomplishment as they learn to sing "Beautiful Savior" with understanding and expression.

Teaching Suggestions:

1. Ask the children to name things in the world that are beautiful, wonderful, or marvelous. Use pictures of such wonders. As you sing the first two verses, ask them to find who the song tells us is the fairest, purest, and brightest of all. They could also discover *why* he is the fairest of all. (Answers are in all three verses.) Explain that this song has been sung for many years by people who love Jesus and are thankful for him.

2. As the accompanist plays verse one, sing "doo-doo" expressively, pitch-level conducting as you sing. Then invite the children to sing and move their arms with you so that they become acquainted with the melody. Introduce the words, a phrase at a time, until they have learned all of the verse. Use pictures of the

26

sun, the moon, the stars, Jesus, and the world to help the children remember the word sequences. Teach the other verses in a similar way.

3. Use meaningful conducting motions to indicate the dynamics desired to help the children sing with expression, majesty, and beauty.

4. Teach the descant to a small group of children, or have one or two instrumentalists play the descant on flute or violin as the children sing the melody.

Beauty Everywhere   232

Words: Matilda Watts Cahoon
Music: Mildred Tanner Pettit
First Line: Skies are fair above us
Topics Indexed: Beautiful World, Creation, Gratitude, Praise

This song reminds children that as they see all the beauties of nature, which are the work of God, they should be thankful for all he gives to them. The accompaniment has been simplified for the *Children's Songbook* to eliminate some heavy-sounding bass notes and to add lightness to the melody. The verse (in 3/4 waltz time) has a joyful, light mood, and the chorus (in 4/4 time) has a more even, marked rhythm with a reverent and majestic feeling. Every other measure in the verse has the same rhythm: a dotted-quarter and three eighth notes. The alternate measures have a half note and a quarter note, or a dotted-half note. Though there are similarities, none of the musical phrases are the same.

Teaching Suggestions:
1. Show pictures of the beauties of nature that are mentioned in the song (skies, trees, flowers, birds, bees, children singing, and so forth). Tell the children that your heart is full of thanks for many things, and you are going to sing a song that expresses your thanks. After you sing, ask them to name the things you are thankful for. Have a few children arrange the pictures in the order in which they come in the song as you sing it again.

2. Teach the chorus first. To help the children understand what "the work of God" means, use the words of the verses as examples. Use questions, pictures, and word strips of keywords to help them remember the sequence of the phrases.

3. Ask the children to clap or tap the rhythm of the melody of

the verse as the accompanist plays the music. They could move from side to side to accentuate the beat. As the pianist goes on to play the chorus, point out that the mood and beat change.

4. Teach the verses as you did the chorus, with word strips, pictures, and questions. Share with the children your love of and appreciation for the beautiful world God has given us.

Because God Loves Me   234

Words and Music: Joleen Grant Meredith
First Line: God planned the day; he planned the night
Topics Indexed: Beautiful World, Cheerfulness, Creation, Family,
  God's Love, Worth of a Child

This song helps younger children understand the wonders of the creation. In the *Children's Songbook*, the music has been condensed in form by creating two verses with two endings instead of one continuous verse that was twice as long.

The music moves easily, mostly by repeated notes and steps and a few small skips. The range of notes is within six tones, from D to B. In teaching the song, avoid rushing the tempo, so that the words can be clearly expressed. It should be sung gently and smoothly.

Teaching Suggestion:

Tell the children that you are going to tell them a wonderful true story. Then sing the song slowly, displaying on a flannelboard pictures depicting the keywords. Repeat the song several times, encouraging the children to sing the words that are illustrated by the pictures as you point to them.

Because It's Spring   239

Words and Music: Faye Glover Petersen
First Line: Why is the sky so blue and clear?
Topics Indexed: Beautiful World, Happiness, Spring

This happy song, written in 6/8 time, expresses the feelings we experience as the world awakens to the wonders of spring. The simplicity of the words and the message make the song most appropriate for younger children. It is included in the *Children's Songbook* with some word and music changes. The left-hand accompaniment now has a simple chord arrangement with two beats to the measure (which is how the song should be conducted).

With only two exceptions, the rhythmic pattern established in the first two measures is repeated through the entire song. Teach this pattern by clapping, tapping, or by using a simple rhythm instrument. The climax of the song is reached in the third line on the high D, which is held with a fermata on the word "sing." The text is written with six "why" questions leading up to the final statement, "Only because it's spring!", which answers all six questions.

Teaching Suggestions:

1. Tell the children that you are going to sing them a riddle, and that they should listen carefully to the clues. Sing the song, humming the last phrase so as not to give away the solution. After they discover the answer to the riddle, have them sing the last phrase with you. Ask them to listen to the song again and count how many questions are asked. Emphasize that the final phrase, "Only because it's spring!", is the answer to each of the six questions.

2. Teach the other lines with a "follow-the-leader" method: sing a phrase, have the children sing the same phrase, sing the next phrase, and so on, without stopping. As each phrase is sung, display pictures or cutouts that illustrate the blue sky, the robin singing, the warm sun, green fields, and clouds.

3. Children will enjoy accentuating the rhythmic pattern by clapping or tapping it. You can also prompt them to notice that the first and third lines have the same melody. Encourage them to hold the word "sing" in the last line. This adds to the suspense in giving the answer to the riddle.

4. Build a nature scene with cutouts placed on a poster as the song is sung. Climax the song presentation by emphasizing that our Heavenly Father has made all these beautiful gifts of nature.

Before I Take the Sacrament 73

Words: Mabel Jones Gabbott
Music: Gladys E. Seely
First Line: Before I take the sacrament, I sit so quietly
Topics Indexed: Jesus Christ — Ministry, Reverence,
    Sacrament

Though the children are not served the sacrament in Primary, the importance and meaning of this ordinance should still be taught. This song teaches simply yet effectively why we take the sacrament and gives children something to think about during the sacrament service. Its uncomplicated melody and words make it appropriate for younger children.

The melody line begins on the third note of the scale, the second phrase begins on the fourth note, and the third phrase on the fifth note. This progression builds to the climax of the song ("I *know* that Jesus came to earth"). The final phrase, "and died for me," is given emphasis through the longer note values. The children can be encouraged to show this emphasis by singing these last three notes more thoughtfully and a little slower.

Teaching Suggestions:

1. Have a child sit quietly in front of the other children. Ask them why this child is sitting so quietly. Have them discover the answer by listening to the first verse of the song. Ask what the child might be thinking about as he or she sits reverently. After they share their ideas, have them listen to you sing the second verse to detect the correct answer. Display pictures showing Jesus with children.

2. Ask questions about the words in the song, and have the children sing the phrases with the answers.

3. Introduce the ideas in verse three with a picture of the sacrament being passed, or show the bread and water trays used in your ward. Ask a question, encourage the children to listen for the answer, and invite them to sing that phrase with you.

Birds in the Tree 241

Words: Glenna Tate Holbrook
Music: Marjorie Castleton Kjar
First Line: We will find a little nest in the branches of a tree
Topics Indexed: Action Songs, Spring

Family love is portrayed in this song as the mother and father bird take care of their family in their nest in the tree. Even the smallest children in the nursery will enjoy doing the actions as the song is sung. The melody is simply constructed, with the first and third phrases the same. The rhythm is even and constant with eighth notes throughout.

Teaching Suggestion:

Little children will learn this song easily as they hear it sung to them several times. Simple actions aid the learning, so there is no need for more formal teaching methods. Visual aids may even detract, since the children are usually intent on acting out the words as they sing.

Book of Mormon Stories   118

Words and Music: Elizabeth Fetzer Bates
Optional Verses: Nancy K. Daines Carter
First Line: Book of Mormon stories that my teacher tells to me
Topics Indexed: Book of Mormon, Freedom, Jesus Christ—
  Blesses Children, Jesus Christ—Ministry, Prophecy,
  Prophets. (Some of these topics refer to optional verses.)

Children around the world enjoy singing this ballad of the stories in the Book of Mormon, which emphasizes that the Lord blesses his people as they learn to live righteously. Elizabeth Fetzer Bates writes, "Any enjoyment of this little song is due to the fact that the Book of Mormon is true. It is the one book in the whole world that we know contains truth, and we can live by its teachings in peace, no matter what happens in the world around us." Nancy Carter submitted additional verses written to help teach her children the stories contained in the Book of Mormon. Each of her eight verses contains the kernel of one of the stories in this book of scripture. As each story is read or taught to the children, the verse that goes with it will help them to remember the important facts.

Teaching Suggestions:

1. Ask the children to listen to the song as it is played on the piano and tell what they think it is about. When they identify it as an "Indian" song, tell them what the connection is between Indians and the Book of Mormon, or have them relate the facts of the relationship. Use pictures of Lehi's family crossing in their ship or other Book of Mormon illustrations.

2. Have the children tap a fist in the palm of the other hand in "tom-tom" style or use simple rhythm instruments to accentuate the rhythm.

3. Invite them to improvise actions to imitate Indian sign language describing such words as "book" (two hands together in

front of you), "Lamanite" (two fingers of one hand behind the head to typify an Indian feather headdress), "crossing the sea" (moving the hand in a wavelike fashion), and "righteously" (arms folded across the chest).

4. Have a group of children softly chant the words "Book of Mormon" over and over as the others sing the song. Chant the words twice to each measure, one syllable with each eighth note, on the following notes: lines one and two — E; line three — G; line four — A (once), G (once), and E (twice).

Called to Serve   174

Words: Grace Gordon
Music: Walter G. Tyler
First Line: Called to serve Him, heav'nly King of glory
Topics Indexed: Commitment, Songs for Leaders, Missionary
  Work, Service

This stirring song reminds us that we are called to the service of our Heavenly Father, to be witnesses for his name, and to proclaim his love. It has been in the children's songbooks of the Church beginning in 1920. In April 1985 it was performed in the Assembly Hall on Temple Square by a group of missionaries from the Missionary Training Center, for all the mission presidents of the Church. These young men and women marched into the building singing. An editorial in the *Church News* stated, "The impact of this experience was so moving that tears were flowing and deep emotions were stirred. It was an unforgettable spiritual moment." (August 11, 1985, p. 16.) Consequently, "Called to Serve" was added to the hymnbook as number 249.

The song as it appears in the *Children's Songbook* has a simplified accompaniment, eliminating the octaves and fuller chording. More advanced pianists may want to add octaves in the left-hand accompaniment, or they may use the version from the hymnbook.

The composer has created a strong rhythmic pattern by using uneven beats in four of the measures of the verse in between measures of even beats. The octave jumps in the melody contribute to the majestic mood.

Teaching Suggestions:

1. Ask someone who has recently received a mission call to help you introduce this song. Have the children guess what the missionary is holding (the letter issuing the mission call). The missionary could read a sentence or two of the letter. Ask the children to listen to you sing a song to discover four things that missionaries are called to do. Sing the first verse and post key-words, such as "serve Him," "witness," "tell the Father's story," and "love proclaim," as they respond.

2. Through questions about the words, continue to provide listening and singing experiences until the children have learned the verse and chorus. Help them understand the significance of the phrases "heavenly King of glory" and "the Father's story," and the meaning of "witness," "proclaim," "glory," "triumph," and "confessing."

3. Invite the children to tap the uneven and even beats of the measures. They can also identify other aspects of the song such as octave jumps and the scalelike progressions. Illustrate the melody and rhythm patterns for them.

4. Invite the children to march around the room as they sing the song, reenacting the special meeting where the missionaries sang it. Remind them that each of us is called to serve the Lord, even when we are not formally called as missionaries. The missionary who told about his or her call could bear testimony of missionary work.

Can a Little Child like Me? 9

Words: Mary M. Dodge
Music: W. K. Bassford
First Line: Can a little child like me thank the Father fittingly?
Topics Indexed: Beautiful World, Gratitude, Prayer Songs,
  Service, Worth of a Child

Even a little child can thank the Father in words and deeds. This song helps give some ideas of what children can do to show their appreciation for blessings. It was first published in the 1920 *Primary Songbook.*

Two of the musically significant features of the song are the rhythmic sequence on the words "fittingly," "do your part," and "all your heart," and the tone movement of the chorus, in which each phrase rises in pitch to the climax on "Father in Heaven."

These phrases also lend themselves to increased volume on each sequence until the last two measures, when the volume decreases to a subdued finish. To create the proper mood for this prayer song, do not sing the phrases at the point of climax too loudly.

Teaching Suggestions:

1. Invite one or two small children to stand before the group and ask them if they can do various acts such as tie their shoes, make their beds, drive a car, swim across the ocean, and so on. After discovering that they can do some things and cannot do others, tell the group to listen to a song that has another question for all of them to ask themselves. They can identify the question in the song and discover the answer.

2. As you sing the song again, ask the children to listen for other things, such as how many times "we thank thee" is sung, what happens to the melody as "Father, we thank thee" is sung, the four things that we can *be* in order to thank our Father, the three things that we should *do,* and some of the things that we thank our Father for (second verse). After each question, sing the song, accept answers, and invite the children to sing that part of the song with you. Post pictures or word strips to help them remember the sequence of the words.

3. Have the children clap or tap the rhythm of the song as they sing, emphasizing the uneven beat patterns.

4. Encourage the children to sing with meaning and with appropriate dynamics (not too loudly). Teach a group of older children to sing the alto part.

Children All Over the World 16

Words: Peggy Hill Ryskamp
Music: Beth Groberg Stratton
First line: All over the world at the end of day
Topics Indexed: Gratitude, Variety of Languages, Prayer, World-wide Church, Worth of a Child

"Somebody ought to write a song to help the children in Primaries all over the world to feel close to each other," thought Peggy Hill Ryskamp as she heard a group of Primary children sing "I Am a Child of God" while she was in France serving a mission. She put into poetry the important message that it doesn't matter in what language it is expressed, Heavenly Father hears and understands when children declare their thankfulness to him, and he loves each one. This is a song of faith that all children can respond to, regardless of their culture. Because the words "thank you" are expressed in several languages in the song, it is particularly enjoyed by older children who love to learn these new words.

There are three musical parts to the song. The first and third parts are the same, with small variations. There is a musical interlude between part A and part B, and a musical postlude as the conclusion. The two most important themes of the song are expressed in repeated sequences: "thank you — thank you" and "loves them — loves them."

Teaching Suggestions:

1. Show pictures of children from other countries in their native dress. Ask the children if they could understand these children if they were to talk to them in their language. Sing the song and hold a picture of a child praying, preferably one from another land. Discuss the fact that Heavenly Father hears and understands each child's prayer, no matter what language is used.

2. Help the children learn the words by giving them listening and singing experiences using questions and pictures. As they hear the phrases sung, have them repeat them with you.

3. Invite the children to tap or clap the rhythm as they sing. Give special attention to the rests and the dotted-eighth-note, six-teenth-note, and eighth-note combinations. The fermata in the middle of the song should also be observed. Lead the song with two beats to the measure.

4. Make word strips of the "thank you" words in other languages. Help the children practice pronouncing them according to the phonetic spellings given within the song.

5. Prepare six paper-sack puppets, each representing one of the countries, with the words meaning "thank you" printed under the mouth of each. The children can make the appropriate puppet "talk" as each language is used in the song.

Choose the Right Way 160

Words and Music: Clara W. McMaster
First Line: There's a right way to live and be happy
Topics Indexed: Choice, Commandment, Happiness, Obedience, Primary Class Songs

This is a straightforward song with an appealing melody; it is easily learned and understood by the children. The central meaning is included in the two phrases of the chorus: "Choose the right way and be happy. I must always choose the right." Though especially appropriate for the CTR classes, for whom the song was originally written, the message applies to many ages and situations.

Teaching Suggestions:

1. There are several suggestions in the CTR lesson manuals for introducing this song to the children. If you teach it to the other Primary children, have a group of the CTR children sing it to them and explain what it means.

2. Teach the chorus first. Discuss with the children the teachings of Jesus and the importance of making right choices.

Christmas Bells   54

Words and Music: A. Laurence Lyon
First Line: Christmas bells are ringing
Topics Indexed: Christmas, Descants

Brother Lyon wrote this song when he was working as a graduate student on a complex orchestra piece for a composition class. He had never written a children's song up to this time. He writes, "In the midst of doing this complex writing, this little tune just popped out of my head and onto the piano, accompaniment, words and all. . . . Then, before I could continue on to my viola concerto, another melody, which seemed to fit the first melody, also seemed to want to be written down. I sang the second melody with the first, and they fit."

The principal melody is written within the accompaniment. Although musically compatible, the melody for the optional descant is not in the accompaniment so must be taught by itself first, and then the accompaniment added when it is securely mastered. The descant could also be played on flute or violin. The piece can be done as either a one-part or a two-part song. To blend the two melodic harmonies, the rhythm of each must be accurate. An interesting syncopation is created when the two voice parts are sung together.

Teaching Suggestions:

1. Show some bells to the children and ring them softly. Ask them to tell in what circumstances they have heard bells ring. Tell them that bells are often rung to announce important events. Ask

them to listen as you sing a song, to discover for what event these bells are ringing. Tell them that it was the most significant event in all the world.

2. The children will learn the song as you sing each phrase, asking them to listen for something specific, and then inviting them to sing that part with you. Display a picture of the nativity as the song is sung.

3. Divide the children into two groups. Ask the first group to sing, "Christmas bells are ringing. Hear what they say to you:" and the second group to sing, "Jesus is born in Bethlehem, in Bethlehem." After they sing the melody several times in this way, the groups could change parts.

4. Teach the optional descant to a small group of children without accompaniment at first. When it is firmly in the children's minds, the accompaniment can be added. Finally, the two melodies can be sung together with the accompaniment added. A soft ringing of bells or an autoharp will add interest to the performance. Or you could have several children strike large nails hung from yarn to get a bell effect.

5. To assist the children in maintaining their parts securely, two song leaders could each direct one of the two groups.

Come with Me to Primary   255

Words and Music: Patricia Critchlow Maughan and Marjorie Castleton Kjar
First Line: Oh, come with me to Primary
Topics Indexed: Friends, Primary, Rounds, Singing, Worldwide Church

The filmstrip "Come with Me to Primary," prepared by the Primary General Board, uses this song as its theme and encourages the children to invite their friends to come to Primary with them. There are four musical phrases in the song, each with a different melody. However, phrase two imitates phrase one, a third higher on the scale. The first, second, and fourth phrases have the same rhythm pattern. Special interest and fun can be created when children sing the song as a round.

Teaching Suggestions:

1. Show the children the filmstrip "Come with Me to Primary," and then teach them to sing the song.

2. Sing the song and invite the children to sing it with you. It can be imitated readily.

3. Divide the children into two, three, or four groups and have them sing this song as a round.

Covered Wagons   221

Words: Anne Kaelin
Music: Richard Randolph
First Line: Day after day the wagons are rolling
Topics Indexed: Pioneers, Singing

This artistically created song gives the feeling of the rolling motion of the wagons and the monotony of the long pioneer trek. There is nostalgia over what has been left behind and thoughts of the pioneers' dreams for their new home. The music in the *Children's Songbook* has been simplified by eliminating the separate staff for the melody and words and including the melody within the accompaniment.

The song form of "Covered Wagons" is A B C B — the last phrase of the verse and the last phrase of the chorus are identical musically. This last phrase of the chorus is a little tricky because of two places where one-syllable words ("take" and "our") must be sung (slurred) on two notes. The leader will need to be sure that the children hear and execute these notes clearly. The singers should give full value to the dotted-quarter notes to add to the rolling effect of the rhythm.

Teaching Suggestions:

1. Teach the chorus of "Covered Wagons" first since its melody is catchy and contains the essence of the message. Display a picture of pioneers with their covered wagons to introduce the song, and invite the children to listen to the pianist play the chorus. Then sing it and invite them to join you.

2. Teach the verses by asking such questions as: "Where must we roam?" "When are the wagons rolling?" "What reminds us of home?" "When do we sit round the campfire?" "Where will we settle and build?" and "Where will we be someday?" After each question, sing the verse, accept answers from the children, and

invite them to join you in singing that phrase of the song. Use word strips of keywords and cutouts or pictures that illustrate the message to help them remember the sequence of the lyrics.

3. Help the children feel the rolling of the wagon wheels and the relentless trial of the long journey by having them sway back and forth to the music as they sing. They could also clap the beats of the notes. For variety, have the girls sing the first verse, the boys the second, and the entire group the rest of the song.

Daddy's Homecoming   210

Words: Anonymous
Music: Frances K. Taylor
First Line: I'm so glad when daddy comes home
Topics Indexed: Action Songs, Fathers, Grandparents, Happiness

This is one of the first songs young children learn as they attend Primary. The message is simply an expression of the joy that a child feels when his or her father returns home. As suggested in the songbook, alternate words may be substituted or added to give the song a wider usage. The children can sing about mother, grandpa, grandma, or others to fit the occasion.

The four musical phrases are marked by a lilting rhythm, with many measures having a quarter note, eighth note, quarter note, eighth note. There is no repetition of melody phrases, but the music flows effortlessly.

Teaching Suggestion:

This song does not require any formal teaching presentation. As you sing the song, adding actions as suggested by the words, the little ones will quickly respond and will soon know it well. It also lends itself to role-playing as dictated by the message of the song.

Dare to Do Right   158

Words: Anonymous
Music: Arranged by A. C. Smyth
First Line: Dare to do right! Dare to be true!
Topics Indexed: Accountability, Choice, Commandments,
    Commitment, Courage, Dependability, Example, Honor,
    Morality

This song comes to mind when temptations entice us to choose a wrong course of action. The frequent use of the word "dare," as it relates to choosing to do the right, provides a positive challenge rather than the negative connotation sometimes associated with taking dares.

The song was included in early editions of the *Primary Songbook,* beginning in 1905. The melody is catchy and rhythmic, mixing measures of even counts with those that have a dotted-eighth note, a sixteenth note, and an eighth note. Singers should be encouraged to make a distinction between these beat patterns and emphasize the contrast.

Teaching Suggestions:

1. Introduce the song by telling a story of someone who took an unwise dare.

2. Invite the children to listen to the message of the song as you sing it, to discover what kind of dares are wise and courageous. Ask questions such as these: "How many times in the chorus do we sing the word 'dare'?" "What words tell what we should dare to do?" "How should we do this work?" and "If we do it bravely, kindly, and well, what will happen?" Help them recognize the phrases in the chorus that are repeated from the verse.

3. Post keywords, such as "right," "true," "work," "bravely," "kindly," and "well," to help the children solidify the lyrics in their minds. Discuss the fact that it sometimes takes courage and bravery to do what is right. Accountability, dependability, and example can also be taught through this song.

4. Encourage the children to notice the melody line by illustrating it on a chart. There are two places where the melody goes step-by-step down the scale, once in the first line of the verse and in the last two measures.

5. Ask the children to clap or tap the rhythm of the song to develop accuracy. Conduct it with two beats to the measure.

Dearest Mother, I Love You 206

Words and Music: Vernon J. LeeMaster
First Line: Gentle words I hear you say
Topics Indexed: Mothers

This simple song is a good one to include in a Mother's Day program where the little children have an opportunity to perform.

It has a straightforward and uncomplicated melody. The feeling engendered is one of gentleness and love.

The rhythm of each of the four phrases is the same, yet the melody is not repeated, although measures one and five are the same. The final phrase includes a scalelike progression from A down to D.

Teaching Suggestions:

1. Tell the children that you are going to teach them a lovely song as a surprise for their mothers. Sing it for them and have them repeat the phrases one by one. Use questions such as these: "What do I hear?" "What helps me each day?" "What two words describe my mother?"

2. Consider teaching the last phrase first. Help the children notice that the melody of the last phrase moves step-by-step down the scale, and that the rhythm of the song consists of even beats.

3. Display pictures of mothers with their children, doing kind and loving things.

Did Jesus Really Live Again? 64

Words: Mabel Jones Gabbott
Music: Royce Campbell Twitchell
First Line: Did Jesus really live again?
Topics Indexed: Easter, Resurrection, Testimony

This song is expressed simply and beautifully so that children and adults alike will be touched by its significant meaning. It bears testimony of the circumstances and physical reality of the Savior's resurrection: that he spoke with his followers, ate with them, and allowed them to touch his resurrected body. There are enough differences in the melody of the third verse that it requires separate staffs. The words to the final measures emphasize the reality of the resurrection — that Jesus did live again and so we shall as well. The mood of the third verse should be reverent and pensive as the serious events of the crucifixion are mentioned.

Teaching Suggestions:

1. Use the questions in the song as the "attention-getter" to introduce it. Post the two questions on a chart or chalkboard and ask the children to turn to their scriptures to find the answers. (John 20:15–16; Luke 24:36–43; 3 Nephi 11:10–14.)

2. Sing the song to the children so they can discover which

parts of the story, as told in the scriptures, are found in the song. Use pictures, of the resurrected Christ, Jesus appearing to Mary Magdalene, and Jesus appearing to the Nephites to illustrate the message of the song.

3. Teach the lyrics by asking questions that can be answered by exact words in the song, singing the song, accepting the children's answers, and inviting the children to sing that part with you. Help them sing the final two measures of the third verse with understanding and firmness. These include fermatas over two notes to emphasize the final declaration: "Oh yes! And so shall I."

Do As I'm Doing 276

Words: Anonymous
Music: Folk style
First Line: Do as I'm doing; follow, follow me!
Topics Indexed: Actions Songs, Example

This activity song offers boys and girls a chance to relax and have fun. In a survey of Primary songs it ranked high as a favorite of children in the Church. It can be used in the home, in the nursery, in Primary sharing time, or in the classroom. There is no end to the actions that the children can originate as they take turns being the leader in performing a movement for all to follow. Even though this tune is especially appropriate for little children, older boys and girls also enjoy participating in this game of "follow the leader."

Teaching Suggestion:
No formal teaching of this song is required. The leader should sing the song, doing various actions, and then invite the children to perform actions of their choosing.

Easter Hosanna 68

Words and Music: Vanja Y. Watkins
First Line: The prophecies of long ago were now at last fulfilled
Topics Indexed: Book of Mormon, Easter, Prophecy,
  Resurrection

The account of Christ appearing to the Nephites in America as told in 3 Nephi chapter 11 is dramatically portrayed in this song.

The words that the people declared, found in verse 17, are used as the text for the chorus. "Easter Hosanna" is exciting and haunting in its melodic construction and could be scheduled for special programs. The minor key adds to the feeling of wonder and sacredness associated with the events of Christ's appearance to the Nephites and of the resurrection.

The verse is written almost entirely with even beats, to be sung smoothly and thoughtfully. The notes move by steps with a few short skips, usually of a third. The chorus is punctuated by an irregular and emphatic beat pattern on the word "Hosanna." The climax of the song is reached on the last chord, where the melodic pattern resolves to the major key.

Teaching Suggestions:

1. "Easter Hosanna" should be taught in association with the story of the coming of Jesus Christ to the Americas. You could tell or read it from the scriptures. The children will enjoy discovering how the important facts of the event are retold in the song.

2. Teach the chorus first as the children read in the scriptures the words that the people cried. Explain the word "hosanna" as a cry of adoration and love. Invite them to lightly clap the rhythm of the chorus.

3. To teach the verse, ask such questions as: "What were now at last fulfilled?" "To whom did he reveal himself?" "How did he look when he came down from heaven?" "Who was it who received their Lord?" With each question, sing the song and invite the children to listen for the answer. Then they could sing the phrase where the answer is found. Explain what is meant by the prophecies now being fulfilled.

4. Draw an illustration of the beginning melody pattern and help the children recognize how it is repeated two times. After they learn the first phrase, they can see that this melody is used again for the second phrase. The third phrase is different, and the final phrase of the verse is much like the first.

5. Use a picture of Christ appearing to the Nephites. Also use keywords posted on word strips or the chalkboard to assist the children in remembering the lyrics.

6. The children will enjoy the feeling created by the minor key and the resolution of the last chord to the major. Encourage them to listen to the music and tell why they think the composer wrote it as she did. Express your testimony of the reality of the resurrection and the appearance of Jesus to the Nephites.

Every Star Is Different   142

Words: John C. Cameron
Music: K. Newell Dayley; arranged by K. Newell Dayley
First Line: Every star is diff'rent, and so is every child
Topics Indexed: Choice, Example, Obbligatos, Special Needs,
Talents, Worth of a Child

This song illustrates the idea that each child is important, of value, and able to serve. Verse one tells about the uniqueness of every child. Verse two tells of the things each can do with his or her own talents to be of service. The message can help build self-esteem in children, especially those with handicaps or those who feel left out because of cultural differences. The last four staffs of the piece are distinct in their composition, changing to the key of B flat from the key of G and forming an ethereal interlude between the first and second verses. The verses can be sung alone, but the last four lines add a charm and lightness to the piece. The optional obbligato can be played on piano, bells, flute, or recorder.

Teaching Suggestions:

1. Introduce this song by identifying some of the many differences among the children. Have them group themselves by color of eyes, color of hair, or by some of their talents (musical, artistic, or personality traits). Emphasize that no one trait is better than another, but that each person is special.

2. Sing the song several times and ask the children to discover what two things it tells us are different (every star and every child), how all children are the same (every one is needed), and if any two are just alike. Invite them to sing the phrases as they learn them. Display pictures of children with different physical characteristics and nationalities.

3. Post keywords to teach verse two to identify what each child can do, even though all are different (shine for others, feel my love, follow commandments, help another, choose the right, have faith and courage).

4. Draw or paste stars of different shapes and colors on a poster and attach a picture of a child to each. Have the faces representative of different ages and various cultures.

5. Express your love for all of the children and your assurance that God loves each one, even though they are different.

Faith   96

Words: Beatrice Goff Jackson
Music: Michael Finlinson Moody
First Line: Faith is knowing the sun will rise
Topics Indexed: Eternal Life, Faith, Heavenly Father, Obedience,
  Plan of Salvation, Prayer, Premortal Existence

This song describes the principle of faith through easily understood examples that even young children experience: sunrise and
prayer. It makes reference to the experiment in Alma 32 of planting
the seed of faith and seeing it grow. Beatrice Jackson says, "Faith
is sometimes difficult to understand. I feel the Lord wants the
Primary children . . . to learn about faith in everyday terms so they
will know that they already have the beginnings of faith. . . . Even
though we can't see our Heavenly Father while we are here on
earth, we can know, through faith, that he is near, he loves us, and
he knows what we're doing."

The music contains four four-measure phrases, none with the
same melody. The ascending melody seems to represent the rising
of the sun, the growing of the seed, and the swelling of the heart.
Phrase one moves stepwise to the end. Phrase two has a quiet,
submissive strain that reminds us of prayer. The third phrase begins
on D, which is repeated eight times, and then rises step-by-step
to emphasize the growth of the seed as it reaches upward. Phrase
four includes the repetition of the notes D and A for emphasis
and a fermata at the point of climax on the word "heart." The song
offers an opportunity for beautiful dynamic expression.

Teaching Suggestions:

1. Ask the children if they have a heart. After they respond, ask
them how they know they have a heart. (Use other such examples.)
Explain that when we know something is true, even though we
haven't seen it, we have faith. Invite them to listen to you sing the
first verse and count how many times the word "faith" is sung.

2. Teach the other verses by asking questions such as these:
"Faith is something that grows larger and larger. Can you find a
word that means growing larger?" (Swelling.) "Faith is also like
something that is very small. What is it?" (Seed.) "Can you listen
for two things that the song tells us faith is?" (Knowing the sun
will rise and knowing the Lord hears my prayers.) After each

question, sing the song, allow the children to answer, and encourage them to sing the phrase of the song in which the answer is found. Ask similar questions to teach verse two. Be sure that the children understand the meaning of all the words, such as "faith," "trust," and "mortal birth."

3. Ask the children to notice that the rhythm is the same for the first two phrases of the song. Point out the interesting rhythm of the third phrase with its sixteenth note. Have them tap or clap these beat patterns.

4. Use visual aids to enhance the learning process, such as pictures of the sun, a child in prayer, a seed, a heart, and Christ. Use keywords, such as "faith," "sun," "prayers," "seed," and "heart." Younger children will enjoy using body actions to portray the rising sun, prayer, planting a seed (in the hand), and the heart.

5. Encourage the children to perform the song with meaning as you direct them to follow the dynamic and tempo markings. (Slower, broadening, a tempo, an increase in volume in the fourth phrase, and a fermata on the word "heart.")

Falling Snow 248

Words and Music: Lois Lunt Metz
First Line: Falling down, gently down
Topics Indexed: Winter

This song is a simple, straightforward expression of the peaceful, joyful feeling associated with the quietly falling snow. When Lois Metz moved to California, she missed the snow that she had enjoyed as she grew up in Utah, so she wrote this song for children everywhere. It is most appropriate for younger age groups and could be used in the nursery and in the Sunbeam and Star classes with lessons about the winter or nature.

The rhythm pattern in the first line is repeated in the second line. The melody and words of the first two measures are duplicated in measures five and six. The melody moves appropriately downward each time "falling down, gently down" is sung.

Teaching Suggestions:
1. Introduce this song by asking the children to solve the riddle: "What is soft and quiet as it falls down?" After the children guess, sing the song to them.
2. Teach "Falling Snow" by rote, singing the first phrase and

having the children repeat it. Sing in this "follow-the-leader" fashion without stopping throughout the song. Use a picture of a snow scene to illustrate the feeling. (The sketch included in the *Children's Songbook* on the same page as the song is ideal.)

3. This song lends itself to expression through extemporaneous movement. Small children in a classroom setting will enjoy moving to the music as they sing.

Families Can Be Together Forever   188

Words: Ruth Muir Gardner
Music: Vanja Y. Watkins
First Line: I have a fam'ly here on earth
Topics Indexed: Eternal Life, Family History, Heavenly Father,
  Plan of Salvation, Preparation, Temples

This song centers on three ideas: that we want to be with our families forever, that Heavenly Father has given us a plan so we can be together, and that we must prepare ourselves so that we can go to the temple. "Families Can Be Together Forever" has been sung for wedding receptions, funerals, and family reunions. Each time it is performed, it brings feelings of love for family and for a kind Heavenly Father who placed us in our families.

The words to the second verse were written to help children understand that even though their parents might not have married in the temple, they can prepare for eternal families themselves by planning for temple marriage. The last phrase of the chorus, "the Lord has shown me how I can," is repeated for emphasis.

Many stories have been told about positive effects of this song. One father, as he knelt with his family at an altar in the Salt Lake Temple, told why he was there. He said that as the Primary children sang this song in sacrament meeting, his heart was touched, and he resolved to prepare himself to be worthy to take his family to the temple so that they could be together forever.

Teaching Suggestions:

1. Show the children a picture of your family, without identifying them, and tell how good these people are to you. Sing the song and ask the children to listen to find out who the people in the picture are. Invite them to sing the first phrase of the song with you.

2. You could also introduce the song by choosing two or three

children to come to the front. Have each of them pick enough children to stand with them to represent the people in their families. Tell the children that even though our families may not be the same in number or in age or sex, they are still our families and are the most important things in the world to us.

3. Ask the children to share ways that their families are good to them. Ask them to listen to you sing the song again and find a word that means "forever and ever." ("Eternity.") After they discover it, invite them to sing the second line with you.

4. Teach the chorus by asking the children, "Do you want to be with your family through all eternity?" Sing the chorus and invite the children to sing the phrases as they learn them.

5. In teaching the second verse, help the children understand that even though their parents might not yet have been married in the temple, they can prepare themselves to go to the temple when they are older.

6. Show a picture of a temple near where you live and explain that Heavenly Father's plan is for our families to be sealed in the temple so that we can be together forever. Place word strips with important words or phrases from the song as stepping stones or stairs leading to the door of the temple.

7. Make paper-doll chains of four or five dolls, each representing a family, connected at the hands and feet. Write keywords on the paper dolls to help the children remember the sequence of the words. Or write words on narrow strips of paper and link them together in a paper chain to show that families can be united together.

Family Night   195

Words and Music: Carol Graff Gunn
First Line: This is the night we've waited for
Topics Indexed: Family Home Evening

Carol Graff Gunn composed this song for her own family to sing on family night. It outlines things families do together and emphasizes the love that grows as they share this special time.

The first two-measure phrase of the melody is repeated in the second phrase, one note lower, and the third phrase is almost the same as the first phrase. The melody of lines one and three is identical, and lines two and four begin the same but end with a variation. Seven measures have a quarter, two eighths, quarter,

quarter rhythm pattern. The repetition makes the song easy to teach and remember.

Teaching Suggestions:

1. Ask the children to listen as you sing a song and see if they can guess what the name of it is. Sing it, leaving out the words "family night" at the end of lines two and four and humming these notes instead. When the children discover the name, display pictures of various family-night activities, or have the children tell what they do when their families gather together. Sing the song and have them join in with the words "family night" as they occur.

2. Ask questions such as these: "Who is together on family night?" "What activities does the song say we do on family night?" After each question, sing the song, receive a response from the children, and encourage them to sing the part of the song that includes the answer to the question.

3. Invite the children to clap or tap the rhythm as they sing. They could pitch-level conduct the song with you to help them feel the direction of the melody.

4. Use keywords and pictures of the activities that the song describes. Encourage the children to sing with enthusiasm and cheerfulness.

Family Prayer 189

Words and Music: DeVota Mifflin Peterson
First Line: Let us gather in a circle and kneel in fam'ly prayer
Topics Indexed: Prayer

The inspiration for this song came from Sister Peterson's childhood. She says, "Our family knelt before meals to pray. We'd turn our plates upside down, turn our chairs away from the table, and then kneel at the chairs for the blessing on the food. At night before bedtime, we knelt with our parents for evening prayer. This time we joined hands in a circle and thanked our Heavenly Father for his many blessings to us. It was easy for me to express my sentiments in words and music because of the example set for me by my family."

This is a reverent song with a strong message of the beauty and warmth felt through prayer in the family. The rhythm moves smoothly and evenly except in the next-to-last measure. It should be sung peacefully, with connected tones.

Teaching Suggestions:

1. Display pictures of several kinds of prayer: blessing on the food, individual, church, and family prayer. Introduce the song to the children by asking them which kind of prayer you are singing about. Or ask a family to attend Primary to sing it to the children. They could introduce the principles taught and tell what a happy experience it is to have family prayer together.

2. An ideal setting for learning "Family Prayer" is in the home as the family gathers together for prayer. The children will quickly learn to sing it by rote as they hear leaders or parents sing it. Sing the first phrase and have them repeat it in "follow-the-leader" style, and so on through the song.

Father, I Will Reverent Be 29

Words and Music: Mildred Tanner Pettit
First Line: Father, I will rev'rent be
Topics Indexed: Chapel, Prayer, Prayer Songs, Reverence

The purpose of this song is to create a feeling of reverence for the Lord's house and to encourage the children to show reverence in their actions. The music has been simplified in its chording and slight changes have been made in the rhythm to make the beat pattern of each line parallel. The rhythm is mostly even and should be sung smoothly, with connected tones. The last line is a prayerful repeat of the words of the first line, to be sung softer and slower. The children may need extra help to learn to sing the difficult octave interval in lines four and five.

Teaching Suggestions:

1. Ask the children what it means to be reverent in church. Ask them to listen to a new song to learn what we should do to be reverent. As the children respond, post word strips or illustrations of the phrases that tell how we can be reverent: walk quietly, fold arms, bow head, close eyes, listen, feel, and speak. Have seven children hold the word strips or pictures and, as you sing the song again, have them hold up the word strips in the order in which they come.

2. Ask: "How should I walk in the Lord's house?" "What do I do when I pray?" "What do I listen to in the Lord's house?" "What should my thoughts and speech be?" After each question, sing the song, receive responses, and ask the children to sing the part of

the song that contains the answer. Have them identify the rhyming words in each line and help them notice that the melody of line one is the same as in line three.

3. Explain that the last line is a special ending (coda) which repeats the words of the first line because they are so important. Encourage them to sing this line thoughtfully, softer and slower.

Father Up Above   23

Words: Mabel Jones Gabbott
Music: Gladys Ericksen Seely
First Line: O Father, look on us today and bless us with thy love
Topics Indexed: Prayer Songs

This eight-measure song elicits a feeling of reverence and love for our Heavenly Father. The words are written as a prayer. The simple melody has been enhanced in the *Children's Songbook* by lightening the left-hand chording.

The smooth, step-by-step melodic progression with few skips creates a lyrical quality. There is no repetition in the four short phrases. The rhythm is the same in lines one and two and is even and connected throughout.

Teaching Suggestions:

1. Have one or two children learn the song before it is presented to the other children, and allow them to introduce this prayer song to the group. After they sing it two or three times, invite all the children to join in.

2. Ask the children to listen to the song and discover to *whom* we pray and in *whose name* we pray. Explain that we pray to Heavenly Father in the name of Jesus Christ. Have a leader or an older child read a scripture that supports this truth. (D&C 88:64; John 16:23.) Encourage the children to sing smoothly, reverently, and with feeling.

Father, We Thank Thee for the Night   8

Words: Rebecca Weston
Music: Grietje Terburg Rowley
First Line: Father, we thank thee for the night
Topics Indexed: Gratitude, Prayer Songs

This is a song of thanks to our Heavenly Father written in the form of a prayer, with words that are understandable even for little children. New music to Rebecca Weston's words has been written by Grietje Rowley for the *Children's Songbook*. The composer tells us that she created a quiet and peaceful feeling in the song to match the emotions we experience at nighttime; but, with the words "and for the pleasant morning light," she changed to a bright, wide-awake sound, and then returned to the night feeling. Sister Rowley accomplishes this change by introducing accidentals that momentarily place us in the key of A-flat major.

Teaching Suggestions:

1. Show the children a picture of a child looking out the window into the night. (One appears with this song in the *Children's Songbook*.) Ask them to share their ideas of what this child might be thinking. After their responses, ask them to listen as you sing a song that tells what the child's thoughts might be.

2. Use simple visual aids illustrating keywords, such as "night," "morning light," "rest," "food," "loving care," and "day."

3. Help the children sing this song with expression and meaning. Emphasize that it is a prayer of gratitude to our Heavenly Father for some of the things that he gives us.

Fathers   209

Words: Dawn Hughes Ballantyne and Joyce Mills
  Jensen
Music: Joyce Mills Jensen
First Line: The father of our home leads our family
Topics Indexed: Bishops, Fathers, Guidance, Heavenly Father,
  Praise

"In trying to describe what our fathers do for us, it soon became apparent that we are blessed with the protection, guidance, and love of more than one father—the father of our home, the father of our ward, and our Heavenly Father," says Joyce Jensen. The words of her composition help all children identify with a loving, caring father, regardless of their circumstances. Many Primary leaders have expressed gratitude for this song because it shows that every child has a father, even though some do not have fathers in their homes.

Each of the musical phrases is different in the song, and there are some unexpected tonal skips. The rhythm of most of the measures has an even beat with four quarter notes. The song has three verses and a chorus.

Teaching Suggestions:

1. Introduce the song with a discussion of what a father is (a parent; a person who is like a father, such as the bishop; and our Heavenly Father). Have the children tell what they think each of these fathers does for us. The bishop and one of the children's fathers could be asked to act as "visual aids."

2. As you sing each verse, ask the children to discover what the song tells us about the father described in the lyrics. Point out that the chorus informs us that fathers love, watch, protect, guide, and direct us, and that these descriptions apply to each of the fathers mentioned in the verses.

3. Help the children follow the direction of the melody by pitch-level conducting it.

4. Conclude by bearing testimony of the reality of our Heavenly Father, that he is the father of us all, and that he does love and care for us.

Feliz Cumpleaños   282

Words and Music: Maurine Benson Ozment
First Line: "Feliz Cumpleaños," that's how they say it in Spain
Topics Indexed: Birthdays, Variety of Languages, Worldwide
  Church

Unique in rhythm and message, this has become a favorite birthday song of children all over the Church. Its message is simply that it doesn't matter where in the world you live, it is always appropriate to say, "Happy birthday to you." Maurine Ozment thought the song would broaden each child's awareness and appreciation for those of other countries and cultures. A second verse has been added for the *Children's Songbook* to include the languages of Samoan, Japanese, and Korean. The accompaniment has been simplified without compromising the charm and interest of the syncopated rhythm and melodic pattern. The key change in the first two measures of the third line has been accomplished through adding accidentals instead of changing the key signature. The unique feature of the music is the uneven rhythm and the variety of beat patterns. Notice particularly the triplets, the dotted-eighth and sixteenth-note combinations, and the measures with syncopation. The pronunciation guide is included below the lyrics to provide easier access to the correct sounds.

Teaching Suggestions:

1. Make word strips for each language and assign small groups of children to each learn to say "happy birthday" in one language. Sing the song to them and have the groups join in with the specific languages they know. After the children master one language, have them exchange word strips and learn a new language, until all have learned every language used in the song.

2. Display cutouts of children from different lands and place them around a birthday cake to illustrate the idea of the song.

3. Practice and learn the various rhythm patterns and where each occurs in the song, so that you can help the children sing it correctly.

Follow the Prophet   110

Words and Music: Duane E. Hiatt
First Line: Adam was a prophet, first one that we know
Topics Indexed: Bible, Guidance, Prophets

This light piece, written with a Jewish folk-song flavor, tells the story of some of the Old Testament prophets. It has nine verses, including ones about Adam, Enoch, Noah, Abraham, Moses, Samuel, Jonah, and Daniel; each details some of the events in the prophet's life. The last verse expresses the importance of following our latter-day prophet. It is not intended that all the verses be sung at one time, but as children learn about a prophet in the Old Testament, they can enjoy singing the verse that goes with the story. Brother Hiatt says, "Trying to entertain, educate, and inspire fifteen children in home evenings over the years has helped me develop an appreciation for what music and rhythm can do in teaching. . . . The song is fun with piano accompaniment. It's also fun accompanied by a guitar, banjo, mandolin, or just hand claps and finger snapping on the off beats. Adding a tambourine or other rhythm instruments also adds life to the song. We've had good times in home evenings pantomiming the situations in the verses and then doing a little shuffle in the choruses." This is a song to be enjoyed in the home, around a campfire, or as a fun song in Primary.

The melody of the first four measures is repeated in the next four measures, and the melody of the first four measures of the chorus is also repeated in the final four measures. Six measures of the chorus contain a syncopated rhythm created by an eighth note, quarter note, eighth note, quarter note, quarter note.

Teaching Suggestions:

1. Teach the chorus first. Have the children clap or tap as you sing the words. Use rhythm instruments to accent the beat and have them count how many times they sing "Follow the prophet."

2. Tell the stories of the prophets, one at a time, and have the children learn the verse that illustrates each story. Use pictures of the prophets.

For Health and Strength 21

Words and Music: Anonymous
First Line: For health and strength and daily food
Topics Indexed: Gratitude, Health, Praise, Rounds

This round is a one-line prayer of gratitude and praise. A simple left-hand chording has been added to provide a supportive accompaniment. The points of entry for each new part in the round come on the fourth beat of each measure. The melody of the song moves down the scale, with some repeated notes, from high C to F. There is an even quarter-note rhythm throughout. Children of all ages will enjoy this simple round with a meaningful message.

Teaching Suggestions:

1. Introduce this song by singing it and then inviting the children to sing it with you. Encourage them to notice that the melody begins with an octave interval, and then the notes move down the scale step by step. Illustrate the contour of the melody on a chart.

2. Post keywords, such as "health," "strength," "good," "praise," and "Lord." Help the children recognize that this song is a simple expression of gratitude and praise to our Heavenly Father who gives us everything.

3. After the children have learned the song well, have them sing it as a round.

For Thy Bounteous Blessings 21

Words: Lester Bucher
Music: Traditional melody, arranged by Vanja Y. Watkins
First Line: For thy bounteous blessings, for thy wondrous word
Topics Indexed: Gratitude, Prayer Songs, Rounds

This is a beautiful prayer song written in a minor mode with an appealing accompaniment. The minor key adds a feeling of greatness and wonder for the blessings we receive from the Lord. The only change in the song for the *Children's Songbook* is that the last chord resolves to the major key with the addition of an A natural. Children of all ages will enjoy singing this lovely song as written or as a round without accompaniment.

Each of the four short musical phrases is different. The rhythm of the first line is repeated in the second line. The melody moves smoothly, with connected tones and an even beat pattern.

Teaching Suggestions:

1. Introduce the song by telling the children that you will sing a prayer song to them, and they should listen for three things that we express thanks for. After they discover the three things, post the word strips "bounteous blessings," "wondrous word," and "loving kindness." Clarify the meaning of these words for the children. As you sing again, ask the children to join in singing the words on the word strips.

2. In order to achieve a reverent feeling, encourage the children to express in song the feeling they have when they pray to their Heavenly Father.

Friends Are Fun 262

Words and Music: Glenn Gordon
First Line: It is fun to have a friend who will play with you
Topics Indexed: Friends

This song of friendship tells that it takes giving and sharing to make friends, and that friends bring happiness. Glenn Gordon skillfully matched the musical setting and message of the song. The lively beat pattern in the first two measures is repeated in measures three and four and in measures five and six. The melody of these measures is similar, but not identical. The use of six eighth notes, moving up and down step-by-step, gives the feeling of a running motion. Several dissonant chords add a playful quality. The song should be sung with a quick pace to support the cheerful spirit intended.

Teaching Suggestions:

1. Introduce the song by asking the children if they like to have friends. Then ask them to listen as you sing the song, and see if they can find the "secret" to having a friend. After they discover the "secret," have them sing that part: "but to have a friend, you must be a friend, too."

2. Ask questions to encourage the children to listen and learn the words of the song: "What two things is it fun to have a friend do with you?" "For how long do you want to have a friend?" After they reply, have them sing that part of the song with you, adding each part to those they have learned. Ask similar questions about verse two.

3. Use pictures of friends doing things together to illustrate the song, or use word strips of keywords.

Fun to Do   253

Words: Rebecca Stevens
Music: Cecilia Johns
First Line: Singing a song is fun to do
Topics Indexed: Action Songs, Friends, Service, Sharing, Singing

This catchy song is a versatile activity melody that can be sung in Primary as a rest song, in the younger Primary classes, and in the home as a song for fun. Many words can be used to illustrate what is fun to do, such as "sharing my toys," "reading a book," "helping a friend," and others that can be created to fit any occasion. "Fun to Do" could also be used to motivate small children to do tasks that are required of them, such as "cleaning my room," "picking up toys," or "making my bed."

The eight-measure melody is easy to learn, with measures one and two the same as five and six. The notes in the final two measures move by steps down the scale to C. The skipping rhythm is accented with the singing of the words "to do" eight times, each with a "short-long" beat. The children will enjoy clapping this snappy rhythm and improvising actions to illustrate the words that they sing.

Teaching Suggestion:

This song requires no formal teaching. The children will sing along with you and do the actions suggested by the words. Invite a child to sing what he or she thinks is fun to do, and then have all of them join in singing.

Genealogy—I Am Doing It   94

Words and Music: Jeanne P. Lawler
First Line: Genealogy—I am doing it
Topics Indexed: Family History

Jeanne Lawler wrote this song after having worked for some time on her four-generation charts. She says it was a "great, lively experience.... I especially liked the idea of meeting every one of [my ancestors] someday, and I could just visualize myself saying, 'You belong to me ... and I belong to you.' " Children will appreciate the significance of the message: by doing genealogy we make a record of our families, and families can be sealed for eternity.

The charm of this song is centered around the catchy rhythm with many dotted-eighth-note/sixteenth-note combinations. This enhances the word "genealogy." The beat pattern is identical in each of the first three lines. The melody contains easy intervals, mostly moving by steps. The repetitions in melody and rhythm seem to invite the children to tap or clap with the music.

Teaching Suggestions:

1. Show a word strip with the letters "Y-E-G-G-E-L-O-N-A" printed on it, and ask the children if they know what it means. Explain that it is not a real word, but that if the letters are rearranged they form an important word. Ask them to discover it in a song you will sing. After they identify the word, arrange the letters correctly.

2. Teach the other phrases of the song by asking questions, having the children listen for the answers, then asking them to sing the phrase that contains the answer. Ask: "What does the song say genealogy is?" "The song mentions something I will keep and something I will write as I do my genealogy. What are these?" "As I do genealogy, what is very clear to me?"

3. Use visual aids, such as a Book of Remembrance, a journal, or a pedigree chart.

4. In a related activity, involve the children in filling in simple pedigree charts of their families.

"Give," Said the Little Stream   236

Words: Fanny J. Crosby
Music: William B. Bradbury
First Line: "Give," said the little stream
Topics Indexed: Cheerfulness, Jesus Christ—Example, Service,
    Sharing, Singing, Talents

This favorite song reminds children that no matter how small they are, they can improve the world by serving and sharing. The song as we know it today appeared in 1920 in *The Primary Songbook* and has been in every children's songbook of the Church since that time, with the exception of the first edition of *Sing with Me*. The second edition of this publication again included " 'Give,' Said the Little Stream," as it was evident that members of the Church were not willing to give up this beloved song. It consists of three verses and a chorus, and there are several phrases where the words and/or music are repeated. The repeated use of the words "give, oh! give" and "give away" is one of the distinctive characteristics of the song. Note that the harmony of the entire song is built on the three primary chords of the D major scale, making it easy to add a guitar or autoharp accompaniment.

Teaching Suggestions:
1. Have several simple items in a basket to give away, such as a pencil, an apple, or other small things. Ask the children how they feel when they receive something. Ask them to tell about a time when they have given something away, and how they felt. Have a child read the scripture from Acts 20:35, "It is more blessed to give than to receive."

2. Show a picture of a verdant landscape with a river flowing through it, and a picture of a desert. Ask the children what could be given to the desert to make it grow beautiful with grass and flowers. Show a wilted flower and a healthy one and ask what could be given to the wilted flower to make it healthy. Ask them to listen to a song that tells how water gives life to the fields and flowers.

3. Teach the chorus first. Show a word strip saying "give" and ask the children to count how many times they hear the word as you sing the chorus. Invite them to sing the chorus with you.

4. Ask: "What happens to the fields where the stream goes?" "What does the little stream say?" "What does the rain do for the

flowers?" After each question, sing the song, invite the children to respond, and then ask them to join you in singing that part of the song.

5. Help the children understand the message — that it is important to give and share. Discuss things that little children can give to others to make them happy, such as hugs, kisses, and kind deeds.

6. Have the children tap or clap the rhythm of the melody, that of the bass line in the accompaniment, or two beats to the measure. Divide them into three groups and have each of the groups tap the song in one of these three ways. Encourage them to clap their assigned rhythms while they sing.

7. As they sing, one child could pass an object to the next child in the row (in rhythm if possible), who gives it to the next child, and so on. The object of the activity is to give the object away before the song stops.

Go the Second Mile 167

Words and Music: Ruth Muir Gardner
First Line: When there is a task to do, do it with a smile
Topics Indexed: Dependability, Happiness, Service, Smiles

The theme of this song is taken from Jesus' Sermon on the Mount, in which he said, "And whosoever shall compel thee to go a mile, go with him twain." (Matthew 5:41.) The meaning is concise and clearly stated in the song so that even little children will understand the message. This cheerful song encourages children to freely serve others.

The melody is straightforward and moves with easy steps and skips. Most of the notation consists of quarter notes.

Teaching Suggestions:
1. Introduce the song by showing a picture of Jesus teaching the people on the occasion of the Sermon on the Mount. Explain that Jesus taught the people how they should live and how they should treat each other. Show the children a chart with the words from Matthew 5:41 printed on it and ask if they know what this scripture means. Tell them that you will sing a song to help them understand the scripture.

2. Divide the children into four groups and play "follow the leader" with them. Sing the first phrase and have group 1 repeat

it after you. Without a pause, sing the second phrase and have group 2 repeat this with you, and continue through the song in this way several times. Ask groups 1 and 2 if they would go the second mile by singing their own part plus another group's part, and ask groups 3 and 4 to go the second mile and sing parts 3 and 4. Finally, ask the children to go the second mile by singing all four phrases in "follow-the-leader" style.

3. Discuss the scripture and song with the children so they can understand the principle of going the second mile and how they can apply it in their lives. Tell them that if a Roman soldier in Jesus' time asked for directions or asked you to walk a mile with him to show him a certain place, you were required to do what he asked. But after the first mile, you were no longer obligated to him. You were the one to decide if you would walk the second mile and do more than you were asked to do.

God Is Watching Over All 229

Words: Nellie Poorman
Music: Franz Schubert
First Line: God has numbered in the sky
Topics Indexed: Creation, God's Love, Guidance, Prayer Songs,
  Worth of a Child

This gentle song teaches that God, in his great love for all his creations, is aware of and watching over each one. Previous versions contained a moving accompaniment in the left-hand staff, characteristic of Schubert's music. In the *Children's Songbook* the music has been simplified, but has retained the beautiful harmony and lovely melodic construction.

The melody carries a straight quarter-note beat pattern with a half note at the end of each phrase. The melody patterns of the first three phrases are identical in form, each starting one note lower on the scale, creating a nice progression. The last phrase follows a similar pattern and resolves smoothly to the first note of the scale.

Teaching Suggestions:

1. Introduce this song as you are teaching about the creation of the earth and all that dwells upon it. Ask the children to discover God's creations that are mentioned in the song as you sing. As they name the various creations, display word strips or pictures

to illustrate them. Ask them to sing the word phrases after they identify them.

2. In order to point out the interesting construction of the melody line, have the children sing "la, la, la," to the tune while you pitch-level conduct, or draw a melody line on a chart to show the progression of the notes.

3. When the children are secure in singing the melody, ask the accompanist to play the song one octave higher on the piano while they sing, to create a light, "music-box" effect.

4. Encourage them to sing reverently and with appreciation for the watchful care of our Heavenly Father and for his great creations.

God's Love 97

Words: Elizabeth Cushing Taylor
Music: Grace Wilbur Conant
First Line: We do not see the wind
Topics Indexed: Faith, God's Love, Prayer Songs

This song of faith teaches that even though we cannot see God's love (like the wind), we can feel it and know that he watches over us. The comparison of the wind with God's love helps even little children understand the actuality of his watchful care. In the *Children's Songbook*, there is some thinning of the accompaniment and a change from 4/4 to 2/2 time, which helps the melody to flow.

Each of the four phrases is unique in melody, yet the first, second, and fourth have the same rhythm. The beauty of the melody and the message are enhanced when the song is sung smoothly and connectedly.

Teaching Suggestions:
1. Introduce the song by telling the children that you are going to read them a beautiful poem that helps us understand God's love for us. While you read the words, have the pianist play the song as a background.

2. Show a picture of trees bending in the wind and ask if the children can see the wind blowing. (Or use a small fan to blow a lightweight object, and ask the children if they can see the wind.) After their responses, ask how they know the wind is blowing when they cannot see it. Sing the first verse and ask them how the song

says we can tell when the wind goes by. Continue to teach the words to the first verse by asking questions and inviting the children to sing the phrases as they learn them.

3. Show a picture of Jesus and ask the children how they know that God loves them. After their responses, ask them to listen to the second verse of the song. Teach the words to this verse through questions that provide listening and singing experiences.

4. Teach the last verse in a similar way. Emphasize that we know that the wind blows and that God loves us through faith. Express your faith in the love that God has for each of his children.

Grandmother 200

Words and Music: Nonie Nelson Sorensen
First Line: You give me a kiss. You give me a hug.
Topics Indexed: Grandparents

Though several songs in the *Children's Songbook* use "grandmother" as an alternate word, this is the only one written primarily about grandmother. The words express feelings of love and companionship enjoyed by a child and his or her grandmother. Sister Sorensen says, "My own mother, now dead, and my dear mother-in-law were and are exemplary grandmothers and were the source of the ideas in the song."

The 6/8 time, to be conducted two beats to a measure, suggests the motion of a grandmother's rocking chair. The repeated use of the quarter and eighth notes in the left hand provides the rhythm for this swaying motion. The song is written with three verses in which the last six measures repeat the words, "I wish every child in the whole wide world had a grandmother just like you." A two-measure introduction and conclusion are played by piano accompaniment.

The catchy rhythm is perhaps the most appealing feature of "Grandmother." Children could clap or tap the rhythm of the melody and/or the rhythm of the left-hand accompaniment. They will enjoy holding the word "just" for its unexpected six counts (or two conducted beats).

Teaching Suggestions:
1. Sit in a chair and move back and forth as if you were in a rocking chair as this song is played. Ask the children to guess what you are doing and to think whom the rocking chair might remind them of. As they respond, show pictures of grandmothers.

2. Ask them how many of them have grandmothers, and how grandmothers show that they love their grandchildren. They could pantomime the things they mention that are also words to the song.

3. Teach the children the words through questions and through actions improvised to match the words.

4. Invite a grandmother to visit the Primary to tell what makes her happy about having grandchildren. Her remarks could tie to the message of verse three.

Had I Been a Child   80

Words: Mabel Jones Gabbott
Music: Darwin Wolford
First Line: Had I been a child when Jesus came
Topics Indexed: Book of Mormon, Jesus Christ—Ministry,
   Jesus Christ—Second Coming, Preparation, Resurrection

This song is an expression of the feelings a child might have regarding the episode told in the Book of Mormon when the Savior visited the Nephites and blessed the children. The first two verses express what a child might wonder had he or she been with Jesus on that special occasion. The last verse shows the child looking forward to the time when Jesus will come again and hoping to be prepared to meet the Savior on that day. The words carry a feeling of the love Jesus has for all children in all times.

The song has a simple but moving melody and can be sung without an accompaniment. However, the piano supplies colorful harmonies that lend beauty and expression to the fine poem. There are several measures of introduction and conclusion. Each of the four phrases is unique in melody and rhythm. The notes of the melody move smoothly by steps and easy intervals.

Teaching Suggestions:

1. Introduce this song by having the children find and read 3 Nephi 17:21–24. (If the children are too young to read, read some of the scripture to them with a picture to illustrate it.) Ask them to tell how they might have felt if they had been with Jesus on that occasion. Ask them to listen to a song that tells how a child might feel.

2. Ask: "To whom did Jesus come, that blessed day?" "What did Jesus show the children?" "Why did Jesus kneel with them?"

"What might Jesus have done to me?" "What might Jesus have said?" "Where might Jesus place his hands?" After each question, sing the song, accept responses, and ask the children to sing the part of the song where the answer is found, each time repeating the parts they have already learned.

3. Use word strips of keywords to help remind the children of the sequence of the words. Use a picture of Jesus blessing the children in Book of Mormon times to help them visualize the event. The illustration found on page 80 in the *Children's Songbook* is a beautiful representation.

4. Express how you feel about Jesus and his blessing of the children and bear testimony of the truth of this wonderful story.

Happy, Happy Birthday 284

Words and Music: Mildred E. Millett
First Line: Happy, happy birthday, children dear
Topics Indexed: Birthdays

The melody of this birthday song is catchy, appealing, and easily learned, and the words are simple and to the point. In a 1983 survey of children's songs, "Happy, Happy Birthday" was found to be one of the most popular with the children of the Church. The words can be individualized by adding the name of the child instead of the word "children."

Four of the eight measures have almost the same rhythm pattern (four eighth notes and two quarter notes). Measures one, five, and seven repeat the same melody with slight variation.

Teaching Suggestions:

1. Introduce the song by asking the children if they like to play follow the leader. Then sing a phrase, have them repeat that phrase, go on to the next phrase, and so on through the song.

2. Use a picture of a birthday cake as a visual aid.

3. Have the children clap or tap the rhythm of the song.

Happy Song 264

Words: Anonymous
Music: Czech folk song
First Line: Ducks in the pond quack a happy song

Topics Indexed: Happiness, Singing, Spring

This piece provides a message of the oneness and happiness all nature expresses through song. The simplicity of the theme makes it appropriate for children of nursery, Sunbeam, and Star age, yet the syncopated rhythm and wordy lyrics can be difficult. However, once they have mastered it, "Happy Song" will be a favorite of all the children.

The rhythm in lines one, two, and four is identical. Eight measures contain the syncopated (eighth note, quarter note, eighth note) rhythm. The melody of line two imitates that of line one, five tones higher on the scale. With a few exceptions, lines three and four move down the scale by steps. The song has identical words in the last line of both verses.

Teaching Suggestions:

1. Capture one or more of the sounds mentioned in the song on a tape recorder (birds singing, ducks quacking, hens cackling, wind blowing). Introduce the song by playing the recording, inviting the children to identify the sounds, and asking them if these are happy or sad sounds. Tell them that they can help you sing a happy song by singing the words, "a happy song," on the correct pitches. Invite them to sing these words each time they occur as you sing the entire song.

2. Tell the children that many of Heavenly Father's creations sing, and that they can discover what some of these are as you sing the song again. Have the children hold pictures of each of the things mentioned (ducks, hens, birds, wind, and children) as they sing.

3. Divide the children into three groups (one for each line) and have each group sing its line, with all groups joining in singing the last line. One child from each group could hold a picture representing the line that group is singing.

4. Encourage the children to tap or clap the uneven beat pattern.

5. Conclude by telling the children how happy it makes you feel to hear them sing in such a cheerful way.

Have a Very Happy Birthday! 284

Words: Mabel Jones Gabbott
Music: Michael Finlinson Moody
First Line: Have a very happy birthday

Topics Indexed: Birthdays

This song wishes children a very happy birthday filled with joy, gladness, and love of friends. It invites them to share their happiness with others. The meaning of each verse stands by itself, so for variety any one of the three verses could be used. The catchy tune is jovial and light-hearted.

The four musical phrases begin with two sixteenth-note pick-ups. The even rhythm of the first three phrases of this song is the same, though each has a different melody. There are several intervals that the children will need to listen to carefully so that they can sing them accurately. The melody moves quickly and with expression to create an exciting birthday song.

Teaching Suggestions:

1. Tell the children that they are going to learn a new birthday song that is filled with good wishes and advice. As you sing the song, ask them to listen for some of the birthday wishes. Display word strips as they identify them (sunshine everywhere, joy and gladness, love of friends).

2. Through questions, listening experiences, and singing of the various phrases, teach the children the rest of the song.

3. Take care to teach the intervals and the rhythm correctly. Pitch-level conduct the song until the children learn it well.

4. Teach each verse as a separate song, so that when all are mastered, the children will know three birthday songs.

5. Use a picture of a birthday cake as a visual aid.

Have a Very Merry Christmas! 51

Words: Mabel Jones Gabbott
Music: Michael Finlinson Moody
First Line: Have a very merry Christmas
Topics Indexed: Christmas

This cheerful Christmas song carries a light-hearted, joyful sentiment with a feeling of reverence at the mention of loved ones and the baby Jesus. Mabel Gabbott says that her words were inspired by the happy experiences in her home and with her own children at Christmastime.

The melody is essentially the same for this song as for "Have a Very Happy Birthday," except in this song each phrase begins on the first beat of the measure instead of the upbeat. The first two notes of each phrase are a dotted-eighth note and a sixteenth note.

Teaching Suggestions:

1. Introduce the song by having the children share some of the things that they do at Christmastime.

2. Direct the children's attention to word strips or pictures displayed around the room to represent parts of the Christmas song. As you sing it, challenge them to find the word strips or pictures that you sing about. (Examples: scatter gladness, sing carols, care for neighbors, ring bell, trim tree.) After you sing each verse, ask several children to each find one of the things mentioned and stand in front of the group with that picture or word strip, in the order that it occurs in the song. Then have all the children join you in singing the verse and checking to see if the children have placed the words and pictures correctly.

3. Encourage the children to sing the intervals accurately and keep the exact rhythm, through listening and then repeating.

4. The children will enjoy tapping the uneven rhythm that occurs in every other measure.

He Died That We Might Live Again   65

Words: Thelma McKinnon Anderson
Music: Charlene Anderson Newell
First Line: He died that we might live again
Topics Indexed: Atonement, Easter, Resurrection

This Easter song was written by a mother and her daughter. Charlene Newell composed the music in Hawaii, and her mother wrote the words in Price, Utah. They consulted day by day, line by line, by telephone across the Pacific Ocean. The important message of praise and gratitude for the Savior's sacrifice will be especially significant for the older children.

The first and second half of the song are almost the same musically. You might teach it in two parts: the first with the message of the death of our Lord Jesus Christ, and the second with that of his resurrection. Sister Newell says, "The Lord must really be happy to hear a special thank you for the great sacrifice made when he gave his life for all of us. It is a wonderful privilege for us to sing our praises to him."

Four measures are the same rhythmically as the first measure (dotted quarter and five eighth notes), and at least three other measures are almost the same. This beat pattern is a major musical element of this song and brings emotion to the important message.

Teaching Suggestions:

1. Introduce the song by placing the following questions on the chalkboard or on a chart: *Why* did he die? *Who* died? *Where* did he die? *What* did he give for me and you? *When* did he rise? *Who* rose? *What* did he show? For *what* do we give thanks and sing? (Teach half of the song at a time.) All the children can listen for the answers, one question at a time, or each Primary class can be asked to listen for the answer to a different question. As they discover an answer, have them sing the phrase that contains it.

2. Ask the children to find out how many different names are used for *Him* in the song. (Lord Jesus, Redeemer, Savior, King.) Use pictures of the Savior on the cross and the resurrected Christ.

3. Illustrate the rhythm of the first measure with long and short lines or by the actual notes (dotted-quarter, five eighth notes, followed by a dotted-half note). Then have them tap this beat pattern and discover where it is found in the song. (In the first half of the song it occurs every other measure, and in the second it is used with variations.) Give attention to the rhythm and notation of the last phrase, the climax to the song, which should be sung slower and with emphasis.

4. Encourage the children to sing with expression and to understand this song's important message. Bear testimony of the truth that Jesus died that we might live again.

He Sent His Son 34

Words: Mabel Jones Gabbott
Music: Michael Finlinson Moody
First Line: How could the Father tell the world
Topics Indexed: Atonement, Christmas, Easter, Heavenly Father,
  Jesus Christ—Example, Jesus Christ—Son of God,
  Plan of Salvation, Resurrection

This song beautifully introduces the meaning of the birth, death, and mission of the Savior. It is appropriate for any occasion where the mission of Jesus Christ is the subject, including Christmas and Easter.

The text asks questions and gives the answers regarding the

purpose of Heavenly Father sending his Son to the world. The questions are about what Heavenly Father wants us to learn; the answers tell us what he did to teach us these important principles. The musical setting has many opportunities for expression through dynamics, tempo changes, fermatas, and high and low tones. The climax of the song comes as the melody descends to the word "death" and then rises as it tells of the resurrection. The final phrases generate the feelings of peace and beauty that come from living like Jesus.

Teaching Suggestions:

1. Introduce this song by relating briefly the story of our premortal existence in which Heavenly Father presented his plan: we would be going to earth to receive a body and to learn many things, we needed someone to show us the right way to live so we could return to our heavenly home, and Heavenly Father would send Jesus Christ to show us how to live.

2. Ask the children to listen to the song and discover what words are used instead of "Jesus Christ." ("His Son.")

3. Tell them that the song is a series of questions and answers. The questions are about what Heavenly Father wants us to learn. The answers tell us what he did to teach us these important lessons. Ask the children to count how many questions they hear as you sing the song again.

4. Display word strips for each of the six questions so the children can see the questions written out as you sing them.

5. Invite them to sing the answers to the questions as they discover them.

6. Use pictures of Jesus' birth, his life, and his death and resurrection to illustrate the answers to the questions.

7. Give attention to the dynamic markings, ritards, and holds to bring expression and understanding to the song. As the children sing the question about death, help them notice that the melody descends, creating a sad feeling, and as they sing the answer about the resurrection, the melody rises with gladness. Show them that the accompaniment rises even higher than the voices as they hold the word "breath." This is the climax and deserves practice to help them feel the beauty of the music.

8. Divide the children into two groups and have one group sing the questions and the other the answers. Have some voices sing the descant in the last two measures.

9. Bear witness of the important mission of Jesus Christ.

Head, Shoulders, Knees, and Toes 275

Words and Music: Anonymous
First Line: Head, shoulders, knees, and toes
Topics Indexed: Action Songs

This little ditty has been a favorite of young children for many years. It provides variety, fun, and relaxation for many situations in Primary and at home, and is included as a rest song in the nursery and other younger age Primary manuals. You can achieve variety by singing the song at various tempos while the children point to the different parts of the body mentioned. Another version is to have them move the various parts of the body as they are mentioned.

Teaching Suggestion:
The little children will quickly learn this song as they listen to you sing it and as they participate in the actions.

Healthy, Wealthy, and Wise 280

Words: Benjamin Franklin
Music: Moravian folk tune
First Line: Early to bed and early to rise
Topics Indexed: Health, Rounds

The message of this song is taken from one of Benjamin Franklin's pithy statements of wisdom. The first phrase of the music is built around F, the first note of the scale; the second phrase is built around A, the third note of the scale; the third phrase is built around C, the fifth note of the scale; and the final phrase is build around F again, almost duplicating the first phrase. This structure makes the piece easily adaptable as a round. Children of all ages will quickly learn and enjoy singing this little ditty.

Teaching Suggestions:
1. Introduce the song by telling the children a little about the author of the words, Benjamin Franklin, and how he wrote and compiled many wise sayings that have been repeated over the years. Invite them to listen to you sing it to discover what the wise saying is.

2. As the children listen to you sing the song several times, they will soon be able to join in singing with you.

3. After they have learned the song thoroughly, divide the children into two, three, or four groups so that they can sing it as a round.

Heavenly Father, Now I Pray   19

Words and Music: Alvin A. Beesley
First Line: Heav'nly Father, now I pray
Topics Indexed: Prayer Songs

This lovely prayer song is written in a hymnlike style. The rhythm incorporates a straight quarter-note beat pattern with a half note at the end of each phrase. The melody moves smoothly by steps, repeated tones, and short intervals. The notes of the last phrase move in steps from G down the scale to D and back to G. The beauty of this children's prayer song lies in its simplicity, pure message, and excellent musical structure.

Teaching Suggestions:
1. Tell the children that you are going to sing a prayer, and that you would like them to listen for three blessings that are asked of Heavenly Father. Use word strips for these blessings (guide, guard me, feel thy love).

2. Sing the song a phrase at a time, with the children repeating each phrase, without stopping.

3. Do not use a picture of Jesus as a visual aid for this song.

Heavenly Father, While I Pray   23

Words and Music: Becky-Lee Hill Reynolds
First Line: Heav'nly Father, while I pray
Topics Indexed: Prayer Songs, Reverence, Sabbath

This simple, sweet song will help small children prepare reverently for prayer. It is suitable to sing in the nursery, in younger Primary classes, or as a prayer song in opening or closing exercises of Primary.

The construction of the melody is an interesting scale study in that the note pattern for all of the phrases is the same, each beginning one tone lower on the scale. Each phrase begins on the same tone as the last note of the preceding phrase. The beat pattern of the phrases consists of six quarter notes and a half note, except for the last measure, in which there are four quarter notes and a whole note. The smooth rhythm and note progression create a peaceful, flowing feeling appropriate for a prayer song.

Teaching Suggestions:

1. Introduce this song by telling the children that you will sing a song to help them get ready for prayer.

2. Ask: "What day does the song say that it is?" "How may I worship?" Sing the song, let the children answer the questions, and then encourage them to sing with you.

3. Use this prayer song frequently for the children in the younger Primary classes, so that when they hear the melody, they will know it is time for prayer.

4. Draw the note pattern for each of the phrases on a chalkboard or chart. Follow this pattern with a pointer as the children sing or hum and help them realize that the phrases all have the same melody pattern. Invite them to pitch-level conduct the song as they sing it.

Hello, Friends! 254

Words and Music: Wilma Boyle Bunker
First Line: Hello, friends! It's nice to be
Topics Indexed: Friends, Primary

This welcome song is appropriate for the nursery, the younger age groups, for the entire Primary, or for singing in the home. For smaller groups, the individual children's names can be substituted for the word "friends," and the song can be repeated until all of them have been named.

The rhythm pattern is the same for each of the four phrases: six eighth notes and a quarter note. The notation for the first and second lines is identical, with the exception of the last measure, where the notes resolve to the first note of the scale.

Teaching Suggestion:

Sing "Hello, Friends" as your greeting to the children, and then invite them to join you in singing it to each other. The song need not be taught formally; as they listen to it a few times, they will soon be singing it with you. Use it to teach the children about friendships and how to treat one another.

Hello Song   260

Words and Music: Maurine Benson Ozment
First Line: Hello! (Hello!) Hello! (Hello!) We welcome you today
Topics Indexed: Friends, Primary, Two-part Songs

This cheerful song welcomes both regular attenders and new-comers to Primary. It is especially appropriate for visitors (including nonmembers). Maurine Ozment has said, "From my training and experience as a schoolteacher, I always sought for ways to enhance a child's self-image. I felt that being welcomed as a Primary visitor with a specific song would help make a child feel important and special."

One appealing feature of the song is the hello "echo," which is sung seven times. A smaller group can sing these echo parts while the main group holds the note on the first "hello." The first, second, and fourth lines are musically the same, with a variation in the last two measures. The third line offers a different rhythm pattern and note progression for variety and interest, but there is repetition within the phrase. Encourage the children to follow the dynamic markings.

Teaching Suggestions:

1. Tell the children that you are going to teach them a song that will be fun to sing to visitors who come to Primary. Ask them to listen for words that will show visitors that we are happy to have them come. Display the words ("hello," "welcome," "glad," "share," "friend") on the chalkboard or as word strips after the children identify them.

2. As you sing the song again, ask the children to discover how many times they hear the word "hello." Since it occurs thirteen times, they might need to listen to you sing it several times to check the number. Ask the children to join in singing the "hellos" — some the first "hello" and others the echo.

3. To help the children learn the words in the third line, ask them to listen and discover two things that we want for our visitors (to share our Primary and to be our friend). Have them join in singing these phrases.

4. The echo can be sung in different ways: a small group or one child could sing from behind the piano or in the back of the room.

5. Help the children learn to sing this song with louds and softs, with variations in tempo, and observing the holds indicated in the music.

Help Me, Dear Father   99

Words and Music: Frances K. Taylor
First Line: Help me, dear Father, to freely forgive
Topics Indexed: Forgiveness, Heavenly Father, Prayer Songs,
   Repentance

This song teaches that as we learn to forgive others and to repent, we will be living closer to our Heavenly Father. The second verse has been added for the *Children's Songbook* to bring together two principles of the gospel that are closely related: that we should learn to *forgive* others, and that we can receive forgiveness from our Heavenly Father for our wrongdoings through *repentance.* There is a note change in the last line to eliminate having three beats on the word "to." The last line now moves smoothly with the words "Help me live nearer, nearer to thee," using three quarter notes instead of the dotted-half note. The accompaniment has also been thinned.

"Help Me, Dear Father" has a 3/4 time signature, so you will need to help children sing it smoothly without a heavy pulsation on the 1–2–3 count. The note progression is simple, with the melody moving by steps and by short intervals. The notation consists mainly of quarter notes, yet the melody of each phrase is different.

Teaching Suggestions:
   1. Introduce the song by having two children role-play a situation where one says something unkind to the other (such as "I won't play with you"). Then ask the children to listen to a song to find something that will help the "actors" know what they should do. After you sing the first verse, have them determine that one of the children needs to forgive the other child (post a word strip that says "forgive"), and the other child should repent (post a word strip, "repent"). The children who acted out the parts should be encouraged to finish the role-playing by expressing forgiveness and repentance.
   2. Teach the chorus by asking questions and having the children listen for and sing the answers. Teach the verses in the same way.

3. Use the scripture from Matthew 6:14–15 to help the children understand the principles of forgiveness and repentance.

Help Us, O God, to Understand 73

Words and Music: D. Evan Davis
First Line: Help us, O God, to understand
Topics Indexed: Atonement, Sacrament

In an article in the *Instructor,* D. Evan Davis tells us that the words of the first verse of this song are a simplification of a sacrament gem quoted by President David O. McKay in *Gospel Ideals*:

Help us, O God, to realize
The great atoning sacrifice.
The gift of thy Beloved Son
The Prince of Life, the Holy One.

Though this was written as a sacrament song, it could be sung on other occasions as the sacrifice and atonement of Jesus Christ are discussed.

The hymn is slow and connected in style, and the harmony is unusual in the richness of the chords written in the minor mood. The last chord resolves to E major. If only the melody tones were heard, they could be in the key of C. It is the harmony that adds the mystical, minor flavor. The notes move by steps, short intervals, and repeated tones, and the rhythm is constant.

Teaching Suggestions:

1. To introduce this song, show a picture of the crucifixion as you sing it.

2. Encourage more thoughtful listening by asking: "What did Jesus do to pay the price for all our sins?" "Why did our Savior die for us?" After they discover the answers in the song, have them sing those parts with you until they have learned all of the song.

3. Add the accompaniment after the children learn the melody. To help them appreciate the beautiful chording and harmony, let them listen to the accompaniment and tell how it makes them feel. Have them listen for the harmony of the last chord to recognize the change in feeling it brings. Encourage them to sing with an ongoing movement in each measure.

4. Express your feelings and testimony regarding the sacrifice our Savior made for us.

Here We Are Together 261

Words: Traditional
Music: Old tune
First Line: Here we are together, together, together
Topics Indexed: Action Songs, Family, Friends, Primary

This familiar and popular folklike tune encourages the feeling of enjoyment as friends and loved ones gather together. The versatility of the melody is unending as the words are changed to accommodate many situations. Several suggestions are included in the *Children's Songbook*. Even though this tune can be sung by even the youngest children, older boys and girls also will find it fun to sing. It is appropriate for home, Primary, activity days, nursery, and the younger age Primary classes.

Teaching Suggestion:
The children will learn to sing this song as parents or leaders sing it to them. No formal teaching is required. Actions can be improvised as the phrases indicate.

Hinges 277

Words: Aileen Fisher
Music: Jeanne P. Lawler
First Line: I'm all made of hinges, 'cause ev'rything bends
Topics Indexed: Action Songs

This song can be sung as a rest or activity tune, just for the fun of it. Jeanne Lawler saw the words in Aileen Fisher's book of poetry, *Up a Windy Hill,* and felt that they would make a wonderful song. It enjoyed immediate success among Primary leaders and children and has been translated into many languages.

The time signature has been changed in the *Children's Songbook* from 3/8 time to 6/8, which establishes an ongoing rhythm. Eighth notes comprise most of the notation, with four quarter and four sixteenth notes added for variety.

Teaching Suggestions:
1. Bring a hinge for the children to see as an attention-getter (or show them a hinge on one of the doors). Ask them to listen to a fun song that describes something that moves like a hinge.

2. Ask the children to listen to find how many times the word "hinges" is sung. Then, as you repeat the song, have them sing the word "hinges" as it occurs.

3. Improvise actions as suggested by the words.

Home 192

Words: Caroline Eyring Miner
Music: K. Newell Dayley
First Line: Home is where the heart is
Topics Indexed: Fathers, God's Love, Guidance, Heavenly Father,
  Mothers

Caroline Miner wrote the words to "Home" when she was recuperating from an illness and feeling great appreciation for the love and care of her family. The order of verses 1 and 2 has been changed in the *Children's Songbook* to present first a message of acceptance for all families, no matter what their situation. Even though not all families have a father, mother, and children present, children can learn about the beauty of this "complete" family and seek to have that kind of family for themselves. At the same time, they can love and appreciate their own families and strive to have peace and the Spirit of our Heavenly Father in their homes.

The musical setting created for the words contributes to the feeling of peace and harmony with a smooth, flowing melody. The most challenging musical aspect of the song occurs in measure six, where the notes skip from B to D and down to A. The slur mark connecting these first two notes indicates that care must be taken to move up to the high note smoothly and in tune. While none of the four phrases of the song are the same, phrases one and three are similar, as are phrases two and four.

Teaching Suggestions:
1. Introduce this song as a riddle by singing the song, omitting the word "home" and humming that note instead. Sing it several times until the children find the answer to the riddle.

2. Place keywords and pictures ("home," "heart," "warmth," "love," "arms") on the chalkboard or on a chart.

3. Ask questions, one at a time, so the children can listen for the answer and then sing that part of the song. Examples: "What two things abound in the home?" "What go all the way around?" (Explain words that the children do not understand.)

4. Use pictures of families participating in various activities to illustrate the song.

5. Teach "Home" as a duet, with older children singing the alto part.

Hosanna 66

Words and Music: Rita S. Robinson; arranged by Chester W. Hill
First Line: Hosanna! Let our voices ring
Topics Indexed: Descants, Easter, Praise, Resurrection, Singing

Rita Robinson tells how "Hosanna" came to be written: "I was searching the scriptures, and it was a spontaneous outburst of praise from my heart. *Hosanna* is a joyful outburst of love and adoration. When we are close to the Lord, we can hardly contain the joy we feel."

The melody of the first four measures is almost duplicated in the second four measures. This is followed by the singing of hosannas with the echo descant. The movement of the melody is almost entirely by steps or by intervals of a third. The rhythm is mostly straight quarter notes, with three instances of a dotted-quarter note followed by an eighth note. With the added descant the song creates an engaging musical number that would be suitable for special programs. Children should be encouraged to sing with expression, following the dynamic markings in the song.

Teaching Suggestions:

1. Briefly tell the children about Jesus' triumphal entry into Jerusalem, as described in Matthew 21:1–11. Ask them to listen to a beautiful song to discover the word that the people used on that occasion. After they identify the word, help them understand the meaning of "hosanna" and why it is used.

2. Ask them to listen to you sing the song again to discover how many times they hear the word "hosanna." As you sing, ask them to join you in singing "hosanna" as it occurs.

3. Ask questions, one at a time, that can be answered by exact words from the song, such as these: "To whom do we sing 'all hail'?" "What does the song say that he brings?" "Who should sing?" After the children find the answer to a question, have them join in singing that part of the song.

4. Use word strips of keywords and a picture of Jesus' triumphal entry into Jerusalem.

5. Teach the descant part separately. When both parts are familiar to the children, divide them into two groups, one for the melody and the other for the descant. Encourage them to sing with expression, noting that the descant is to be sung softer than the rest of the song for an echo effect.

How Dear to God Are Little Children 180

Words: Jaclyn Thomas Milne
Music: Carol Baker Black
First Line: How dear to God are little children
Topics Indexed: Eternal Life, God's Love, Guidance, Heavenly Father, Songs for Leaders, Parents, Plan of Salvation, Premortal Existence, Worth of a Child

This beautiful song reminds parents and teachers of their sacred responsibility in raising God's children. It appears in print for the first time in the *Children's Songbook* and can be sung by or to parents, leaders, and teachers of children to inspire them to magnify their callings. It is suitable for performance for meetings or programs where the focus is on teaching children. The music is written for ladies' voices in an easy three-part arrangement. The song's poignant message will have an emotional impact on singers and listeners.

How Will They Know? 182

Words and Music: Natalie W. Sleeth; arranged by A. Laurence Lyon and Natalie W. Sleeth
First Line: How will they know, the ones for whom we care
Topics Indexed: Choice, Forgiveness, God's Love, Guidance, Songs for Leaders

Natalie Sleeth said, "When my son had young children of his own, I became aware of how the way he was raised (by my husband and me) was reflected in the way he and his wife were raising their children. . . . I generalized this idea into an expression of the need for teaching those within our care what we feel is important in life." The music was originally written as a four-part piece for the Mormon Tabernacle Choir, but has since been arranged in several other voicings by the composer. The arrangement in the *Children's*

Songbook is for three-part women's voices with an optional descant. Verses one and two are contained within the same staff, with a descant to be sung with the second verse. This is followed by sixteen measures of a second theme, and then the music returns to the original melody, which is much like a third verse with variations. This beautiful song, performed with meaning and expression, will provoke thoughts regarding the importance of teaching children.

Hum Your Favorite Hymn   152

Words: Marilyn Price Adams
Music: K. Newell Dayley
First Line: If on occasion you have found
Topics Indexed: Choice, Morality, Singing

This energetic, catchy song can be a valuable tool in teaching children to overcome ugly words and thoughts by substituting the message of a beautiful hymn. Sister Adams says that the inspiration for the words came from a powerful message by Elder Boyd K. Packer in which he admonished us to replace evil thoughts that come into our minds with a favorite hymn.

The music of the first four-measure phrase is duplicated in the second phrase except for the last three notes. The rhythm of these phrases is mostly a straight beat pattern. Three measures of the chorus contain the unique musical feature of the song: two eighth notes, two sixteenth notes, and an eighth note, followed by a dotted-quarter note in the next measure. This rhythm pattern sets the lively mood for the song.

Teaching Suggestions:

1. To introduce this song to the children, show them a picture of Elder Boyd K. Packer and give a brief part of the message from "Worthy Thoughts, Worthy Music" (*Ensign*, January 1974).

2. Show the hymnbook and ask the children to name their favorite hymn. Tell them that you are going to sing a song, and they should listen to discover when it is a good time to hum their favorite hymn. Accept their answers and discuss the message.

3. Teach the chorus first. Have the children find out how many times the words "Hum your favorite hymn" are sung, and then, as you sing the chorus again, have them join in singing these words. By asking questions that can be answered by exact words in the song, teach the rest of the chorus.

4. To teach the verses, use word strips and questions for which the children can discover the answers by listening to you sing the song. Have them join you in singing the phrases as they learn them.

5. Invite the children to tap or clap the rhythm of the chorus. Help them sing the large intervals accurately.

I Am a Child of God 2

Words: Naomi Ward Randall
Music: Mildred Tanner Pettit; arranged by Darwin Wolford
First Line: I am a child of God, and he has sent me here
Topics Indexed: Descants, Eternal Life, Guidance, Obedience,
    Parents, Plan of Salvation, Prayer Songs, Teachers, Testimony,
    Worth of a Child

Neither Naomi Randall nor Mildred Pettit ever dreamed that they were creating a masterpiece in Church music when they began working on "I Am a Child of God" in 1957. It has had an unbelievable influence on the members of the Church in countries all over the world. It has become a favorite song of children, young people, and adults and has been performed by many groups, including the Mormon Tabernacle Choir. Naomi Randall has written, "It is my desire that this song will be a witness to each child that our Heavenly Father loves us and that he truly is the divine Father of each one of us. Being a precious child of God, each individual has great potential and needs to realize his or her self-worth."

When Sister Randall began working on the words for this song, she went off by herself and prayed aloud, pleading that the song our Heavenly Father wanted to have for his children would be given to them. She retired to her bed and went to sleep, but awakened during the wee hours of the morning. There, in the quiet darkness, she again began to ponder and pray. All at once the lines began to form in her mind. She arose from her bed, went to another room, and began to write as fast as she could. She read over what she had written, dropped to her knees, and said a fervent prayer of thanks.

Sister Pettit also had a beautiful spiritual experience as she composed the music. Her son recalled some of the events during the week she worked on it: "Mother worked when the inspiration came to her. Sometimes it was at midnight. . . . She had us sing it over and over. She'd play the piano, and we'd sing it until she was satisfied. She felt it was necessary to have the music the way the

Lord wanted it. She mentioned one time that she felt she knew how the song was supposed to go." Within a week the song—words and music—was finished.

A few years later President Spencer W. Kimball, who was then an apostle, expressed his love for the song, but stated that there was one word in the chorus that concerned him. He wondered if Sister Randall would consider changing the line "Teach me all that I must know" to "Teach me all that I must *do*." He explained that just knowing the gospel is not enough. It is *doing* the will of our Heavenly Father that prepares us to return and live with him someday. President Kimball enjoyed telling people that Sister Naomi Randall and he wrote the beautiful and inspired lyrics to "I Am a Child of God." He said, "Of course, Sister Randall wrote most of the words, but I wrote one!"

"I Am a Child of God" is included in *Hymns,* number 301, in a hymnlike arrangement with four complete voice parts. The arrangement in the *Children's Songbook* has been transposed to the key of C, and the accompaniment has been thinned. Darwin Wolford prepared a descant for a few high voices or flute or violin to accompany the third verse.

Teaching Suggestions:

1. Introduce the song by bearing testimony that we are children of our Heavenly Father and that he loves each one of us. Sing the first verse and teach it to the children through listening and singing experiences.

2. Ask the children if it is enough to *know* what is right. Then sing the chorus, receive answers from them, and teach the chorus. Tell them about President Kimball's contribution to the song. Use key action words—"lead," "guide," "walk," "help," "teach," "do," "live"—to help them remember the words.

3. Teach each verse by asking questions and by using word strips of keywords.

4. Encourage the children to sing with meaning and expression, pausing slightly after "Lead me" and "Guide me" and holding the word "do" on the last line momentarily.

I Am Glad for Many Things 151

Words and Music: Moiselle Renstrom
First Line: I am glad for many things
Topics Indexed: Gratitude, Happiness

This is a happy tune for little children to sing to express gladness for their many blessings. It moves mostly by steps and by repeated notes. The second line begins the same way as the first, but the last two measures are different. Many repeated words are included in the lyrics: "many things," "thank you," and "my heart sings." This simple song is particularly appropriate for the nursery and the younger classes.

Teaching Suggestions:

1. Name several things that you are thankful for; then sing the first verse of the song. Encourage the children to name things they are thankful for, and invite them to sing this verse with you.

2. Ask the children to listen to the second verse to discover what our heart sings, when we are glad for many things.

3. Ask them to listen and count how many times they hear the words "many things," "thank you," and "my heart sings."

4. Ask several children to stand in front of the others and name something that they are glad for. Have the children repeat the song after each child's expression. You could name the thing a child mentions in place of "many things." (For example, "I am glad for mother dear.")

5. Prepare a large heart from posterboard, with a circle cut out of the center large enough for a child's head to show through. Use this visual aid to illustrate the second verse in which the words say, "Thank you, thank you, my heart sings."

6. Use pictures of some of the things children are thankful for or have them draw pictures of these things.

I Am like a Star   163

Words and Music: Patricia Kelsey Graham
First Line: I am like a star shining brightly
Topics Indexed: Example, Happiness, Smiles, Worth of a Child

This charming little piece, the class song for the four- and five-year-olds, reminds children of how our Heavenly Father's love helps us shine. As Patricia Graham thought of music that would be appealing to this age group, the nursery tune "Twinkle, Twinkle Little Star" came to her mind. She played it high on the piano to sound like a music box. This was the mood and format that she used to write "I Am like a Star."

The construction of the song is simple, but with an interesting melody line. The prevalent feature is the four eighth notes that begin on one note, move up a step, return to the first note, and step up again. This occurs five times, each time on a different note of the scale. The right-hand score of music can be played an octave higher than written to give the music a "twinkle" effect.

Teaching Suggestions:

1. Cut a star-shaped hole in a posterboard (about ten inches square) and cover the hole with yellow cellophane or fabric. Use a flashlight to make the star shine as you tell the children that when we remember that Heavenly Father loves us, we smile and do happy things, and we are like shining stars. The opposite is true when we forget about Heavenly Father's love for us. (Turn off the flashlight as you give this example.) Have the children read Matthew 5:16 to learn how Jesus taught us about this principle.

2. Ask: "Who does the song say loves us?" "What does the song say I can do and say?" "What do I do for the world to see?" and "What does the song say I am like?" Each time you ask a question, sing the song, allow the children to respond, and then encourage them to sing the part in which the answer occurs.

3. Prepare a melody chart for each musical phrase using stars on a musical staff. As the children sing each phrase, have a child follow the melody by pointing to the stars on the chart. Show all four of the charts and have the children arrange them in the order in which they come in the song.

4. Make several large posterboard stars, each with a hole cut out for a child's face to show through. Invite the smaller children to be shining stars while the others sing the song.

5. Have the children pitch-level conduct the song with their hands or their bodies, beginning in a sitting position and rising up and down as the melody moves higher and lower.

I Believe in Being Honest 149

Words: Ruth Muir Gardner
Music: Lyall J. Gardner
First Line: I believe in being honest
Topics Indexed: Accountability, Commitment, Courage, Honesty, Honor, Morality, Preparation

This spirited song emphasizes in the minds of the children that it is important to be honest and fair in all of their dealings.

The melody and lyrics are straightforward. The first two lines state the message clearly, the third and fourth lines expand on the theme, and then a return to the first two lines gives a strong conclusion. Five measures contain the rhythm of a dotted-quarter note, an eighth note, and two quarter notes. Most of the remaining measures have an even quarter-note beat, which creates an almost marchlike meter. The children will enjoy clapping or tapping the uneven beats in contrast to the straight beat pattern in the rest of the song.

Teaching Suggestions:

1. Show the children a word strip with the letters "T-H-O-N-E-S" printed on it and tell them that if they rearrange the letters, they will discover something that you believe in. Ask them to discover the word as you sing the song; then write the word "honest" on the chalkboard. Tell a story about honesty from a Primary manual or the *Friend*.

2. Invite the children to clap the rhythm of the first phrase as you sing it. Then have them clap and sing the phrase. Sing the song again and encourage them to listen for another phrase that has almost the same rhythm and that tells something else we believe in being.

3. Ask the children which article of faith the first two phrases of the song remind them of. Have a child repeat the first part of the thirteenth article of faith. This song uses the word "I" instead of "we"; have them tell why they think the author wrote it this way.

4. Teach lines three and four by asking the children to listen for four habits that will help us to be honest. Display word strips as they respond. ("Keep my word," "Tell the truth," "Speak up in defending right," and "Keep my name and honor bright.") Divide the children into four groups and invite each to sing one habit.

5. Help the children understand the principles expressed by explaining their meaning and giving examples of each. Tell them that you believe in being honest, and that it is important for them to form the habit of always being honest. Quote King Benjamin (Mosiah 4:10), "If you believe all these things see that ye do them." Tell them that President Benson, our prophet, has said, "The Lord expects us to be honest."

I Feel My Savior's Love 74

Words: Ralph Rodgers, Jr., K. Newell Dayley, and Laurie
  Huffman
Music: K. Newell Dayley
First Line: I feel my Savior's love in all the world around me
Topics Indexed: Guidance, Jesus Christ — Blesses Children,
  Jesus Christ — Example, Peace, Prayer

The beautiful melody and words of this song are acutely moving and bring feelings of love and reverence for our Savior, making it a worthy number for special meetings and programs. It is especially appealing to the older boys and girls. It has been printed in several arrangements; for the children, it is lovely with a simple alto part added.

The melody of the song is written in A A B A form; the first, second, and fourth phrases are essentially the same, and the third phrase is different. The song is intended to be sung in a smooth and connected style. Laurie Huffman says, "The expression 'I' says it all, not the universal 'we.' The song represents the simple outpouring of a child's gift of faith. It should be sung reverently and lovingly."

Teaching Suggestions:

1. Show a picture of the Savior blessing the Nephite children and read 3 Nephi 17:11–12, 21. Ask the children to think quietly about how this event makes them feel. Tell them that you will sing a song that tells how you feel about the Savior.

2. Teach the song in several teaching periods, perhaps one verse at a time. Give the children opportunities to listen to the song with a purpose in mind and then sing it phrase by phrase until they have learned the entire verse.

3. Display pictures of the Savior to illustrate the ideas in the song. You could use the picture in the *Children's Songbook* that accompanies the song.

I Have a Family Tree 199

Words: Mary Ellen Jex Jolley
Music: Darwin Wolford
First Line: I have a fam'ly tree with branches by the dozens

Topics Indexed: Action Songs, Family History, Grandparents

Mary Ellen Jolley came from a large family, with some 125 first cousins, who had many get-togethers and reunions. Her strong love for her relatives provided the inspiration for this song. Darwin Wolford's catchy melody is easy to sing and play. It can be enjoyed in the home, in Primary as a rest song, or in the younger age-group classrooms.

The bouncy rhythm of the first measure, with its dotted-eighth notes and sixteenth notes, is one of the song's appealing characteristics. This rhythm is repeated twice more in the composition. There is no repetition of the melody phrases. The first verse ends on the second note of the scale (the first ending), so that it is necessary to go to the second verse for a resolution and conclusion.

Teaching Suggestions:

1. Introduce the song by showing an illustration of a family tree. Ask the children to listen to a song that tells what kind of a tree this is.

2. Have them listen for the five kinds of relatives that are mentioned. (Grandpas, grandmas, uncles, aunts, cousins.) Ask them to arrange word strips, with these five relatives printed on them, in the correct order as they listen to the song again.

3. Use word strips of keywords to help them remember the word sequence.

4. Invite a child to come to the front of the group; place finger puppets, each representing one of the five relatives mentioned, on the child's hand. As the group sings the song, ask the child to point to or move the puppets in turn.

5. Have the children clap the rhythm and find the words that they sing when the syncopated beats occur. ("have a family tree," "with branches by the," "uncles, aunts, and").

6. Explain what a reunion is and show pictures to illustrate families getting together. Emphasize that when there are only a few members in a family, it is still just as important. Have the children tell about their families and their family reunions.

7. Encourage the children to improvise actions as suggested by the words. Mary Ellen Jolley has suggested the following actions:

"I have a fam'ly tree" (Place arms above head with hands closed in fists.)

"With branches by the dozens." (Move arms back and forth to the side and extend fingers.)

"I have grandpas. I have grandmas." (Point to thumb and pointer finger.)

"I have uncles, aunts, and cousins." (Point to remaining fingers in turn.)

"When it's reunion time," (Nod head forward and back.)

"No matter what the weather," (Move head side to side.)

"It is such a happy day" (Smile a big smile.)

"When the fam'ly gets together." (Bring hands down in front and move them swiftly in winding fashion.)

I Have Two Ears 269

Words: Georgia Maeser
Music: A. Laurence Lyon
First Line: I have two ears to hear the truth
Topics Indexed: Action Songs, Commitment, Creation, Gratitude, Kindness, Morality

This cheerful message of thankfulness for our bodies is especially notable since Georgia Maeser, the author, was physically handicapped from an illness she suffered at age three, which caused permanent injury to her spine. The composition is an unusual mixture of a playful activity song and a song of gratitude for blessings received from our Father.

In the first and fifth measures, an unexpected E flat adds a playful and dissonant sound to the song. The music includes other accidentals so that the listener is carried from one key to another. The rhythm is primarily an even quarter-note beat pattern with a few variations. The melody of each of the four phrases is different, but the first measures of the first and second phrases (measures one and five) are identical.

Teaching Suggestions:

1. Tell the children that our bodies have two of several parts and ask them to identify as many of these pairs as they can. Then sing the song and ask them to find the "twos" that are named. Display pictures of them, or have children hold the illustrations.

2. Use a drawing of a child's silhouette. As you sing the song, add the parts of the body to the figure as they are mentioned (ears, eyes, feet, lips, and hands). Invite the children to take turns placing the parts of the body as the song is repeated.

3. Ask: "What do my two ears hear?" "What do my two eyes see?" "What do my two feet do?" "How will I try to use them?" "What do I thank my Heavenly Father for?" After the children

discover the answer to a question, have them sing that part of the song with you, continuing until all the words have been learned.

4. Express your thankfulness to Heavenly Father for creating our wonderful bodies.

I Have Two Little Hands 272

Words: Bertha A. Kleinman
Music: William Frederick Hanson
First Line: I have two little hands, folded snugly and tight
Topics Indexed: Action Songs, Obedience, Service

This favorite song has been included in the children's songbooks of the Church since 1920. It is often sung as a reverence or "get quiet" song for the younger children. The first and third phrases have the same melody, and the second and fourth phrases are different. The rhythm is even, with an eighth note for each beat, except in three measures where two sixteenth notes are needed to accommodate the words. The melody should be sung smoothly with connected tones, and the singers should not exaggerate the swaying beat. The last phrase contains some difficult intervals, so the leader should help the children, probably through pitch-level conducting, to reach each tone accurately.

Teaching Suggestions:

1. To draw attention to the hands, wear gloves to introduce the song. Hold up your hands and tell the children some things that your hands can do. Invite them to name things their hands can do. Then sing the song to them. Let the children take turns wearing the gloves as you repeat the song several times.

2. Have each child trace the image of his or her hands on a piece of paper and invite a few of them, in turn, to stand in front with their pictures as you sing the song to them. Encourage the children to join you in singing.

I Hope They Call Me on a Mission 169

Words and Music: Newel Kay Brown
First Line: I hope they call me on a mission
Topics Indexed: Missionary Work, Preparation, Service

This popular piece has become a song of commitment that

contributes to a greater desire for missionary service among the youth of the Church. Since its publication, it has been translated into eighteen foreign languages and sung by tens of thousands of Latter-day Saint youth. The infectious melody brings a feeling of excitement to the missionary theme. Newel Kay Brown has said, "The enrichment that I and the members of my family have enjoyed [through this song] can hardly be measured. My dream of a song which would play a part in the motivation of young men and women to share the gospel has been realized. The children of the first crop of youth which sang it are already humming the little 'cowboy' tune which was written in Arkadelphia, Arkansas, some twenty years ago."

The significant characteristic of the piece is its "cowboy" feeling, primarily set by the repetitious swinging rhythm in the lower staff created by dotted-eighth-note/sixteenth-note combinations, followed by two quarter notes. Every measure but one in the bass clef has the same rhythm. The melody form of the song is A B A C — the first and third phrases are the same and the second and fourth are different. There have been some changes in the presentation of this song in the *Children's Songbook*: the melody is now part of the accompaniment instead of the three-staff arrangement; the notation on the words "mission" and "ready" is changed from two eighth notes to a dotted-eighth note and sixteenth note, so that the melody matches the rhythm of the left-hand accompaniment; the beginning F of the left hand in each measure is now a dotted-eighth note instead of a whole note.

Teaching Suggestions:

1. Use pictures of missionaries, men and women, to introduce this song. Discuss briefly with the children the things that they do.

2. Ask a recently called or recently returned missionary to visit the children and tell what he plans to do (or what he did) on his mission. The missionary could show or read a part of his mission call. Allow the children to ask questions.

3. Ask the children questions, one at a time, that can be answered by words in the song. Sing it for them, accept answers, and have them join in singing the part of the song in which the answer occurs. Examples: "What three things does the song say that missionaries do?" "What do I hope for?" (There are two answers to this question.) "When do I hope that they call me on a mission?"

4. Use word strips of keywords to help them remember the text.

5. Encourage them to tap or clap the rhythm of the melody and the rhythm of the left-hand accompaniment. Divide the children into two groups and have them tap the two rhythms at the same time. The left-hand rhythm provides an interesting background to the singing as it is clapped, tapped, or beaten lightly on a drum or tom-tom.

I Know My Father Lives 5

Words and Music: Reid N. Nibley
First Line: I know my Father lives and loves me too
Topics Indexed: Faith, God's Love, Holy Ghost, Obedience, Plan of Salvation, Prayer Songs, Testimony, Worth of a Child

This little two-verse song is a priceless gem that combines a simple, sweet message of testimony with a pure and uncomplicated melody. Reid Nibley said, "When I hear children sing it, I realize it is not my piece but theirs. . . . I was touched when a father told me that he sings the song every night with his daughter as he puts her to bed." "I Know My Father Lives" is included in *Hymns*, number 302, in its original form. The version in the *Children's Songbook* is a two-part arrangement with a moving accompaniment that does not include the melody. Leaders can choose from the two versions.

The song includes two four-measure phrases and a two-measure phrase. The climax of the song occurs in the seventh and eighth measures, where the music builds in volume and emphasis on the words "tells me it is true." The last two-measure phrase restates and reaffirms this message in a more subdued tone.

Teaching Suggestions:

1. Ask the children if they have heard the people of the ward bear testimony during fast meeting. Explain that a testimony is an expression of how we feel in our hearts. Tell them that Reid Nibley wrote a beautiful song in which he declares his testimony for all the children of the Church. Then sing the song for them.

2. Ask them to listen to the song again and discover *what* I know and *how* I know it is true. As they respond, write the words "Father lives," "loves me," and "Spirit whispers" on the board to emphasize these words. (Explain that the Holy Ghost does not usually speak in whispers that we hear, but that he communicates through the mind and heart as though it were a whisper.) Teach verse two through questions and listening and singing experiences.

3. Pitch-level conduct to establish correct rhythm patterns as well as to indicate pitch direction.

4. Encourage the children to sing the song smoothly, with conviction.

5. Express your testimony to the children.

I Like My Birthdays 104

Words: Wallace F. Bennett
Music: Tracy Y. Cannon
First Line: I like my birthdays, ev'ry one
Topics Indexed: Birthdays, Gift of the Holy Ghost, Jesus
Christ — Baptism, Preparation, Priesthood

This cheerful song expresses the happiness a child approaching his or her eighth birthday might feel when looking forward to baptism and confirmation. The song is suggested for some Primary lessons on baptism. For the *Children's Songbook* it has been changed from the key of E flat to C, the accompaniment has been simplified, and there are a few word changes in the third verse. The skipping rhythm of this song, created by the quarter-note/eighth-note combinations, is consistent through the piece. The notation is different for each of the four phrases, and the melody moves effortlessly by steps and short intervals.

Teaching Suggestions:

1. Tell the children that you are going to sing a song about a very special day, and that you want them to discover what this special day is and why it is so special.

2. Teach the song with questions, word strips, and pictures. For verses two and three use pictures of Jesus' baptism and of a confirmation.

3. Show a picture of a birthday cake with eight candles on it. To provide more opportunities for repetition, ask the children to remove a candle from the cake and discover a special message written on it, such as: "Those who have not been baptized yet, sing the first verse." "The boys sing the first two phrases, and the girls sing the last two phrases." "Four Primary classes each sing one of the phrases of the song."

4. Invite children who have been baptized to express briefly the feelings they had when they were baptized.

I Lived in Heaven 4

Words and Music: Janeen Jacobs Brady
First Line: I lived in heaven a long time ago, it is true
Topics Indexed: Atonement, Eternal Life, Plan of Salvation,
    Premortal Existence

This lovely song tells about the plan of salvation, that we once lived in heaven with people we loved, and through Heavenly Father's plan we can receive eternal salvation and live with him again. The text is fresh and appealing.

The first and second phrases of the melody are identical, the third phrase is a variation of the same melody, and the fourth phrase is unlike the other phrases. The rhythm pattern is the same for all four phrases: twelve eighth notes and a dotted-half note. The melody flows smoothly in 6/8 time with uncomplicated intervals. An unusual harmony occurs in the third line with the introduction of accidentals that create a mysterious feeling; it resolves in the last line to the calm mood introduced in the beginning phrases.

Teaching Suggestions:

1. Introduce this song by telling the children that you are going to tell them a beautiful story in a song. (Teach the concepts one verse at a time.)

2. Ask them to listen while you sing it again and see if they can find the answers to the following questions: "*Where* did I live?" "*When* did I live there?" "*What* did I do besides live there?" "*Who* lived there with me?" Place four cards with the above italicized words on a chart or have children hold them. Repeat the song until they discover the answers. Ask additional questions about the words: "What did Heavenly Father present to us?" "What is the word that means 'forever' that was part of his plan?" Have them sing each phrase as they learn it. (Help them understand the meaning of "eternal salvation" and other difficult words.)

3. Read the following scriptures, or have children read them, to help them to understand the principles in this song: Moses 1:39; Moses 4:1–2; Abraham 3:24–28.

4. Express your conviction that our Heavenly Father lives, that Jesus Christ did come to earth to live and die for us, and that through this plan we can receive eternal life.

I Love to Pray   25

Words and Music: Moiselle Renstrom
First Line: In the morning when I wake, before I work or play
Topics Indexed: Gratitude, Prayer

This quiet, peaceful song reminds children of the importance of morning and evening prayer. In the *Children's Songbook* there are some changes in the accompaniment and a word change in verse two: "Thank thee, Heavenly Father" instead of "Thanks, dear Heavenly Father." The melody of the first line hovers around the tone of A. The second line includes a step-by-step progression from D down to E with a resolution to F. The simple melody adds to the clarity of the message.

Teaching Suggestions:
1. Ask the children to name various times when we offer prayers. Ask them to listen for when the song says we might offer prayers.
2. Display pictures of children offering their morning or evening prayers.

I Love to See the Temple   95

Words and Music: Janice Kapp Perry
First Line: I love to see the temple. I'm going there someday
Topics Indexed: Commitment, Family, Family History, Temples

Sister Perry says that the inspiration for this song came because she grew up where there was no temple, and for her the chance to see one occasionally was a sweet experience. She also says, "A child born to us lived only one day. The temple always gives me comfort because our sealing there ensures we will have that child again in eternity if we are worthy."

The rhythm set in the first measure (two eighth notes and two quarter notes) is felt, with some variation, throughout the song in the melody or accompaniment. The melody is different in each of the four phrases, even though there are many similarities and repeated patterns. The climax comes in the last line where there is a fermata on the word "young," and then the melody rises to D, the highest note of the song, on the word "this." There are many dynamic possibilities in the piece that will enhance its presentation, some of which are noted in the music.

Teaching Suggestions:

1. Show a picture of a temple (probably the one that is situated closest to you) and ask the children why we go to the temple. List their responses on a chalkboard or a chart. Sing the song, one verse at a time, and see how many of the reasons that the children named are found in the song. Add to the list any that they discover from hearing it.

2. Teach the words through asking questions, one at a time, that can be answered with exact words in the song, singing it, receiving the answers, and then having the children sing that part with you. Examples: "What does the song say is my sacred duty?" "What does the song say that the temple is a place of?" "When I go to the temple, what am I going to feel and do?" Ask similar questions for the second verse.

3. Show word strips of keywords to help the children learn the words.

4. Help them feel the rhythm by having them clap or tap the beat of the various measures. (Seven measures contain two eighth notes and two quarter notes. The first measure of the third line has a dotted-quarter note followed by three eighth notes.)

5. Help the children sing the song with love and reverence for the sacred temple. Ask children who have visited a temple, before its dedication or to be sealed to their parents, to express the feelings they had when they were there.

6. Describe the peace and love found in the temple and stress the importance of the children's preparing to go there while they are still young. Tell a story of a touching temple experience, such as a family gathered to witness a marriage or to be sealed together.

I Need My Heavenly Father   18

Words and Music: Judith Wirthlin Parker
First Line: I need my Heav'nly Father to help me ev'ry day
Topics Indexed: Choice, Guidance, Happiness, Prayer Songs

This simple piece can be used as a reverence or prayer song. It has been included in Primary lessons for four- and five-year-olds. Sister Parker, the composer, said she was especially moved when she made an unannounced visit to a Primary in Perth, Australia, and, as she came up the walk to the little chapel, heard the children singing "I Need My Heavenly Father" in their Scottish-like brogue.

The song has three phrases in A B B form; the last two begin the same, but have some variation. The repetition of "He wants me to be happy and choose the righteous way," in phrases two and three, adds emphasis to the message. The most difficult interval occurs in the fifth and ninth measures when the notes jump from F up to D.

Teaching Suggestions:

1. Prepare a box with a mirror in the bottom of it. Allow several children to look into the box and describe what they see. Tell them that you love to see their happy faces and so does our Heavenly Father. Express your assurance that he loves each one of them and wants them to be happy. Immediately following this activity, sing the song.

2. Display a drawing of the melody that goes with the words "He wants me to be happy," and ask the children to discover what words you sing when this melody pattern occurs. When they discover the words, have them pitch-level conduct and sing this part with you. Let them discover what word is sung on the highest note, and encourage them to sit tall and sing this high tone in tune.

3. Ask the children to listen to the song to discover what Heavenly Father wants us to do. (Choose the righteous way.) Ask them to find out if the melody is the same or different each time "choose the righteous way" is sung. Invite them to sing these phrases, noticing the difference.

4. Post keywords ("need," "help," "happy," "choose") in random order and ask the children to determine the correct order by listening to the song.

5. Encourage them to sing with expression and understanding. The last phrase should be sung a little slower and with emphasis.

I Often Go Walking 202

Words: Phyllis Luch
Music: Jeanne P. Lawler
First Line: I often go walking in meadows of clover
Topics Indexed: Mothers

Children of all ages enjoy singing this wonderful song about the beauties of nature and their love for their mothers. For the *Children's Songbook* the accompaniment has been thinned and restructured slightly, but the lovely harmony has not been lost.

Phyllis Luch says of her inspiration for the words: "My mother was mentally ill. . . . Nearly the only time she was at peace was in the fields and meadows. . . . She knew the names of wildflowers, which as a child I thought was amazing."

The melody form of "I Often Go Walking" is A A B B (the first two phrases are the same, and the third and fourth phrases are the same), with slight variations in the final notes of the phrases to allow for suitable resolutions. The intervals that occur in the first two phrases are the most difficult, and the leader should practice to teach them correctly. Two major rhythm patterns are found in the measures: uneven patterns of quarter, dotted-quarter, and eighth notes, and even patterns of three quarter notes.

Teaching Suggestions:

1. Present the melody with a violin and piano playing. Discuss with the children the mood of the song, and how it makes them feel.

2. Speak the words as a poem, using appropriate pictures to illustrate. (The double-page picture at the beginning of the section "My Heavenly Father" in the *Children's Songbook* is a good choice.) For young children, use arm and hand actions to dramatize "arm-fuls," "gather," "whole meadow over," and "remind me of you."

3. Teach the words, phrase by phrase, through questions, pictures, keywords, and hand actions.

4. Invite the children to clap the rhythm of the uneven and even measures. Help them reach the notes of the octave and sixth intervals by pitch-level conducting or illustrating the intervals.

5. Have the children act out the song by handing flowers to a mother to make a bouquet. As an activity for younger children, have them walk around pretending to gather flowers or actually gathering flowers previously placed around. Real flowers or paper cutouts could be used.

6. Help the children capture the mood of the song by encouraging them to sing sweetly, smoothly, and with expression. It should be sung in moderate tempo, the third line increasing somewhat in momentum and the final phrase slowing again.

7. Show a picture of your mother and tell how she helped you love and appreciate the beauties of nature.

I Pledge Myself to Love the Right 161

Words: Margaret Mann
Music: Wolfgang Amadeus Mozart
First Line: I pledge myself to love the right
Topics Indexed: Commitment, Honor

This song of commitment is appealing and applicable to all ages. Its four short phrases are each distinct in melody and rhythm. The rhythm includes two quarter notes followed by four eighth notes (measure three) and a dotted-quarter note followed by five eighth notes (measure six) that will require practice for accuracy. The intervals of a seventh (C to B flat on the words "the good" and "to keep") will need special attention. The tempo is marchlike, and the song should be sung with spirit and commitment.

Teaching Suggestions:

1. Show a picture of a Church leader and relate a short story or example of how he taught honesty. Then tell the children that you will sing a song that includes a promise to love the right. Ask them to listen for a word in the song that means "promise."

2. Ask the children to listen again and find four things that I promise or pledge to *love*. As the children answer, post the words on a chart after the words "I pledge to love:" Have them join you in singing this part of the song.

3. Ask them to listen again and discover two things that I pledge to *keep*. As the children answer, post these words on the chart following the words "I pledge to keep:"

4. Have the children tap the beat as they sing, noticing how the marchlike quality and the majestic sound of Mozart's music reinforce the message. Direct their attention to the one-syllable words that are sung on two notes ("fair," "and," "bright," "in") and help them to sing these correctly.

5. Discuss the meaning of such words as "pledge" and "to keep my faith and honor bright." Express your feelings about the importance of being honest and true and keeping our promises.

I Pray in Faith 14

Words and Music: Janice Kapp Perry
First Line: I kneel to pray ev'ry day
Topics Indexed: Faith, Prayer, Prayer Songs, Revelation, Two-part Songs

This melodic duet helps teach children the parts of prayer. The two distinct tunes can be sung together or separately. The piano part is a quiet accompaniment that does not contain the melody line of either of the parts. Older children will enjoy the challenge of this song as they master the two verses and learn to sing them together. At the same time they will be learning some important principles about prayer.

Verse one contains many half notes and dotted-half notes and should be sung smoothly in a connected style. The message of this verse sets the mood of the song by talking of how we pray. Verse two contains a melody of more motion, much of it in an even quarter-note rhythm with a few measures of uneven beats (a dotted-quarter note and eighth note). This verse mentions the four parts of prayer: (1) addressing our Heavenly Father, (2) expressing gratitude, (3) asking for needed blessings, and (4) closing in Jesus' name. None of the musical phrases are repeated.

Teaching Suggestions:

1. Ask the children to think of how they might teach someone who had never prayed to say a prayer to our Heavenly Father. As they give their ideas, write them on the board. Sing the song and ask if they can find other ideas from the song that could help teach someone about prayer; add these to the thoughts they mentioned. Use keywords such as these: verse one—kneel, every day, speak to Heavenly Father, hears and answers, faith. Verse two—Heavenly Father, thanks for blessings, ask for needs, in Jesus' name, Amen.

2. Tell the children that Sister Perry wrote this song to help children learn the four parts of prayer. Ask them to identify these parts when you sing verse two. Invite them to look up references in the scriptures that emphasize these points. (See Psalm 50:14; D&C 136:28; 3 Nephi 18:20; Psalm 55:17; James 1:5–6.)

3. Continue to teach the song by asking questions about the message, singing the song, receiving responses from the children, and encouraging them to sing the parts as they learn them.

4. Illustrate the melody pattern for some of the phrases and have the children identify the words that are on the high and low notes. Help them feel the direction of the melody by pitch-level conducting. Invite them to clap the beat patterns in verse two.

5. While you sing one verse, play a recording of the other verse so the children can hear the two verses together. Direct the children in singing one verse while the recording plays the other.

6. When the children have learned both verses well, divide them into two groups and have them sing the two verses together. Add variety by having different groups or individuals sing the two verses, such as boys on verse one with girls on verse two, or leaders and teachers on verse one with children on verse two.

7. Encourage the children to sing the song with meaning and expression and to think of its message.

I Thank Thee, Dear Father 7

Words: Anonymous
Music: George Careless
First Line: I thank thee, dear Father in heaven above
Topics Indexed: Gratitude, Kindness, Obedience, Prayer Songs

The composer of this song has skillfully taken the sweet message of the lyrics and given them a gentle musical setting that enhances the mood and feeling. The melody form of the song is A B A C (the first and third phrases are the same except for the last note). There is a repeated rhythmic sequence of a half note and two quarter notes throughout the song, except for the last measure of each phrase. The time signature is 2/2, and the leader should conduct the song with two beats to the measure. A beautiful alto harmony that older children would enjoy singing is part of the notation.

Teaching Suggestions:
1. Ask the children to listen as you sing verse one to discover what you are thanking our Father in Heaven for. (There are eight things mentioned.) As they respond, give eight children pictures or word strips that identify these things and have them stand in front of the group. Sing the song again and let the children in front arrange themselves in the order in which their pictures or word strips come in the song. With the help of the visual aids, invite all the children to sing this verse with you.

2. Tell the children that verse two tells us some of the ways in which we need Heavenly Father's help. As you sing, post key-words that will help them remember these.

3. Illustrate with a melody line the contour of the phrases and help the children identify the two phrases that are the same and the phrase that moves step by step down the scale.

4. Encourage the children to sing reverently and smoothly with connected tones. Teach some of the older children the alto part.

5. Express your love for Heavenly Father and your appreciation for all he gives to us.

I Think the World Is Glorious 230

Words: Anna Johnson
Music: Alexander Schreiner
First Line: I think the world is glorious and lovely as can be
Topics Indexed: Beautiful World, Gratitude, Parents, Singing,
    Teachers

The words to this song are based on the message in Psalm 100:1–5. The musical setting is light and lyrical and fits the joyous message of the text.

The song has been changed from 3/4 to 6/8 time in the *Children's Songbook*, with quarter and eighth notes instead of half notes and quarter notes. The leader should conduct it with two beats to the measure to produce a lilting and moving melody. The accompaniment has been thinned and some harmony notes transferred from the left hand to the right, making it easier to play.

The first and second lines are identical in rhythm and similar in melody. The same is true of lines three and four. The many quarter-note/eighth-note combinations generate the skipping beat. The melody moves smoothly by steps and easy intervals. Of interest is the alliteration (several of the words begin with the same sound) in line two of the first verse.

Teaching Suggestions:

1. Ask the children how it makes them feel when they see the beautiful world in which we live. Sing the song to them to demonstrate your feelings about the glorious world.

2. Ask them to listen again and find out what I do when I think of the beautiful world. After the children answer, ask them to listen to discover how many times the word "sing" occurs; invite them to sing that part of the song with you.

3. Ask: "What two things do I sing?" "What three things bring sweet messages to me?" (Lead them to discover that these three things all begin with the letter B.) "What do I think the world is?" Support the answers with pictures or word strips of keywords.

4. Teach the second verse by asking the children to listen and raise their hands when they hear new words in the song. They will discover that only one line is different from the first verse. Encourage them to sing the parts that they know, while you sing the new line.

5. Cut a large circle like a world and place pictures of hills, birds, blossoms, teachers, parents, and other beautiful things around the world. Allow the children to express their appreciation for the things that they most enjoy in the world.

I Think When I Read That Sweet Story   56

Words: Jemima Luke
Music: Leah Ashton Lloyd
First Line: I think when I read that sweet story of old
Topics Indexed: Bible, Jesus Christ — Blesses Children,
   Jesus Christ — Ministry

The impact of this little song rests in the emotion that is created through the message of love that the Savior gave to the children, combined with the beautiful, simple melody. It has become one of the most familiar and choice children's songs in the Church. In the *Children's Songbook* it has been transposed to the key of G from A flat, and the chording has been thinned slightly. The less familiar third verse was eliminated.

The melody in each of the four phrases is unique, with little repetition. The song contains mostly an even eighth-note rhythm and should be sung rather slowly in a connected style.

Teaching Suggestions:

1. Open your scriptures to one of the accounts of when Jesus blessed the children and explain that you are reading a very beautiful true story. Tell the children that you are going to sing a song that will tell them what story you are reading. After you sing, ask them to identify the story and display a picture of Jesus with the children.

2. Ask the children questions, one by one, that can be answered with exact words from the song. Sing it for them, accept answers

to the questions, and invite the children to join in singing that part of the song. Examples: "Where would I like to have been?" "Whom did he call?" "Where was Jesus?"

3. Encourage the children to sing the song sweetly and with a feeling of love for Jesus.

I Want to Be a Missionary Now   168

Words and Music: Grietje Terburg Rowley
First Line: I want to be a missionary now
Topics Indexed: Book of Mormon, Commitment, Example,
   Missionary Work, Testimony

Grietje Rowley, a convert to the Church, wrote this song to show children that they can begin to be missionaries now, and that each one can be a lifelong missionary who brings joy and happiness to many people.

The charm of the song is created by the uneven beat pattern, with many dotted-eighth-note/sixteenth-note combinations. The melody pattern is A B C A—the first and fourth phrases are the same, except for the pick-up notes. The third phrase begins with even beats, unlike the other phrases. An extended last ending for the third verse begins with even notes and then incorporates the same melody as in the first and fourth phrases.

Teaching Suggestions:

1. Have two or three children dress in simple costumes, such as a suit coat and tie for a boy and badges for boys and girls, and have each carry scriptures. Ask the group who these children are pretending to be. After you receive responses, ask if these children are really missionaries. Help them understand that they cannot receive formal calls to be missionaries until they are grown, but they can do missionary work with their friends and neighbors now. Sing the first verse of the song to them.

2. Show two or three pictures of children playing together and ask them if these children are missionaries. Help them understand that they can be missionaries by what they say and how they act while they are with their friends. Sing verses two and three.

3. Ask the children to notice how the melody bounces with long and short sounds on the word "testimony" in the last line. Sing this line for them while they tap the rhythm. Invite them to sing the line with you. Prepare a chart that shows a picture of the melody line of this last phrase.

4. Ask the children to listen to you sing the song again and discover if the notes in the first line are the same as or different from those in the last line. (They are the same except for the pick-up notes.) Then ask them to join in singing the first and last lines as you sing the entire first verse.

5. Tell the children that most of the song has long and short sounds, but that there are five tones that are even. Ask them to find the words that you sing on these five even notes. ("I want to share the.") Ask them to join in singing the parts they have learned while you sing the song again.

6. Continue teaching the song through questions about the words and melody. Teach all verses so the children can understand the full message.

7. Invite the children to tap or clap the rhythm while they sing.

I Want to Be Reverent   28

Words: Primary Committee
Music: Vanja Y. Watkins
First Line: I want to be rev'rent
Topics Indexed: Example, Reverence

This is an uncomplicated and lovely song that can be used to help children, especially the younger ones, remember to be reverent. The music contains interesting progressions created by the use of accidentals that carry the listener momentarily to the keys of A and G and back to D. There are four short phrases in the two lines, each one different from the others. The notes of the third phrase are all the same (D), and in the fourth phrase the notes move by repeated notes from G to D. Though the rhythm pattern moves smoothly to match the proper word emphasis and accents, there is little repetition in beat patterns.

Teaching Suggestions:

1. Introduce the song by talking to the children about what it means to be reverent. The idea that each one must be responsible for his or her own actions is an important part of the message.

2. Teach this song by singing it, one phrase at a time, and having the children repeat each phrase, in a follow-the-leader fashion, without stopping.

3. Ask them to "quietly listen" to you sing and find the words that are all on the same note of the scale. ("I will quietly listen.") Pitch-level conduct to help them find these words.

4. Encourage the children to sing the song with expression: the third line softly and the final phrase with a slower tempo.

I Want to Give the Lord My Tenth   150

Words and Music: Lonnie Dobson Adams
First Line: I want to give the Lord my tenth
Topics Indexed: Gratitude, Tithing

When Lonnie Adams was young, her grandmother gave her a lovely mosaic container to keep her tithing in, and told her that if she would faithfully pay her tithing, she would always have enough money. She has found that great blessings come through keeping the law of tithing, and she expresses her testimony of the principle in this song.

The words of the first verse have been revised for the *Children's Songbook*, and the second verse has been rewritten. Musically, the song moves smoothly and easily, with three of the eight measures using an even quarter-note beat pattern and three an uneven beat pattern. None of the four phrases is the same melodically, but there is a repetition of one melody pattern in phrases one and three with the notes of the tonic chord, D, F sharp, and A.

Teaching Suggestions:
1. Tell the children that you are going to sing a song about tithing that uses another word instead of "tithing." After you sing and they discover the word "tenth," ask them why these two words mean the same thing. Tell them that some of the members in the early days of the Church paid their tithing "in kind," giving a tenth of their vegetables, fruit, eggs, or crops that they raised. Illustrate through the use of coins or other objects that tithing represents one out of ten, or a tenth.
2. Use scriptures to help the children understand that the law of tithing is a commandment of the Lord. (See Genesis 28:22; Malachi 3:10; D&C 119:1–7.)
3. Help them learn the words through questions and keywords.
4. Help them sing the rhythm by clapping or tapping the beats.
5. Express your belief in the principle of tithing, or tell why Lonnie Dobson Adams wrote the song.

I Want to Live the Gospel   148

Words: Naomi Ward Randall
Music: Roy M. Darley
First Line: I want to live the gospel
Topics Indexed: Commitment, Example, Morality, Obedience

Naomi Randall, the author of this song, says, "My deep conviction that all children have an innate desire to learn of our Heavenly Father and to live by his teachings prompted the lyrics. Even though we sometimes make mistakes, we try again and again to do as our Savior taught." If the children learn to sing the piece thoughtfully and expressively, it can greatly influence them in making good choices.

The song is written with two verses and a chorus. The chorus is made up of two short phrases that are the same, words and music, emphasizing the statement of commitment to live the gospel. The melody moves smoothly by steps and natural intervals, with no repetition of phrases in the verses. However, the rhythm for phrases two, three, and four is similar, with eighth notes on the second and fourth counts of these measures.

Teaching Suggestions:

1. Tell the children that you will sing a song that tells four things you want to do. As they identify the four things, post word strips: "to live," "to know," "to follow," and "live." Discuss with them the meaning of these four phrases.

2. Divide the children into four groups and give a word strip to each. Have each group learn to sing the phrase that matches its word strip. After they have sung the verse several times, each group singing a phrase, have the groups exchange word strips and learn to sing another phrase, continuing in this way until they have learned all the phrases. Teach the second verse in a similar way.

3. Sing the chorus and ask the children if they notice anything unusual. (The same phrase is sung two times in the chorus.) Ask them why they think the writers repeated this phrase. Discuss ways that they can try to live the gospel, using pictures of children being kind, helping their parents, going to Church, and so on.

I Wiggle 271

Words: Louise B. Scott
Music: Lucille F. Wood
First Line: I wiggle my fingers. I wiggle my toes
Topics Indexed: Action Songs, Quiet

This song can be sung to help restless children relax and prepare to sit quietly. It is a playful piece that little ones will enjoy singing again and again.

Each of the first five measures begins on a successively higher note of the scale, starting with G and moving up to D. The melody in each of these measures follows a similar pattern. The melody then moves down again to G. The last two measures repeat the lower D tone until the last note, which moves back to G. The rhythm of the song is developed around the way the words might naturally be spoken. The dynamic markings indicate that the last two measures should be sung slower and softer to create a quiet mood.

Teaching Suggestion:

Introduce "I Wiggle" to the children by singing it to them while improvising some actions. Encourage them to do the actions with you. With several repetitions, they will soon know the song.

I Will Be Valiant 162

Words and Music: Vanja Y. Watkins
First Line: The Lord needs valiant servants
Topics Indexed: Commitment, Courage, Dependability, Primary Class Songs, Service, Worth of a Child

Vanja Watkins wanted to create a song that would have vitality and appeal for the eight- and nine-year-old Valiant classes and that would contain a message of commitment to live righteously. One day she went to her bedroom and found on top of her dresser a small paper with this quotation from Joseph Fielding Smith:

"Our young people are among the most blessed and favored of our Father's children. They are the nobility of heaven, a choice and chosen generation who have a divine destiny. Their spirits have been reserved to come forth in this day when the gospel is on earth, and when the Lord needs valiant servants to carry on his great Latter-day work."

She didn't know where the paper came from, but she knew it was the answer to her prayers.

The construction of the melody is clever, with many of the phrases repeated with slight variation. The climax is reached in the last line as the melody begins on the first note of the scale, F, rises to the highest note, D, and moves back to F. This phrase should begin softly and increase in volume as it reaches the high note. The tempo of the song should be consistent throughout, and notes with triplet markings should flow easily. The lively accompaniment contributes to the energy and briskness of the piece, stirring feelings of resolution.

Teaching Suggestions:

1. Bring a "Help Wanted" section of the newspaper and ask the children what jobs they think are listed. Tell them that employers need secretaries, truck drivers, nurses, teachers, and babysitters, but that there is no listing for the most important job of all. Sing the song and ask them to determine what the most important job is.

2. Show pictures of some of the Lord's servants and let the children identify who they are. (David fighting Goliath, Good Samaritan, the 2,000 stripling warriors, pioneers, Joseph Smith, missionaries, the present prophet.) Ask the children to listen again and find the word that describes these servants. Discuss the meaning of "valiant."

3. Continue teaching the song by asking questions, having the children listen for the answers as you sing, and inviting them to sing that part with you. Examples: "On whom can the Lord depend?" "What two things do we stand for when we are valiant servants?" "If you are his valiant servant, what will you keep?" "How should valiant servants serve other people?" "What should valiant servants follow?" "What do valiant servants do?" (These questions teach the phrases of the song starting at the end and working backward to the beginning.)

4. Encourage the children to sing the song with vigor and expression, following the dynamic markings in the music. The accompaniment can be added as a culmination after the words and melody are learned. Ask them to notice how the accompaniment adds to the majestic feeling of the song.

5. Invite them to march to the rhythm of the song while they sing and carry pictures of some of the Lord's valiant servants.

6. Read and discuss scriptures that tell of valiant servants, such as Alma 53:20–21, John 13:13–17, and Matthew 25:34–40. Tell the children how you feel about being a valiant servant, and that we can all be valiant servants if we serve the Lord and our fellowmen.

I Will Follow God's Plan 164

Words and Music: Vanja Y. Watkins
First Line: My life is a gift; my life has a plan
*Topics Indexed: Choice, Commitment, Guidance, Happiness,
    Morality, Obedience, Plan of Salvation, Premortal Existence,
    Primary Class Songs, Worth of a Child*

This class song for the ten- and eleven-year-old Merrie Miss girls in Primary expresses the truth that there is great purpose and meaning in their lives, and that they should find that purpose and follow the plan that God has for each of them.

The song is written with a four-measure introduction, a verse, and a four-line chorus. The verse states what my life is and why I am here, and the chorus declares what I will do with my life. Seven of the first eight measures begin with a quarter note and two eighth notes. The chorus flows, reaching a climax in feeling and volume on the high note, D, on the word "walk." As the markings indicate, there is a great opportunity for dynamic expression to accentuate the feelings of the song.

Teaching Suggestions:

1. Introduce the song to the girls in connection with lessons that teach that God has a plan for each one of them. Show them the plans for a house or a pattern for a dress and ask them what the purpose is for a plan. Ask them what might happen if they sewed a dress or built a house without knowing what it would be like or what the measurements should be. Explain that our lives also need to be planned so that the end result will be good. Point out that when we follow a plan, we can usually be sure of the results.

2. Stage a demonstration by asking a girl to come to the front and bake a cake from ingredients that you have assembled. Tell her that she doesn't have any directions, but that she should bake a delicious cake. Discuss the fact that the cake would probably be a failure without a recipe, and that when we have a plan, our results will be better.

3. Explain briefly that God has a plan for us and this plan is found in the scriptures. The plan is to come to earth, get a body, and choose to keep the commandments so that we can return to him. God has plans and desires for each one that can be discovered through prayer and through the Holy Spirit.

4. Sing the chorus and ask them to listen for all the things the song says "I will do." Sing it again and ask them to discover what blessings they will receive if they follow God's plan. Invite them to join you in singing this part of the song.

5. Teach the other words using keywords and questions, such as these: "What three things does the song say about my life?" "What was my choice?"

6. Encourage them to sing with expression and with the dynamics indicated in the song. Bear witness that as the girls follow God's plan for them, they will find happiness on earth and in the life to come.

I Will Try to Be Reverent   28

Words and Music: Wilma Boyle Bunker
First Line: I love my Heav'nly Father
Topics Indexed: Reverence

This lovely, simple song with its meaningful message is appropriate for all ages. The older children will enjoy singing the alto part on the last four notes.

The song should be sung smoothly with connected tones to bring about the desired reverent feeling. The first and second phrases are almost the same. The rhythm is a simple, even beat pattern with a majority of quarter notes. The tone A in the fourth measure should be held for four counts, and the next word ("rev'rent") should be sung without a breath between. The leader should help the children sing with expression, noting the fermata on the word "house" and singing the last phrase slower.

Teaching Suggestion:

This song can most easily be taught by having the leader or a small group of children sing it as a prayer song for the others to hear. It is simple enough that all will learn it after hearing it a few times.

If with All Your Hearts   15

Words and Music: From Elijah *by Felix Mendelssohn*
First Line: If with all your hearts ye truly seek me
Topics Indexed: Prayer Songs, Revelation

This is a classic melody known and loved throughout the world. This children's version is shortened and simplified from the original in *Elijah,* but the essence of Mendelssohn is retained. The arrangement that has been prepared for the *Children's Songbook* places the melody within the staff and simplifies the accompaniment. The melody conveys a beauty to the important message, that as we truly seek the Lord, we will find him.

The secret in performing this piece well is in capturing the feeling and expression required. It calls for smooth, connected tones with slight crescendos as the melody rises in pitch, and a brief hold at the point of the fermata on the last "our." At the climax in the first measure of the last line, where the notes move from F up to E flat, the children will need a nice head tone to reach the pitch accurately and without strain. In the last line the words of the previous line are repeated, with a different melody, to emphasize the message. This phrase should be sung a little slower.

Teaching Suggestions:

1. Tell the children that you are going to sing a beautiful song about prayer. Ask them to discover a word that is used instead of the word "prayer." Discuss with them what it means to seek the Lord with all your heart. Tell them that we also seek the Lord when we read scriptures, obey his commandments, and attend Church.

2. Ask them to find Jeremiah 29:13 and compare the words of the scripture with the words in the song as they listen to it again.

3. Tell the children that the composer, Felix Mendelssohn, wrote a great oratorio about the prophet Elijah that is still being performed over a hundred years later. Explain that this song, "If with All Your Hearts," is a piece from that oratorio.

4. Help the children sing accurately and with expression and meaning, as noted above.

If You're Happy 266

Words and Music: Anonymous
First Line: If you're happy and you know it, clap your hands
Topics Indexed: Action Songs, Happiness

This happy, fun song is printed in the Nursery manual for the little ones to use in their classes; it is best suited to the younger age groups. It can be sung as a rest song in Primary or in the classroom for a change of pace or activity. Families will also enjoy singing it in the home, especially for family home evening.

The catchy rhythm of the song incorporates an uneven beat pattern throughout, with the repetition of a dotted-eighth note followed by a sixteenth note. None of the melody phrases are repeated.

Teaching Suggestion:

This song need not be formally taught. As you sing it to the children, executing the actions, they will follow you, first by imitating the actions and later by participating in singing the words.

I'll Walk with You 140

Words: Carol Lynn Pearson
Music: Reid N. Nibley
First Line: If you don't walk as most people do
Topics Indexed: Accountability, Commitment, Example,
  Jesus Christ—Example, Kindness, Love, Service, Special
  Needs

This song was written to teach children to treat those who seem different with love and understanding. Author Carol Lynn Pearson says, "My own experience and those of others make it so clear that many are left out or made to feel less because they are different or have unusual problems." Composer Reid Nibley says that the message had special significance for him because he has a daughter with Down's syndrome.

This moving piece appeals both lyrically and musically to the inner feelings of love that we experience when we read of the ministry of the Savior. The poem was originally thought of as two verses and a chorus, but Reid Nibley was impressed to compose the music as a continuous melody with the last phrase repeated. He wanted the lyrics regarding the ministry of Jesus to have a unique mood. If the phrases are considered as six measures long, the form of the music is A A B C D B. The "B" part can be considered as the chorus. When the lyrics say "I won't, I won't" or "I will, I will," the melody and rhythm are the same (with one variation). Most of the rhythm has smooth, even beats that flow easily. "I'll Walk with You" is especially appropriate for meetings involving leaders of children with special needs, but it can have great significance for children in any setting.

Teaching Suggestions:

1. You will probably want to teach this song in two parts. Divide the suggestions that follow according to the ones that fit each part.

2. Ask the children with blue eyes to stand, those with brown eyes to turn around, and all others to stay seated. This focuses on some of the differences they have. Illustrate other differences such as birthdays, color of hair, color of clothes, and so on, in a similar way. Emphasize that though we are all unique in many ways, these characteristics do not make us better or worse, nor do they affect our Heavenly Father's love for us. Invite the children to listen to a beautiful song about people who may be different from us and how they should be treated.

3. Show pictures of Jesus' ministry as he dealt with people, healing the sick, blessing the children, forgiving the sinner, and so on. Ask the children how Jesus treated everyone. Then sing the second part of the song, beginning with "Jesus."

4. Show pictures of people with handicaps, such as someone in a wheelchair, and discuss how we should act toward them.

5. Teach the last phrase first, by asking questions one at a time: "When I walk and talk with you, what am I showing?" "What two rhyming words tell what I will do with you?" Ask the children to join in singing the parts as they learn them.

6. Tell the children that the first part of the song names some things that I won't do. Sing this part and hold up a card with the words "I won't" printed on it to indicate that they should join you in singing these words. Have them count how many times they sing "I won't." Use the same technique with the words "I will."

7. Use questions to teach the other phrases. Write keywords on cards or on the chalkboard to help the children remember the lyrics.

8. Watch for kind acts that the children do for each other and

commend them for these actions. Emphasize that we are following Jesus when we treat others with kindness.

I'm Glad to Pay a Tithing   150

Words and Music: Ruth Benson Lehenbauer
First Line: My Heav'nly Father gives me all good and lovely
   things
Topics Indexed: Gratitude, Tithing

This song provides an important message that can be the basis for teaching children the principle of tithing. Ruth Lehenbauer says, "The thought that children need to understand the reasons behind paying tithing, one being gratitude and the other being to acknowledge God in all things, was the source of inspiration for the words." For the *Children's Songbook* the title has been changed from the original "I Pay My Tithing," the key has been transposed from E flat to D, and the pick-up note has been moved to the third note of the scale from the fifth. There are also a few word changes.

The smooth melody line is enhanced by the uneven beat pattern in measures five and seven in contrast to the rest of the song. Measures five, six, and seven have a nice musical progression: each has the same note pattern built on a successively lower tone of the scale.

Teaching Suggestions:

1. Sing the song and post on a chart or flannelboard pictures of the sun, rain, a bird, ten pennies, and a tithing receipt to illustrate the message.

2. Teach the words by asking questions, singing the answers in the song, and inviting the children to sing with you.

3. Help the children appreciate the tonal progression and the even and uneven beats in the second line by having them pitch-level conduct with you and then clap or tap the rhythm.

4. Discuss the meaning and purpose of tithing and how it is used (to build temples, chapels, schools, and assist in the missionary program). Testify of the importance of the principle of tithing as taught in the scriptures. (See D&C 119:1–7; Malachi 3:10.)

I'm Thankful to Be Me   11

Words: Joy Saunders Lundberg
Music: Janice Kapp Perry
First Line: At night, when I'm alone in bed
Topics Indexed: Gratitude, Talents, Worth of a Child

This little song of gratitude reminds children of the many blessings God has given them. Joy Lundberg says, "I decided this could be an opportunity for children to feel good about themselves, to build a little self-esteem . . . also, I thought it to be an advantage to their well-being if they filled their minds with pleasant thoughts of gratitude as they fell asleep each night. I love to sing it to my little grandchildren when they come to spend the night. . . . Now they are learning to sing it and feel those good feelings about themselves and the love Heavenly Father has for them."

The soothing and flowing melody matches the quiet, comforting message. Although there is no repetition of the melody, the beat pattern is basically the same for each of the four lines. The leader should help the children sit tall and use a good head tone to reach the high notes and large interval skips. The climax occurs in the third line, where the dynamics call for more volume. The last measures should be sung more slowly.

Teaching Suggestions:

1. Ask the children to close their eyes and think of something that they are thankful for. After a few share their thoughts, sing the song to them.

2. Display pictures of blessings — friends, loved ones, teachers, the beautiful world, and so on — and ask the children to listen to the song again and find how these blessings make us feel. Invite them to sing the last line with you.

3. Teach the other phrases with questions and listening and singing experiences. Teach the last phrase first.

4. Help the children remember the sequence of the words with pictures or keywords. Help them sing the music accurately, using pitch-level conducting and diagrams of the melody.

5. Encourage the children to think each night before they go to sleep of something that happened that day that they are thankful for. Tell them that by thinking of happy things, they will be happier.

I'm Trying to Be like Jesus 78

Words and Music: Janice Kapp Perry
First Line: I'm trying to be like Jesus; I'm following in his
  ways
Topics Indexed: Choice, Commitment, Friends, Holy Ghost,
  Jesus Christ — Example, Jesus Christ — Second Coming,
  Kindness, Love, Morality, Service

This lovely song won first place in the *Ensign* song-writing contest and was printed in the April 1983 issue. Janice Kapp Perry has said of the song, "When we think of kindness and loving, Jesus is the one perfect example for children to emulate. This song describes a child's way of fulfilling the sacrament covenant, to take his name and always remember him and keep his commandments." Except for the very little ones, children of all ages can learn and appreciate its message.

The catchy beat of the first measure is repeated in four other measures, and in an additional four measures it is almost the same. The melody pattern of the verse is A A B, considering the phrases as four measures each. The two four-measure phrases of the chorus are similar. The chorus presents an excellent opportunity for teaching children to sing an alto part.

Teaching Suggestions:

1. Tell the children that as we are growing up, we often look at people that we admire and want to be like them, such as sports heroes, favorite relatives, or television stars. Sometimes these people are worthy of our admiration, and sometimes they are not. Ask them to think of someone who is always a good example for them to follow. Display a picture of Jesus and sing the song.

2. Involve the children in listening and singing experiences by asking questions, using keywords, and showing pictures to illustrate the ideas of the phrases. Teach the verse one week and the chorus the next.

3. In teaching the chorus, emphasize that it mentions three important messages that the still small voice will whisper. Have the children listen for these messages, and post word strips as they find them. ("Love one another," "show kindness," "be gentle and loving.")

4. Clap the rhythm of the first phrase ("I'm trying to be like

Jesus"). Draw a diagram of it using long and short lines, and ask the children to discover other places where this rhythm occurs. (The rhythm is the same for the first four phrases.) Invite the children to tap this rhythm with you as they sing the words.

5. Have the children share examples of times when others showed love and kindness to them. Show pictures of children doing kind acts and relate an experience when someone showed kindness to you. Express your conviction that Jesus wants us to be loving to all.

In the Leafy Treetops 240

Words and Music: Anonymous
First Line: In the leafy treetops, the birds sing "Good morning"
Topics Indexed: Beautiful World, Cheerfulness, Summer

This song is included in the Primary manual for three-year-olds. It has been sung and enjoyed by the younger Primary children for many years. Its imaginative message, with the birds singing "Good morning" and the flowers saying "How do you do," seems to capture the children's fancy. For the *Children's Songbook* the score has been lowered to the key of D from E flat, and the accompaniment has been thinned and refined to eliminate a heavy bass chording.

The musical form of this four-phrase song is A B B A: the first and fourth phrases are identical in words and music, and phrases two and three are the same musically. The beat pattern is even throughout, except in the first and ninth measures, which contain a dotted-quarter and an eighth note.

Teaching Suggestions:

1. Tell the children that you love to go outdoors and look at the beautiful flowers and listen to the happy birds singing. Say that even though the birds and flowers do not really talk, sometimes we almost feel that they are speaking to us. Sing the song, one verse at a time, and ask them to find what the birds and the flowers seem to be saying. Have them sing these parts with you.

2. Use pictures of birds, trees, and flowers, or real leaves and flowers, to illustrate the song.

3. Invite some of the children to take the part of the birds and others the part of the flowers. Have them sing their greetings while the others sing the rest of the song.

4. Discuss with the children how the singing birds and beautiful flowers make them feel. Express your love for the beautiful creations that the Lord has given us.

It's Autumntime   246

Words and Music: Rita Mae Olsen; arranged by Vanja Y. Watkins
First Line: It's autumntime. It's autumntime
Topics Indexed: Autumn

This song was inspired by the beautiful autumn colors that Rita Mae Olsen saw around her Idaho home. She says, "I wanted to emphasize the beauty of nature in the fall as being part of God's creation. I wanted the children to notice the autumn colors and the beautiful time of year." The lyrics are simple, with several repetitions, and the melody invites a swaying motion. The song is quickly learned and easy to sing, with a catchy rhythm and message. In the *Children's Songbook* the accompaniment has been simplified, and the words of the last phrase of verses one and two have been exchanged.

With the exception of the last note of each line, the rhythm is the same throughout the song (long-short, long-short). The melody and words of the first measure are repeated in the second measure. Measures five and six are also the same.

Teaching Suggestions:
1. Bring some beautifully colored autumn leaves and ask the children what season of the year it is. Invite them to sing the words "It's autumntime" with you as you pitch-level conduct and sing the song. Ask them to count how many times they sing these words in the song.

2. Invite the children to sway with the rhythm of the music as they sing, to represent a breeze going through the trees. Have them use arm actions as suggested by the words ("leaves are falling down," "all around the town").

Jesus Has Risen   70

Words and Music: Thelma Johnson Ryser
First Line: Jesus has risen, Jesus, our friend
Topics Indexed: Easter, Resurrection, Testimony

This lovely song is a majestic yet peaceful proclamation of the reality of the resurrection. It is a natural choice for an Easter program. There are many opportunities in the piece for interesting dynamics and poignant expression.

The arrangement in the *Children's Songbook* has been altered slightly to accomplish some harmonic improvements. The introduction is now in 3/4 time like the rest of the music, and the beginning pitch is given in the introduction. The melody in line three has been modified to match the first phrase of the song, so that the pattern of the phrases is now A B A C D.

The smooth, even rhythm of each of the five phrases is identical, with the exception of measure two of the third phrase ("sing to him"), which contains uneven beats. The last phrase includes the climax of the song, a reaffirmation of the words "Jesus has risen, Savior divine!" There is one high E that the leader should help the children reach with good head tones and exact pitch.

Teaching Suggestions:

1. Ask the children to pretend they are living at the time when Jesus was crucified. The disciples are very sad, as are all his followers and loved ones. Ask them to imagine how everyone would have felt if someone said to them . . . (then sing the song). After you sing, ask them to express how they would have felt.

2. Show several pictures of the resurrected Christ and ask the children to describe the pictures and why so many artists have painted pictures about the resurrection. Emphasize that the resurrection is one of the most important events that has ever happened on the earth.

3. Use a word strip, "Jesus has risen," and hold it up each time you sing this phrase. Have the children join you in singing this phrase as you repeat the song. Have them raise their hands or stand up each time they sing the phrase. Teach the other words with word strips of keywords and with questions.

4. Use pitch-level conducting to help the children sing the high notes with good head tones and accuracy. Help them sing with expression, observing the fermata and the slower tempo in the last three measures.

5. Have someone play the introduction on tone bells.

Jesus Is Our Loving Friend   58

Words: Anna Johnson
Music: Alexander Schreiner
First Line: Jesus is our loving friend
Topics Indexed: Guidance, Jesus Christ—Blesses Children,
  Praise, Prayer, Worth of a Child

This uncomplicated two-line song presents for children a comforting message of Jesus' love and tenderness. It is included in several of the Primary class manuals for younger children. For the *Children's Songbook* the key has been changed from A to G to simplify the accompaniment, and the meter has been converted from 3/4 to 6/8 time. The melody now flows more naturally, but the leader should be careful not to rush the tempo when conducting it with only two beats to a measure.

The song form is A B A B. Line one (phrases one and two) is the same musically as line two (phrases three and four) except for the last note, where the melody resolves to the first note of the scale. A swaying motion is created by several measures of long-short beats (a quarter and an eighth note). Children will quickly learn this tune by rote and will find it one of their favorite "quiet" songs.

Teaching Suggestions:
1. Invite the children to think of someone who is their friend and share why that person is their friend. Tell them that you are going to sing a song about a special, loving friend. Display a picture of Jesus while you sing. Equate the way Jesus feels about us to the way we feel about our friends.

2. Ask questions to encourage them to listen to the song, such as: "What will Jesus do when we pray?" "How do we raise our voices?"

3. Place on a flannelboard or chart a cutout figure of Jesus and, around him, figures of children from different countries. Explain that every child is precious to Jesus.

4. Invite the children to pitch-level conduct the song while they sing it, to help them see that the first phrase moves down the scale in steps and the second phrase moves back and forth from D to E. Point out that the melody line in two of the phrases moves down, just as we kneel down or bow our heads when we pray.

Jesus Loved the Little Children   **59**

Words and Music: Moiselle Renstrom
First Line: Jesus loved the little children
Topics Indexed: Honesty, Jesus Christ — Blesses Children,
  Jesus Christ — Ministry, Kindness, Worth of a Child

This song, with its simple melody and message, is most suitable for younger children. It engenders feelings of love and peace as little ones sing of Jesus' love for them.

Lines one and two are the same musically, with the exception of the final note. The first phrase is built on the tonic or I chord (E flat, G, and B flat), beginning on B flat. The beat pattern is even, with many quarter notes, and should be sung smoothly with connected tones.

Teaching Suggestions:

1. Display pictures of Jesus with children and ask the group to identify what Jesus is doing in each. Ask them how they think Jesus feels about children. Read 3 Nephi 17:21 and sing the song.

2. Sing the first phrase, have the children repeat the phrase, and then go on to the next phrase in the same way without stopping. Point to yourself when it is your turn to sing and to the children when they should sing.

3. Make line drawings of the two melody phrases in line one and line two, each on a separate piece of paper. As you sing, move your finger along the lines and have the children determine which phrase comes first. Have a child follow the melody phrases with a finger while the others sing the song.

4. Invite younger ones to pantomime simple actions to go with the words, such as hugging themselves by crossing their arms or putting their hands on opposite shoulders for "Jesus loved the little children," and pointing to themselves for "little ones like me."

5. The melody of the song is childlike, one that a beginning piano student might learn. Ask a child who is learning to play the piano to practice the melody line and play it for the children. Ask them to decide if the song sounds like it is meant for adults or for children to sing. Have them sing as the child plays.

Jesus Once Was a Little Child   55

Words: James R. Murray
Music: Joseph Ballantyne
First Line: Jesus once was a little child
Topics Indexed: Honesty, Jesus Christ—Example

The example of the Savior as a child helps little children of today relate to the experiences and life of Jesus. This favorite song portrays him as a gentle, loving child. It is suggested for use with some of the Sunbeam and Star lessons. It has been through several key changes over the years—from E flat to D and now to C—putting it in an easier range.

The melody of the song has motion and appeal. The verse contains two four-measure phrases that are almost the same. The rhythm of the first two measures of the chorus is repeated twice, yet the melody is not duplicated within the eight measures.

Teaching Suggestions:

1. Ask a child to come to the front and *try* to perform a stunt, such as a somersault. Ask another to *try* to stack several blocks, one on top of another, and a third to *try* to read a difficult word. Explain to the children that it is good to *try* to do different things, even though they may seem difficult. Sing the chorus and ask them to listen for what the song says we should *try* to do.

2. Ask a child to learn the words of the first verse as a poem and another child to learn the second verse. Have them recite these verses and you sing the chorus after each. Then ask the two children to repeat the verses and have all the children join in singing the chorus.

3. Teach the words to the verses through pictures of Jesus as a child and through questions such as these: "How was Jesus once like you and me?" "What three words describe Jesus and show us how a little child should be?" "What did he do that little children do?"

4. Explain the meaning of difficult words, such as "pure," "meek," "mild," and "vexed." Have the children think of modern words to substitute for them, such as "perfect," "gentle," "thoughtful," or "angry." Ask a child to pantomime the way a person might look who was meek, mild, or vexed, and have the others guess what word the child is pantomiming, using the words from the song.

5. Teach the alto part to the older boys and girls.

6. Emphasize that we all, including parents and teachers, should *try* to be like Jesus.

Jesus Said Love Everyone 61

Words and Music: Moiselle Renstrom
First Line: Jesus said love ev'ryone; treat them kindly, too
Topics Indexed: Jesus Christ — Ministry, Kindness, Love

This simple song is a classic for clarity of text and melody. Children as young as nursery age can learn to sing it and understand its message. Parents will find that the song will bring a feeling of peace and love as they sing it in the home.

The song has four short phrases, each one musically different, yet the first and third phrases begin alike. The beat pattern is even and smooth, with mostly quarter notes.

Teaching Suggestions:

1. Display a picture of Jesus and tell the children that Jesus taught us a very important truth. Read (or have a child read) John 13:34; then sing the song and have the children identify the truth.

2. Show the children a cutout of a heart and ask what word it makes them think of. Ask them to listen again to find how many times the word "love" is sung.

3. Teach the words to the song through questions: "What does the song say that Jesus said?" "How should we treat everyone?" Each time you ask a question, invite the children to listen to you sing so they can discover the answer, and then have them join you in singing the phrase in which the answer occurs.

4. Show pictures of children being kind to others. Discuss how being kind makes them and others feel. Encourage them to always be kind and loving to everyone.

Jesus Wants Me for a Sunbeam 60

Words: Nellie Talbot
Music: Edwin O. Excell
First Line: Jesus wants me for a sunbeam, to shine for him each day
Topics Indexed: Cheerfulness, Commitment, Example, Happiness, Kindness, Love, Primary Class Songs, Service, Worth of a Child

This longtime favorite piece is the class song for the three-year-old Sunbeams. In a 1983 survey of Primary songs, it rated sixth in familiarity and eighth in song favorites. For the *Children's Songbook* it has been lowered to the key of F from the key of G, placing it in a more singable range. The accompaniment has also been thinned and the left-hand chords altered to provide a lighter arrangement. Verses three and four, which were seldom sung, have been deleted.

The verse has four two-measure phrases, with the musical form A B A B (the first two phrases are repeated in phrases three and four). The form of the chorus is A B A C. There is repetition and variety in rhythm and pitch throughout. The melody flows with the 6/8 time signature and is easy to learn and to sing. Leaders should help the children avoid overemphasizing the second syllable of "sunbeam."

Teaching Suggestions:

1. Show a picture of a large sun with beams projecting from around it. Explain to the children that the rays or beams of the sun send out light and warmth to all the world. (On each of the sunbeams write the name of one of the children so that all the names are included.) Display a picture of Jesus and tell them that he wants each one of them to shine and be an example of love and helpfulness to others, like the beams of the sun. Sing the chorus and invite them to sing with you several times.

2. Make a poster with a picture of Jesus in the center and small suns (or beams) around the picture. Write the name of one of the children on each sun, or place a picture of a child on each sun.

3. Help the children learn the words to the verses with questions and illustrations, such as a home, a school, and a child at play.

4. Make small cutouts of suns with beams for the children to hold or pass around while they sing the song.

5. Ask the children to name something that they can do to be a sunbeam for Jesus. Then encourage them to sing the song sweetly, without shouting, to show Jesus that they can be loving, kind, and helpful.

Keep the Commandments 146

Words and Music (including obbligato): Barbara A.
McConochie; arranged by Darwin Wolford
First Line: Keep the commandments; keep the commandments!

Topics Indexed: Commandments, Obbligatos, Obedience, Peace, Prophets

The inspiration for this song came from a statement of President Harold B. Lee that by keeping the commandments we can have peace and safety. Sister McConochie also leaned on scriptures, including D&C 59:23 and Mosiah 2:22. The simple but strong message of the importance of keeping the Lord's commandments is as vital for adults as for children.

Much of the strength of the song comes from repetition of significant words and musical phrases. The first part states that there is peace and safety in keeping the commandments, the next part reassures us that blessings come from doing this, and the final phrases reemphasize the plea to keep the commandments. The melody begins quietly on lower tones and rises to the climax as "keep the commandments" is sung firmly, for the third time, on the highest pitches in the song, with a fermata on the high D. Finally, the melody moves down peacefully and concludes on the tonic tone (F), with the words "in this there is safety and peace." The second verse, which has been added by Sister McConochie for the *Children's Songbook*, presents the idea that we are on earth to be tested, and that as we remember the Lord's promises, listen to the prophets, and keep the commandments, we will find safety and peace.

An arrangement of "Keep the Commandments" appears in *Hymns*, number 303, as a vocal duet with one verse. The two-verse version in the *Children's Songbook* is for one voice with an optional obbligato for flute or soprano voice. Primary leaders can choose either arrangement.

Teaching Suggestions:

1. Ask the children what it would be like to live without traffic laws — no lights, stop signs, or other regulations. Explain that laws help keep us safe and our lives in order. Tell them that commandments are also laws — spiritual laws — which, like traffic laws, help us have safety and peace. Sing the song and ask them to discover how many times you sing "keep the commandments." Hold up a sign with the words "keep the commandments" printed on it each time you sing these words.

2. Tell the children that Barbara McConochie received the inspiration for writing this song from the words of the prophet, Harold B. Lee, and from scriptures, Mosiah 2:22 and D&C 59:23. Have them look up these scriptures and read them together. Then

ask them to listen to the song again and see if they hear any of the words that are in the scriptures.

3. Display pictures of President Harold B. Lee, the present prophet of the Church, and other prophets. Use quotations from them showing that all the prophets have said to keep the Lord's commandments.

4. Help the children learn the words through questions, key-words, and pictures.

5. Bear testimony that the words of this song are true, and that we will be blessed with peace and safety as we keep the commandments of the Lord.

Kindness Begins with Me 145

Words and Music: Clara W. McMaster
First Line: I want to be kind to ev'ryone
Topics Indexed: Accountability, Example, Kindness

Clara McMaster wrote this two-line song to help children acquire an individual feeling for being kind. It reminds them that they should not wait for kind acts to come to them first, but that they can be the ones to initiate kindness.

The song form is A B A C. The rhythm is moving and lilting, with a catchy beat. The dotted-quarter note on the word "this" indicates a slight pause before the final words, "kindness begins with me," which should be sung more slowly and with emphasis. The song should be conducted two beats to the measure, with a moderately fast tempo.

Teaching Suggestions:

1. Use this song to reinforce stories from the scriptures about kindness, such as the Good Samaritan or stories of Jesus' life. Use pictures of these stories.

2. Help the children recognize that kindness is contagious by having a child demonstrate a sad face and then a happy face. Point out that kindness and happiness are contagious, and that as they do kind acts, others will want to do them, too. Invite them to play "pass a smile" by having one child smile at the child sitting next to him or her, and having this child smile at the next child, and so on, until the smile has spread among all the children.

3. Ask the children to listen to the song several times to find answers to questions such as these: "To whom should I be kind?"

"Why should I be kind?" "What do I say to myself?" Use keywords to help them remember the sequence of the words.

4. Help the children internalize the message of the song by using examples of kindness that you observe and pictures of children doing kind acts. Discuss these examples and pictures.

Latter-day Prophets   134

Words: Cynthia Lord Pace
Music: Vanja Y. Watkins
First Line: Latter-day prophets are: number one
Topics Indexed: Prophets

Children of all ages can learn and enjoy singing the names of the prophets in this clever song. Cynthia Pace relates this story: "In Primary one of the courses of study was about the latter-day prophets. One very dedicated and concerned mother came to me, knowing of my love of music, and asked me to write a song so her daughter could remember the names of the prophets. . . . I knelt down and poured out my heart to my Father in Heaven [in thanks] for my many blessings. I also asked him to help me write a little song to help this girl. At the close of my prayer the words to the first line of the song came: 'Latter-day prophets are: number one, Joseph Smith, then Brigham Young,' with the impression, 'I have given you the first line, you write the rest!' "

An indication of the great popularity of "Latter-day Prophets" came at the death of Spencer W. Kimball. The Primary office received many requests and suggestions for a revision to include the new prophet, Ezra Taft Benson. This updated version is the one included in the *Children's Songbook*.

The music has a whimsical mood with a few dissonant chords and syncopated beats in the beginning measures. The melody of the first and fifth lines is similar, but other musical phrases are not alike. A variety of rhythms allows the beats to match the accents and syllables in the prophets' names.

Teaching Suggestions:

1. Use a string stretched across the front of the room and clothespins to display pictures of the latter-day prophets with name cards attached to each. Ask the children to arrange them in the correct order, according to the time when they served. After they do this, sing the song and let them check to see if they are correct. Sing it several times until they find the right order.

2. Have several children hold the name cards of the prophets in the correct order across the front of the room. Ask others to place the pictures of the prophets by the correct names as you sing the song again. You can repeat this activity several times. Encourage the children to join in singing or humming as they learn the song.

3. Teach the children the words in three parts. The first two lines introduce the first five prophets, the next two lines the next five, and the last two lines name the last three prophets.

4. Introduce the latter-day prophets in Sharing Time by having someone dress up as each prophet and tell a little about what he did during his life. Have the children sing the song.

5. Express your belief that the Lord chooses his prophets to lead us, and that we should listen to and follow their words.

Lift Up Your Voice and Sing 252

Words and Music: Richard C. Berg
First Line: A song is a wonderful kind of thing
Topics Indexed: Singing

Richard C. Berg, a professor of music at the college level, says that this song expresses his feelings about the joys of singing in showing gratitude for the blessings of living. He has experienced great pleasure in hearing large festival children's choruses, as well as classroom groups, sing this song beautifully and expressively.

The musical form of the first half of the song is A B A C, the first two-measure phrase being repeated in the third phrase. No other phrases are duplicated. The double bar in the third line separates the verse and the refrain, as it was labeled in the first printing. In the last line the repetition of "Lift up your voice" reaches a climax as it is sung the third time. The dynamic markings suggest that these words are sung softly the first time, medium loudly the second, and loudly the third time. The children should be encouraged to sing with enthusiasm and joy at the blessing of being able to express glad feelings through music.

Teaching Suggestions:

1. Ask the children to listen to the accompanist play the song and then describe how the music makes them feel. Express how music makes you feel. Then sing the song for them.

2. Find scriptures that tell about singing, such as D&C 25:12–

13; Mosiah 12:22; Ezra 3:11; Psalm 100:2; and Isaiah 49:13, and read or have the children read them to show that the Lord talks of singing songs of praise on many occasions in the scriptures.

3. Draw a picture to illustrate the movement of the melody in the last line and follow the contour of the drawing with your finger as you sing. Encourage the children to discover what words are sung on the highest notes, what words are on repeated notes, and where the tones step down the scale. Have them join in singing this line.

4. Teach the words to the rest of the song with keywords and questions such as these: "What is a song?" "How should we sing?" Make a word strip of the words "lift up your voice" and hold it up each time these words are to be sung. To help the children remember the order of the phrases "brighten the day" and "lighten the way," point out that the letters B and D come before L and W in the alphabet.

5. Encourage the children to sing with enthusiasm and expression, following the dynamic markings in the music.

Listen, Listen 107

Words and Music: Merrill Bradshaw
First Line: Listen to the still small voice!
Topics Indexed: Choice, Guidance, Holy Ghost, Rounds

Through its simplicity and gentle beauty, this little melody helps us understand the workings of the Holy Ghost. It expresses in word and music the spirit of D&C 8:2, "I will tell you in your mind and in your heart, by the Holy Ghost, which shall come upon you and which shall dwell in your heart."

The melody is interesting because it appears to be written in C major and yet has the feeling of a minor key. There is really no tonal center. The melody moves smoothly and gently. The words "listen, listen" in measures three and four should be attacked softly and released so that the tones are not sustained through the eighth rests. This gives importance and emphasis to these words. "Listen, Listen" can be sung straight through as printed, or as a two-part round. The beginning point for the second group is marked in the music. The first group holds at the fermata on "you" until the second group joins them on this note, and then both groups sing "always" together. There should be no accompaniment since the point of the song is to listen to the voice.

Teaching Suggestions:

1. Discuss the difference between easy choices, such as what to wear, and difficult choices. Give an example of when you or someone you know was directed by the Spirit to make a right choice. Ask the children what we should do when we have an important choice to make, and have them listen to the song for the answer.

2. Ask: "How many times do we sing 'listen'?" "If you listen to the still small voice, what will he do for you?" "When do you listen to the still small voice?" "What word is held longer than any other in the song?" Each time you ask a question, sing the song and have the children listen for the answer. Accept responses and invite them to join you in singing the part that gives the answer.

3. Point out that two of the "listen" words come together, and that there is "listening space" between these words. Invite them to listen for the "listening space," and then ask them to sing those two words with you.

4. Ask the children how the melody moves when they sing the words "Listen to the still small voice." Sing this phrase using the words "down, down, down, down, down, up, up," to emphasize the direction, and invite them to do the same. Display a melody chart of this phrase. Sing the phrase again using the real words.

5. Display the chart again and ask the children to find another place in the song that has the same melody pattern. ("When you have to make a choice.") Repeat activity 4 with this phrase. Point out that this phrase has the same melody direction, but begins lower.

6. When the children have learned to sing the song well, invite them to sing it as a two-part round. Have them practice holding the word "you" until you give them the signal to sing the last notes. Show a picture of a fermata while they hold the tone. They may need to take a quick breath, but should continue singing until the fermata chart is put down.

7. Encourage them to "feel the song inside" by following your directions, listening to the words, and singing with expression.

Little Jesus 39

Words: Marilyn Curtis White
Music: Mark Newell and Charlene Anderson Newell
First Line: Fairest little Jesus child

Topics Indexed: Christmas

When Mark Newell was ten years old, he wrote a lovely little melody in his music theory book. His mother, Charlene Newell, liked it so much that she asked a friend to write some words to the melody. Charlene took the words and the melody and put it all together, adjusting the rhythm and adding the harmony. The result is a beautifully simple Christmas song that younger children can learn and enjoy.

The rhythm of the song is even and smooth and should be sung with connected tones. Each of the four phrases is different, yet the first and third begin the same. The melody moves by steps, repeated notes, and natural intervals. The octave skip from C to high C in the first line will be the most difficult interval for little ones to master. The words of the first phrase are the same for both verses; this is also true of the final phrase. The leader should help the children sing the song sweetly and with expression.

Teaching Suggestions:

1. Teach the song to the younger children by rote, singing it for them and then having them repeat after you. Use pictures of the baby Jesus, or wrap a doll in a blanket and let them take turns holding the "baby Jesus" while they sing.

2. Help the children understand such words as "fairest," "meek," "mild," and "praise." Remind them that Jesus had an earthly mother and father who cared about him and taught him to love Heavenly Father.

Little Lambs So White and Fair   58

Words and Music: Anonymous
First Line: Little lambs so white and fair
Topics Indexed: Guidance, Jesus Christ—Example,
   Obedience, Worth of a Child

Even though the name of Jesus is not mentioned in this song, the metaphor of the shepherd who watches over his sheep is unmistakably a reference to the Savior who cares for his flock. The melody and words are childlike and easy to sing. In the *Children's Songbook* the key has been lowered from A flat to G.

The melody form is A B A C; the first and third phrases are the same and the second and fourth are similar. The rhythm is constant and steady and should be sung smoothly and evenly.

Teaching Suggestions:

1. Introduce this song by showing the children a picture of the Good Shepherd with his sheep. Tell them that the shepherd watches over and cares for his sheep, and that they follow him wherever he goes. Then sing the song to them.

2. Invite the children to play "follow the leader." You sing one phrase, the children repeat that phrase, and you sing the next phrase, and so on without stopping. Point out that they are following you like the little lambs follow the shepherd. Tell them how Jesus is like a shepherd watching over us, his flock, and guiding us so that we can return to Heavenly Father.

3. Tell the children that the shepherd, in Bible times, would call his sheep, sometimes by whistling, or sometimes with a little instrument. Have someone play the melody using a flute, a recorder, or some other flutelike instrument to simulate a shepherd's pipe.

4. Lead the song with pitch-level conducting until the children learn to sing the intervals accurately.

Little Pioneer Children 216

Words and Music: A. Laurence Lyon
First Line: Little pioneer children gath'ring berries for food
Topics Indexed: Happiness, Pioneers, Rounds, Singing, Work

This is a happy song about the life of a pioneer child in the trek across the country. There are a few word changes in the *Children's Songbook*, and the melody has been written within the accompaniment. The optional music for round accompaniment or musical instrument is placed on a third staff.

The song has a swinging rhythm with a 6/8 beat that gives the feeling of wagons rolling across the plains. The chord progression in each line is almost the same—F, C7, F, C7, F—which creates a harmony that is conducive to "round" music. Each phrase has a different melody, though there is a similar melodic pattern in the first measures of lines one and two.

Teaching Suggestions:

1. Ask the children to name some of the things they do each day. Ask them to listen as you sing a song that tells some of the things that pioneer children did. Discuss the difference between their activities and those of pioneer children.

2. Teach the lyrics through questions and pictures of pioneer activities, giving listening and singing opportunities.

3. Have the children clap the rhythm of the first two measures, and then sing the words as they clap. Tell them that there are two other phrases that have the same rhythm and that they should listen to find them. ("See the pioneer children" and "gladly helping each other.") Have them clap and sing these phrases. They will also enjoy clapping the rhythm to the last line. Divide the children into two groups, one group clapping the rhythm of the melody and the other clapping two beats to a measure, while they sing.

4. Have the children dress in simple costumes and pantomime the actions mentioned in the song. (Use pioneer bonnets, hats, and baskets for gathering berries.)

5. Younger children could join hands and walk in a circle while singing, changing directions at the beginning of each phrase.

6. After the children are familiar with the song, divide them into two, three, or four groups and help them sing it as a round.

Little Purple Pansies 244

Words: Anonymous
Music: Joseph Ballantyne
First Line: Little purple pansies, touched with yellow gold
Topics Indexed: Cheerfulness, Spring

This song likens the little pansy that brightens the garden to the small child who brings happiness to others. The tune is cheery and catchy. For the *Children's Songbook* the key has been changed from D to C.

The song form is A B A C: the first two phrases are similar and the first and third phrases are the same. There is an interesting scale descent in line four. The melody includes many repeated tones with a moving harmony beneath that forms an interesting melody of its own. The same words are used in the last line for both verses to emphasize the message, "just one spot to gladden, you and I." The rhythm is identical for each of the phrases, with a dotted-eighth/sixteenth-note combination prevalent throughout. The song is most appropriate for younger children, but the addition of an alto part could effectively involve the older ones.

Teaching Suggestions:
1. Bring some fresh pansies, or show a picture of pansies, and tell the children how much happiness and beauty these flowers have brought to you. Tell them that where they grow, they brighten that

spot and bring joy. Tell them that you are going to sing a song that tells how the pansy brings happiness.

2. Ask the children to clap the uneven beat pattern of the song, while you and the teachers sing it. Encourage them to realize that the rhythm is the same for each of the four phrases.

3. Help the children understand that they, too, can bring happiness to others, even though they are small, like the little pansy does.

4. After the children have learned the song well, have a group of teachers or older children sing the alto part.

Little Seeds Lie Fast Asleep   243

Words and Music: Moiselle Renstrom
First Line: Little seeds lie fast asleep in a row, in a row
Topics Indexed: Action Songs, Spring

This lovely song is perfect to help small children visualize and act out the growth process of the seed as it sprouts and reaches up toward the sun. Each of the four phrases has a different melody, yet there are many repeated note patterns. The rhythm is smooth and connected. Children in the nursery and the younger age groups will learn it quickly by listening to it and acting out the lyrics.

Teaching Suggestions:

1. Teach the song by inviting a few of the children to curl up on the floor in a row pretending to be seeds. As you sing the song, you, or other children, can touch each of them in turn and invite them to slowly stand and stretch up tall. After a few repetitions, the children will begin to sing with you.

2. The instructions for actions that accompanied the first printing were:

Verse one: Line one — bend head to left and rest on folded hands. Line two — make a circle with arms.

Verse two: Line one — rise quietly. Line two — stretch high and make a circle with arms.

Love Is Spoken Here   190

Words and Music: Janice Kapp Perry
First Line: I see my mother kneeling with our family each day
Topics Indexed: Example, Fathers, Love, Mothers, Obedience,
   Parents, Prayer, Priesthood, Two-part Songs

Janice Kapp Perry wrote this song for the *Ensign* song-writing contest of 1980. It received a first-place award and was printed in the March 1981 issue. The song has become a favorite because of the interesting melody construction, the meaningful text, and the beautiful harmonies. It is frequently performed by children's choirs. Janice Kapp Perry says, "I wrote about two things I loved in my family—hearing my mother pray for us daily and seeing my father give strong priesthood leadership in our home."

In verse one, the song form is A A B C. The first two phrases are the same except for the last note. The melody moves smoothly by steps and short intervals. In the third phrase, the word "plea" is sung on the highest note of the verse. The leader should help the children reach this tone accurately. The melody of verse two seems to indicate strength and power as the message refers to the priesthood. Though a different melody from verse one, it also has the A A B C song form. The interesting rhythm pattern on the words "father and mother leading the way" is repeated on "teaching me how to trust and obey." This verse also includes an accidental in the melody on the word "to" (C sharp); the leader should have the children listen carefully to this sound so that they can sing it on pitch. The directions in the *Children's Songbook* indicate that the verses should first be sung separately, then combined using the third ending. This last line, with its appealing two-part harmony and important message, should be sung more slowly and with emphasis.

Teaching Suggestions:

1. Ask the children a riddle: "There is a special place where we can eat, sleep, have family prayer, and hold family home evening. What is this special place?" Post a picture of a home and tell the children to listen to a song that tells about some important things that can happen in the home.

2. Ask them to find some of the things that the song says happen in my home. As these are named, post word strips: "family prayer," "love is spoken," "priesthood power," "father and mother leading," and "the Savior near." You could also use pictures of these concepts.

3. Teach the words through questions: "What am I thankful for?" "What does the song say that I see?" "What do I hear in my home?" "How does her plea make me feel?" "What is my home blessed with?" Ask each question, have the children listen to the song, accept responses, and have them join you in singing that part of the song.

4. Teach both verses to all of the children, and then divide them into two groups and have them sing (or hum) the verses together. You could have two leaders, each directing one of the groups.

5. To teach the last line, ask the children to listen to two leaders sing the line together. Tell them to listen to how the two parts are on the same notes for the first few tones, and then they separate into harmony. Ask them to see if they can find the first word that the leaders sing in harmony ("near"). Use a picture of the Savior while teaching the last line.

6. Help the children sing this song with expression and conviction.

Love One Another 136

Words and Music: Luacine Clark Fox; arranged by Jo Marie Borgeson Bray
First Line: As I have loved you, love one another
Topics Indexed: Commandments, Example, Jesus Christ—Example, Love, Obbligatos

Though this song is simple, children and adults alike feel satisfaction and joy in singing these beautiful words of the Savior, set to an appealing melody. It can be particularly moving when the children execute the sign language (included in the *Children's Songbook*) to express the meaning of the song.

This is one of the children's songs included in *Hymns* (number 308). The arrangement in the hymnbook is in duet form. For the *Children's Songbook*, the time signature has been changed to 6/8 from 3/4 time to enhance the flow of the melody. The optional obbligato has also been included.

Even though each melody phrase is different in the song, there is a repeated beat pattern. The first two measures contain a dotted-quarter note, a quarter note, an eighth note, and two dotted-quarter notes. This pattern is duplicated four times, and variations of it are also present. There are no difficult intervals, pitches, or rhythms. The melody should flow smoothly and expressively, with connected tones.

Teaching Suggestions:

1. Show a picture of the Last Supper and tell the children: "Jesus met with his disciples in the upper room the night before he gave up his life for us. He spoke to his disciples with love, saying . . . " (Sing the song to the children.)

2. Teach the words through questions such as these: "How many times do I sing the words 'love one another'?" "What was the new commandment that Jesus gave?" "What word means that you are a follower of Jesus?" "How will people know you are a disciple of Jesus?" As the children discover each answer, invite them to sing that part of the song with you, adding one phrase at a time to the ones already learned.

3. Have the children compare the words of the song to the words of the scripture in John 13:34–35. Have them use their scriptures, or write these verses on a chart. Point to the words as they sing the song.

4. Illustrate the message of the song by showing pictures of Jesus showing love to others or pictures of children demonstrating love.

5. Invite a guest to teach the actions for "signing" the song. (See *Children's Songbook*, page 137.) Add a violin or flute obbligato to the singing.

6. Express your belief that by following the teachings and example of the Savior, we can become his disciples, or followers. Encourage the children to sing the song with love and reverence for Jesus.

Mary's Lullaby 44

Words: Jan Underwood Pinborough
Music: German folk tune; arranged by Darwin Wolford
First Line: Lullaby, lullaby, my little one
Topics Indexed: Christmas, Descants, Lullabies

Jan Pinborough has said of this song, "I wanted this to be not only the tender lullaby of a loving mother, but also Mary's acknowledgment of her tiny son's divine mission, of which she was quite aware. At the time I wrote this, I was expecting our second child, which provided some of the tenderness I felt for this lullaby." Darwin Wolford simplified the accompaniment to include the pitches of the descant and the melody so that the parts can be sung more easily.

Considering the music in four-measure phrases, the song form is A A B A. The endings of the A phrases have some variation. The rhythm flows smoothly, and the melody moves by steps and effortless intervals. The jump of an octave in the fourth line is the most difficult interval for the children. The optional descant on the second page imitates the melody two beats later and offers an interesting challenge for the older children.

Teaching Suggestions:

1. Tell the children that you will sing a lullaby that a mother sings to her baby. Ask them to listen and discover who the mother and baby are. After they identify the mother as Mary and the baby as Jesus, ask them what words help them know that it is Mary and Jesus that are being sung about. Sing the song again so they can discover that it mentions "Joseph" and the "star."

2. Ask the children to tell what a lullaby is and then listen to find out how many times they hear the word "lullaby." Invite them to sing the word "lullaby" with you each time it occurs.

3. Teach the words to the children through questions that can be answered by exact words in the song, with word strips of keywords, and with pictures. Use pictures of Mary with the baby Jesus, Joseph, the star, a baby's head, and a baby's hands.

4. After they learn the song, teach a group of older children the descant. You could have two leaders direct the two parts.

5. For variation, have a flutist play the alto part and the descant as the children sing the melody. Have some older children and teachers match tones with the instrument.

6. Have two children take the parts of Mary and Joseph while the song is sung. Encourage them to sing sweetly and with expression.

Mother Dear 206

Words: Maud Belnap Kimball
Music: Mildred Tanner Pettit
First Line: Mother dear, I love you so
Topics Indexed: Mothers, Smiles

"Mother Dear" is a simple two-line song with sweet expressions about love for mother. Minor word, rhythmic, and melodic changes were made in the song for the *Children's Songbook* to improve the word accents and musical resolutions.

There are no repeated musical phrases in the song, but it moves easily with repeated notes, steps, and short intervals. All of the notes are within a five-tone spread, except for the high D in the middle of the second line. The rhythm is mostly even until the next-to-last measure, where four eighth notes make the pronunciation of the words a challenge. "Mother Dear" is a pleasing song that is suitable for the little children to sing for Mother's Day.

Teaching Suggestions:

1. Tell the children that you are going to sing a song about someone they love very much, and that you want them to guess who it is. Sing the song, humming the first two words so as not to reveal the answer. After they guess the riddle, invite them to sing the first phrase with you as you sing it again.

2. Display pictures to help them remember the words, such as a smiling mother, a home, eyes, and stars.

3. Ask questions for them to answer each time they listen to the song, such as these: "What does mother's smile make the home?" "What is such a joy to look at?" "What are mother's eyes like?"

4. Ask them to clap or tap the rhythm of the last phrase to reinforce the beat pattern of these notes.

Mother, I Love You   207

Words and Music: Lorin F. Wheelwright
First Line: Mother, I love you; mother, I do
Topics Indexed: Mothers

Lorin F. Wheelwright said that "Mother, I Love You" is a tribute to his mother, Valborg Rasmussen, whom he loved dearly. The song form is A B A B (C). The first and third phrases, which are the same, contain two smaller identical phrases. The fourth phrase is like the second with a variation in the last two notes. The final phrase, to be sung after the second verse, restates the expression of love for mother. This is to be sung more deliberately and slowly. The most difficult musical intervals for children to sing occur with the first three notes (and subsequent repetitions); they should execute these accurately, without sliding to reach the tones. The rhythm has a lilting beat that flows with smooth, connected tones. For versatility the word "daddy" can be substituted for "mother."

Teaching Suggestions:

1. Show the children pictures of mothers of various ages, young mothers to grandmothers. Ask them what all these women might have in common. After they identify them as mothers, tell them that everyone has a mother, and that you are going to sing a song that tells how we feel about our mothers.

2. Make charts showing pictures of the melody of the three musical patterns in the song: the first phrase (first four measures), the second phrase (second four measures), and the final phrase (last four measures). Teach the song by showing one chart at a time; follow the melody on the chart with a pointer as you sing. Ask questions about words that are sung at high and low points. Help the children notice how the melody moves and where they hear the same melody repeated. As they listen and answer questions, invite them to sing the phrases.

3. This melody also lends itself to having the children move their bodies up and down to the pitches.

4. Ask the children to find words that rhyme. ("Near" and "hear," "mind" and "find.") Ask them to place the rhyming words on the melody charts where they occur.

5. Encourage them to pitch-level conduct the song with you to help them reach the notes accurately. Remind them to sing with love and expression.

6. Invite the mothers to visit so the children can sing to them.

Mother, Tell Me the Story   204

Words and Music: Janice Kapp Perry
First Line: Mother, tell me the story that I love to hear
Topics Indexed: Jesus Christ — Blesses Children, Lullabies,
  Mothers, Two-part Songs

This beautiful, comforting lullaby is one of five counterpoint duets by Janice Kapp Perry included in the *Children's Songbook*. The first verse contains a child's questions and pleas; in the second, the mother offers responses and reassurance of her love. Sister Perry says, "I remembered the many times my mother told me of where I came from, why I'm here, where I'm going, and how she loved me. I always felt peace at these times." This song is challenging and appealing for older children, and yet the message is appropriate for the little ones. It can been performed on Mother's Day by a mother and child or by a larger group.

The child's part is somewhat demanding musically because the range is extensive—from B below middle C up to high D. The child's melody in the top staff is sung first, the mother's part follows, and finally the two melodies are sung together. After the two voices sing the "1, 2, 3" ending, they return to the D.S. al fine sign and sing through to the last ending. The accompaniment complements both melody lines, but does not include either one. An optional second verse is printed at the bottom of the page.

Teaching Suggestions:

1. Teach the song to the children using the follow-the-leader method. Sing the first phrase of the song, have them repeat that phrase, you sing the next phrase, and so on, without stopping, until they have sung the entire verse. Encourage them to listen to the pitches of the notes so that they sing them accurately, without sliding into the tones. Pitch-level conduct to help them.

2. Each of the four phrases of the song expresses a specific thought. Use word strips of keywords in each phrase to help the children remember the sequence of the lyrics.

My Country   224

Words: Mabel Jones Gabbott
Music: Newel Kay Brown
First Line: This is my country! I sing it with pride
Topics Indexed: Accountability, Country, Freedom

Mabel Jones Gabbott says, "The words of the song refer to geographical differences in the lands we live in, not political boundaries; children everywhere can find kinship with the descriptions of these lands." The spirited, marchlike beat of the music matches the sentiments of the patriotic words.

The song has four two-measure phrases written in A B B C form. The melodic intervals move easily, many times with steps and repeated tones. Newel Kay Brown said, "The mildly syncopated rhythm of the song results from an attempt to match the natural spoken rhythm of the text; therefore, it might help to speak the words together, then again while the song is played. Such phrases as 'I sing it with pride' will fall very naturally into place when the children are asked to sing the words."

Teaching Suggestions:

1. Display a map of your country and ask the children what it is. Tell them that you are going to sing a song that answers this question.

2. Show pictures of some landscapes as described in the song, and ask the children which look most like the place where they live. Explain that in many countries there can be a wide variety of landscapes from one place to another and from one season to another.

3. Teach the words by using pictures and questions that can be answered with exact words from the song, such as these: "What two things are found here?" "What three kinds of places are described in the song?" (You may need to sing the song several times so the children can identify all three types of lands. Pictures of each will help them remember the words.) After the children answer a question, have them join you in singing that part of the song.

4. Help the children feel the syncopated rhythm by following Newel Brown's suggestion described above.

5. Have them march around the room or in place as they sing the song to the accompaniment. Help them sing with feeling and love for their country. Express your devotion to your country and the importance of being loyal and true to it.

My Dad 211

Words and Music: Carol Graff Gunn
First Line: My daddy is my favorite pal, and I help him ev'ry day
Topics Indexed: Fathers, Honesty

Carol Graff Gunn wrote this song for her three little boys to sing because they "loved their dad and wanted to be with him every chance they got." The first, second, and fourth lines begin with the same melody, but end with variations. The third line contains an interesting musical progression where the pattern of the first measure is repeated twice, each time on a lower note of the scale. The rhythm is even and constant throughout, with few deviations from the straight quarter-note beat pattern. The rhyming words will help the children learn and remember the song. The climax is reached on the word "dad," where a hold is indicated.

Teaching Suggestions:

1. Tell the children that you are thinking of a very special person that you would like them to guess from the song that you will sing. As you sing, hum when you come to the words "daddy" and "dad" so they can guess the special person.

2. Show pictures of some fathers and ask the children to tell some of the things that they like to do with their dads and some things that their fathers teach them.

3. Ask: "What does the song say I know?" "Why am I very glad?" "What does my dad teach me?" "What do I want to be?" "What do I do every day?" Each time the children discover an answer, have them join you in singing that part of the song, adding it to the ones they know, until they have learned all of the phrases.

4. Show pictures of some of the repeated melody patterns, such as on the words "my daddy is my fav'rite pal" and "teaches me that," and encourage them to listen for repetitions of these note patterns and to identify words that are sung with the melodies.

5. Invite the fathers to join the children so that they can sing "My Dad" to them, or the children could perform the song for a Father's Day program.

My Flag, My Flag 225

Words: Anna Johnson
Music: Alexander Schreiner
First Line: My flag, my flag, my country's flag
Topics Indexed: Country, Freedom

This is a song that stirs feelings of loyalty and devotion for flag and country, a patriotic song that could be used worldwide. It has been transposed to the key of G from the key of A, and some left-hand notes have been added to fit the regal, dramatic mood of the song.

The musical pattern of the two-measure phrases of the first half of the song is A B A C, the first and third phrases being the same. The fourth phrase ("the banner of the brave") moves down the scale by steps from B to D. The pattern of the last half of the song, or chorus, is also A B A (with variation) C. The rhythm includes some measures of even beats and some of uneven beats, with the use of dotted-quarter and eighth notes.

Teaching Suggestions:

1. Show a flag of your country and ask a child to wave it. Ask the children what their flag reminds them of. Post word strips (the shape of flags) with the words "brave," "free," and "liberty" printed on them. Have the children listen to you sing the song while three children arrange the word strips in the order in which they are sung. Have the child with the flag wave it while the song is sung.

2. Sing the song again and ask the children to discover a word that means the same thing as "flag." Repeat the song and ask them to join you in singing the word "banner" when it occurs.

3. Draw a melody line for the two musical phrases in the chorus, sung on the words "wave on, wave on forever," using dots to represent the notes. Sing the two phrases and have the children determine which melody line matches the phrase that you sing.

4. Teach the remaining words with word strips of keywords and with questions. Each time the song is sung, ask a child to stand in front and wave the flag, or give each of the children a small flag to wave.

5. Express your love and reverence for the flag and encourage the children to always respect and honor the flag of their country.

My Hands 273

Words: Louise B. Scott
Music: Lucille F. Wood
First Line: My hands upon my head I'll place
Topics Indexed: Action Songs, Quiet

This is a lively activity song that helps little children get rid of the "wiggles" and settle down for quiet listening. The first, second, and fourth lines are musically the same; the third line contains two phrases with the same melody, the second a step lower in the scale. The melody frequently features intervals of a third: F to A, E to G, B flat to D, A to C. The other notes move naturally by steps and repeated notes, providing a catchy and easily learned song that can be sung frequently to provide a change of pace, especially in the nursery and the younger-age classes.

Teaching Suggestions:

1. Little children will learn "My Hands" quickly just by listening to you sing it. Sing the song, improvising actions suggested by the words and inviting them to follow.

2. In the classroom, use this song each week as a signal that it is time for the children to listen quietly to the lesson.

My Heavenly Father Loves Me   228

Words and Music: Clara W. McMaster
First Line: Whenever I hear the song of a bird
Topics Indexed: Beautiful World, Creation, God's Love,
  Gratitude, Heavenly Father, Summer, Worth of a Child.

This wonderful song generates emotions of love and gratitude for all that our Heavenly Father does for us. The lyrics include many descriptive phrases: "wind as it rushes," "touch a velvet rose," and "magical sound." The children will enjoy "feeling" the expression that these words suggest. Clara McMaster said, "As I thanked my Heavenly Father for his guidance and the direction I had felt from the Holy Ghost [in writing the song], I prayed in my heart that children who sang my song might have a beautiful feeling of our Heavenly Father's love for them and gain a testimony such as had come to me."

A few changes have been made in the version printed in the *Children's Songbook*. The key was changed from F to E flat, the pick-notes to measures one and nine have been raised an octave, and the higher pitches in the third-to-last measure are indicated as optional notes. The musical range is now from middle C up to high D.

Dividing the song into four four-measure phrases, the musical form is A B A C (the first and third phrases are almost the same). The last phrase ascends up the scale to a climax on high C (and the optional high E flat), and then moves smoothly down the scale to E flat. There is a fermata on the high note of climax for emphasis. The rhythm has an uneven beat pattern alternating with an even sequence of eighth notes. It should be sung smoothly, with a slight rocking feeling. The accompanist should seek to achieve the lilting feeling of the melody and a legato touch in the bass, following the words that are sung so that the tied notes match the lyrics in each verse.

Teaching Suggestions:

1. Express your belief that our Heavenly Father loves each of us, and that he shows his love in many ways. Then sing the song, play a recording of it, or have a child or group of children sing

it. (Several recordings have been made of the song, including the tapes that accompany the Sunbeam and Star A lessons.) After they listen to the song, have the children name the things mentioned that show that Heavenly Father loves us.

2. Teach the last phrase first. Draw an illustration of the melody line of this phrase, including an indication of where the fermata occurs, and ask the children to listen and discover what words are sung with this melody pattern. Then have them sing the phrase with you, holding the word "world" until you direct them to move to the end.

3. Teach the other words and phrases with questions, pictures, and keywords to help them remember the correct sequence. Place the pictures and words in a flip chart, on a scroll or roller box, on sticks, or on a flannelboard; or have the children hold them and arrange them in the correct order as the song is sung.

4. Help younger children learn the words by following improvised actions to illustrate the words, especially for verse two.

5. Help the children express their feelings about the beauty of the world with such questions as: "How do you feel when you hear the singing of birds?" "What colors do you see when you look at the sky?" "How does it feel to have the rain splash on your face?" Remind them that Heavenly Father gave us this beautiful world because he loves us so much.

My Mother Dear 203

Words and Music: Becky-Lee Hill Reynolds
First Line: Like sunshine in the morning
Topics Indexed: Mothers

This happy, sweet song fits nicely into any Mother's Day program. Becky-Lee Reynolds was a new missionary in France when she wrote it, and says it did not take her long to write down her homesick feelings about her own mother in words and music.

The melody moves smoothly and evenly with quarter notes. The melody of the first phrase is imitated in the second phrase, one pitch higher on the scale, and the third phrase is the same as the first. Each of these phrases begins with a skip up of a sixth, and then the notes move down the scale by repeated tones and steps. The last phrase includes the climax of the song and the highest note, C. The children should be encouraged to sing with love and expression.

Teaching Suggestions:

1. Tell the children that a sister missionary was living far away in France when she wrote this song. She was homesick for her family, so she wrote a lovely song telling how she felt about her mother, whom she loved very much. Tell them to listen to the song and find some things that reminded the missionary of her mother.

2. Ask questions that can be answered with exact words of the song, such as these: "What two words in the last part of the song describe what kind of a person my mother is?" "What do the songs of the bluebirds do?" "What words describe the flowers in the springtime?" "What does the sunshine do?" As each question is answered, have the children sing that phrase with you until they have learned all of the words.

3. Display pictures that illustrate each phrase: a happy mother, bluebirds singing, flowers, and the sun. Ask the children to hold the pictures and raise them as each is mentioned.

4. Divide the children into three groups, to take the part of the sun, the flowers, or the bluebirds. As the song is sung, have the groups stand and sing their phrase in turn. All should join together to sing the last phrase. Use the pictures described above to cue the groups when it is their turn to sing.

5. Invite the children to think of happy things around them that remind them of their mothers.

Nephi's Courage   120

Words and Music: Bill N. Hansen, Jr., and Lisa T. Hansen
First Line: The Lord commanded Nephi to go and get the plates
Topics Indexed: Book of Mormon, Choice, Commandments,
  Commitment, Courage, Faith, Obedience, Prophets

Lisa and Bill Hansen wrote "Nephi's Courage" because of their love for the scripture from 1 Nephi 3:7. They said, "We knew there was a need for songs about scriptural heroes, and we also knew that the Primary children would enjoy a vigorous melody to go along with the message. We hope the Primary children will want to know the Lord through the scriptures." The third verse has been added in the *Children's Songbook* to add the thought that, like Nephi, we are asked by the Lord to do certain things, and we too need to respond to the Lord courageously.

The song form of the verse is A A (with variation) B A. The

first, second, and fourth phrases are alike except that the second phrase changes to the minor mode, which creates an ominous feeling as the wicked Laban is mentioned. The third phrase, which is different from the others, introduces Laman and Lemuel and remains in the minor mode. This change of mode from major to minor and back to major generates interest and sets the stage for the strong and determined tone of the chorus. The chorus contains four phrases: the first two state the message, and the next two repeat it for emphasis. It is introduced with a strong melody statement on "I will go; I will do" with interval jumps of a fourth and of an octave. Within the chorus is a skipping pattern where the melody moves down the scale with jumps of a third, then an interval jump of a sixth back up to D and back down the scale to G, with hardly time to breathe. This is a rather demanding exercise for the singer, but even young children seem able to learn it.

Teaching Suggestions:

1. Display a chart with the words from 1 Nephi 3:7, beginning with "I will go . . . " Ask the children to read it and to tell what they think it means. Then tell them that you are going to sing a song that was written from that scripture, and ask them to listen for the words that are the same as the scripture. Then sing the *chorus.* Teach the chorus by asking the children questions, singing, and having them join in singing with you.

2. Help the children notice the melody pattern of the chorus by pitch-level conducting or by moving their bodies as they sing.

3. Ask them if they know what prophet is quoted in the scripture. Briefly tell the story of how the Lord asked Lehi to send his sons to Jerusalem to get the brass plates and how Nephi accepted the commandment by using these words. Ask them to listen as you sing the story to them. Invite them to join in singing the chorus.

4. Continue teaching the verses by asking questions, singing the song, accepting answers, and inviting the children to sing the part that contains the answer. Ask: "What big word describes Nephi?" "Who were afraid to try?" "Where was 'wicked Laban'?" "What did the Lord command Nephi to do?"

5. Post pictures of Nephi obtaining the brass plates and Nephi building the ship.

6. Review the stories of Nephi in a Sharing Time through reading or dramatization, and then sing "Nephi's Courage."

7. Help the children understand that they can also be courageous, like Nephi, in keeping the commandments of the Lord.

Oh, How We Love to Stand 279

Words and Music: Olga Carlson Brown
First Line: Oh, how we love to stand and turn ourselves around
Topics Indexed: Action Songs

This activity song can be used for a rest or change-of-pace number for the younger children. The children's names can be substituted for words in the first line. Alternate actions are suggested in the songbook for variation.

The uncomplicated melody line moves easily by repeated notes and steps. The rhythm is bouncy, with recurrent uneven beats of a quarter note and eighth note.

Teaching Suggestions:

1. Teach the song by simple rote methods, singing the song while doing the actions and inviting the children to join you. Try to use as many of the children's names as possible as you sing.

2. Invite the children to clap, tap, or beat the rhythm of the song as they sing it.

Oh, Hush Thee, My Baby 48

Words and Music: Joseph Ballantyne
Ostinato: Patricia Haglund Nielsen
First Line: Oh, hush thee, my baby; a story I'll tell
Topics Indexed: Christmas, Lullabies, Ostinatos

This beautiful Christmas melody has long been a favorite of the children, especially the little ones. A few changes have been made for the *Children's Songbook*: the key is now E flat instead of F, and the chorus is written in 3/4 time like the rest of the piece, instead of 6/8 time. The word "Jesus" in the last line is now sung on even beats. An ostinato is added for variation and interest. It is meant to be sung with the verse only (not the chorus) and should be performed smoothly and sweetly, without loud or harsh tones.

The melody pattern of the first three phrases in the verse is the same, with the second phrase placed one step higher on the scale. The alto part of the verse is a third below the melody, providing a lovely and simple harmony that the older children will enjoy learning. The song form of the chorus is A B A C; the first and third phrases are identical in words and music. The alto part of the chorus becomes the melody, and the upper voice is like a descant. Children seem to sing the melody part most readily, though the notes descend to a B flat below middle C. The song is especially beautiful when the children learn to sing both parts. The melody moves smoothly with connected tones and almost entirely by steps and repeated notes. The rhythm also contributes to the smooth flow.

Teaching Suggestions:

1. Tell the children that you are going to sing a lullaby that tells a very special story. (Bring a new baby or a doll to sing to.) Ask them to listen and discover what story you will tell the baby.

2. Teach the chorus first by asking questions such as these: "Who will care for his little one?" "What does the baby have to fear?" Each time you ask a question, sing the chorus, accept answers, and sing the chorus again, inviting the children to sing the words as they learn them. Teach the words to the verses in the same way.

3. Use pictures of the baby Jesus, angels, the star, and shepherds to illustrate the ideas. Have children hold the pictures.

4. Teach the alto part by having the children listen to you sing it (and the descant of the chorus) as you pitch-level conduct. Then invite them to move their hands up and down to the notes while singing with you. Ask a leader or other group to sing the melody while the children sing the harmony.

5. Dramatize the song by having the children rock imaginary babies in their arms while singing; or invite a child to come up front and rock a doll.

Oh, What Do You Do in the Summertime? 245

Words and Music: Dorothy S. Andersen
First Line: Oh, what do you do in the summertime
Topics Indexed: Summer

This is a recreational song about the sights, sounds, and "feel" of summer. The melody and lyrics are catchy, and children of all ages enjoy singing it.

There are two fermatas, and in the third line a slower tempo is noted. Sister Andersen indicates that the leader should encourage the children to watch carefully after the question, "Is that what you do?" so that they all come in together with the answer, "So do I."

In measures four through seven the melody pattern is repeated three times as summertime activities are described. The melody range is one octave, from D to high D, and two intervals of an octave are included. Eight of the twelve measures use the same lyrics for all three verses, so that learning the song becomes quite simple. Several music leaders have reported that the children like singing this song so much that they have written additional words to ask "What do you do in the wintertime?" and "What do you do in the autumntime?"

Teaching Suggestions:

1. Introduce the song by asking the children to think of things that they enjoy most about the summer—things they like to do, see, hear, smell, and "feel." Sing the first phrase ("Oh, what do you do in the summertime, when all the world is green?") and stop to let them express their thoughts. Then sing the last phrase of the song, "Is that what you do? So do I!" Repeat this several times until many ideas have been voiced. Display pictures or drawings of the activities that are mentioned in the song (fish, dream on the banks, swim, swing, march in parades, drink lemonade, count the stars).

2. Tell the children to join you in singing the parts of the song that they know, but to listen to the rest of the words to find which activities you like to do.

3. Dorothy Andersen tells us that she teaches this song by placing four pictures, one on each side of a box, to illustrate the lyrics of each verse. As they sing, a child rotates the box to display the image that the words mention. The box could be placed on a stick.

4. Encourage the children to experience the fun that comes from singing with expression, noting the pauses and the slower tempo.

On a Golden Springtime   88

Words: Virginia Maughan Kammeyer
Music: Crawford Gates
First Line: On a golden springtime, underneath the ground
Topics Indexed: Easter, Heavenly Father, Jesus Christ—Son
*   of God, Joseph Smith, Missionary Work, Plan of Salvation,*
*   Restoration of the Gospel, Resurrection, Spring, Testimony*

This song likens important events that took place in the springtime (Jesus' resurrection and Joseph Smith's First Vision) to the little seed that reaches forth to the sunlight. Virginia Kammeyer says, "Two years ago my husband and I went to Israel. We saw the tomb which Church leaders feel is the place where Christ was resurrected. There was the same holy feeling there as in the Sacred Grove where Joseph prayed." Crawford Gates said he hoped to give the children a touch of "richness of imagination with a unique flavor." The beautiful harmonies and lyrics of "On a Golden Spring-time" do just this — add meaning to sacred and momentous events, bringing simple but deep feelings about these occurrences within the understanding of the child.

The melody flows smoothly and easily, with most of the rhythm in an even beat pattern. There are no repetitions of musical phrases. In the last line there is an upward melodic progression in which several accidentals are introduced. This sequence seems to achieve the feeling of the seed that is pushing upward toward the light, building to the high C at the end. The children can be encouraged to listen to these sounds before they attempt to reproduce the notes.

Teaching Suggestions:

1. Tell the children that springtime is a wonderful time of year in which many special events have occurred. Encourage them to share their ideas of what happens in the spring. Then sing the first verse. (Teach each of the verses at a separate time and yet help the children see the relationship of the message of all three.)

2. Have children act out the first verse, with a child or children as the seedling(s) and another as the sun. As you sing the first verse, the seeds should awaken and begin to reach upward while the sun shines over them. Have the children join you in singing as they repeat the actions several times.

3. Prepare a poster of an outdoor scene with the sun shining in the background. Include a seedling, which is attached to a string that goes around the poster, just peeking out of the ground. As the song is sung, move the string so that the plant appears in the scene.

4. Teach the second and third verses by reading the message, discussing the significance of the event, and showing pictures that illustrate it. Then, as you sing the verse, ask questions that can be answered by words of the song, and invite the children to sing the phrases as they learn them.

5. Help the children learn to sing the melody accurately and

with expression. First have them listen carefully to the note progression and then invite them to sing. If they move their arms up and down with the notes of the song, they will be able to feel the melody and pitches more easily.

6. Express your belief in and appreciation for the resurrection of the Savior and the restoration of the gospel through Joseph Smith.

Once There Was a Snowman   249

Words and Music: Moiselle Renstrom
First Line: Once there was a snowman, snowman, snowman
Topics Indexed: Action Songs, Winter

This is an appealing activity song that children seem to relate to no matter where in the world they live. Even in countries where there is no snow, this is one of the most requested songs. There is much repetition of the melody phrases in the song. The first and third lines are identical. All of the notes are within a five-tone range from F up to high C, and the rhythm is even, with each line starting with four running (eighth) notes moving up the scale. The melody line rises as the snowman becomes taller and descends as the snowman melts.

Teaching Suggestions:
1. The children will quickly learn this song just by hearing you sing it a few times. No formal teaching is required.

2. As they sing the song, have them improvise the actions, moving tall, tall, tall on the second line and crouching small, small, small on the last line.

3. Prepare cutouts of various sized circles to form a snowman, and let the children build a snowman "tall, tall, tall." Post a sun and have a child remove circles to make the snowman "small, small, small."

Once within a Lowly Stable   41

Words and Music: Patty Smith Hill and Mildred Hill
First Line: Once within a lowly stable
Topics Indexed: Christmas

This beautiful Christmas lullaby was written some years ago by two sisters, Patty and Mildred Hill, who were active in the education of small children. Appropriate for children of all ages, it is a wonderful addition for any Christmas program. For the *Children's Songbook* the repeated tones in the bass chords have been eliminated to provide a smoother presentation.

If it is considered in two-measure phrases, the song form is A B A C D E—the first phrase is repeated in the third phrase and the other phrases are different. The melody moves smoothly by steps and natural intervals to produce the feeling of peaceful beauty surrounding the sacred event of Christ's birth. The climax occurs in the last line as the notes rise to high E and D on the words "the Christ," which should be sung more slowly and with emphasis.

Teaching Suggestions:

1. Introduce the song to the children by singing it and placing cutouts on a flannelboard, as if you are telling a story. The cutouts could be of a stable, sheep, oxen, Mary, Baby Jesus, and the manger. If the group is small, use a crèche (manger scene with movable figures).

2. Teach the words by asking questions, having the children listen to the song to discover the answers, and then inviting them to sing that part of the song with you.

3. Ask several children to hold cutouts of the things mentioned in the song and to raise them as each is mentioned. Or pin the cutouts to a line stretched across the room.

4. Have children take the roles of Mary and the angels to dramatize the song.

Our Bishop   135

Words and Music: Robert P. Manookin
First Line: Busy as a man can be, he's our bishop
Topics Indexed: Commitment

This song helps children understand the role and calling of the bishop. The author, Robert Manookin, was serving as a bishop at the time he composed the song. Once his ward's Jr. Sunday School surprised him by singing it for him in a sacrament meeting. Brother Manookin revised the accompaniment for the *Children's Songbook* and added a second verse. The time signature has been changed to 2/2 from 4/4 and should be conducted with two beats to the measure.

The melody is the same in lines one, two, and four except for some variation in the last measures. The third line introduces a melody pattern in the first two measures which is imitated in the next two measures a third lower on the scale. The rhythm has an even beat with quarter and half notes throughout. The third line should be sung with a ritard in the last measure and a fermata on the last note, moving to the original tempo in the last line.

Teaching Suggestions:

1. Tell the children that you will sing a riddle for them and that they should guess what special person you are singing about. Sing the song, humming the notes when the word "bishop" should be sung. After they solve the riddle, have them tell some things they know about the bishop and what he does. List these ideas on a chart or chalkboard. Sing the song again and ask them to see how many of the things that they named are found in the song.

2. Show three melody charts illustrating the three different ways in which the words "he's our bishop" are sung. Sing the first line and ask the children to choose the song chart that goes with the words "he's our bishop" in that line. Have them sing this phrase, following the song chart. In the same way, continue to teach these words in lines two and four, matching the song charts to the tune. Sing the entire song, inviting the children to sing the phrases they know while you point to the melody chart for each one.

3. Teach the other lyrics through questions, and with pictures of a bishop doing some of the things that are mentioned in the song.

4. Plan to have the bishop visit Primary so the children can sing the song to him as a surprise. Help them prepare to sing the song cheerfully and with love and expression to show their appreciation for him.

Our Chapel Is a Sacred Place 30

Words: Polly Bourgeous
Music: Darwin Wolford
First Line: Our chapel is a sacred place; we enter quietly
Topics Indexed: Chapel, Prayer Songs, Reverence

Polly Bourgeous, a Primary music leader in Phoenix, Arizona, wrote the words to this song to help the children in her ward achieve an attitude of reverence in the chapel. It consists of four different musical phrases with many skips. There are three places with intervals of a sixth (measures one, five, and six); the children will need to hear and practice these notes to sing them accurately. The melody moves smoothly, with an even quarter-note beat pattern, except for three dotted-quarter/eighth-note combinations.

Teaching Suggestions:

1. Show the children a picture of a meetinghouse and remind them that this is a special building where we meet to worship our Heavenly Father. Ask them to name the different parts of the building, and when they mention the chapel, place the words "a sacred place" on the picture. Tell them that the chapel is sacred because it is there that we take the sacrament, sing, and pray. Ask them how we should enter the chapel. Then sing the first line of the song and invite them to sing it with you.

2. Ask them to listen to the second part of the song, which is like a prayer, and to find two things it says we can do while we think of our Heavenly Father. Have them sing that line with you.

3. Encourage the children to listen to each of the difficult intervals and practice singing them accurately.

4. Use other pictures to help teach the song, such as children entering a chapel quietly, people singing, and people praying. Encourage the children to sing the song reverently and thoughtfully.

Our Door Is Always Open 254

Words: Anonymous
Music: French folk tune
First Line: Our door is always open to our friends who pass this way
Topics Indexed: Friends, Rounds

Children of all ages can enjoy singing this happy round for themselves or for visitors who come to see them. All of the four musical phrases are different. However, the chording moves back and forth from the D to the A7 chord, which makes it singable as a round. For the *Children's Songbook* a simple accompaniment has been added and some note changes have been made in the next-to-last measure.

The children can clap or tap the syncopated beat pattern to feel the uneven and catchy rhythm of the song. For added enjoyment, the leader can divide the children into two, three, or four groups to sing the song as a round.

Teaching Suggestions:

1. Ask the children what they might do to welcome a friend or visitor to their home or to Primary. Ask two children to take the parts of visitor and host, and have them dramatize different ways they can welcome a friend as you sing the song.

2. Invite the children to clap or tap the rhythm as you sing the words. You may need to repeat this several times to help them clap the syncopated beats in the second line correctly. Encourage them to sing the words with you.

3. After the children have learned the song, divide them into groups and help them sing it as a round.

Our Primary Colors 258

Words and Music: Marzelle Mangum
First Line: Our Primary colors are one, two, three
Topics Indexed: Courage, Happiness, Honesty, Morality, Primary, Service

This song teaches children the symbolism of our Primary colors: red standing for courage, yellow for service, and blue for truth. The words have been altered slightly in the *Children's Songbook* to match the wording in the current Primary Handbook as to the significance of the Primary colors. The meter has been changed from 3/4 time to 6/8.

The first four phrases have the song form A B A C—phrases one and three are the same and phrases two and four are different. The four phrases in the last eight measures are each different, but the beat patterns are the same: nine eighth notes followed by a dotted-quarter note. The last phrase is the climax and should be emphasized.

Teaching Suggestions:

1. Show pictures of the following symbols and ask the children what these symbols stand for: + − =. After they identify them, tell the children that you will sing a song that tells about three other symbols, and that they should listen and discover what these are.

2. After the children identify the symbols as the colors red, yellow, and blue, display (or have children hold) three pieces of paper or banners of the Primary colors and three word strips with

the meaning of the colors printed on them: courage, service, and truth. Sing the song several times until the children can correctly match the words with the colors. Ask them to join in singing after they have heard the song several times.

3. Help the children learn the lyrics with word strips of key-words, and questions such as these: "When will we be happy?" "What is blue for?" "What is yellow for?" "What is red for?" "What does each one have for you and me?" After you ask a question, sing the song, receive their answers, and invite them to sing the part that includes the answer.

4. For older children, ask them to explain the two meanings of "Primary colors" (the three basic colors from which all colors are made and the three colors of the Primary organization). Help them understand the meaning of such words as "symbol," "cour-age," "service," "truth," "thought," "deed," and "creed."

5. Help the children understand the last phrase, "We will be happy when this is our creed." Tell them that Heavenly Father wants all his children to be happy, and that as we learn to have courage, to perform service, and to be truthful, we will be happier people.

6. Have the children make small banners of the three colors with the words that they represent printed on them, and place them on sticks or tongue depressors. As they sing the song, have them hold up the colors as they are mentioned.

7. For variety, have the children who are wearing red, yellow, or blue stand and sing the phrase corresponding to their color.

Picture a Christmas 50

Words and Music: Patricia Kelsey Graham
First Line: Picture a stable in Judea
Topics Indexed: Christmas

This Christmas song lends itself to a simple dramatization of the story of the Nativity. The overall effect is one of reverence and awe for the wondrous events of that first Christmas night.

One sister tells of the special experience she had in West Germany when she used this piece, along with other Primary songs, for a Christmas program she presented at a U.S. military installation. Fifteen Primary children along with fifteen children of other religions sang together for the performance. The director, Sandy Fugal, said of the event, "What a powerful testimony these thirty children will carry with them throughout their lives. They may not remember their director ..., but they will always remember to 'sing praise to Him, remember Him,' as they picture Christmas every year."

The song consists of two verses and a chorus. A notable feature is the use of eighth-note triplets as pick-up beats (four times in the song). The rhythm is mostly even, with quarter notes, a few eighth notes, and a syncopated beat in the next-to-last measure. The verse and chorus each contain four melodic phrases. The first two phrases of the verse have almost the same melody as the first two phrases of the chorus. The other musical phrases are different. The melody flows smoothly with many scale-line steps and a few larger intervals.

Teaching Suggestions:

1. Ask the children to picture in their minds the things they recall when they think of Christmas. Invite them to share their thoughts. After they respond, tell them that there are many wonderful ways to picture Christmas, but the true picture of Christmas is of the birth of Jesus. Then sing the song.

2. Sing the song several times, encouraging the children to listen by using questions, such as these: "Where was the stable?" "What two words describe the kind of a night it was?" "What can you hear?" "What can you see?" "When we picture the baby Jesus, what should we think of?" "As you picture Christmas this year, what should you do?" After they discover an answer, invite them to sing that part of the song.

3. Make a picture of the Nativity by placing cutouts of the scene on a flannelboard as they are mentioned in the song — or have the children hold the cutouts.

4. For a Christmas program, have the children dress in costumes and stand inside a large frame to form a nativity scene; or enlarge nativity pictures to posterboard size and hold them in the frame.

5. Encourage the children to sing the song thoughtfully and with expression. There are several dynamic markings that should be observed. A violin accompaniment would be a beautiful addition.

Pioneer Children Sang As They Walked 214

Words and Music: Elizabeth Fetzer Bates
First Line: Pioneer children sang as they walked and walked
Topics Indexed: Pioneers, Sabbath, Singing

Elizabeth Bates tells how this song came to be written: "I visited Ruth May Fox when she was 104 years old. . . . I asked her to tell me about when she was a pioneer in 1864. She said they enjoyed walking across the plains, sang as they walked, sang and danced in their group in the evenings, and held meetings on Sunday. When I returned home, I wrote the song." Sister Bates feels that though children of this era do not have to walk across the country, they are pioneers in many other ways, and that they will enjoy learning about these early pioneers.

The melody form of the song is A B C A. The first and fourth phrases are the same except for the final two notes. The first and second phrases have the same melody pattern, except that the second is higher on the scale. The third phrase includes two smaller phrases that are similar in structure. The words to lines one and two are identical, and the words to line four are almost the same. The rhythm, which is repeated throughout, imitates a swaying, walking beat to help the singers feel what it must have been like to walk across the plains day after day. Sister Bates feels that even though the words may convey the pioneers' weariness in the long trek, these people were cheerful and contented, and the song should be sung happily and at a good tempo. She quotes from 2 Nephi 8:11, "The redeemed of the Lord shall return, and come with singing unto Zion."

Teaching Suggestions:

1. Ask the children if any of them have gone on a hike and walked for a long, long time. Invite them to express how they felt after the hike. Tell them that there were some children who lived many years ago who walked and walked and walked for many days. Ask them to listen to a song to find out who these children were.

2. Tell the children that the writer of the song wanted them to understand that pioneer children had to walk many hours almost every day for weeks and weeks, so she used the word "walk" many times in the song. Ask them to listen as you sing it again to see if they can count how many times this word is sung. Point out that the word "walk" is sung four times in the first phrase, four times in the second, and five times in the last phrase. Sing it again and hold up your fingers to count the times it is sung.

3. After they have heard the song several times, invite the children to sing the first, second, and fourth lines with you as you sing the entire song. Ask them what the pioneer children did while they walked, and why they think that the pioneers sang.

4. To teach the words to the third line, ask such questions as: "What did they do on Sundays?" "What else did they do on the other days?" Use word strips ("washed," "worked," "played," "camped," "read," "prayed") and pictures of the activities.

5. Invite the children to imagine that they are pioneers and walk around the room as they sing the song. Encourage them to sing with enthusiasm and energy as the pioneers might have done.

Pioneer Children Were Quick to Obey   215

Words: Virginia Maughan Kammeyer
Music: Lynn Shurtleff
First Line: Pioneer children were quick to obey
Topics Indexed: Cheerfulness, Obedience, Pioneers, Work

This song helps children apply the example of the pioneers in their own lives. The first two verses convey the idea that pioneer children were willing to do all that was needed to help. The third verse expresses that children of today can also be pioneers, by being willing and cheerful and walking with heaven in view. Lynn Shurtleff says, "The stories of the pioneer children had an influence on my childhood. I always used to wonder if I could ever be like those children. This song gave me a chance to express some of that admiration."

There is a walking motion in the song provided by the lilting 3/4 rhythm. Though there are some dotted-quarter/eighth-note combinations, the beat pattern is mostly smooth and even. Each of the four musical phrases is different, yet the second and fourth lines both include a series of steps that move down the scale from C to F. Lynn Shurtleff advises the song leader to concentrate on the feelings of the text and to sing it without rushing the tempo so that the children can feel the walking motion in the rhythm.

Teaching Suggestions:

1. Ask the children to imagine that their parents have decided that they should leave their home and travel a long way to a new land. They can take only a few of their toys or other possessions and will need to walk all the way. Ask them how they would feel, and what they think would happen if they did not obey their parents along the way. Ask them to listen to a song to discover some of the things that pioneer children did on their journey.

2. Show pictures of pioneers that illustrate the words in the

song, and use questions that can be answered by exact words in the song, such as these: "What did they do in the firelight?" "What did they walk by?" "What were pioneer children quick to do?" After each question is answered, have the children join you in singing the parts of the song that they learn. Continue to ask similar questions for verses two and three.

3. Invite the children to dress in simple pioneer costumes (hats and aprons) and pantomime the actions suggested by the lyrics.

4. Before teaching the third verse, ask the children in what ways they could be like the pioneers, without walking across the plains. After listening to their responses, sing the third verse and ask them questions regarding the message. Emphasize that whether we are pioneers who walked across the plains or children of today, it is important for us to be helpful, cheerful, and obedient to the commandments of the Lord.

Popcorn Popping   242

*Words and Music: Georgia W. Bello; arranged by Betty Lou
    Cooney*
First Line: I looked out the window, and what did I see?
Topics Indexed: Action Songs, Spring

This is a lively song that children will continue to request again and again; they never seem to tire of it. In the children's music survey conducted in 1983, "Popcorn Popping" registered number one on the favorites list and number three in both frequency and familiarity. Georgia Bello tells how it came to be written: "There was a beautiful apricot tree in our yard while we were living in Magna, Utah. My second son, who was four years old, came running into the house excitedly announcing that popcorn was popping on the apricot tree. Six years later in our home in Salt Lake City, I was standing at my kitchen window and looked out and saw the fruit trees in the orchard across the street all in bloom. I attribute to inspiration the words that came to mind after six years: 'popcorn's popping on the apricot tree.' I didn't have a piano at the time, but I used my daughter's toy piano and wrote the music and words in half an hour. I still feel to this day that this was a special gift." The rhythm has a catchy, uneven beat with many dotted-eighth/sixteenth-note combinations. The leader should encourage the children to sing this crisply so that the long-short patterns are emphasized. The musical form of the song is A B A B C D E B.

The first and third phrases are the same; the second, fourth, and last phrases are the same; and the C and D phrases in measures nine through twelve are very similar. The E phrase in measures thirteen and fourteen contains two smaller phrases where the melody pattern is repeated a step higher on the scale.

Teaching Suggestions:

1. Introduce this song by telling the story of how it was written. Sing it for the children and invite them to join you in singing the parts they remember. They will quickly learn to sing this song after hearing it a few times.

2. The children, particularly the younger ones, will enjoy participating in actions suggested by the words as they sing. Bring a bouquet of apricot blossoms when available.

Quickly I'll Obey   197

Words: Thelma J. Harrison
Music: Russian folk tune
Ostinato: Patricia Haglund Nielsen
First Line: When my mother calls me, quickly I'll obey
Topics Indexed: Fathers, Heavenly Father, Mothers, Obedience,
  Ostinatos, Parents

This song of obedience has a lilting charm that makes it appealing for even little children. Thelma Harrison said that in her home she was taught that children should obey their parents— that this is one way of being obedient to our Heavenly Father and of having a happy life. So the words to this little song came easily to her. Parents will find that it can emphasize the importance of obedience during a relevant teaching moment. The words in the *Children's Songbook* have been altered slightly so that the second line is the same for all three verses. The eight-measure tune is written in an A A B B form, with slight modifications in the repeated phrases. The beat pattern is mostly even, and the melody moves smoothly. The simple optional ostinato that is included in the *Children's Songbook* offers an appealing variation for the children.

Teaching Suggestions:

1. Teach this song by singing it to the children as part of a teaching situation without formally presenting it. After several repetitions, they will be able to sing it with you.

2. In the classroom, ask each of the children to tell an expe-

rience when he or she obeyed a parent. After each child has responded, have all the children sing the song.

3. Teach the ostinato to a group of children and have them sing it softly as the rest of the children sing the song.

Rain Is Falling All Around   241

Words and Music: Moiselle Renstrom
First Line: Rain is falling all around
Topics Indexed: Autumn, Spring, Summer, Winter

This charming song is skillfully geared to the interests and abilities of little children. The melody almost feels like rain falling. For the *Children's Songbook* the key has been changed from E flat to F, and versatility is provided with the suggested alternative phrases: "Sun is shining," "Wind is blowing," "Leaves are falling," and "Snow is falling."

The melody of the song hovers around high C, with E the lowest note. The song form is A B A C; the first and third phrases are the same. The rhythm is mostly even, with many eighth notes, and is the same for each of the four phrases. The last phrase moves down the scale from D to F. The words are simple and the melody moves easily, making the song appropriate for the younger children. Actions can be improvised as the words suggest.

Teaching Suggestions:

1. This song need not be taught formally. Sing it several times to the children, and they will soon be singing along.

2. Encourage them to follow you as you improvise actions to go with the words. Introduce the alternative phrases to them as the weather or season dictates.

Remember the Sabbath Day   155

Words and Music: Clara W. McMaster
First Line: Remember the Sabbath day, to always keep it holy
Topics Indexed: Sabbath

This beautiful two-line song shares the straightforward, simple message taken from the Ten Commandments. (See Exodus 20:8–11.) The melody phrases are each different and move with a natural ease, with intervals of a third and fourth occurring throughout the song. The rhythm flows smoothly with mostly even beats and two dotted-quarter/eighth-note combinations. The melody should be sung steadily, with connected tones.

Teaching Suggestions:

1. In teaching this song to older children, ask them if they know where in the scriptures the Lord gave us a commandment to "keep the Sabbath day holy." As they answer, ask them to turn to Exodus, chapter 20, and find the Ten Commandments. Ask them to listen to you sing a song about the Sabbath day and compare the words of the song to the scripture. Write the words to the song on a chart and ask a child to underline or mark in color the words that are found in the scripture.

2. For younger children, tell them that you will sing a song about a special day of the week, and that you would like them to tell what day it is. After you sing the song, help them understand that "Sabbath" is another name for Sunday. Review briefly the creation and how the Lord rested on the seventh day, the Sabbath day. Tell them that the Lord gave us a commandment that we should "Remember the Sabbath day, to keep it holy."

3. Teach the song through questions such as these: "What should we remember about the Sabbath day?" "What does the song say we should always do on the Sabbath?" "What two words explain what the Lord did to the Sabbath?" "What should we do on the Sabbath?" After they answer each question, have them sing that part of the song with you.

4. Have the children explain what they can do to keep the Sabbath day holy, and help them understand what "hallowed" and "worship" mean. Encourage them to sing this song reverently, smoothly, and with expression.

Repentance   98

Words: Sylvia Knight Lloyd
Music: Robert P. Manookin
First Line: "I am sorry" is not always easy to say
Topics Indexed: Heavenly Father, Repentance

This song encourages children to repent and try to do better, with Heavenly Father's help. The lyrics are easy to understand, so that children of all ages can relate to the message.

"Repentance" is characterized by several interesting harmonic progressions, some of which have a dissonant tone but resolve beautifully to provide an almost haunting musical sound. The accompaniment has a few contemporary-sounding chords. The melody flows smoothly, with mostly eighth notes throughout. The melody line in each of the four phrases is different, but the rhythm is the same for the first three lines. In the last line, two dotted-eighth notes followed by a sixteenth note match the emphasis of the words. The climax on the highest note in the song, high E, occurs in the last line, on the word "Father," after which the song should be sung more slowly to the conclusion.

Teaching Suggestions:

1. "Accidentally" bump into someone, lightly step on a child's toe, knock a book to the floor, or some such blunder, and then say, "I'm sorry." Ask the children, "When is the right time to say 'I'm sorry?' "

2. Discuss when it might be easy to say "I'm sorry" and when it might be more difficult. Lead the children to understand that it is hard to say "I'm sorry" when "I know I've been thoughtless" or "done something wrong." Ask them to listen to find out when the song says it is not easy to say "I'm sorry."

3. Ask the children to listen to you sing the song and discover three things that I will try to do when I've done something wrong. Then invite them to sing this part of the song with you.

4. Ask other questions to help them learn the words and the message of the song, such as these: "What is not always easy to say?" "What do I pray that Heavenly Father will help me to be?"

5. Let the children move an arm from side to side to the beat of the music, or have them conduct the two counts to a measure. They could also clap or tap the rhythm of the last line.

6. Ask a child, or a class, to repeat the Fourth Article of Faith, and ask them to discover what the second principle of the gospel is. Tell them that this song helps us understand the important principle of repentance.

Reverence 27

Words: Ruth H. Chadwick
Music: Leah Ashton Lloyd
First Line: Today, dear Father, I will show how quiet I can be
Topics Indexed: Gratitude, Quiet, Reverence

"Reverence" is a simple, lovely song that will help the younger children prepare for prayer or for other quiet times. Prayer language ("thee" and "thou") is used so that the song is like a prayer to our Heavenly Father. This feeling is emphasized by a few word changes in the first phrase: "Today, dear Father, I will show" instead of "Today, dear Lord, I'll try to show." The accompaniment in the *Children's Songbook* has also been altered slightly, to strengthen the movement of the inner harmonies.

The melody in the two phrases is not repeated. It moves smoothly, with connected notes. The successive quarter notes create a calm, quiet feeling that is not disturbed by the two dotted-quarter/eighth-note combinations in the last measures and the dotted-half notes at the end of the phrases.

Teaching Suggestions:

1. Ask several children to come before the group and demonstrate a way they can be quiet in Primary. Whisper instructions to each one if necessary, such as "fold arms," "sit still," "bow head," and "don't talk," and let the others guess what they are demonstrating. While the children continue to be examples of reverence, sing the song.

2. Ask the children to name some of the blessings Heavenly Father has given them, and display pictures they have drawn (during an activity period or at another time) to illustrate these blessings. Ask them to listen as you sing the song to find a way that they can show thankfulness to Heavenly Father for their blessings.

3. Sing the first line and ask the children to repeat it, then go on to the second line and have them repeat this one, without stopping, singing the entire song in follow-the-leader fashion.

4. Explain to the children the meaning of "thee" and "thou" and tell them that this song is like a little prayer to our Heavenly Father.

Reverence Is Love   31

Words and Music: Maggie Olauson
First Line: Rev'rence is more than just quietly sitting
Topics Indexed: Love, Reverence

The message of this song is particularly valuable in teaching children the true meaning of reverence—that it signifies much more than simply sitting quietly. It had a profound effect on the Primary children in the author's ward, who had been experiencing some problems with irreverence. She says that the spirit of the song seemed to touch their hearts, and they were more reverent after learning it.

The melody moves smoothly, with an even beat pattern and connected tones. The notes range between middle C and high C, with much of the melody moving by steps and hovering between D and G. The song has eight four-measure phrases. The first four are each different, and the second four repeat many of the melody patterns of the first part. The same note sequence is used at the beginning of four of the phrases.

Teaching Suggestions:

1. Ask several children to come to the front of the group and show how they can be reverent. Then ask each one to hold a word strip that describes the thoughts he or she might have, such as: "I wish I could be outside playing." "I had a lot of fun yesterday at my party." "I wonder what we will eat for dinner today." "I want to tell my friend a joke." "I am thankful for the many blessings that I have." "I love the story of how Jesus blessed the children." Explain that all of the children are quiet, yet some have more reverent thoughts. (For little children, describe the thoughts that each child might have.) Explain that reverence is more than just quietly sitting. Sing the song for them.

2. Show a picture of Jesus and have the children express their feelings about him. Explain that the feelings they have for Jesus are reverent feelings.

3. Sing the song again and ask the children to listen for other ways that they can show reverence. (Thinking, feeling, showing in words and deeds, knowing in their heart that Heavenly Father and Jesus are near.)

4. Teach the words by using word strips of keywords and asking questions that the children can answer by listening to the song, such as these: "What do I know in my heart?" "What is clear?" "In what two ways does my reverence show?" "What do I think of when I get a reverent feeling?" After they discover an answer, have them sing that part of the song with you.

5. Discuss with the children some words and deeds we could say and do to show reverence. Discuss the blessings we have received that give us grateful, reverent feelings. Have them draw pictures of their blessings and show and tell the others about their pictures.

Reverently, Quietly   26

Words and Music: Clara W. McMaster
First Line: Reverently, quietly, lovingly we think of thee
Topics Indexed: Prayer Songs, Quiet, Reverence

This song, with its beautiful melody and simplicity of construction, is appealing and moving. It has become a favorite of leaders and children everywhere, and in the Primary music survey of 1983 it ranked in the top ten of favorite and familiar Primary songs. Sister McMaster studied and prayed that she would be prompted to write what would be best for the children. She felt strongly that if she prepared well and asked for the Lord's help, he would guide her. As she was pondering, some thoughts came to her mind, and she went to the piano and wrote them down. This was the beginning of her new song, "Reverently, Quietly." In the *Children's Songbook* it has been lowered to the key of C from D, and the lower octave notes have been eliminated from the accompaniment.

The melody of the first line is repeated in the second, one note lower on the scale. The third line begins like the first, but changes in the last two measures, and the final line is different from the others, ending with a G repeated for the last six notes. The song should be sung smoothly and with subdued tones, and with a slower tempo and softer voice in the final phrase.

Teaching Suggestions:

1. Ask the children to mimic your actions: fold your arms, bow your head, whisper the words "reverently, quietly," sit down quietly, and then sing the first phrase of the song.

2. Display a word strip with the words "reverently, quietly" printed on it. Sing the song and ask the children to raise their hands each time they hear these two words. Sing it again and invite them to sing this phrase as it comes in the song.

3. Show three pictures: children singing, someone praying, and a heart. Sing the song again and ask the children to arrange the pictures in the correct order according to the message of the song.

4. Ask questions to teach the words, such as: "How do we think of Heavenly Father?" "How do we sing our melody?" "How do we pray?" "What do we want to dwell in our hearts?" Ask the children to sing the phrases as they learn them.

5. Ask the children to describe how it feels to have the Holy

Spirit with them. Tell them that we can pray to have this special feeling with us when we are in church and at other times, and that the Spirit can be felt more easily when everyone is being reverent. Encourage them to sing reverently and with expression.

Roll Your Hands 274

Words: Traditional
Music: Old tune; arranged by Grietje Terburg Rowley
First Line: Roll your hands, roll your hands
Topics Indexed: Action Songs

This activity song is appropriate for the nursery and the younger age groups to provide a change of pace. It is easily learned and offers variety as the tempo of the song changes to fit the words. In the *Children's Songbook* the notes in the next-to-last measure have been changed to move by steps down the scale, which produces an inversion of the scale that is introduced in the first two measures. The piano part has been simplified slightly; however, children usually sing it without accompaniment.

Teaching Suggestion:
Teach this song by rote, inviting the children to follow your actions.

Samuel Tells of the Baby Jesus 36

Words: Mabel Jones Gabbott
Music: Grietje Terburg Rowley
First Line: Said Samuel, "Within five years a night will be as day"
Topics Indexed: Christmas, Prophecy, Prophets

This is a wonderful program song for Christmas events. It is also a great teaching tool to help children understand the relationship between the events of the Savior's birth as told in the Book of Mormon and in the Bible. It is simple enough musically and in lyrics for children of all ages to sing.

Grietje Rowley said of the song, "Every Christmas our family reads the Christmas story from the New Testament. We also read in the Book of Mormon about the first Christmas in America. We try to imagine how the people felt about Jesus' birth. . . . I tried to make the music sound a little like both Jewish and Indian music." The music moves from the minor key to the major and back to minor, which creates an intriguing and joyous feeling. This is an appropriate background for relating the significant events that took place at the time of the Savior's birth, as told in the Book of Mormon and in the New Testament. The first two lines are written in C minor, which is the related minor to the key of E-flat major, so the music moves effortlessly between these two keys. The last two lines are written in the major key, with a few minor chords slipped in, and the song ends on the E-flat major chord.

None of the musical phrases are repeated, although the last two lines include many similar patterns. The melody moves by repeated tones, steps, and short intervals throughout, creating a connected, smooth feeling. The music does have a strong Indian sound without a heavy tom-tom beat, and the minor melody scale is typical of Jewish music. The chorus has a joyous presentation in declaring the birth of the Savior.

Teaching Suggestions:

1. Tell briefly the story of Samuel the Lamanite and his predictions of the birth of the Savior, while the two events are simply dramatized. On one side of the room a child could take the part of Samuel the Lamanite as recorded in the Book of Mormon. On the other side of the room, children could dramatize the nativity scene as recorded in the book of Luke. Use a world globe to show the distance between the two places. Explain that Samuel was able to tell the people about Jesus' birth five years before it actually happened because he was a prophet. Discuss how the people in America knew that Jesus had been born even though there were no televisions, satellite transmissions, or telephones in Book of Mormon times to tell people what was happening around the world. After you relate these two events, tell the children that you will sing a song that tells the story in music. Sing the two verses.

2. Have a child move a cutout picture of the sun across the sky, having it set and then rise again, to help the children imagine a day, a night, and a day without darkness.

3. Have the children listen to the accompaniment to the first two lines and ask them what the music reminds them of. Tell them that the composer wanted the music to sound like Indian music and like Jewish music, and discuss why she did this. Invite them to beat the rhythm on their laps as they sing the verse several times.

4. Ask the children to notice the difference in the mood between the verse and the chorus. The verse is written in the minor mode, and the chorus has a happy feeling as the birth of the Savior is announced. The word "hosanna" is sung twice to express this joy.

5. Help the children learn the words with questions, word strips of keywords, and pictures of Samuel the Lamanite and the birth of Jesus.

6. Bear testimony to the actuality of these events and encourage the children to sing the song with expression and conviction.

Saturday 196

Words and Music: Rita S. Robinson; arranged by Chester W. Hill
First Line: Saturday is a special day
Topics Indexed: Preparation, Sabbath, Work

This song is an effective tool to teach children to prepare for the Sabbath day, so that Sunday can be reserved for more spiritual and worshipful activities. Rita Robinson says, "My son and daughter wanted to go somewhere after Primary [then held on Saturday]. I explained to them that we must first return home and get everything ready for Sunday. Then we could go. I then sang the line to them: 'Saturday is a special day . . . ' The melody came by inspiration."

The 6/8 time signature establishes a lilting rhythm that produces a song of motion and action to match the lyrics. The melody of the first two measures is repeated in the beginning measures of the last line, and the final two measures are a repeat of measures seven and eight. The climax occurs in the fourth line as the melody moves up the scale to high D and then jumps down an octave. There is a fermata on the lower D.

Teaching Suggestions:
1. Ask the children to name all the things that they and their parents do to get ready for church, and show pictures of some of these things. Ask which of these things they could do on Saturday, and why it would be a good idea to prepare on Saturday for Sunday. Sing the song and let them discover things that they have not mentioned that they could do on Saturday to prepare for Sunday.

2. Invite some children to come to the front to pantomime the activities mentioned in the song while you sing it again. Invite them to sing with you as they repeat it with the actions.

3. Draw a fermata on the chalkboard or on a small chart. Ask the children to hold the note with the fermata (on the word "day") as long as a selected child holds up the chart or points to the fermata on the chalkboard.

4. Have them move their bodies up and down to the pitches of the music. Then have them sing the music in various styles, such as staccato, legato, whispered, and so on.

Search, Ponder, and Pray 109

Words: Jaclyn Thomas Milne
Music: Carol Baker Black
First Line: I love to read the holy scriptures
Topics Indexed: Guidance, Holy Ghost, Prayer, Revelation,
  Scriptures, Testimony

"How can a child, or an adult for that matter, know for sure that the scriptures are really true?" When Jaclyn Milne asked herself that question, her search for answers led her to *Teachings of the Prophet Joseph Smith,* compiled by Joseph Fielding Smith. She read: "Search the scriptures—search the revelations which we publish, and ask your Heavenly Father, in the name of His Son Jesus Christ, to manifest the truth unto you, and if you do it with an eye single to His glory nothing doubting, He will answer you by the power of His Holy Spirit." (Page 11.) While she was considering these words, the answer clearly came, and she began singing her thoughts: "Search, ponder and pray are the things that I must do . . . "

The rhythm of the song matches closely the emphasis and pauses used in speaking the words, with no duplication of beat patterns. None of the melody phrases are repeated. The melody of the verse hovers around the notes of D, E, F, and G, in contrast to the notes of the chorus, which move with larger intervals in a wider range. The song should be sung thoughtfully and with feeling. It is probably more appropriate for older children.

Teaching Suggestions:

1. Place a card with the word "testimony" printed on it inside the scriptures. Show the scriptures to the children and tell them that there is a word hidden inside that describes what they can have if they really study the scriptures. Tell them that you will sing a song to them to help them discover what the word is. After you

sing, accept responses and have a child open the scriptures and find the word.

2. Ask the children to listen to the song again to find the three things that we must do to gain a testimony of the truthfulness of the scriptures. After they have identified "search," "ponder," and "pray," invite them to think of an action they can do to represent each of these words, such as putting a finger to the forehead to think, and bowing the head as if in prayer.

3. Show a picture of Joseph Smith reading the scriptures and briefly tell the story of how his searching and pondering the scriptures led him to pray to the Lord for knowledge. Ask a child to read one of the scriptures listed with the song in the *Children's Songbook* that tells how other prophets felt about the help the scriptures can give.

4. Help the children learn the words through questions that can be answered with words in the song, through word strips of keywords, and with charts that show the movement of the phrases or melody patterns. If this last suggestion is followed, ask them to identify words that are sung on high and low notes of the phrases, and place word strips of these words in the appropriate spots on the melody chart.

5. Ask the children to listen for rhyming words *within* the lines. (See lines two and five: "start" and "heart," "guide" and "inside," "understand" and "command.")

6. Tell of a time when the scriptures helped you solve a problem. Express your testimony that the scriptures have been written by prophets through the direction of the Lord.

Seek the Lord Early   108

Words and Music: Joanne Bushman Doxey
First Line: I'll seek the Lord early while in my youth
Topics Indexed: Commandments, Commitment, Obedience,
   Prayer, Prayer Songs, Preparation, Prophets, Revelation,
   Scriptures

Joanne Doxey says, "I was impressed as I read the scriptures while on a mission in Barcelona, Spain, that if children learned early to seek the Lord, they would be guided and protected throughout their lives." Her song teaches children to seek the Lord through reading the scriptures, praying, obeying the prophets, and keeping the commandments.

Musically the first half of the song is almost the same as the second, except for the last phrase. The notes move smoothly by repeated tones, steps, and short intervals, with much of the melody within a five-note span from E flat to B flat. The rhythm has a lilting beat created by the long-short meter of the half-note/quarter-note measures intermixed with the three even quarter-note beats. The climax is reached in the next-to-last line with the words "his love will abound," after which there is a slight pause, and the last line is sung more quietly, slowly, and deliberately. The song invites some contrasts in dynamics and expression to communicate the deep feelings of the message. The volume should increase as the notes rise, and the tone should become more subdued as the melody descends.

Teaching Suggestions:

1. Have one child be "it" and quickly find another who is hiding somewhere in the room. Ask the children what the name of this game is. After they identify it as "Hide and Seek," discuss the meaning of the word "seek." Tell them that they are going to learn a song about seeking the Lord, but that seeking the Lord is different than this game. The Lord does not hide from us, because he *wants* us to find him, and when we find the Lord, we do not see him in person, but we "feel" his presence.

2. Sing the song several times, encouraging the children to listen by asking such questions as: "Can you find four things we should do to seek the Lord?" "What word means that the Lord's love is everywhere?" "When does the song say we should seek the Lord?" "If I seek the Lord, what will he help me know?" When they discover an answer, invite them to sing that part with you, adding one phrase at a time to the ones they know. Use four pictures to illustrate the things we should do to seek the Lord. (A child reading the scriptures, a child in prayer, the prophet, and a child being baptized.)

3. Ask the children to listen to find out how many times in the song they hear the words "I'll seek the Lord early." Help them recognize that twice these words are sung on the same notes, and the third time the melody and rhythm are different. Invite them to clap the two rhythms as they sing these phrases.

4. Help them find the rhyming couplets by drawing eight arched phrase lines and writing the ending word of phrases 1, 3, 5, and 7 ("youth," "there," "obey," "abound") at the end of these lines. Sing the song and invite the children to find the rhyming words that go on the ends of the other phrases.

5. Help the children internalize the message by inviting them to share how they feel when they read the scriptures, pray, follow the prophet, and keep the commandments. (There is a strong correlation between the message of this song and that of "If with All Your Hearts.")

6. Help the children sing expressively. Instruct them to sing softly as you hold your hands closely together, and then to increase their volume as you move your hands farther apart.

Shine On   144

Words and Music: Joseph Ballantyne
First Line: My light is but a little one
Topics Indexed: Example, Worth of a Child

This lovely song has long been a part of the musical heritage of Latter-day Saint children. Beginning in 1905, it has been included in all the Primary songbooks. Its message can help children learn that as they help, share, and are obedient, they can make their "lights" shine brightly.

The melody of the verse is written in A B A C form — the first and third phrases are the same and the second and fourth are different. The children will need help in singing the rhythm accurately by distinguishing between the eighth notes in measures 1 and 5, the dotted-eighth and sixteenth notes in measures 2, 3, 6, and 11, and the triplets in measures 7 and 15. Many of the notes hover in the higher range, so the leader should encourage the children to have good posture and attack these notes with a clear head tone, without straining. Essentially the song is targeted for younger children, but the harmony is appealing for the older ones who can learn to sing the alto part.

Teaching Suggestions:
1. Turn on a small flashlight and ask the children which makes more light, the flashlight or the sun. Ask them how the flashlight is helpful, even though it is not as bright as the sun. Tell them that they can be a light to help others when they try to follow the Savior's example. Sing the song and ask them to discover what the light is that is mentioned.

2. Teach the song by rote, chorus first, by asking questions that the children can answer by listening to it. Use word strips of keywords, such as "shine on" and "light," and a picture of a sun. Have them count how many times the words "shine on" are sung.

3. Have the children clap the beat patterns where there are three eighth notes, dotted-eighth notes and sixteenth notes, or triplets; say or sing the words as they clap the beat.

4. Encourage the children to relate ways they can be helpful and make their lights shine. Show pictures of children helping or sharing, and ask how they feel when they do kind acts.

5. Teach leaders or older children the alto part and have them join with the others who are singing the melody.

Sing a Song 253

Words and Music: Ingrid Sawatzki Gordon
First Line: Sing, sing, sing
Topics Indexed: Rounds, Singing

Ingrid Gordon says, "Singing is a fun thing to do. . . . This song is supposed to be fun and easy to sing. It's an instant involvement song and children of all ages seem to enjoy it."

"Sing a Song" is a simple eight-measure piece with chording that moves back and forth from the F chord to the C7 chord. It can be sung as a two-, three-, or four-part round. The accompaniment to the round can be played on the piano, or the chords could be played on another instrument such as guitar or autoharp.

Teaching Suggestions:

1. Sing the song, moving your hands up and down your body according to the pitch. For example, in the first phrase move your hands from your waist to your knees and back to your waist; in the second phrase touch shoulders, shoulders, waist, and knees, and so on. Challenge the children to mimic your actions and at the same time listen to the song several times. They will soon be able to join in singing it.

2. After the children have learned the words and the melody, divide them into two, three, or four groups and invite them to sing the song as a round.

Sing Your Way Home 193

Words and Music: Traditional song
First Line: Sing your way home at the close of the day
Topics Indexed: Cheerfulness, Singing, Smiles

This lighthearted song reminds children that singing and smiling can help drive troubles away and make us happy. It has appeared in various books of songs for school children and was printed for the Primary in 1964 in a music envelope of fun songs. In these and other printings the melody was not contained within the accompaniment, so a new Church copyrighted arrangement was written for the *Children's Songbook*.

The beat pattern of five of the nine short phrases has two eighth notes, three quarter notes, and a half note; the other phrases have a variation of this rhythm. The last three phrases all follow the same melody pattern, each beginning on a lower tone of the scale. The last phrase has some optional descant notes for an enjoyable harmonic addition.

Teaching Suggestions:

1. Choose a few of the younger children to join hands and move to a corner of the room. Ask one child to be the leader, and to lead the others around the room while you sing the song, until they find their way "home" to their chairs. Explain that when we sing happy songs and smile, it helps us to forget unhappy things.

2. Prepare three large, brightly colored music notes and one large smile. As you sing the song, post a music note each time you sing "Sing your way home," and the smile for "Smile every mile." Sing the song several times, inviting the children to sing with you.

3. Draw a picture of the last musical phrase on a chart or chalkboard while you sing the words, and ask the children to listen to the song again and find other places where this musical pattern is sung (in the last three phrases, each a tone lower). Invite them to pitch-level conduct these phrases as they sing them.

4. Ask the children to clap or tap the rhythm of the last two-measure phrase and to find other places in the song where this rhythm is found (fourth, sixth, seventh, and eighth phrases). They could sway or swing their arms from side to side to the beat of the music, one beat to a measure.

5. Teach the descant to some of the older children and have them harmonize on the last four notes. For variety, add an alto part by having some of the children sing the word "sing" at the beginning of each of the first eight measures, sustaining it for all three counts on the tones as follows: (1) G, (2) D, (3) F sharp, (4) D, (5) F sharp, (6) D, (7) G, (8) D. Beginning with measure nine ("smile every mile"), they would join the others in singing in unison to the next-to-last measure, then divide again and sing the descant on the last four notes.

Sleep, Little Jesus   47

Words: Mabel Jones Gabbott
Music: Michael Finlinson Moody
First Line: Sleep, little Jesus, Lord of the earth
Topics Indexed: Christmas, Lullabies

This melodic lullaby will be a beautiful addition to any Christmas occasion. It is a simple expression of the love, joy, and peace accompanying the Savior's birth. The arrangement has been simplified and the melody line combined with the accompaniment for the *Children's Songbook*.

The music flows smoothly, with a lilting rhythm characteristic of lullabies. None of the phrases is repeated. Seven measures contain the predominant beat pattern of quarter note, dotted-quarter note, and eighth note. In the third line the melody rises to its highest pitch, E, and the song reaches its climax on the words "Bringing thee love. Bright shines ..." These higher notes are probably the most difficult to sing. The one-syllable words "love," "bright," and "star" are each sung on two tones. The leader will need to help the children effectively perform these with ease and with true tones. The song should be sung sweetly and with feeling, with some increase in volume as the melody rises and more quietly when it descends.

Teaching Suggestions:

1. Ask the children what happens when a new baby is born to their family. Whom do they tell and how does it make them feel? After they share their ideas, discuss what happened when the baby Jesus was born and how the news of his birth was told. Sing the song and ask them to discover what three things happened when Jesus was born. (Angels tell the news, shepherds bring their love, and star shines above.) Show pictures that illustrate these three occurrences.

2. Teach the words by showing pictures and asking questions, such as these: "What is another name for Jesus?" "What are the angels telling?" "What do the shepherds bring?" "Where does the star shine?" After each question, sing the song, accept answers, and invite the children to sing that part of the song with you.

3. Have the children clap or tap the pervasive beat pattern (quarter, dotted-quarter, eighth note) and identify where they hear this rhythm in the song.

4. Help the children sing the last phrase smoothly and accurately by having them sit up straight, take deep breaths, and sing the high notes with clear head tones. Help them notice where they must sing the slurred notes with two tones to a one-syllable word.

5. Invite younger children to pretend to rock a cradle or rock a baby in their arms as they sing.

Smiles   267

Words: Daniel Taylor
Music: Anonymous
First Line: If you chance to meet a frown
Topics Indexed: Action Songs, Cheerfulness, Happiness, Smiles

"Smiles" is a classic children's activity song that the little ones usually learn as they first enter the nursery. The children love to respond to the words with frowns and smiles. The song was printed in the 1939 *Primary Songbook* with the initials H.S.L.-E.H. denoting the composer; the correct name has never been found. For the *Children's Songbook* the key has been changed from E flat to D.

The melody is lively and bright, with many interval jumps that give it a jovial air. Most of the notes are eighth notes. Children readily learn to sing it by rote after hearing it a few times.

Teaching Suggestions:

1. Ask the children to follow your example, and frown and smile as the words of the song indicate.

2. Ask two children to lock arms back to back, and have one of them display a smiling face and the other a frowning face. These children could turn around to show the group the correct face as the song indicates.

3. Make out of cardboard a smiling face that turns into a frown when turned upside down. (Eyes should be drawn in the center and half circles drawn above and below them as a forehead and a mouth.)

Springtime Is Coming   238

Words: Fannie Giralda Pheatt
Music: Alsatian folk tune
First Line: Springtime is coming, is coming today

Topics Indexed: Spring

This little song expresses the happiness that comes with spring. The waltzlike rhythm and cheerfulness of the message make it appealing to the children. The accompaniment has been simplified and the key changed from D to C for the *Children's Songbook*.

The melody of the first line is almost the same as that of the second. The four staccato eighth notes in the second line (instead of two quarter notes) are a unique and surprising feature of the song. This rhythm should be sung gracefully and unhurriedly so the words can be enunciated clearly.

Teaching Suggestions:

1. Ask the children to name some things that tell them that springtime is coming. Tell them that in some places when the robins come back, this means springtime is near. Ask them what a robin sounds like and show them a picture of one.

2. Sing the song several times, each time asking a question that the children can answer with the words from the song, such as these: "What was the robin doing?" "How do we know springtime is coming?" "When is springtime coming?" Ask the children to join you in singing as they learn each phrase.

3. Help them feel the waltzlike rhythm by clapping the beat as they sing, with emphasis on the first count of each measure. They can clap the song in two ways: with an even three beats to the measure, or following the rhythm of the melody. Some of the children could clap the even beats while the others clap the rhythm of the melody as they sing.

4. Invite the children to make up actions to the song, as suggested by the words. In the classroom or the home, younger children might hop around like robins to the beat of the music, hunting for materials to build a nest or looking for worms.

Stand for the Right   159

Words and Music: Joseph Ballantyne
First Line: Our prophet has some words for you
Topics Indexed: Accountability, Commandments, Courage,
    Dependability, Example, Guidance, Honor, Morality,
    Obedience, Prophets, Testimony

This song is a straightforward declaration of the importance of being true and standing for the right at all times. It has been sung by children all over the world.

The song form of "Stand for the Right" is A B A C—the first and third phrases are almost the same. The notes of the last phrase move down the scale from high D to F sharp, up one tone to G, and down again to D. Every measure has uneven beats until the last four measures. Eight measures have a long-short count with a half note and quarter note, and three measures have a dotted-quarter, eighth, and quarter note. The last phrase has all quarter notes on the descending scale, to add strength to the message of being true and standing for the right. This should be sung deliberately and with emphasis.

Teaching Suggestions:

1. Briefly tell the children the story of Helaman's stripling warriors (Alma 53:16–23) and show a picture. Ask them what it means to be "true at all times in whatsoever thing they were entrusted," and what they can do to be true. Show a picture of the current prophet and tell them that he has a message for all children. Then sing the song and encourage them to find out what he wants them to do.

2. Show four word strips with the words "who," "what," "where," and "when" printed on them. Sing the song several times until the children can find the who (the prophet), what (some words—be true), where (at work or at play), and when (in darkness or light). Invite them to join you in singing the phrases as they learn them.

3. Ask the children to listen to discover how many times you sing "be true." Tell them that this must be a very important message, since it is repeated four times.

4. Help the children feel the rhythm of the song by clapping or tapping the notes as they sing. Ask them why they think the composer made the beats in the last phrase even and strong. Have them listen to find out how the melody moves on the last phrase, and invite them to pitch-level conduct it.

5. For review, ask the children to sing "be true" when these words occur, while you sing the rest of the song. Ask them to stand up as they sing the words "stand for the right," and sing with conviction and emphasis.

6. Encourage the children to share experiences of times when it took courage to be true and stand for the right. You might have them role-play situations in which they can stand for the right. (For example, you could have one child ask another to go to the store with him or her and "take" some candy and gum. The other could respond with, "No, I don't want to.")

Stand Up   278

Words: Glenna Tate Holbrook
Music: Marjorie Castleton Kjar
First Line: I will stand up when "stand up" is said
Topics Indexed: Action Songs

This is a happy and bright action song that younger children learn easily and enjoy. It can be sung in the nursery, the Primary classroom, in singing time, or in the home to help restless children "get the wiggles out."

Considering the melody as six two-measure phrases, the last two phrases are very similar to the first two phrases. There is no other repetition of melodies. The rhythm is lilting and light, beginning with even eighth-note beats and moving to uneven quarter-note/eighth-note combinations.

Teaching Suggestion:

Teach this song by singing it to the children several times and encouraging them to participate in the actions suggested by the words.

Stars Were Gleaming   37

Words: Nancy Byrd Turner
Music: Polish carol; arranged by Darwin Wolford
First Line: Stars were gleaming, shepherds dreaming
Topics Indexed: Christmas

This beautiful old Polish Christmas carol has had several lyrical settings and musical arrangements. The first verse tells of the experience of the shepherds on the hillside, and the second verse refers to the wise men and the star they followed. The new musical arrangement by Darwin Wolford in the *Children's Songbook* changes the delineation of the measures by beginning with two eighth notes as a pick-up beat. This places the accent on "gleaming," "dreaming," and so forth, a more natural word emphasis.

One of the song's appealing features is the unusual use of rhyming sequences. The last words of the first, second, and fourth phrases rhyme ("chill," "hill," "still"), and within each of the first three phrases there is a series of rhyming words ("gleaming" and "dreaming"; "story" and "glory"; and "singing," "ringing," "winging," and "bringing"). These euphonious expressions bring a feeling of beauty to the composition. The musical form of the four phrases is A A B C; the first two phrases are identical. Within the third phrase is an interesting musical progression: the first four notes are repeated three times, each time a step higher on the scale. In the last four-measure phrase, the voices sing "Hearken! we can hear it still!" after which the accompaniment alone repeats this melody to complete the musical phrase. It is as though the singers are silent so that they can listen for the singing of the angels. There is a marvelous opportunity in "Stars Were Gleaming" to magnify the impact and feeling of the song with dynamic expression. Especially in the third line the leader should encourage the children to begin softly and build with each musical progression to the end. Then the accompaniment adds its soft postlude.

Teaching Suggestions:

1. Ask the children to imagine that they are shepherds on the hillside the night of Jesus' birth. Have them describe what they might have seen and felt that night. As they share their ideas, display a piece of black paper or posterboard and add stars, angels, shepherds, sheep, an outline of the city, and so on, to complete the picture. Then sing the first verse.

2. Ask the children to listen to discover the rhyming words in the first verse. They could find the words that rhyme with "singing," then with "story," then with "gleaming," and finally the words that rhyme with "chill." Sing the song for them each time they listen for a new rhyming word. Post word strips of the rhyming words to help them remember the sequence. As the children learn them, have them join in singing the rhyming words. When reviewing the song, have the children arrange the word strips in the correct order and sing the song to check their accuracy. Help them appreciate the beauty of these poetic phrases that set the stage for the story.

3. Have the children find the rhyming words in the second verse as they have done in the first. Use figures of wise men to "travel" from one word strip to another as you sing it.

4. Draw illustrations of the various melody phrases and help the children identify which illustrations go with the phrases as they sing them. Help the children enjoy the musical progression of the third line by following the illustration of the pattern and by pitch-level conducting this melody.

5. Help the children sing with expression and meaning, observing the dynamic markings as printed in the music.

Teach Me to Walk in the Light   177

Words and Music: Clara W. McMaster
Obbligato: Darwin Wolford
First Line: Teach me to walk in the light of his love
Topics Indexed: Choice, Commandments, Commitment, Eternal
  Life, God's Love, Guidance, Heavenly Father, Leaders,
  Obbligatos, Parents, Prayer, Teachers

This is a meaningful song in which a dialogue between the child and the parent or leader highlights the importance of teaching children to walk in the light of Jesus Christ and the Father. The first verse is a plea from the child for direction, the second is the parent's response, and the third is a prayer of thankfulness from the child and the parent. Few Primary songs have been as frequently performed, especially for programs and meetings where the focus is on teaching children.

This is one of the twelve children's songs printed in *Hymns*. The arrangement in the *Children's Songbook* is the same as in the hymnbook, except that an optional obbligato for flute or violin has been added, and the key has been changed from E flat to D.

The melody of each of the four-measure phrases is different, with tones in the octave range from D to high D. The rhythm is mostly even quarter-note beats, with one dotted-quarter/eighth-note combination. The song should be sung in a smooth and flowing legato style.

Teaching Suggestions:
1. Ask a few teachers to come to the front of the room. Ask the children to tell what these teachers teach when they come to Primary each week. Tell them you will sing a song that tells of three things teachers or parents can teach children, and ask them to listen for these things (walk in the light, pray, know). Compare these with the suggestions that the children have mentioned. Invite them to participate by singing "teach me" as these words come in the song. Have them count how many times they sing these words.

2. Ask the children if they have ever been somewhere where it was so dark that they couldn't see anything. Ask them what they

would have to do to find anything in that dark place. Explain that it is much easier to find our way when we have a light to guide us. Jesus has given us a light, the light of his love and example, so we will know what way we should go and how we should live. Invite the children to join you in singing the phrase "Teach me to walk in the light" as you sing the entire song.

3. Tell the children that the leaders will learn the second verse, and everyone will sing the third verse together, which is like singing a prayer to our Heavenly Father. Teach the words to this verse with questions, pictures, and word strips of keywords.

4. The older girls and boys could add a harmony on the final "walk in the light" by singing a third above the melody (B, A, G, F sharp) or by singing the printed alto line on the last phrase.

5. Express your belief that Heavenly Father has called parents and teachers to teach children how to keep the commandments and to pray to him, and that we should be grateful to Heavenly Father for those who have been called to guide us.

Teacher, Do You Love Me?   178

Words and Music: Michael Finlinson Moody
First Line: Teacher, do you love me?
Topics Indexed: Choice, Guidance, Jesus — Example, Leaders,
  Love, Teachers

This piece was written as the theme song for a fireside broadcast by satellite in 1986 to Primary leaders and teachers. It was subsequently chosen by the National Federation of Women to be performed for their Mother of the Year award program. In the first two verses, the child pleads for the teacher's love and guidance, even in times of wandering or disobedience. The teacher responds in the next two verses with assurances of love and expressions of desire to teach the child to live like Jesus. The child sings the first chorus alone, and the second time the child and teacher sing the chorus together.

Teaching Suggestions:

1. Ask the children who loves them more than anyone else (Jesus and Heavenly Father). Then ask them who else loves them very much, and show pictures of parents, teachers, and other loved ones as they respond.

2. Teach the verses by asking the children to listen while you

sing the song to find the things a teacher might do to show he or she loves them (care for me, teach me, help me choose the right, take my hand and lead me). Use pictures to illustrate these points.

3. Teach the chorus by asking the children to listen for two things the song says I need to show me how to be like Jesus (love, light). Explain that this light is the teacher's example.

4. If possible, show the film "Teacher, Do You Love Me?" during sharing time before teaching the song to the children.

5. Teachers could learn their part of the song at another time so they are prepared to sing with the children. The teachers could sing the alto part for the final chorus.

Tell Me, Dear Lord 176

Words: M.E.P
Music: C. Harold Lowden
First Line: Tell me, dear Lord, in thine own way I pray
Topics Indexed: Guidance, Leaders, Prayer Songs, Revelation

This song is a prayer for guidance to do the Lord's will and understand his word. The text is somewhat difficult for younger children, but the last line has been simplified for the *Children's Songbook*. The words have been changed from "anoint my eyes to understand thy word" to "help me to understand thy loving word." The time signature has also been changed, from 4/4 to 2/2, so the leader will conduct two beats to a measure for a smoother flowing melody.

Each of the four phrases has a different melody pattern, but the first measure of lines one and three is the same. The rhythm is the same in the first three lines. The notes of the final phrase move from high E flat down the scale by steps to E flat, with the B flat repeated along the way. The melody should be sung reverently and with smooth, connected tones.

Teaching Suggestions:
1. Display a picture of Joseph Smith reading the scriptures and briefly review the story of how he read James 1:5. Emphasize that Joseph was questioning and wanted to do what was right. Tell them that we, like Joseph, can know Heavenly Father's will for us if we will ask him. Then sing the song to the children.

2. Tell the children that there are some special words that start with "th" that we use when we pray (thou, thy, and thine). Ask

them to discover these words as you sing the song. Have them hold up cards with these words printed on them as they find the words.

3. Ask questions to help the children listen to the song and understand its meaning, such as these: "What do we ask the Lord to help us understand?" "What do we ask the Lord to teach us?" "When are we asking for the Lord's help?" "In what way does the Lord tell us his will?" After they find the answer to a question, have them sing that part of the song with you.

4. Draw arched phrase lines for each of the four phrases and let the children place word strips of keywords on the phrase lines where they occur. Teach the first two lines of the first verse together to achieve a continuity of thought. Do the same with the last two lines of verse two.

Tell Me the Stories of Jesus 57

Words: W. H. Parker
Music: F. A. Challinor
First Line: Tell me the stories of Jesus I love to hear
Topics Indexed: Bible, Jesus Christ — Ministry

This traditional song describes events in the Savior's life which are especially meaningful to children. The original text with six stanzas was written by W. H. Parker for the Sunday School anniversary of the Chelsea Street Baptist Church in Nottingham, England, in 1885. Frederic Challinor composed the music, and it was the prize-winning tune in a competition sponsored by the National Sunday School Union, London, in its centennial year, 1903. For the *Children's Songbook* the key is changed from C to B flat, and the accompaniment has been thinned. There are also a few word changes in verse two.

The melody is written with a 6/8 meter. Six measures contain a dotted-quarter note, quarter note, and eighth note, and four measures have two dotted-quarter notes. Lines one and two begin with the same musical phrase of six eighth notes; otherwise there are no repetitions in the melody. The climactic point occurs in the first measures of the last line, which should be sung slower and with emphasis, observing the fermata and then softening and ritarding to the end.

Teaching Suggestions:

1. Introduce this song by having a parent and children drama-tize family story time. As the children gather around the parent, they could sing the first verse.

2. Show a copy of the New Testament and ask the children to briefly tell some of the stories about Jesus that are found there. Show pictures of scenes by the wayside (Jesus at the well, Sermon on the Mount), tales of the sea (Jesus walking on water, calling the fishermen), Jesus with the children, calming the storm, and so on. Then sing the song to them.

3. Ask the children to express how they might have felt if they had been one of the children that Jesus gathered and blessed. Sing the second verse and display a picture of Jesus with the children.

4. Help the children understand unfamiliar words or phrases, such as "accents of wonder," "tempest," "Galilee," and "chided the billows."

5. Invite the children to clap the rhythm — dotted-quarter, quarter, eighth, and dotted-half (or two dotted-quarters) — that oc-curs six times in the song. Have them repeat the claps each time this rhythm occurs.

6. Encourage the children to sing the song with expression and meaning. The older children may enjoy singing the alto part.

Thank Thee, Father 24

Words: Alice C. D. Riley
Music: F. Remsen
First Line: Thank thee, Father, for this day
Topics Indexed: Gratitude, Prayer Songs

The lyrics of this song are written as though the child were singing a prayer, thanking Heavenly Father for his blessings and love, and asking for help and guidance. Some word changes have been made for the *Children's Songbook* to clarify for children that we pray to the Father and not the Lord, Jesus Christ. The beat has been changed from 2/4 to 4/4, and the key lowered to D from E flat.

The first three phrases begin with the same tones, A A G F, and the last phrase begins with A D G F, which contributes to the continuity of the melody. There is an even quarter-note beat pattern throughout, with half notes at the end of the phrases. The song should be sung slowly, reverently, and smoothly, with connected tones and a ritard in the last measure.

Teaching Suggestions:

1. Introduce the song by asking the children to share some of the things they thank Heavenly Father for when they pray. Then sing the first verse and invite them to discover some of the things it says we thank the Father for; compare these with the things they mentioned. Use pictures to illustrate.

2. Make a clock with hands that move. As you move the hands from hour to hour, ask the children what they often do at that time. Tell them we should thank Heavenly Father in prayer for all that we do during the day, whether at work or play.

3. Draw a diagram of the melody pattern of the first measure. Sing and pitch-level conduct these tones. Invite the children to raise their hands when they hear this melody pattern repeated as you sing.

4. Tell the children that the second verse names some things they ask the Father to help them do. Have them discover what these things are as you sing it again.

5. Encourage the children to sing reverently and sweetly, as if they were offering a prayer to the Father.

Thank Thee for Everything 10

Words: Vanja Y. Watkins
Music: Wilford A. Beesley, Jr.
First Line: Father, please hear us sing
Topics Indexed: Beautiful World, Gratitude, Praise, Prayer Songs

This song is a beautiful expression of praise to our Heavenly Father for the good world he has given to us. The mood of the text and music blend to create a feeling of peace and gratitude. The melody is written in A B A B form with an added two-measure ending — the first four-measure phrase is the same as the third phrase, and the second and fourth phrases are almost the same. In the first and third phrases the first four tones are repeated one tone higher on the scale. The second and fourth phrases include a complete scale movement from high D down to D. The rhythm patterns are also repeated. The song should be sung smoothly, with connected tones.

Teaching Suggestions:

1. Show the children pictures that illustrate the seasons of the year. Ask them to describe what the world looks like during the different seasons. Explain that each season is beautiful, and that

Heavenly Father planned for us to live in this lovely world. Ask them to listen to a song of thankfulness for our beautiful world.

2. To teach the words, ask questions that can be answered with words from the song, such as these: "Where is beauty?" "What two words describe the trees?" "What two words describe the skies?" "What do we thank Heavenly Father for?" Sing the song for the children each time you ask a question. Accept their answers and then invite them to sing that part with you.

3. Ask the children to listen to discover what words you sing when the melody moves down the scale step by step. You may need to sing it several times for them to find these two phrases. Invite them to pitch-level conduct these phrases with you.

4. Show a picture you have drawn of a bare tree with a gray sky. Divide the picture in half and put green leaves and blue sky on one half. Or you could use a box and place a winter scene on one side and a summer scene on the other, turning it as the words are sung.

Thanks to Our Father   20

Words: Robert Louis Stevenson
Music: Franz Joseph Haydn
First Line: Thanks to our Father we will bring
Topics Indexed: Family, Gratitude, Prayer Songs

This charming melody and text combine to create a lovely song of thanks as well as an opportunity for the children to become familiar with a classic composer, Haydn. For the *Children's Songbook* the key has been changed from G to F. The song is sweet and light, though not easily sung accurately. Many of the syllables must be sung on two notes. The words to verses one and four are the same, and verses two and three introduce the things for which we give thanks.

The melody is composed of two phrases that are identical for the first two measures and similar for the last two measures. The eighth notes and interval skips provide a lot of motion. The children should be encouraged to sing smoothly, connecting the tones as much as possible to avoid a disjointed effect. They should be taught to sing each note directly, without sliding into the pitch.

Teaching Suggestions:

1. Ask the children to name some things they see in the room, or saw on their way to church, and list them on the chalkboard. Ask them who gave them these things. Help them understand that Father in heaven gives us everything. Sing the first verse of the song.

2. Ask the children to listen to the accompanist play "Thanks to Our Father" to see if the music reminds them of any other music they have heard. Tell them that it was written by a famous composer, Joseph Haydn, who was born over 250 years ago, and that much of his music was written in this style.

3. When teaching the song to younger children, invite them to improvise actions for verses two and three. Invite children to draw pictures for these verses, or use pictures from the library.

4. Have the children move their hands or their whole bodies up and down according to the pitch of the music while they sing the song.

Thanks to Thee   6

Words: Mary R. Jack
Music: Darwin Wolford
First Line: When I'm home or far away
Topics Indexed: Family, Gratitude, Prayer Songs

This is a lovely, simple song written as though a child were singing a prayer to our Heavenly Father. It was first printed in the July 1965 issue of the *Children's Friend*. The melody in the first two measures of lines one, two, and four is identical. The even rhythm pattern, six quarter notes and a half note, is repeated throughout the song, adding steadiness and interest.

Teaching Suggestions:

1. Ask the children to think of all of the places they might be when they pray. Ask them if Heavenly Father can hear them if they pray when they are hiking in the mountains, by a swimming pool, in school, or on a vacation. Explain that it is a great comfort to know that Heavenly Father always hears prayers, whether we are at home or far away. Then sing the song to the children.

2. Ask the children to share some of the things they say to Heavenly Father in their prayers. Show pictures of some of these

things that are also part of the song. Make an accordion poster of pictures (a home, a family, pets to love, things to do, a family praying, and so on) to help them remember the word sequence.

3. Ask the pianist to play the complete song as you sing "loo" in measures 1 and 2, 5 and 6, and 13 and 14. (This melody is the same in each case.) Repeat this procedure, asking the children to join you in singing "loo." Then ask them to listen as you sing to discover what words you sing with this melody. Have them join in singing these words with you. Then they could sing each of these phrases while you sing the other phrases.

4. Ask the children to listen for the rhyming words in the song. You may need to sing it several times until they find the four pairs. Sing the song again and challenge them to sing the rhyming words while you sing the rest of the song.

5. Encourage the children to sing the song reverently, in an attitude of prayer.

The Articles of Faith   122–133

Words: Joseph Smith
Music: Vanja Y. Watkins

It has long been a standard procedure to have Primary children memorize and learn the meaning of the thirteen Articles of Faith. Elder Bruce R. McConkie wrote, "Joseph Smith wrote 13 brief statements which have become known as the *Articles of Faith,* statements which summarize some of the basic doctrines of the Church. These Articles of Faith are scripture and are published as part of the Pearl of Great Price." (*Mormon Doctrine* [Salt Lake City: Bookcraft, 1966], p. 53.)

In 1977, Patricia Maughan, a member of the Primary general board music committee, reported that she had visited a Primary for handicapped children in which the leaders were teaching the children to sing the Articles of Faith to music that the leaders had composed. They found that these children, who had many disabilities, could learn to recite such scriptures (or names of the presidents of the Church) more easily when the words were set to music. Subsequently the general Primary presidency asked the Church music chairman if someone could write a musical setting for the Articles of Faith so that children all over the Church could benefit from this effective teaching method. Several composers submitted music for these scriptures. Among them was Vanja Watkins, who wrote the melody line for each of the thirteen Articles of Faith, and approval was given for her music to be included in the Primary music resources. Some of the numbers were performed in the Tabernacle by a group of mentally handicapped children for a Primary conference, an achievement for these special children that would have been almost impossible without the musical setting. Sister Watkins, who has a feeling for the harmony of music and words, showed great respect for the rhythm of the words as she set them to music. They are sung just as one might speak the words. The inspired melodies and rhythms of these songs will help anyone who learns them to recall each word in order, without hesitation.

Seven of the articles are written in the key of C major, three in F major, and three in D minor. The songs should be taught by rote. Effective aids for learning could be charts on which these scriptures are written, keywords for each article, pictures that illustrate the meaning of the Article of Faith, and illustrations of the melody line and/or rhythm patterns to assist the children in accurately mastering the music. The leader usually cannot teach all the important principles relating to these scriptures. The songs are primarily a means of remembering the words, the meaning of which should be introduced to the children in the home, in Primary classes, or in Sharing Time.

The First Article of Faith 122

First Line: We believe in God, the Eternal Father
Topics Indexed: Heavenly Father, Holy Ghost, Jesus Christ—
Son of God

Teaching Suggestions:

1. Show a picture of Heavenly Father and Jesus appearing to Joseph Smith in the grove, and ask the children to recount something that Joseph Smith found out about God when he had this vision. (That Heavenly Father and Jesus are separate beings, and that they look alike.) Ask a child to read from D&C 130:22 to learn something about the Holy Ghost, the third member of the Godhead. Tell the children that Joseph Smith wrote in the first Article of Faith what he had learned about the Godhead. Sing the song, and then invite them to sing it with you.

2. Ask the children to listen to the pianist play the music to this song and share how the music makes them feel. Tell them

that the composer wanted to create a feeling of reverence and sacredness to talk about Heavenly Father, Jesus Christ, and the Holy Ghost, so she wrote the music in a minor key to establish this sacred attitude.

The Second Article of Faith 122

First Line: We believe that men will be punished for their own sins
Topics Indexed: Accountability

Teaching Suggestions:

1. Write thirteen dashes on the chalkboard to represent the letters for the word "transgression." Tell the children that these lines represent a very big word that you want them to discover. Give hints, such as, "This word means doing something that you shouldn't do," or "This word means 'sin.'" They could also guess some letters that are part of the word. When the entire word is discovered, tell them that you are going to sing the second Article of Faith, which speaks of men's sins.

2. Show a picture of Adam and Eve and briefly tell the story of Adam's transgression by asking such questions as: "Who was the first man who lived on the earth?" "What was his wife's name?" "Where did they live?" "A serpent came and asked Eve to do something. What was it?" "What did Adam do when Eve told him she had eaten of the forbidden fruit?" "Do you think Heavenly Father would punish us for a transgression that Adam committed?" Sing the song and ask the children to find the answer to the last question.

3. Draw an illustration of the melody on a chart and ask the children to notice the octave jump in the first measure and the repeat of the last phrase. Encourage them to sing the octave jump accurately and the final repeated phrase more softly and subdued.

The Third Article of Faith 123

First Line: We believe that through the Atonement of Christ
Topics Indexed: Atonement, Obedience, Plan of Salvation

Teaching Suggestions:

1. Ask the children if they ever got into trouble or were punished for something that they didn't do. Let them give some examples. Tell them that Jesus was perfect and never did anything

wrong, but he voluntarily suffered for the sins of everyone in the world so that we wouldn't have to suffer, if we repented. This was called the Atonement. Post this word on the chalkboard and show a picture of Jesus in Gethsemane.

2. Ask the children to listen as you sing "The Third Article of Faith" and find what we need to be obedient to, to be saved (the laws and ordinances of the gospel). Explain what some of the laws of the gospel are (paying tithing, keeping the Sabbath day holy, being honest, and so on), and what ordinances we must obey (baptism, confirmation, taking the sacrament, endowment).

3. Display, in random order, word strips of some of the important words in the song. As you sing, pause before each important word and have a child choose a word he or she thinks will fit into the song at that point. Sing the phrase again to check if the word fits, and then invite the children to sing the phrase.

4. Through melody charts, help the children discover the three places where the melody moves down the scale on four eighth notes, or on quicker notes, and the two places where one syllable is sung on two tones. Have them identify the word sung at the climax and highest tone of the song; let them discover that the melody moves down the scale from high D to F in the last line. In each case, have them listen to you sing the song, and place word strips of the words that are sung in these particular musical sequences in the correct places on the melody chart.

5. Encourage the children to sing this song smoothly, with connected tones, and with conviction.

The Fourth Article of Faith 124

First Line: We believe that the first principles and ordinances
Topics Indexed: Baptism, Faith, Gift of the Holy Ghost,
    Repentance

Teaching Suggestions:

1. Ask the children what they could tell someone who wanted to know what to do to become a member of The Church of Jesus Christ of Latter-day Saints. Tell them that you will sing "The Fourth Article of Faith" and want them to listen to find four things a person must do. As they name them, post word strips of each. Repeat the song as necessary.

2. Tell the children that there are two words that describe the four things, and we hear these two words in the first line. Sing

the song and let them name the two words ("principles" and "ordinances"). Ask them whether these two words are sung on even or uneven beats. Have them listen to find out, and then sing that line with you. Post word strips of the two words, invite them to listen again and place the four word strips (from suggestion number one) under "principles" or "ordinances." (Faith and repentance would go under "principles," and baptism and laying on of hands would be posted under "ordinances.")

3. Tell the children that the composer put a rest, or a place where there is no sound, after each of the numbers in the song. As you sing it, invite them to tap quietly on their laps on the rests.

4. Continue to teach the song by asking questions such as these: "What gift do we receive by the laying on of hands?" "What two big words describe how baptism should be performed?" "What is the second principle that is required?" "In whom must we have faith?" After each response, have the children join you in singing that phrase.

5. Point out interesting rhythms that they will enjoy clapping, phrases where the melody is similar (measures one through four and nine through twelve), or places where there is a big jump in the melody.

6. Express your testimony regarding the importance of the four principles and ordinances of the gospel, and encourage the children to sing the song with confidence and conviction.

The Fifth Article of Faith 125

First Line: We believe that a man must be called of God
Topics Indexed: Authority, Missionary Work, Priesthood, Prophecy

Teaching Suggestions:

1. Tell the children that when a person is called of God to serve in special callings in the Church, three conditions must be met. Tell them that the fifth Article of Faith names these three things, each preceded by the word "by," and that you want them to discover them as you sing (prophecy, laying on of hands, those in authority). Use word strips of these keywords or a picture to illustrate the laying on of hands.

2. Draw an illustration of the melody line of the first two-measure phrase, ask the children to find the words that fit in this phrase, and have them sing it. ("We believe that a man must be

called of God.") Sing the song again and ask them to find another phrase that has the same melody and discover the words of that phrase. ("By those who are in authority.") As you sing the entire song, invite them to join you in singing these two phrases. They could pitch-level conduct as they follow the melody line.

3. Teach the rest of the song by emphasizing and illustrating unusual melody patterns, such as the scale line on the words "laying on of hands" and the interesting pattern on "Gospel and ad- ." Ask questions about the words, and when they discover an answer have them join in singing that phrase. Continue until they can sing the entire song.

4. Help the children understand that this Article of Faith refers to the authority of the priesthood, which many of the youth and men of their ward hold, even though it does not use the word "priesthood." If possible, have the bishop visit and tell about his calling to this important assignment.

The Sixth Article of Faith 126

First Line: We believe in the same organization
Topics Indexed: Church Leaders, Prophets

Teaching Suggestions:

1. Have a child hold the word strip "We believe" and ask the children to name some of the things that we believe as members of The Church of Jesus Christ of Latter-day Saints. After you accept responses, tell them that you are going to sing a song about one thing that we believe, and that they should listen to discover what it is. After you sing the song and accept answers, explain that you have just sung "The Sixth Article of Faith" and invite any of the children that have memorized this article to stand and repeat it.

2. Explain to the children that one way they can learn this song and the sixth Article of Faith is to remember that it names six things that existed in the Primitive Church. Sing it again and have them count the six things. Explain the meaning of such words as "Primitive Church," "pastor," "evangelist," and "so forth." Invite children to post word strips of the six things as they are sung. Have them repeat this part of the song until they can sing it well.

3. Tell the children that the first part of the song is like climbing up and down a mountain. Demonstrate by pitch-level conducting the accented notes (beats one and three) of the first three measures, moving upward and then quickly coming down again. Have them

sing and pitch-level conduct this phrase. Ask them to repeat it several times until they can sing the entire phrase with the accompaniment.

4. Demonstrate the unusual rhythmic qualities of the song by having the children clap to the melody or march quietly as they sing.

5. Share your testimony about the organization of the Church.

The Seventh Article of Faith 126

First Line: We believe in the gift of tongues
Topics Indexed: Prophecy, Revelation

Teaching Suggestions:

1. Tell an experience of one of the early prophets of the Church where speaking in tongues was manifest or when a vision or healing occurred. Tell the children that the seventh Article of Faith names seven special gifts the Lord has given to his people to experience. Ask them to count these gifts as you sing the song and discuss their meaning. (The "so forth," counted in the seven, indicates other gifts that he gives to us.) Post word strips to help them remember the gifts and the order in which they come. Invite seven children to each hold one of the word strips and to arrange themselves in the correct order as the song is sung.

2. Draw a curved line representing the melody of each phrase. (Think of the notes as dots arranged up or down by pitch and connected with a curved line.) As you sing the song, trace the melody pictures with your finger, and then encourage the children to trace the melody line in the air or on the chalkboard. Have them place word strips of important words on the melody line in the appropriate places. Encourage them to find interesting features on the melody chart, such as the complete scale from middle C to high C and how the first tones (the accented notes) in measures three through eight move down the scale from A to C.

3. Ask the children to listen to the melody played on the piano to find out if the rhythm is mostly even or uneven. Have them clap the uneven rhythm while they sing the song.

4. Express your belief in the reality of these great gifts the Lord has given to us.

The Eighth Article of Faith 127

First Line: We believe the Bible to be the word of God
Topics Indexed: Bible, Book of Mormon

Teaching Suggestions:

1. Hold up a sack or box and tell the children that there are two very important things hidden in it. Tell them that you are going to sing a song that will give them a clue. After they identify the Bible and the Book of Mormon, have two children remove the books from the sack. Ask them what these books are and how they came to be written. After they express their ideas, clarify misunderstandings and emphasize that God directed prophets throughout the ages to write his teachings for us. These writings are our scriptures. Sing the song again and invite the children to sing the phrases "We believe the Bible" and "We also believe the Book of Mormon" as children hold up these books.

2. Ask questions such as these: "What does the song say that we believe the Bible and Book of Mormon to be?" "What is the phrase after 'We believe the Bible to be the word of God'?" Invite the children to sing these parts after they give the answer. Help them understand the meaning of the phrase "as far as it is translated correctly."

3. Help the children listen to the melody and discover that the first and third phrases are almost alike. You could draw patterns of these phrases and other melody patterns, such as the triplet in the second phrase. Have them listen to the piano accompaniment and describe the feeling of the minor key of this song.

4. Express your feelings about the truthfulness of the Bible and the Book of Mormon and encourage the children to read from the scriptures.

The Ninth Article of Faith 128

First Line: We believe all that God has revealed
Topics Indexed: Revelation

Teaching Suggestions:

1. Place an object, such as a copy of the Book of Mormon, a CTR ring, or a Gospel in Action card, in a paper bag or other container and tell the children that you are going to *reveal* what

is inside. Allow several children to look into the bag, and tell them that what is in the bag has been *revealed* to them. Open the bag for all the children to see and emphasize that now the object has been *revealed* to everyone. Ask them what it means to *reveal* (to make known or to show). Tell them that you are going to sing a song about what God *reveals*. If some of the children have already memorized this Article of Faith, let them repeat it for the others.

2. Ask three children to hold word strips that say "has revealed," "does now reveal," and "will yet reveal." As you sing the song, have them hold their word strips up as their words are sung.

3. Sing the song again and invite three children to hold a picture of Joseph Smith receiving the gold plates, a picture of the present prophet of the Church, and a blank piece of paper with a large question mark on it. Ask the children in the group to match the pictures with the word strips (from suggestion number two) and explain why they matched them the way they did.

4. Help the children learn the last line by drawing a diagram of the melody. Explain that singing this line is like running up and down mountain peaks—that the word "many" begins at the top of a peak and the notes move down and up forming five peaks. Invite them to pitch-level conduct this line as they sing it. They could also move their bodies up and down as they sing, or you could invite eight children of different heights to represent the mountain peaks and the valleys of the last line.

5. Divide the children into three groups and have one group sing the first phrase ("We believe all that God has revealed"), another sing the second phrase ("all that He does now reveal"), another the third phrase ("and we believe that He will yet reveal"), and all join together for the last phrase ("many great and important things pertaining to the Kingdom of God").

6. Show other pictures depicting revelation, such as Noah building the ark, Moses and the Ten Commandments, the present prophet, or Lehi with the Liahona. Ask the children to name something that God has revealed in the past and something that God has recently revealed through his prophet. Ask them if they know what God will yet reveal; point out that we do not know exactly what he will reveal, but the song tells us he will reveal "many great and important things pertaining to the Kingdom of God."

The Tenth Article of Faith   128

First Line: We believe in the literal gathering of Israel
Topics Indexed: Jesus Christ—Second Coming, Prophecy

Teaching Suggestions:

1. The children should have a lesson in Sharing Time or in the classroom to teach the concepts of this Article of Faith before they are taught the song.

2. Explain to the children that there are many important things that this song says that we believe. Ask them to listen to you sing the song while they count the things we believe; then have them listen again to see if they can name the five things. You may need to sing it several times so that they can repeat all five; post word strips of keywords to help them remember the points.

3. Assign each of five groups one of the things that we believe and have a leader for each group discuss with them their assigned concept. Suggest that each group draw a picture to represent that concept. Have them learn the music for their phrase and prepare to explain the pictures they have drawn. Have the groups sing their phrases in turn, putting together the whole song.

4. Help the children notice the uneven rhythm patterns in the first half of the song, and point out that the last part, which talks of Christ reigning on the earth, has a more even rhythm and should be sung majestically. Invite them to clap or tap these rhythms and observe how the beat of the notes fits the words of the Article of Faith. Point out that the melody of the first four measures is repeated with variation in measures six through nine.

The Eleventh Article of Faith   130

First Line: We claim the privilege of worshiping Almighty God
Topics Indexed: Freedom

Teaching Suggestions:

1. Briefly tell stories of people who have been persecuted for their beliefs: the pilgrims, the Anti-Nephi-Lehis (see Alma 24), and the early Mormons. Ask the children if they think it is fair for people to be persecuted for their beliefs. Emphasize that it is a privilege to worship God the way one believes. Tell them that

Joseph Smith wrote an Article of Faith about the privilege we have to worship God as we wish. Sing "The Eleventh Article of Faith."

2. Ask the children to name some of the religions of their friends or associates. Tell them that there is a five-word phrase in "The Eleventh Article of Faith" that means to worship the way one chooses; invite them to listen for this phrase as you sing the song ("dictates of our own conscience"). Repeat this phrase several times, inviting them to sing it with you.

3. Ask the children to find the words that tell how they should respond to their friends who belong to other religions. ("Let them worship how, where, or what they may.") Invite them to sing this phrase with you until they have learned it well.

4. Help the children learn the melody through illustrations of the melody phrases. Allow them to discover which words are sung on the low and high places and where there are similar melody patterns.

The Twelfth Article of Faith   131

First Line: We believe in being subject to kings
Topics Indexed: Country, Obedience

Teaching Suggestions:

1. Show the children a map or world globe and have them identify several countries where the gospel is being preached. Ask them if they know what kind of government the people have in each of these countries (kings, presidents, rulers, or magistrates). Tell them that the leaders of our Church talk to the leaders of countries to make sure that we obey the laws of those lands in our missionary work. Our leaders are careful to honor and sustain the law of each land. Ask the children if they know which Article of Faith tells about honoring and obeying the law. Then sing "The Twelfth Article of Faith."

2. Ask the children to listen to the song and find three things they should do regarding the law of the land. After they have responded, help them understand what these words mean. Ask them to describe some of the laws of their land (paying taxes, observing traffic signals, and so on), and ask if there is ever a time when they don't have to obey the law. Tell them that Heavenly Father always expects us to obey, honor, and sustain the law. If we have laws that we don't like, we should work to change them, but we must always obey them while they are the laws.

3. Have the children clap the uneven rhythm of this song, noticing the beat of the triplets. Illustrate the melody pattern, noting that the melody moves up and down all through the song.

The Thirteenth Article of Faith 132

First Line: We believe in being honest, true, chaste, benevolent
Topics Indexed: Honesty, Kindness, Morality, Service

Teaching Suggestions:

1. Introduce this Article of Faith by telling the children that the Lord has told us how we should act and treat others while we live on this earth. Sing the song and ask them to find six things it tells us we believe in being (honest, true, chaste, benevolent, virtuous, doing good); four things that are the admonition of Paul (believe all things, hope all things, endured many things, and hope to be able to endure all things); and four kinds of things we seek after (virtuous, lovely, good report, praiseworthy).

2. Prepare a melody chart that divides the song into six phrases, ending with the words "virtuous," "men," "Paul," "things" (with the fermata), "praiseworthy," and "things." Sing the song several times, each time asking the children information about the melody. Ask, for example, where the breathing places occur in the phrases; what words occur on the repeated notes in phrase four; what word is sung on the high point in phrase four ("hope"); what long word occurs in the third phrase that means "suggestion" or "direction"; and places where the melody goes up the scale at the end of a phrase (end of first and fifth phrases). Help them discover the features of the melody by listening to you, singing with you, following the melody chart, adding word strips to the chart, and repeating the phrases until they learn to sing the song correctly.

3. Help the children sing this song with expression and appropriate dynamics as indicated in the music. Encourage them to build in volume in the fifth line, reach a climax in line six as they sing these notes with emphasis ("hope to be able to endure all things"), and hold the word "things" (with the fermata).

4. Bear testimony that the thirteenth Article of Faith is a code for living, and that when we are faced with decisions about where we should go, what we should listen to, what we should see, or how we should treat others, we can use this as a guide.

The Books in the Book of Mormon 119

Words: Daphne Matthews (adapted)
Music: "Ten Little Indians" (adapted)
First Line: First and second books of Nephi
Topics Indexed: Book of Mormon

Sister Matthews thought it would be helpful to have a song with the names of the books in the Book of Mormon so children could easily learn them. She adapted the words to fit a tune that would be familiar to even the little ones.

It is interesting to note that the melody for measures one and two is the same as in measures five and six, and there is a descending scale in the last two measures.

Teaching Suggestions:

1. Hold up a copy of the Book of Mormon and ask the children how many books they see. Tell them that there are fifteen smaller books that make up the larger book, each one written by one or more men, usually prophets. As you sing the song, have them count the books to see if this is the correct number.

2. Write the names of the books, each on a separate piece of paper. Give these papers to fifteen children and ask them to arrange themselves in the correct order as you sing the song. You may need to sing it several times until the papers are arranged in the correct order. Clip these papers to a clothesline that is stretched across the front of the room. Continue teaching the words by removing one or two of the papers each time the children sing the song.

3. Pass out copies of the Book of Mormon to the children and have them sing the song by looking at the title page.

The Books in the New Testament 116

Words: Anonymous
Music: Scottish folk song; adapted by W. W. Phelps
First Line: Matthew, Mark, Luke, John, the Acts and Romans
Topics Indexed: Bible

Primary children some forty years ago learned the names of the books in the New Testament by singing them to the familiar

tune used for the hymn "Praise to the Man." The seminaries also taught their students to recite the names of the books through this song. The repetition in much of the melody line makes learning the music easy. The melody of lines one and two is repeated in lines three and four and again in lines seven and eight. The challenge is fitting the names of the books to the notes. Some syllables are sung on more than one note, and some quarter notes are divided into two eighth notes to accommodate the pronunciation. The leader should learn to sing it accurately before teaching it to the children.

Teaching Suggestions:

1. Hold up a copy of the Bible and tell the children there are two parts to this book, the Old and the New Testaments. Ask them to name any of the books they might know in the New Testament. As they respond, write the names on large pieces of paper. Invite the children to look in their Bibles to discover other books they had not thought of.

2. Display the names of each of the books of the New Testament on separate sheets of paper, in random order, on the flannelboard or chalkboard. As you sing the song, have some of the children rearrange the names in the correct order. You may need to sing it several times until they do this correctly. After they begin to learn the song, take away the name of one book at a time, until they can sing the song completely without the help of the written names.

The Books in the Old Testament 114

Words: Anonymous
Music: George Kaillmark
First Line: Genesis, Exodus, Leviticus, Numbers
Topics Indexed: Bible

The origin of this song is probably similar to that of "The Books in the New Testament"; a teacher in seminary or in Sunday School likely decided to put the names of these books to music so the children could learn to recite them more easily. The music is that of the well-known hymn "Do What Is Right"; one verse and two choruses are used to contain the names of the thirty-nine books of the Old Testament. If we consider the music in eight-measure phrases, the musical form is A A B A B A: there are four phrases

that are the same, and the remaining two are alike. The rhythm of the A phrases includes even and uneven beats, and the rhythm of the B phrases is even. The melody of the original song has been altered somewhat to accommodate the syllables of the names.

Teaching Suggestions:

1. Hold up a copy of the Bible and tell the children that there are two parts to this book, the Old and the New Testaments. Ask them to name any of the books in the Old Testament that they know. As they mention some of the books, write them on pieces of paper. Have them look in the Bible to discover the names of books that they had not thought of.

2. You will probably want to teach this song over several weeks because of its length and the difficulty in pronouncing the names accurately and in their correct order.

3. Taking two eight-measure phrases at a time, assign one or several children to represent each book and let them practice the melody and name for their book only. Have each group sing their part, in order, until the two phrases are sung. Ask them to repeat this several times, and then have two groups join together to sing the names of two books, then have four groups join together, and so on. Do the same for the next two phrases. The repetition will help the children pick up the song more readily.

The Chapel Doors   156

Words and Music: Dorothy Little Read
First Line: The chapel doors seem to say to me
Topics Indexed: Chapel, Quiet, Reverence, Sabbath

Dorothy Read, concerned about the irreverence she observed in many ward Primaries, searched for a song that might help the children overcome this problem. One day, when walking into her own chapel, she became aware of the automatic door closure that shut the doors with a distinct "sh—" sound. Later that "sh" sound from the chapel doors came back to her and in just minutes this song came to her mind. The song is popular with children all over the world, rating number ten of favorite songs in the Primary survey of 1983. Though it is about being reverent, it is not a somber number. The melody seems to portray that being reverent in the chapel can be a happy experience.

The music form of "The Chapel Doors" is A A B A—the first,

second, and fourth four-measure phrases are the same (with slight variation). The 6/8 time signature lends a swinging motion to the music, and the leader should conduct it with two beats to the measure. The "sh" that occurs three times is the unique feature and is more naturally whispered than sung. There are also two fermatas that should be observed.

Teaching Suggestions:

1. Draw a simple outline of a church building on a large piece of paper and cut out opening flaps for two doors. Draw a picture of the inside of the chapel and paste it behind the doors so that when the doors are open, you can see the chapel. Show the picture to the children and ask them to guess what is inside the doors. After opening the doors, discuss why the chapel should be a sacred, reverent place. Invite the children to listen to the song and discover the reasons given for reverence in the chapel ("to learn of Jesus, to sing and pray"). Have them sing this phrase with you.

2. Teach the phrase "Sh, be still," and have the children sing it several times. Draw a picture of the melody patterns where these words occur and show the children that the notes sung on these words are not the same each time. As you sing the entire song, have them join in singing "sh, be still" the three times it occurs.

3. Divide the children into two groups and have one sing the "sh, be still" phrases and the others sing the remaining phrases. Hold up a picture of a reverent child each time they come to the phrase "sh, be still." Help them feel the spirit of the song by encouraging them to sing joyfully, but with reverence, and observing the fermatas that are marked in the music.

The Church of Jesus Christ 77

Words and Music: Janice Kapp Perry
First Line: I belong to The Church of Jesus Christ of Latter-day Saints
Topics Indexed: Accountability, Commitment, Example, Jesus Christ—Example, Missionary Work, Testimony

Janice Kapp Perry says she felt that children needed a song telling the name of our church. The piece she wrote to fill that need engenders spirit and strength of conviction with its strong statement of the beliefs of members of the Church. Even very little children can sing it out powerfully.

The melody phrases are each distinct and are not repeated. There is also variety in the rhythm patterns, with very little repetition and a mixture of even and uneven beats. The children will enjoy clapping or tapping the various sections; this will also help them to sing the notes to the correct rhythm. The solid melody and rhythm are easily learned and remembered by children of all ages.

Teaching Suggestions:

1. Post the word "belong," and ask the children to name some of the groups they belong to, such as family, Primary class, sports team, scout group, ward, or school. Ask them what it means to belong to something. Ask them to name the church they belong to. Display a picture of Jesus and read D&C 115:4.

2. Tell the children that you are going to sing a song about being a member of The Church of Jesus Christ of Latter-day Saints, and that you would like them to listen to find two things they "know" because they are members of the Church. After they respond, invite them to sing these two phrases with you as you post two word strips with "know who I am" and "know God's plan" on them.

3. Ask the children to listen to the song again and find six things we do because we belong to The Church of Jesus Christ of Latter-day Saints. Post word strips for these ("follow," "believe," "honor," "do," "follow," "proclaim"). Tell them that these are action words, and that as members of the Church we should be willing to act and do many important things. As you sing the song again, invite them to sing as much of the song as they can remember.

4. Draw illustrations of the four musical phrases (each four measures long) on the chalkboard or on a poster. Invite the children to imitate your arm actions as you sing the song and trace the lines. Challenge nine children to place the action words on the phrase chart as you sing. Have all the children sing the song with you to see if the words are placed correctly.

5. Express your feelings about membership in the Church and invite some of the children to voice their feelings.

The Commandments   112

Words: Anonymous
Music: Charlene Anderson Newell
First Line: Thou shalt have no gods but Me

Topics Indexed: Bible, Commandments, Honesty, Love, Morality, Parents, Sabbath, Ten Commandments

This song paraphrases the Ten Commandments so children can learn and remember them. It also includes Jesus' statement regarding the "great commandment," as recorded in Matthew 22:35–40. For the *Children's Songbook* the last note of many of the phrases has been dotted, which provides more "breathing room" between phrases, and the time signature has been changed from 4/4 to 2/4.

The first eight measures are written in the minor mode. The first and second two-measure phrases are the same, as are the third and fourth phrases. The remainder of the song changes to the major key. In this part of the song there is also some repetition of musical phrases. The melody line includes many repeated notes, notes that move by steps, and intervals in which the tones jump as much as an octave. The rhythm is made up of mostly even beats with a few dotted-eighth/sixteenth combinations. The climax is reached in the next-to-last line on the word "all," which is held before moving to the last phrase.

Teaching Suggestions:

1. With pictures, questions, and discussion, briefly tell the story of Moses and how he received the Ten Commandments on Mount Sinai. Ask the children if they can name any of the Ten Commandments. Write their responses on the chalkboard. Tell them that you will sing a song that mentions all the Ten Commandments. Encourage them to listen to find the commandments that are listed on the chalkboard and others they did not mention.

2. Cut out a simple outline of "tablets" on paper and number from one to ten down one side. After each number, put one or two keywords for each commandment. Sing the song again, and point to each of the numbers and keywords.

3. Prepare to make two lists on the chalkboard labeled "Do" and "Don't." As you sing the song, have the children listen for things they should and shouldn't do and list them under the appropriate heading.

4. Tell the children that the words in the last two lines are what Jesus replied when he was asked what the greatest commandment was. Tell them that if all people truly loved the Lord and their neighbors as themselves, they would easily be able to keep all of the Ten Commandments. Sing these phrases to the children and invite them to sing with you.

5. Older children will enjoy comparing the words of the song with the words in the scriptures, as found in Exodus 20:3–17 and Matthew 22:35–40. Help them understand all the words and phrases, such as "idols," "bow thy knee," "vain," "profane," "wanton ways," "marriage trust," "unjust," and "covet."

The Dearest Names   208

Words and Music: Frances K. Taylor
First Line: I know a name, a glorious name
Topics Indexed: Fathers, Mothers, Parents

This popular song shares the simple message that the dearest names to a child are "mother" and "father." Younger children, especially those in the nursery, will ask to sing it again and again. For the *Children's Songbook*, the accompaniment has been simplified to eliminate some repetitive patterns, and the time signature has been changed from 3/4 to 6/8. It should be conducted two beats to the measure. The accompaniment is supportive, yet allows the melody to receive lyric emphasis.

There are no identical musical phrases within the four lines, but lines one and three have some similarities, as do lines two and four. The appealing feature occurs in the second line with the words "Listen, I'll whisper the name to you . . . " These should be sung in more hushed tones and with added expression.

Teaching Suggestions:

1. Bring one child to the front and sing the first two lines just to this child, whispering "mother" in his or her ear so that no one else can hear this word of the song. Ask the other children to guess what word you whispered. The child in front could report when the correct answer is given. Invite all the children to sing the first verse with you. Use the same procedure to teach the second verse.

2. Ask two or three mothers to come to the front. Tell the children that these women are tender, kind, and true, and that there is a special name that they all have. Ask them to guess what the name is. When the children have found the name "mother," ask them to whisper it. Then sing the phrase, "Listen, I'll whisper the name to you . . . ," with the children joining you to whisper "mother."

3. Teach the children to sing the phrase "I love you, I love you." Then sing "Mother so tender and kind and true," and invite them to add their phrase. Teach the last line in the same manner.

4. Ask the children to play "fill in the blank" with you. Sing the song, but stop on important words, and encourage them to sing the word that goes in the blank.

The Family 194

Words: Mabel Jones Gabbott
Music: Richard Clinger
First Line: When the fam'ly gets together
Topics Indexed: Family Home Evening, Parents

This song is spirited and full of fun. Mabel Jones Gabbott wrote the words to express her happy feelings about her family as they read, played, and learned the gospel in family home evening. She says, "This is one of my favorite songs because it is so personal. Though my five are grown now and enjoying families of their own, they still come together on Monday nights to my home in Bountiful. We still believe that when the family gets together, it seems that nothing can go wrong."

The musical form of the song is A B A C—the first and third phrases are the same and the second and fourth are each distinct. The rhythm is bouncy and uneven; twelve measures contain a quarter/eighth, quarter/eighth pattern. Each of the musical phrases is the same rhythmically. The climax comes in the last measure of the third line when the notes skip from E up to high C on the word "song." This note has a fermata, after which the tones move downward with the closing phrase.

Teaching Suggestions:

1. Invite a few children to come to the front to pantomine a situation for the other children. Quietly whisper to these children that they are to act out a family home evening in which the father tells a story and the mother leads them in song. Simple props could be used, such as a tie for father and an apron for mother. After the children have completed their demonstration, ask those who have been observing to guess what the actors have been portraying. Tell them that you are going to sing a song about some of the things that families do for family home evening. Encourage them to listen to discover some of these things.

2. Teach the words by asking questions, such as these: "What does it seem like when the family gets together?" "What does mother do?" "What does father do?" "What two things do we do

to learn to know each other?" "When does the family get together?" After asking each question, sing the song, accept answers, and invite the children to join in singing that phrase with you.

3. Invite the children to tap or clap the rhythm that goes with each of the phrases.

4. Display pictures of families doing things together to illustrate the lyrics of the song. Invite the children to share some of the things they do when their families get together.

The Golden Plates 86

Words: Rose Thomas Graham
Music: J. Spencer Cornwall
First Line: The golden plates lay hidden
Topics Indexed: Book of Mormon, Joseph Smith, Restoration of the Gospel

This appealing song ranked number four in familiarity and in popularity in the 1983 Primary music survey. The two short verses tell briefly the story of the coming forth of the Book of Mormon, translated from golden plates hidden many years before. The song has a new straightforward musical arrangement in the *Children's Songbook*, and in the second verse, measure three, the words have been changed from "A godly man of old" to "Written in days of old," to bring about a more natural word emphasis.

The music has little repetition of musical phrases or rhythmic patterns; the entire song moves smoothly and effortlessly. The third measure, "deep in the mountainside," should be sung softly and mysteriously.

Teaching Suggestions:

1. Introduce the song by speaking the words to the two verses as though telling the children a special story. Use expression, contrasting the mystery of verse one with the climax of verse two. Use pictures of the golden plates, Joseph Smith, and Nephi, and a copy of the Book of Mormon to illustrate the story as you repeat the verses. Discuss briefly the events described, touching on the meaning of difficult words ("confide," "record"). Then sing the song to the children.

2. Invite the children to tap or softly clap the rhythm as you sing it. They will soon learn to sing the song by rote as they hear it sung by you and other children in the group.

3. Bear testimony of the divine coming forth of the Book of Mormon; encourage the children to share their feelings about these events.

The Handcart Song 220

*Words: John Daniel Thompson McAllister and Lucile
 Cardon Reading*
Music: John Daniel Thompson McAllister
First Line: When pioneers moved to the West
Topics Indexed: Descants, Pioneers, Singing

This is truly one of the "heritage" songs of the Church, having been written in the early 1850s. From a biography of John Daniel Thompson McAllister by Lucile McAllister Weenig we read, "While John was in Belfast [on a mission] in December 1855 . . . he preached a discourse which he called a 'Telegraphic Handcart' on emigration. He wrote, 'The Saints got the Spirit of it, and rejoiced to think the time was coming when they would have the privilege to push or draw a handcart to Zion.' This may have been the time when John wrote the words to the Handcart Song that he later put to music." In 1856, John McAllister was helping a handcart company to prepare to journey to the Salt Lake Valley. "Before the handcart company left Iowa, he did take time to teach his 'Handcart Song' to the handcart pioneers who sang it as they pushed and pulled their carts across the plains and mountains to Zion." Evidently many of the handcart groups that followed also sang the song along the way. The music had six verses and was later arranged by Frederick Beesley. Three of the original verses (dropped in subsequent printings) are as follows:

> *Ye Saints who dwell on Europe's shore*
> *Prepare yourselves for many more,*
> *To leave behind your native land,*
> *For sure God's judgments are at hand.*
> *For you must cross the raging main*
> *Before the promised land you gain,*
> *And with the faithful make a start,*
> *To cross the plains with your handcart.*
>
> *As on the road the carts are pulled*
> *'Twould very much surprise the world*
> *To see the old and feeble dame*

Thus lend a hand to pull the same;
And maidens fair will dance and sing;
Young men more happy than a king.
And children, too, will laugh and play,
Their strength increasing day by day.

And long before the valley's gained
We will be met upon the plains
With music sweet and friends so dear
And fresh supplies our heart to cheer.
And then with music and with song
How cheerfully we'll march along
And thank the day we made a start
To cross the plains with our handcart.

In the *Children's Songbook* the song is printed with a simplified arrangement and an interesting optional descant to accompany the chorus.

The melody of the chorus is the same as that of the verse, with the exception of three eighth notes on the word "merrily." Otherwise, the rhythm is the same in every measure (quarter note, eighth note, quarter note, eighth note), creating a constant uneven beat pattern. The children will enjoy clapping this rhythm. The addition of the descant in the chorus provides an interesting variation.

Teaching Suggestions:

1. Introduce this song by telling about the pioneer John McAllister, who himself crossed the plains to Salt Lake City as a young man, and then later wrote this song to help the handcart companies that followed to have the courage to walk the long way to the valley. Show the children pictures of the handcart companies as they struggled along the way. Then sing the chorus of the song. Help the children understand how hard it would have been to pack all their belongings in a handcart and walk every step of the long journey.

2. Have the children clap or tap the rhythm of the song while you sing it. Have some of them clap an even two counts to a measure while the others clap the uneven beats of the melody.

3. Teach the chorus first by singing it several times and asking the children to repeat it.

4. Have the children listen to you sing the verse to hear how the melody is the same as for the chorus. Teach the words to the verse with questions such as these: "What did they do as they

216

pushed?" "How long did they push their handcarts?" "What did they have to have to meet the test?" "Where did the pioneers move?" Ask the children to join you in singing the phrases after they answer each question.

5. Younger children will enjoy dressing in simple pioneer costumes — a bonnet, hat, or neckerchief — and improvising some of the actions that the words suggest.

6. Teach a group of older children the optional descant. Encourage the children to imagine that they are pioneers crossing the plains as they sing the song with energy and enthusiasm.

The Hearts of the Children   92

Words and Music: Patricia Kelsey Graham
First Line: The hearts of the children turn to their fathers
Topics Indexed: Bible, Family History, Prophecy, Obbligatos

This song invites feelings of love and assurance with the wonderful message that families can be sealed for eternity because of the power that Elijah brought to the earth. The words are based on two scriptural passages, Malachi 4:5–6 and D&C 2:2.

The opening musical phrase is repeated with variation in the third and fourth measures of the third line. Otherwise there is no restatement of the melody. The music moves evenly and smoothly throughout and should be sung with connected tones. It should begin rather softly and build to the climax in the fourth line on the word "prophecy." An optional obbligato can be played on an instrument or sung by a few high voices as the song is repeated.

Teaching Suggestions:

1. The composer suggests making a poster booklet of three large hearts joined together at the side by rings so the pages will turn. Illustrations and keywords that would be placed on the six pages are as follows: (1) picture of a child or children and the word "children"; (2) old-time picture of ancestors and the word "fathers"; (3) picture of an ancient prophet and the words "Malachi prophesied"; (4) the word "turn," with each letter placed in a small heart; (5) picture of an ancient prophet and the words "Elijah, prophecy"; (6) picture of a family in front of the temple and the words "sealed, eternity." Show the picture of the children and explain that there is a picture of some special people on the other side. After you have encouraged the children to guess who these

people might be, "turn" the heart page to reveal the picture of ancestors. Tell the children that even though they have not met their great-great-grandparents, they can get to know and love them. Tell how we have been blessed with temples where families can be sealed to ancestors who lived long ago.

2. Sing the song to the children, turning the pages of the heart-shaped book as you sing. Explain briefly that the prophet Malachi prophesied many years ago (about 430 B.C.) that the Lord would send Elijah to turn the hearts of the children to their fathers. Then Elijah did appear in the Kirtland Temple to Joseph Smith and Oliver Cowdery and gave them the power to seal families together in the temples. Have two children read the scriptures from Malachi 4:5–6 and D&C 110:13–16.

3. Help the children learn the words through the booklet and by asking questions, encouraging them to listen to the song to discover the answers, and inviting them to sing the phrases as they learn them. Ask: "For how long are families sealed?" (Explain that "eternity" means "forever," and that it is such an important word that it is held for a long time.) "To whom have the hearts of the children turned?" "Who prophesied that the hearts shall turn?" "Who was the prophet who fulfilled the prophecy?"

4. Help the children understand the message of this song: that our hearts will have a growing desire to find out who our "fathers" or ancestors are, and we will want to be sealed to them forever.

The Holy Ghost   105

Words and Music: Jeanne P. Lawler
First Line: When Christ was on the earth
Topics Indexed: Choice, Gift of the Holy Ghost, Guidance, Holy Ghost

This song explains the role of the Holy Ghost: to comfort and guide us with a still, small voice, and to testify to us of God and Christ. It is appropriate for performance at baptisms, to underscore the significance of the ordinances of baptism and confirmation. In the *Children's Songbook* the words of verse one have been altered, and verses two and three have been replaced by a new second verse, more practical and applicable to the understanding of the children.

The music seems to be divided into two eight-measure sections, each with its own musical pattern. The first two measures introduce a musical figure that is repeated twice, each a note higher on the scale. The first two measures of the third line (the beginning of the second eight-measure section) introduce another musical figure that is also repeated twice, each a note *lower* on the scale. These progressions capture attention and make the melody more memorable. The last two measures in each of the two eight-measure sections are the same. The rhythm is mostly even, and the notes fall within the octave range from C to high C.

Teaching Suggestions:

1. Introduce the song by repeating in a very soft voice some instructions to the children, such as, "Everyone who can hear my voice, put your finger on your nose," "If you can hear my voice, put your hand on your head," and so on. Explain that even though you were speaking very quietly, they could hear and obey instructions if they were listening. Tell them that you are going to sing a song about someone who has a still, small voice and tells us important things. Ask them to listen and identify the person the song tells about.

2. Teach the song in two parts. Sing each half of the song several times, encouraging the children to listen by using questions: "What did Christ promise he would send?" "What did Jesus say the Holy Ghost will do for us?" "What two words describe what kind of a friend the Holy Ghost is?" "Who whispers with a still, small voice?" "What is another word for the 'Holy Spirit'?" "What does he testify of?" After the children have answered a question, have them join in singing that phrase, continuing until they have learned the entire section. Teach the second verse in a similar way.

3. Help the children hear and feel the interesting musical progressions by having them move their hands or whole bodies up and down with the melody. Illustrate the musical patterns on a chart or chalkboard.

4. Explain that when the Holy Ghost whispers, we usually cannot hear a voice at all, but it is like he is whispering to our minds. Tell the children that the Holy Ghost will tell them important things and that he tries to guide them to do what is right.

The Lord Gave Me a Temple 153

Words: Donnell Hunter
Music: Darwin Wolford
First Line: The Lord gave me a temple to live within on earth

Topics Indexed: Commandments, Creation, Eternal Life, Health, Morality, Premortal Existence, Preparation, Temples

This song teaches that the body is the temple of the spirit, and if we keep it clean and pure, we can claim blessings Heavenly Father has promised. Darwin Wolford says, "Though this song deals with the Word of Wisdom, its subject is broader than that. It talks about the comparison of the physical body (a temple) and Father's temple." In the *Children's Songbook* the song has been lowered half a step, and the pick-up notes have been raised to bring all the tones within an easy range. Donnell Hunter expressed these sentiments on hearing his song performed: "I remember once driving home on a Saturday afternoon after my temple assignment and hearing a children's chorus sing this hymn at general conference and thinking if I never wrote another thing and if this song helped one child somewhere in the world to stay pure, it would be worth more than anything I have ever done."

The first and second four-measure phrases begin similarly and include notes that move almost entirely by steps. The next two phrases are each different, with several scalelike progressions. The rhythm is even and should be sung smoothly, in a flowing manner. As the melody line approaches the climax, there could be a slight increase in volume, bringing out in firmness the commitment, "I'll make my temple brighter; I'll keep my spirit free." This should be followed by a slight ritard in the last two phrases.

Teaching Suggestions:

1. Hold up your hand with a glove on it and tell the children that Elder Boyd K. Packer has said that the hand can represent your spirit, and the glove can represent your body. "While you are alive the spirit inside the body can cause it to work and to act and to live. When I separate them, the glove, which represents your body, is taken away from your spirit; it cannot move anymore." (*Ensign,* July 1973, p. 51.) Ask the children to listen to you sing a song that mentions another name for the body. After they hear it, explain to them that Heavenly Father's temples and our bodies are alike in that they both need to be kept clean and pure so that we can have the blessings that have been promised.

2. Teach the words by asking questions that can be answered with words of the song. Sing the song, accept answers, and invite the children to sing the phrases as they are identified. Ask: "Who gave me a temple?" "What was I in heaven?" "When did I leave my heavenly home?" "What am I going to do with my temple?"

"What will I do with my spirit?" "What is the temple my Father gave to me?" Use word strips of keywords to help the children remember the sequence of the lyrics. Ask similar questions to teach the second verse.

3. Invite the children to pitch-level conduct the melody as you sing. They might identify the words that are sung on the descending scale ("make my temple brighter" and "keep my spirit free") and other melodic patterns, such as how the first, second, and fourth phrases begin with the same three notes. Illustrate these musical phrases on a chart or chalkboard.

4. Encourage the children to sing with conviction and determination to keep their "temples" clean and pure. Direct them to sing the third phrase with increased volume and firmness and then ritard on the last phrase. Explain any unfamiliar words or phrases.

The Nativity Song   52

Words and Music: Patricia Kelsey Graham
First Line: This is the season beloved of the year
Topics Indexed: Christmas

This song tells the story of the Savior's birth in a simple and loving way. It can be effectively used to dramatize these events in a classroom, for a Primary group, or in the home. The author envisioned the figures of the Nativity being put together in a scene as the song was sung. Posterboard figures may be used, or children can be dressed in costumes to form the scene.

The song has five verses, with a four-measure introduction that is also used as an interlude between verses to allow time to place figures for the next verse. There are four musical phrases in the song. The first two measures of phrases one and three have the same melody, and the first two measures of phrases two and four are the same. The melody flows smoothly with mostly even beats, and the 3/4 time lends a lilting motion. The song works well for small children to pantomime, yet its tenderness has appeal for children of all ages.

Teaching Suggestions:

1. Ask the children to name the figures that should be present to portray the story of the birth of Jesus. As they make suggestions, show pictures, figures, or flannelboard cutouts of those that are mentioned in the song. Give the figures or pictures to various

children and ask them to come to the front as you sing about the persons or pieces that they are holding. Encourage the others to make suggestions as to where each of the figures should be positioned. Then repeat the song, having other children hold the figures.

2. Help the children learn the words with questions, pictures, and word strips. Alternate the singing of the verses by different groups — teachers, boys, girls, left, right, and so on.

3. For a more formal presentation of the nativity scene, make large figures from posterboard for each of the people and items mentioned in the song. Have several children hold the figures to form the scene as it is sung. Or have children dress in simple costumes and form a live nativity scene.

The Oxcart 219

Words and Music: Anonymous
First Line: Here comes the oxcart, oh, how slow!
Topics Indexed: Pioneers

"The Oxcart" first appeared in LDS music resources in the *Children's Friend,* July 1949. Little is known of its origin or writers except that it was probably an early pioneer song. Its appealing melody is written in the minor key, giving it a slow and mournful tone.

The melody of measures one and three is the same, and other melody patterns are different in the song. The uneven and sometimes unpredictable rhythm is the unique feature. This rhythm is syncopated in measures five and seven. In the next-to-last measure, the words, melody, and rhythm imitate the sound of the wagon wheels as they roll along.

Teaching Suggestions:
1. Ask the children if they know how the pioneers carried their supplies and belongings across the land. They might name covered wagons and handcarts. Show them pictures of these modes of travel and tell them that some pioneers traveled another way. Ask them to listen to a song you will sing that tells how some pioneers carried their supplies across the plains.

2. Show the children a picture of oxen and describe how these animals could pull heavy loads, but that they moved very slowly along the way. Chant the words to the song as the piano accompaniment is played. Ask them to tap the rhythm as the song is sung.

3. Ask the children what sound the wheels of the oxcart made as it rolled along. After they find the answer, have them sing the "creaks" in the next-to-last measure. To help them feel the rhythm, encourage them to tap the beats as they sing.

4. Divide the children into three groups and have each group sing one of the first three phrases and all groups join together to sing the last phrase. Have the groups exchange the phrases they sing until they know all of the words.

The Priesthood Is Restored   89

Words: Joan D. Campbell
Music: Hal K. Campbell
First Line: The priesthood is restored
Topics Indexed: Priesthood, Restoration of the Gospel

This song is a compact, precise statement about the restoration of priesthood power to the earth. It is intended for older children, and although the words are brief, a wealth of information is contained in the four lines. Hal Campbell made the accompaniment sound like a trumpet fanfare heralding the important occurrence so as to appeal particularly to the older boys who would learn it. There is a key change from B flat to G for the *Children's Songbook*, and the accompaniment has been thinned, yet the contemporary tonality and interesting harmonics are retained.

By itself, the melody is quite simple, with long, sustained notes on the phrase endings. In the third line the tones move down the scale from high C to E. There is no repetition of musical phrases. The rhythm is steady and even, with four strong beats per measure. The challenge for music leaders will be to help the young people hold the phrase endings while the accompaniment plays the "fanfare," and to incorporate the suggested dynamic markings to produce an impressive presentation.

Teaching Suggestions:
1. Ask the children, "If there were some very important news that was to be told, how would it be announced?" (Newspaper, television, radio.) Explain that long ago when an important event was announced, trumpets would sound, and someone would read a proclamation from a scroll. Ask them to close their eyes and listen to the pianist play the accompaniment and imagine they are hearing trumpets. Tell them that this song announces a very im-

portant event, and that as you sing it, you want them to discover what the event is. (You could sing the song while reading from a scroll of paper.) Post a word strip of the proclamation: "THE PRIESTHOOD IS RESTORED." Show a picture of the restoration of the Aaronic Priesthood and tell briefly how it was given to Joseph Smith.

2. Teach the phrases by encouraging the children to listen as you sing the song, asking questions that can be answered by exact words in the song, and inviting them to sing the phrases as they learn them. Display pictures of priesthood holders performing ordinances such as baptism, confirmation, blessing the sick, blessing the sacrament, and so on, to help them understand the importance of the priesthood restoration.

3. Ask the children to listen to the song again and discover the three words that are held the longest. Have them detect how many counts each of these notes is held. Help them sing these notes with sustained breaths (taking a deep breath before each phrase and taking a breath before the word "again"), holding the words on the vowel sound and singing the consonant sound at the end. Direct the singing so that they observe the dynamic markings as indicated.

4. Ask an older boy to read D&C 13:1 and tell briefly how the Aaronic Priesthood was restored. He could refer to the explanation that precedes section 13 of the Doctrine and Covenants. Ask the children to share experiences of when their lives have been blessed by priesthood power.

The Prophet Said to Plant a Garden 237

Words and Music: Mary Jane McAllister Davis
First Line: The prophet said to plant a garden
Topics Indexed: Health, Obedience, Preparation, Prophets,
*   Sharing, Work*

Prophets have frequently encouraged members of the Church to be frugal and, if possible, to grow some of the food they eat. When President Spencer W. Kimball spoke out on this subject, Mary Jane Davis felt impressed to write the admonition in a song for children. Her joyful composition presents the message on a child's level and is appealing for children of all ages.

Each of the four musical phrases is different except that the first and third phrases begin alike. The rhythm is even and straightforward, with mostly quarter notes. The melody includes some repeated notes and many jumps, including a skip of an octave and several skips of a sixth. The leader should help the children sing these notes accurately and with a good head tone.

Teaching Suggestions:

1. Introduce the song by telling the children that God has given us the things that are needed to grow good food to eat. Ask them to name these things. Then sing the song and ask them if it names the things they thought of (rich soil, rain, sunshine, seeds).

2. Make a string poster, so that as things are mentioned in the song the strings can be moved to reveal them. The poster should include green grass and brown soil at the bottom, forming a pocket in which to hide the other figures. The background can be simply a blue sky. A cloud with rain coming out of it, the sun, the seed, and the crops should each be taped to strings that go around the posterboard; these cutouts will be hidden in the pocket at the bottom of the poster until it is time to move them into view by moving the strings. After you have manipulated the figures once or twice to demonstrate, give a few children a turn as everyone sings the song.

3. Sing the song several times, each time asking the children a question that can be answered by words in the song, and inviting them to join in singing the phrases as they learn them.

4. Invite the children to pitch-level conduct the song with you so that they will feel the skips in the melody and sing the tones correctly. Younger children could dramatize the action of planting the seed and its growing into the good things to eat.

5. You can emphasize several gospel principles in singing this song, as noted above in "Topics Indexed."

The Sacrament 72

Words and Music: Vanja Y. Watkins
First Line: As I take the water and bread
Topics Indexed: Sacrament

When writing this song, Vanja Watkins had a strong feeling that the words should reflect those that the Savior declared when he asked us to partake of the sacrament in remembrance of him. She later added a second verse that would include words of commitment to the idea that was presented in the first verse.

The melody flows smoothly, mainly by steps, and with even rhythm. There is no repetition of melody in the four phrases, but the words of the third phrase are repeated for emphasis in both verses. In the final phrase, the voice part begins and then stops for five counts, while the piano plays an interlude, before the phrase is finished. This seems to allow "thinking time" for the singer to contemplate the meaning of the sacrament and the importance of remembering Jesus.

Teaching Suggestions:

1. Ask the children to suppose that a grandparent whom they loved very much was soon going to die. Ask them what they might want to have to help remember him or her (pictures, tapes, videos, journals). Tell them that when Jesus knew he was going to die, he wanted us to have something to help us remember him. He gathered his apostles around him and blessed and passed the bread and water. This was the first sacrament. Ask the children to listen as you sing a song to discover what Jesus said about taking the sacrament. Display a picture of the Last Supper as you sing.

2. Tell the children that the composer felt that the words that Jesus said were so important that she stated them twice in the song. Ask them to listen and raise their hands when they hear you repeat Jesus' words, "This do in remembrance of me." Sing these words again and ask the children what happens in the last phrase. (There is a pause in the singing but the accompaniment keeps going.) Tell them that during this pause we can fill our minds with thoughts of Jesus: of Jesus sitting at the sacrament table, gathering the children around him, healing the sick, or teaching the people. Invite the children to sing the last two phrases with you, counting five counts of rest time after the last "do."

3. Continue to teach the words to both verses with questions, such as these: "What name is sung instead of Jesus?" (Point out how the name "Savior" is sung on the highest note of the song.) "Which comes first in the song, the bread or the water?" "Whom will I remember?" "How do we want to serve him?" "What did Jesus give for me?" Have them sing these phrases as they learn them.

4. Invite the children to read some of the scriptures about the sacrament, such as Matthew 26:26–28; 3 Nephi 18:7, 11; Moroni 6:6; and D&C 20:75–79. Bear testimony of how the sacrament is a great blessing to help us remember the Savior and his sacrifice for us.

The Sacred Grove 87

Words: Joan D. Campbell
Music: Hal K. Campbell
First Line: The Sacred Grove was green and fresh
Topics Indexed: Heavenly Father, Jesus Christ — Son of God,
*   Joseph Smith, Prayer, Restoration of the Gospel*

This majestic number teaches of Joseph Smith's First Vision. The composer said, "This song is intended to examine the setting of the lovely spring morning and the sacred encounter with deity by the young boy, Joseph Smith." The accompaniment has been simplified in the *Children's Songbook* and lowered from the key of E flat to C. The song is most appropriate for older children who will understand its message; it can be an impressive addition for special programs.

The melody should flow smoothly, yet it is unusual in structure, with many uneven beats, accidentals, and unusual intervals. There are five musical phrases, each one different from the others. The words of phrase four are a repetition of phrase three, with the same melody one note higher on the scale. The music should build to a climax in this fourth phrase with increased volume and intensity, and the final phrase should be slower and more subdued. The 9/8 time signature is not difficult to follow if conducted three beats to the measure.

Teaching Suggestions:

1. Ask the children to close their eyes and imagine they can see Joseph Smith going into the Sacred Grove to pray to the Father. Describe briefly the events and the scene in the beautiful grove of trees on a lovely spring day. Have an older child read the scripture from Joseph Smith — History 1:14 and part of verse 15. While their eyes are still closed, sing the song to the children.

2. As you sing again, place cutouts or pictures of the First Vision on a board or chart, or have children hold them.

3. To help the children learn the words, ask a question, sing the song, receive answers, and invite them to sing that part with you. Ask: "Where did Joseph kneel?" "What word describes Joseph's prayer?" (Help them understand the meaning of "fervent.") "What phrase of the song is repeated?" (Explain that the author wanted to emphasize this important phrase.) "What did the morning sun do?" "What two words describe the Sacred Grove?"

4. Help the children sing the difficult intervals in the second line (F sharp to D sharp and G to D sharp) by asking them to listen as these notes are sung or played and then imitate the tones. Encourage them to sing with expression and meaning, emphasizing the words and increasing the volume when the phrase is repeated.

5. Bear your testimony of the reality of the First Vision, that Joseph Smith truly was visited by the Father and the Son.

The Shepherd's Carol 40

Words and Music: Daniel Lyman Carter
First Line: Mary, Mary, hush, see the Child
Topics Indexed: Christmas, Rounds

This four-part round was published in the *Friend*, December 1981, with one verse and the melody line only. For the *Children's Songbook* a second verse and a simple accompaniment have been added, and there are slight revisions in the melody. The minor key, coupled with the sacred theme, contributes to the haunting mood of the song.

This uncomplicated and beautiful composition moves smoothly and effortlessly. A distinctive characteristic is the uneven beat pattern throughout, created by quarter-/eighth-note combinations or dotted-eighth/sixteenth-/eighth-note patterns. The first three short phrases each have the same rhythm. The harmony produced when the piece is sung as a four-part round is lovely and appealing.

Teaching Suggestions:

1. Teach the song by rote, singing it and inviting the children to repeat it after you. Use pictures of Mary with the baby Jesus for the first phrase, Joseph for the second, and Jesus Christ for the final phrases.

2. Divide the children into four groups and have each sing one of the phrases. Each could hold a picture or cutout to remind them of the phrase they will sing. Have the groups exchange parts until all of them have learned to sing the entire song.

3. Invite the children to clap or tap the rhythm of the melody as they sing. Direct them to clap the uneven beat patterns correctly and to feel the swaying motion.

4. After they have learned to sing "The Shepherd's Carol," divide the children into two, three, or four groups, and have them

sing it as a round. Encourage them to sing with love, reverence, and awe for the holy event of the Savior's birth.

The Still Small Voice 106

Words and Music: Merrill Bradshaw
First Line: Through a still small voice, the Spirit speaks to me
Topics Indexed: Choice, Guidance, Holy Ghost

This sensitive and skillfully written number has a peaceful and somewhat mysterious feeling created by the atonal chording (a definite key signature is purposely avoided) and the use of accidentals. It has great appeal for children and provides a wonderful message of how the Holy Ghost operates in our lives.

There are many repeated tones and several repetitions of phrases that will simplify the learning of this composition. The melody line in measures one through six is similar to that in measures nine through fourteen. The first two measures of the next-to-last line are almost the same as the first measures of the last line. The "listens" should be sung in a hushed voice, the second time very softly. The composer repeats notes in some phrases to emphasize the words "Through a still small voice," "try to do what's right," and "Holy Spirit whispers." A number of accidentals transport the song from the key of F to B flat, with suggestions of other keys in between.

Teaching Suggestions:
1. Tell the children that Heavenly Father has given us some special people to guide us here on the earth, and have them name some of them (parents, teachers, grandparents, and so on). Ask them to listen to a song that tells about another special guide that Heavenly Father has sent to help us; then sing the song. You could invite someone to play the melody on a flute or violin so the children can enjoy the peaceful, quiet feeling this music provides.

2. Show the children a picture of a child being confirmed, or invite a child who has recently been baptized and confirmed to stand in front of the group. Ask what a person who is being confirmed is told to receive. Explain that the Holy Ghost is sometimes called the "still small voice," and discuss briefly with the children what we can do to have this Holy Spirit guide us.

3. Ask the children to listen to you sing the song to discover four ways that the Holy Ghost can help them (guide me, save me,

direct me, and protect me). Post word strips as they respond. Draw a simple melody chart of the tones on which these words are sung and ask the children to notice that the melody is the same for these four short phrases. Sing these phrases, while four children arrange the word strips in the correct order.

4. Invite the children to listen to the song and determine what word is repeated four times. Show an illustration of the melody pattern sung with the word "listen," and encourage them to sing the first phrase of "listens" softly and the second very softly.

5. Draw another melody pattern for the phrases where there are repeated notes and ask the children to listen and find the words that are sung with these melody patterns.

6. Share your feelings about how the Holy Ghost has helped you to know what choices you should make. Have a child read D&C 8:2. Help the children sing "The Still Small Voice" with expression and beauty.

The Things I Do 170

Words: L. Clair Likes
Music: Vanja Y. Watkins
First Line: I'm much too young to go abroad
Topics Indexed: Accountability, Chapel, Example, Friends,
*   Missionary Work, Preparation, Reverence*

This missionary song provides a valuable lesson to help boys and girls realize that their actions can influence those around them. Brother Likes says, "James and Paul seemed to point out the best, perhaps the only way that children could be missionaries: James with his 'Shew me thy faith without thy works, and I will shew thee my faith by my works' (James 2:18), and Paul with his admonition to Timothy, 'Be thou an example of the believers, in word, in conversation, in charity, in spirit, in faith, in purity' (1 Timothy 4:12). Hence the words of the song."

Vanja Watkins says that the melody is built upon the pentatonic scale — a five-tone scale with the same interval spacing as the notes played on a piano's five black keys. The first, second, and fourth verses are in the key of C and have an uneven rhythm pattern created by a quarter-/eighth-note combination throughout. The melody and rhythm of the fourth verse are the same as in the first two verses except for the final four measures. The third verse is prefaced by an interlude that modulates to the key of F, and, in contrast to the other verses, the beat is even with quarter notes for every tone. The melody of this verse is similar to the other verses.

Teaching Suggestions:

1. Fill a jar with water and ask the children how many drops of water they think are in the jar. Ask them, "If you were one drop of water, could you make a difference to the rest of the water in the jar?" Illustrate how one drop can make a difference by adding a drop of dark food coloring and pointing out how it flows through the whole jar. Help the children understand that what they do influences others. Sing the song for them, using a few simple pictures to illustrate the ideas. (Teach one verse at a time.)

2. Teach the verses, directing the children's listening and singing with questions such as these: "How does the song say I can show I know the word of God is true?" "The song says you are too young to go far away on a mission. What word does it use that means to travel far away?"

3. Invite the children to tap the uneven beat of verses one, two, and four. Help them notice that the third verse has a very even rhythm, and discuss why they think the composer might have written it this way. (It has a more dignified sound, going to church is special so the words about going to church have different music, it sounds more like a hymn.) Ask them if they notice anything else about verse three. (The melody is higher and somewhat different.)

4. After the children have learned the song, invite them to stand to sing the three verses with the uneven beat and sit with their arms folded on the verse with the even rhythm. Challenge them to decide when to sit and when to stand by listening to the music.

The Wise Man and the Foolish Man   281

Words and Music: Southern folk song
First Line: The wise man built his house upon the rock
Topics Indexed: Action Songs, Bible

This popular song is based on the parable that Jesus told of the wise man who hears the Lord's word and follows it, versus the foolish man who hears His word and does not follow it. (See Matthew 7:24–27.) It is a traditional Southern folk tune that is now in public domain. Some refinement in notation and accompaniment has been made on the version in the *Children's Songbook*.

Children of all ages love to sing the four verses of this song and participate in the suggested actions.

The song form is A B A C, with the first and third phrases being the same and the second phrase imitating the first phrase one tone lower on the scale. This repetition of melody makes the song easy to learn and remember.

Teaching Suggestions:

1. Read Matthew 7:24–27 and invite discussion about the meaning of Jesus' parable. Then sing the song to the children and invite them to join you as they become familiar with the words and melody.

2. Children will learn to sing this song quickly after hearing it a few times. Encourage them to participate in the actions that are suggested; this will help them respond to the message of the song.

The Word of Wisdom 154

Words and Music: Janice Kapp Perry
First Line: The Lord has revealed the Word of Wisdom
Topics Indexed: Health, Joseph Smith, Morality, Obedience,
    Two-part Songs, Word of Wisdom

The first verse of this song tells how we got the Word of Wisdom, and the second names the blessings promised to those who live it. Sister Perry says she received the inspiration for the words from a book by John A. Widtsoe, *A Principle with a Promise,* in which he listed the promises from living this commandment as (1) a clean body, (2) a clear mind, and (3) a spirit in tune with the Lord.

There are two verses in the song, each with a different melody, to be sung separately and then together in harmony. This device is an excellent one for teaching children to sing "parts." Older children particularly enjoy the challenge of the harmonization. The two verses include similar melody and rhythm patterns, but there is no repetition. The song moves smoothly, with sustained tones and somewhat of a swaying motion. All the tones are within the middle C to high C range.

Teaching Suggestions:

1. Draw lines on the chalkboard to represent the letters in "The Word of Wisdom." Challenge the children to discover what words these lines represent, giving them some clues as needed.

Tell them that the Doctrine and Covenants, section 89, tells about this principle, and that it is a principle with a promise. After they find the answer, help them understand what the "principle" (good health habits, especially regarding foods to eat) and the "promise" (a clean body, a clear mind, and a spirit in tune with the Lord) are in the Word of Wisdom.

2. Sing the first verse, asking the children to listen to find out how we got the Word of Wisdom. Invite them to sing the first phrase with you.

3. Teach the other words by asking the children a question, inviting them to listen to the song and find the answer, and encouraging them to sing that part with you. Questions might include these: "What does the song say we are promised?" "What two things must we do to get the beautiful blessings?" "What three blessings are promised to all who follow the word?" Use word strips to identify the three blessings stated in verse two.

4. After the children have learned the song, divide them into two groups and have them sing verse one, verse two, and then both verses together. You could teach verse one to one group and verse two to another group, and then bring them together to sing the song.

The World Is So Big 235

Words: Beverly Searle Spencer
Music: K. Newell Dayley
First Line: The world is so big and, oh, so round
Topics Indexed: Beautiful World, Creation, God's Love

With a background in teaching little ones in school and as a chorister and coordinator in Jr. Sunday School, Beverly Spencer recognized the need to include activity songs during the time young children attend church.This song is most appropriate for younger ones and could be sung in the nursery, in Primary, and in the home. Actions could be improvised, if desired.

For the *Children's Songbook*, the musical notation for "The World Is So Big" is simplified, the melody is incorporated into the accompaniment, and the time signature is changed from 3/4 to 6/8. This helps the melody flow smoothly and lightly.

The song has two verses; the second verse uses the same words as verse one except for four measures. The melody and words of measures one and two are repeated in measures nine and ten. Otherwise each musical phrase is different.

Teaching Suggestions:

1. Sing the song for the children on several occasions and invite them to join you as they learn it. Invite them to improvise actions as the words suggest. Display pictures that illustrate the things mentioned in the song to help them remember the words.

2. Encourage the children to name some of their blessings and some of God's beautiful creations each time they sing the song. Help them sing the notes accurately by pitch-level conducting and inviting them to conduct it with you.

The World Is So Lovely 233

Words and Music: Moiselle Renstrom
First Line: The world is so lovely! I'm glad as can be
Topics Indexed: Beautiful World, Creation, Family

This is a simple two-line melody that expresses, in childlike words, appreciation for our lovely world. Leaders, teachers, and parents will find that the song fits many teaching moments to emphasize the beauties of the world and the Lord's creations. Alternate words can be substituted in the first phrase of the second verse to include other things for which children can express gratitude: the day and the nighttime; the trees and the flowers, the fish and the animals; the birds and the insects, and so on. There is some alteration of the words for the *Children's Songbook* to name additional blessings and to identify that these are creations of the Lord.

The melody of the first line is built on the descending scale, and the melody of the second line is built on the ascending scale. The notes move steadily and smoothly on even beats and should be sung with connected tones.

Teaching Suggestions:

1. The little children will learn to sing this song quickly after hearing others sing it a few times. As you tell the story of the creation, sing the song as part of the lesson.

2. Tell the children how thankful you are for our beautiful world, and then sing the song for them to express your appreciation. Display pictures to illustrate the message.

3. Ask the children to tell what they are thankful for, and have the group sing the song after each child's expression. Use alternate words as suggested above, including children's ideas.

There Was Starlight on the Hillside 40

Words: Mabel Jones Gabbott
Music: Michael Finlinson Moody
First Line: There was starlight on the hillside
Topics Indexed: Christmas

This lovely Christmas song, with its beautiful harmony, paints a picture of the wonder and awe of the sacred night when Jesus was born. It is appropriate for children of all ages. The key has been raised from D to E flat in the *Children's Songbook*.

The first measures of lines one and two have the same melody, yet the harmony in the accompaniment makes them seem different. The tones of the last phrase move down the scale from B flat to E flat. The beat pattern of the first and third phrases is the same, and the others are similar. Even though there are several uneven beats created by a dotted-quarter note and an eighth note, the song flows smoothly in a connected style.

Teaching Suggestions:
1. Recite the three verses as a poem, displaying pictures of the events occurring at Jesus' birth as they are mentioned. Tell the children that the writers of this song wanted to tell their friends of the wonders of Jesus' birth through this Christmas carol. Sing the song and let some of them hold the pictures as you sing.
2. Let the children dramatize the song by dressing in simple costumes as shepherds, angels, Joseph, and Mary with the baby Jesus.
3. Help the children feel the sacredness of the events on the night of Jesus' birth by encouraging them to sing sweetly and softly, with expression.

This Is God's House 30

Words: Louise M. Oglevee
Music: William G. Oglevee
First Line: This is God's house, and he is here today
Topics Indexed: Chapel, Prayer, Prayer Songs, Reverence

This song creates a peaceful and reverent mood as a prayer song in Primary opening or closing exercises or in the classroom.

It was written in the early 1900s when Dr. Oglevee was pastor in the Presbyterian Church in Rock Island, Illinois. Mary Louise Oglevee Rack, a granddaughter of the Oglevees, says, "As a granddaughter, I attended Sunday School in his church from earliest childhood. Each Sunday the hour was begun with this song . . . a reminder of what was most important about our being gathered at that time and place."

The melody of the song is mostly within the five-note range from F up to high C. In the first line the notes move from F up to C, with some repeated tones. In the second line the notes move down from C to F, with some skips and repeated tones. Each phrase is different melodically and rhythmically, yet the song moves smoothly and naturally.

Teaching Suggestions:

1. Show the children a picture of a meetinghouse and ask them whose house it is. After they respond, sing the song to them, repeat the question, and invite them to sing the answer with you. Ask them if Father in heaven hears us sing and pray. Sing the answer and encourage them to join you in singing this last phrase.

2. Discuss with the children appropriate behavior in the meetinghouse, which is Heavenly Father's house. You could have them sing the song each week for several weeks, in the opening or closing exercises or in the classroom, to remind them to sit reverently and prepare to listen to the lessons that are taught.

This Is My Beloved Son 76

Words: Marvin K. Gardner
Music: Vanja Y. Watkins
First Line: Jesus entered Jordan's waters
Topics Indexed: Book of Mormon, Heavenly Father, Jesus
    Christ — Baptism, Jesus Christ — Son of God, Joseph
    Smith, Restoration of the Gospel, Scriptures, Testimony

Marvin Gardner tells how he came to write the words to "This Is My Beloved Son": "As Church members, we often bear our testimonies of the Savior. In the scriptures, our Heavenly Father has also borne his testimony of Jesus Christ: 'This is my Beloved Son. Hear Him!' One day, I was thinking how wonderful it would have been to be present at the River Jordan, in the Nephite city of Bountiful, or in the Sacred Grove, and to hear the Father speak these words of testimony. And then I realized that as we read of these events in the scriptures, we can be there in our minds and hear the Father's words. More importantly, any time we read the scriptures with a sincere heart, the Holy Ghost can bear witness to us of the Father's testimony of Jesus Christ. 'This Is My Beloved Son' tells stories from the New Testament, the Book of Mormon, and the Pearl of Great Price—and then applies the principle of revelation and testimony to our lives today."

Each of the four verses tells a story of its own, but the final phrase unites them all with, "This is My Beloved Son. Hear Him!" There is a two-measure introduction, a one-measure interlude between verses, and a final ending for verse four that concludes on F instead of A. The piano part incorporates a flowing accompaniment with simple but rich harmony. The song could be performed as a special program number. All but the very young children can learn to sing it.

Teaching Suggestions:

1. Have three children or three leaders each tell briefly one of the following stories: the baptism of Jesus, the first appearance of the resurrected Jesus to the Nephites, and the appearance of the Father and the Son to Joseph Smith in the Sacred Grove. Each should end his or her story by reading the words from the scriptures that the Father spoke to introduce the Son. After each story is told, sing the verse that tells of the event. Ask the children how these stories are the same. Explain that the Father showed his great love for his Son when he introduced him in this way. Post a word strip: "This is My Beloved Son. Hear Him."

2. Teach the first three verses (probably in more than one teaching session) by asking questions, using pictures of the events, and posting word strips of keywords. Invite the children to sing the last phrase of each verse with you as you pitch-level conduct it.

3. Tell the children that even though we were not present at Jesus' baptism, at his appearance to the Nephites, or in the Sacred Grove, we can still have the Father witness to us that Jesus is his Beloved Son. Ask them to listen to the fourth verse to learn how. After they have responded, explain that as we read Jesus' words in the scriptures, the Father can tell us in our hearts that Jesus is truly his Beloved Son and that we should listen to his teachings. Invite the children to sing the words of the last verse with you.

To Be a Pioneer 218

Words and Music: Ruth Muir Gardner; arranged by Vanja Y. Watkins
First Line: You don't have to push a handcart
Topics Indexed: Descants, Pioneers

This is a spirited number with an optional descant that adds rhythm and appeal, especially for the older children. The idea that pioneers have special qualities, other than pushing a handcart, makes their example more relevant for children today.

The melody of the song is uncomplicated and natural. The musical phrases are each different, and there are few repetitions of rhythm patterns. The first verse names some things the early pioneers did that children today do not have to do. The second verse names qualities, such as courage and faith, that children do need to have to be pioneers today. The melody is within the octave range from middle C to high C. The optional descant includes some repetition of rhythm and notes.

Teaching Suggestions:

1. Ask the children to discover what attributes you need to be a pioneer from stories you will briefly tell. Tell a story about courage, such as "She Walked Across the Plains," Valiant B manual, p. 124, and a story about a modern pioneer, such as "Manu," Valiant B manual, p. 230.

2. Post two words on the chalkboard: "do" and "don't." Ask the children to find three things that you *don't* have to do to be a pioneer while you sing the first verse. Then ask them to discover three things that you *do* have to have to be a pioneer as you sing the second verse. Post word strips under the words "do" and "don't" as they respond.

3. Teach some of the children the marchlike chant of the descant. Have them march in place or around the room as they sing it. After both parts are learned, have the children sing the parts together.

To Get Quiet 275

Words and Music: Moiselle Renstrom
First Line: One, two, I stretch up tall
Topics Indexed: Action Songs, Quiet

This is a simple rest tune for the children in the nursery or the younger age classes. It invites them to participate in a musical activity in preparation for sitting quietly.

The two-line song includes some repetition of melody and rhythm and moves smoothly within a six-note range. It is easily learned by rote as the little ones imitate the leader's words and actions.

Teaching Suggestion:

Sing the song for the children, improvising actions as suggested by the words, and invite them to participate with you as you sing it several times. They will enjoy singing it often.

To Think about Jesus 71

Words: Mabel Jones Gabbott
Music: Robert Cundick
First Line: It shouldn't be hard to sit very still
Topics Indexed: Atonement, Jesus Christ — Ministry, Quiet,
  Reverence, Sacrament

This beautiful sacrament song has an almost haunting mood and is appropriate for a reverence song or as an Easter number. For older children the words "though I am small" could be changed to "when I've grown tall." Mabel Jones Gabbott says, "After much prayer and study, I said to myself, 'It shouldn't be hard to write about Jesus and reverence.' The words gave me my first line, and the ideas and words followed quickly."

The song is in the key of C minor, ending with a C major chord. Composer Robert Cundick points out, "The music is reminiscent of music written many years ago in modal harmony. The melody uses several repetitions of phrases to help children learn it with comparative ease. It is written in the style of a folk song." The musical form of the piece is A, A, B, B; A, B. Phrases one and two are the same, and phrases three and four are the same. These two phrases are repeated in the chorus (except for the last measure). The melody moves smoothly with connected tones. The dynamic markings, "slower," "a tempo," and fermata will help the singers perform the song with expression and meaning.

Teaching Suggestions:

1. Ask several children to come to the front and try to do some things that are hard to do, such as unscrew a tight lid from a jar or solve a math equation. Ask them to name things that are hard

for them to do. Then post the word strip, "It shouldn't be hard," and ask them to listen to a song that tells what shouldn't be hard to do.

2. Show a picture or pictures of Jesus, sing the chorus for the children, and invite them to sing it with you. Teach the other phrases by asking questions, singing the song, accepting answers, and inviting the children to sing that part with you. Use pictures that are suggested by the lyrics.

3. Divide the children into two groups and have one sing the words "It shouldn't be hard" and the other finish each phrase. They could count how many times these words are sung in each verse.

4. Draw an illustration of the two two-measure melody phrases and help the children notice that the first phrase has notes that move downward, like climbing down stairs. The other phrase, introduced in line two, measure two, moves upward in steps. Ask them to find the words that are sung when they move up the steps and those sung when they step down. Point out the identical sounds of the phrase endings, except for the last phrase. Invite them to pitch-level conduct the song to help them feel the direction of the melody.

5. Invite the children to listen to the piano accompaniment and ask them how the music makes them feel. Tell them that the composer wrote the music in a minor key to suggest the sacredness and wonder of Jesus' life and death. Have them listen for the last chord of the song, which changes to the major key to suggest the peace that comes from thinking about Jesus.

6. Show a picture of the sacrament being passed, or show real sacrament trays, and discuss with the children why we should be reverent during the sacrament. They might conclude that we are quiet and reverent because we take the sacrament to remind us of what Jesus did while he was on the earth.

Truth from Elijah   90

Words and Music: Vanja Y. Watkins
First Line: The hearts of the children have turned to their fathers
Topics Indexed: Bible, Family History, Temples

This song about genealogy work has a Jewish (Old Testament) flavor to evoke the image of the prophet Elijah, who was the last one before Christ to hold the sealing power of the Melchizedek

Priesthood. He appeared to Joseph Smith to restore this power to the earth again. The music is written in E minor with the last chord resolving to the major. The song is probably more suitable for older children because of the mature message that it presents. However, all children will enjoy the interesting musical phrases and the repeated and rhyming words.

The musical form is A A B B A. The song has five four-measure phrases; the first, second, and fifth are the same, as are the third and fourth phrases. There are some variations in the phrase endings. Because of the interesting sequences and musical progressions in the song, there is a feeling of motion and turning, which relates to the message of the lyrics. The harmonies in the accompaniment follow the pattern. The climax of the song is reached in the middle of the sixth line on the word "eternity," which should be sung with emphasis.

Teaching Suggestions:

1. Show the children a picture of a family tree or a pedigree chart. Tell them that trying to find our ancestors is called family history or genealogy work. Have a child read D&C 2:1–2, and ask the children to find words in the scripture that mean being interested in family history. ("And the hearts of the children shall turn to their fathers.") Ask them to listen to you sing a song that uses these words, and also listen to discover the name of the prophet from whom we have learned this truth.

2. Invite the children to clap the rhythm of the third and fourth phrases, beginning with "And we as the children" and going through "us for eternity." Write the words to these phrases on the chalkboard and have the children underline or circle the words that come on the first beat of each measure. Ask a child to shake a tambourine on these downbeats as you or the children sing.

3. Teach phrases one and five (which are almost the same) first, and have the children sing these with you as you sing the entire song. Teach the other words through questions, pictures (children, ancestors, heart, Elijah, the temple), melody illustrations, and by listening for rhyming words.

4. Explain to the children that the music has a Jewish or Israelitish flavor because the story of Elijah is in the Old Testament. Invite them to move to the music—they could turn their bodies to the phrases with "turned" and "learned" in them.

Two Happy Feet 270

Words: Norma Madsen Thomas
Music: Barbara Boyer Obray
First Line: I have two happy little feet to take me where I go
Topics Indexed: Action Songs, Happiness, Quiet, Reverence

Norma Madsen Thomas wrote the words of this happy action song while she was a Primary president in San Diego, to help the children to be more reverent. Her inspiration was her own little children and her love of reverence for the house of the Lord. A Primary co-worker and friend, Barbara Obray, set the words to music, and they used the song in their Primary, where the children enjoyed singing and moving to the little composition. "Two Happy Feet" is especially enjoyed by the younger children in the nursery, the younger Primary classes, and in Sharing Time.

The first and third musical phrases are the same and the second and fourth are similar. The rhythm has mostly even beats, with some dotted-quarter/eighth-note combinations to add variety. The composer achieved the feeling of a walking motion in the music.

Teaching Suggestions:
1. Small children will learn to sing this song as they hear it sung. Improvise actions to help them learn it more quickly.
2. Have the children hold hands and follow the leader around the room as they sing the song. They could skip, hop, and be very quiet as the words suggest.

Two Little Eyes 268

Words and Music: Moiselle Renstrom
First Line: Two little eyes that blink, blink, blink
Topics Indexed: Action Songs

This charming activity song has become a favorite of young children everywhere. It is most often sung in the nursery and in the younger age classes.

The melodies of the first and third lines are very similar, as are the melodies of the second and fourth lines, so that the song is easy for little ones to learn and remember. They enjoy the actions that the song generates.

Teaching Suggestions:

1. Sing the song to the children, improvising actions suggested by the words. They will soon participate in doing the actions and singing the song.

2. Make a poster with a picture of a child's head with "blinking eyes," made by taping on cardboard eyelids that can be moved up and down by strings. The children can take turns making the eyelids "blink" while they sing the song.

We Are Different   263

Words and Music: Patricia Kelsey Graham
First Line: I know you, and you know me
Topics Indexed: Friends, Kindness, Love, Service, Special Needs

This song teaches that although we are different, we can know, help, and love each other. It celebrates the uniqueness of each person and is appropriate for children with special needs. The syncopated, calypso beat is catchy and very appealing. Although the rhythm is different and unusual, children will be drawn to the song as they hear it and learn to sing the beats. This idea correlates with the message of the song.

Lines one and three are identical, both in music and words, and lines two and four contain musical patterns that are the same. The syncopated rhythm is the distinctive characteristic. The children will learn to feel comfortable with it as they clap or tap while it is sung or played. The leader should learn it thoroughly before introducing it to the children.

Teaching Suggestions:

1. Show pictures of the sun and the sea and ask the children to tell how they are different. Invite two children to come to the front, and ask the group to tell how these children are the same and how they are different. After the children respond, say, "That's the way it is supposed to be," and then sing the first verse.

2. Bring a child to the front and face him or her while you sing the song and do simple actions such as pointing to the child, pointing to yourself, holding hands, and so on. Repeat this presentation with other children, and then invite them to turn and sing the song with a partner close by, using the same actions.

3. Tell the children that there are three things we can do to

understand other people: know them, help them, and love them. Teach the first line of all verses (with the help of word strips "know," "help," and "love"), the third line, and the last line, which is the same for all three verses. Invite the children to sing these parts, with you singing the second line alone, until they learn all the words.

4. Divide the group into two sections, or pair the children off with partners, and have them face each other. Have the first group or person sing the first part of the phrase ("I know you"), and the second group or person sing the last half of the phrase ("and you know me"). Then have both groups sing the second and last lines together.

5. Invite the children to tap the rhythm with you and have some of them play rhythm instruments to the syncopated beat.

We Are Reverent 27

Words: Mabel Jones Gabbott
Music: A. Laurence Lyon
First Line: Quiet as deep waters run
Topics Indexed: Quiet, Reverence

Laurence Lyon says, "There need to be more quiet moments in life, moments to reflect and meditate about the important things of life, such as the life of the Savior. . . . This song teaches reverence through a comtemplation of the quiet things in nature as an example to remember when one is being quiet." Though the song is short and uncomplicated, children will appreciate the beauty of the music and the imagery that the words bring to mind.

There are no repetitions of melody phrases, though the first and second measures are similar; there are some lovely harmony and chordal progressions in the song. The rhythm of the first, second, and fourth measures is the same. The leap of a sixth downward and back up (B down to D) in the first and second measures will need to be practiced. There are three sequential broken triads, in measures three and four (D, B, G; C, A, F sharp; and B, G, E) that will be an interesting teaching element. The song should be sung peacefully and unhurriedly, and the accompanist should be aware of the quarter notes in the alto voice that should be held while two eighth notes are played.

Teaching Suggestions:

1. Ask the children how they would sound if they were a shadow or a distant star. Ask them to name some things that are very quiet and draw pictures or pantomime their ideas. (These activities make the idea of being quiet more interesting.) Ask the accompanist to share something quiet and beautiful with them by playing the song. Comment on the peacefulness of the music and the reverent feeling it gives, and ask the children to name the quiet things that they thought of. Tell them that you know three things that are quiet that you will sing about. Sing the first verse and post pictures of deep water, a sunny meadow, and a reverent child. Include word strips of keywords.

2. Invite the children to sing the first verse with you. Pitch-level conduct to help them sense the big skips. Invite them to move their arms with you. Teach the second verse in a similar way.

3. Using four small charts, make a bar graph of the melody of each of the four measures, each horizontal bar representing one note. Mix the charts up and have the children listen to you sing the song to determine the order in which the musical phrases come.

4. Encourage the children to sing "We Are Reverent" softly and slowly and with expression.

We Bow Our Heads 25

Words: Anna Johnson
Music: Alexander Schreiner
First Line: We bow our heads and close our eyes
Topics Indexed: Gratitude, Prayer, Prayer Songs

This is a familiar reverence song for little children in the Church and is outlined to be sung in preparation for prayer in several of the younger-age Primary manuals. It is simple and singable, with a message that the children quickly understand.

There are four melodic phrases in the song. Though there is some similarity in phrases one and three and in phrases two and four, each is different. Measures three and seven contain several repeated F notes. Except for one note, the rhythm of line one is the same as line two.

Teaching Suggestions:

1. Ask one or two children to pantomime bowing their heads and closing their eyes, and ask the others to guess what these children are doing. Invite all the children to bow their heads and close their eyes as you sing the song. Repeat it, and encourage them to sing with you.

2. Ask the children to listen to verse one again and find four things we do when we pray (bow heads, close eyes, say prayer, thank Father). Teach the words to the second verse by asking questions, singing the song, accepting answers, and inviting the children to sing that part of the song with you.

3. Show pictures of a child bowing his or her head in prayer, of blessings we share, and of children's activities at home, school, or play, and discuss with the children what is portrayed in the pictures. Sing the song several times as part of the discussion to clarify the meaning of the words.

We Welcome You 256

Words: Ruth Muir Gardner and Lois Coombs Sprunt
Music: Marjorie Castleton Kjar
First Line: We welcome you today to Primary
Topics Indexed: Primary, Teachers, Worldwide Church

This song was originally written for the celebration of the 100th birthday of the Primary organization. It began with the words "A happy birthday to the Primary," and became the theme song of birthday celebrations in Primaries all over the world. For the *Children's Songbook,* the music and Primary committees wanted the song to have a wider application, and so the writers composed additional words for the first eight measures to give it an added dimension as a welcome song. The original words are printed at the bottom of the page so Primaries can continue to use it for Primary birthday celebrations. The song brings feelings of history as it recounts an important occasion and opens opportunities for leaders to talk about the early Primary organization and how the Church has grown. Children of today like hearing about the lessons that were taught in those early pioneer days. The first eight measures of the song can be sung alone when a short "welcome to Primary" message is appropriate.

The song is written with an introductory eight-measure section that is repeated for the conclusion. The largest segment, beginning with "When Primary first had its start," is sixteen measures long and has an A B A B song form. The first four of these measures are the same as measures nine through twelve, and measures five through eight are the same as measures thirteen through sixteen, with minor variations in the last two measures. The rhythm is mostly even, with an ongoing beat that gives the music energy and motion. There are no difficult intervals or challenging melody patterns, except for two octave skips in the beginning segment. Three fermatas and a slower tempo are indicated in the music to encourage emphasis and expression.

Teaching Suggestions:

1. Briefly tell the story of how Aurelia Rogers organized the first Primary. Sing eight measures of the song, beginning with "When Primary first had its start" (through "choose the right"), and ask the children to identify five things that children in that first Primary were taught. You may need to sing this section several times for them to discover all five (do his part, use good manners, be polite, love the Lord, choose the right). Post word strips of keywords to help them. Invite them to listen to the song again, arrange the word strips in the correct order, and then sing this part of the song with you, repeating as necessary.

2. Ask the children to think of what they are taught in Primary today. Ask them if they learn the same things as in the first Primary. Then sing the next eight measures, beginning with "Now every week in Primary" (through "who come that day"). Ask the children to discover four things the song says we do in Primary today (learn the gospel, sing, pray, share). Post word strips of keywords to represent these things. Invite the children to sing this part of the song with you, repeating as necessary.

3. To teach the first section of the song, you and some of the teachers could sing as you go around the room, shaking hands with each child in rhythm to the music. Then assign one child to be the greeter on each row and have this child shake hands with each of the other children on the row in rhythm to the music. Invite the children to join in the singing as they repeat this several times and choose additional children to be the greeters. This part of the song could be sung to children who visit the Primary.

4. Discuss briefly with the children how they show good manners, how to be polite, how they show love for the Lord, and so on. A child or children could stand in front and pantomime a behavior for each one of these actions to remind them of the words.

5. In celebration of the birthday of Primary in August, draw a picture of a birthday cake with candles. Use the candles as word strips for important words and phrases.

6. Draw pictures of red, yellow, and blue balloons, or blow up real balloons, and tie words of the song to the balloons or write them on the paper ones. Have some of the children come to the front and hold the balloons in the order in which the words come in the song.

We'll Bring the World His Truth   172

Words and Music: Janice Kapp Perry
First Line: We have been born, as Nephi of old
Topics Indexed: Book of Mormon, Commitment, Missionary
Work, Obedience, Parents, Preparation, Prophets, Worldwide
Church, Worth of a Child

Janice Kapp Perry wrote this song in 1983 in response to the request of a stake in Provo, Utah, for a "missionary fight song" for a 200–voice children's choir to perform at stake conference in BYU's Marriott Center. Later she was asked to add a fourth verse to express the idea that we have the obligation of spreading the gospel to the world because we are of the seed of Abraham. This verse is not printed in the *Children's Songbook*. It reads as follows:

> *We are God's children. We have received*
> *The blessings promised to Abraham's seed.*
> *We'll share the gospel. This is our quest*
> *'Til ev'ry nation on earth is blessed.*

The verse and the chorus each contain sixteen measures with the musical form of A B A C—the first and third phrases are the same, and the second and fourth phrases are different. The notes flow smoothly and naturally within the octave from middle C to high C. The rhythm is mostly even. Of rhythmical interest are the two eighth notes on the word "Helaman" in the chorus. The children will learn these beat patterns more easily if they clap or tap them several times. The largest interval in the music is the sixth from middle C up to A that occurs twice in the chorus. The song includes a four-measure coda that completes it with firmness and conviction. This should be sung slowly, broadly, and emphatically.

Teaching Suggestions:

1. In a Sharing Time, discuss Nephi and Helaman's army so that the song will have more significance for the children.

2. Show a map of the world, or bring a world globe. Tell the children that there is something very important that they can bring to the world. Have them guess what it might be. Have the scriptures in a covered basket or box and invite them to open it to discover what they can bring the world. Invite them to sing the last phrase with you: "to bring the world his truth." Then sing the entire chorus and direct them to join you on the last phrase.

3. Display a sheet of paper on which are drawn 100 stick figures. Discuss how many people this is. Then unfold nineteen more sheets with 100 stick figures on each to help them imagine how many were in Helaman's army. (Draw the figures on one sheet of paper and photocopy it to make the twenty sheets, or you could have the children help draw the figures.) Emphasize that none of these warriors was harmed because they obeyed the teachings of their parents and of the Lord. Have the children sing the first phrase of the chorus.

4. Teach the chorus by asking questions, singing, accepting answers, and inviting the children to sing these parts. You could ask: "What will we bring the world?" "Whose missionaries will we be?" "When have we been taught?" "What are we like?" Draw illustrations of the four melody phrases in the chorus, and ask the children to discover which two phrases have the same notes and what words are sung with each of the phrases.

5. Teach the words to the verses in the same way, with questions and by helping the children observe the movement of the melody. Post colored paper circles representing the notes of the verse, placed high or low to represent the melody line. Using a small paper world globe, move it along the notes as they hum the tune (like "follow the bouncing ball"). When the globe comes to a stop on a note, ask them to identify the word sung with that note.

6. To help the children sing the song with expression and dynamics, have them hold their hands close together and move them farther apart as the melody moves up the scale, singing with more volume. As the melody moves down the scale, have them move their hands closer together and sing more softly.

We're All Together Again   259

Words: Traditional; adapted
Music: Satis N. Coleman
First Line: We're all together again
Topics Indexed: Singing

This is an activity song of welcome for children of all ages. The copyright goes back to 1963 when it was published in the school series *Music for Young Americans*.

The melody and words introduced in the first line are repeated in the second line with notes one tone higher on the scale. The rhythm is the same in lines one, two, and four, and the words in these lines are almost the same. The leader could use this as an activity song by having the children clap the rhythm, tap their feet, or march around the room.

Teaching Suggestions:

1. The children will learn to sing this song by rote as they hear it repeated several times.

2. Divide the children into two groups and have one group sing "We're here, we're here!" the three times that it occurs. Have the other group sing the other phrases.

3. Have the children lock elbows and move from side to side during the words "We're all together again," then stamp their feet on the words "We're here, we're here."

Westward Ho!   217

Words: Miriam H. Kirkell
Music: Marcia Davidson
First Line: Over the winding trail forward we go
Topics Indexed: Ostinatos, Pioneers

This is a pioneer song that the Church has published by permission. For the *Children's Songbook* the key has been lowered from G minor to E minor. There are also a few word changes so that the syllables match the notes more closely. The minor key captures the feeling of weariness and hardship that the pioneers experienced, yet the melody and steady accompaniment seem to typify their determination and strength. The song is appealing and challenging for older children. The lyrics might be difficult for younger children, but they can join in singing the "Westward ho's." The ostinato will offer an opportunity for the older boys and girls to sing a two-part harmony.

The rhythm is steady and even, and yet the music has a swaying motion with the accompaniment imitating the rocking action of wagon wheels. The melody of the first and fifth measures is the same, as is the melody of the third and seventh measures. There are two octave jumps in the first line. The climax is reached in the last line of verse three, which should end with two strong "Westward ho's."

Teaching Suggestions:

1. Draw a simple outline of the United States with a trail marked from the midwest to Utah. Put a covered wagon on the trail and decorate the map with word strips made in the shape of bushes, buffalo, Indian teepees, rivers, and so on. Draw the children's attention to the word strip that says "Westward ho" and explain to them that the pioneers used these words to encourage each other as they traveled west. Ask them to count how many times you sing these words in the first verse.

2. Make four small melody charts, each one showing the direction of the notes for one of the "Westward ho's." Help the children discover that two of these melody patterns are the same and the others are different. Sing the song again and have the children arrange the charts in the correct order. Then ask them to sing these words as you pitch-level conduct. Sing the three verses and have them join in singing the "Westward ho's." For variety ask the girls to sing the first set of "Westward ho's" and the boys the second.

3. Prepare six word strips, each containing the words of the first half of a line from the song, and give them to six Primary classes. Have the classes sing their lines in turn, with everyone singing the "Westward ho's." Ask them to exchange word strips until they learn all the words to the song.

4. Teach the optional ostinato to a small group of older children and have the children sing the two parts together.

When Grandpa Comes 201

Words and Music: Marian Major
First Line: It's always fun when grandpa comes
Topics Indexed: Grandparents

This well-loved song is about the happy times when grandpa comes to visit. Alternate words allow the children to sing about grandma also. The catchy, playful music is fun to sing.

The rhythm is the same in almost every measure—quarter/eighth, quarter/eighth note—which produces a bouncy pulse throughout. Although there are many similarities in the note patterns, the only duplicate melodies are in the first two measures of lines one and three. Of interest are the repeated notes that occur six times in the first three lines, giving emphasis to the words sung with these notes. There is a wide tonal range in the song, from middle C up to high E, and the notes seem to bounce up and down within this range.

Teaching Suggestions:

1. Sing the song for the children omitting the word "grandpa" each time it occurs. Ask them to guess what the missing word is. After they find the answer, insert the word "grandpa" as you repeat the song. Ask them to sing the song and substitute "grandma."

2. Ask the children to share what they do with their grandpa or grandma when they visit with them. Bring the discussion around to the point that it is "always fun for everyone when grandpa comes." Invite them to sing this last phrase with you.

3. Tell the children that there are six times in the song when a note is repeated three times. Draw this pattern on the chalkboard six times and ask them to clap with you each time these repeated notes come in the music. Challenge them to discover what words are sung on these notes as you sing it again. Write the words (or place simple pictures) above the note patterns as the children detect what they are. You may need to sing the song several times for them to find all six. Have them join you in singing the last line each time you sing the song.

3. Make simple circle puppets, two for each child. Let them draw faces of grandpa and grandma in the circles and mount them on wooden craft sticks or tongue depressors.

When He Comes Again 82

Words and Music: Mirla Greenwood Thayne
First Line: I wonder, when he comes again
Topics Indexed: Example, Jesus Christ—Blesses Children,
  Jesus Christ—Second Coming, Preparation, Service

Some years ago, Mirla Greenwood Thayne was asked to compose and direct a presentation for her Provo ward's annual children's spring conference. The final scene was of Jesus' visit to the Nephites, his blessing the children, and the prophecies that he would return to the earth. Realizing that she must include some speaking parts for the tiny tots, she quickly wrote twelve two-line parts for them. Together they became one poem about the anticipated Second Coming. Some time later, after the successful presentation of the program, Sister Thayne sat at her piano. "A tune formed in my mind to be transferred to my fingers," she recounts. "I played the melody over and over. 'A song without words?' I questioned. Then the words, spoken by the little children in the Primary presentation, were rekindled in my memory. There was a wedding of words and of music as I found them to be a perfect match." The song quickly became a favorite in Primaries all over the world.

One Sunday morning in April 1961, when Mirla Thayne was very ill with cancer and waiting for surgery, she turned on her television to watch general conference. She says, "I . . . turned on the television just in time to hear the soul-stirring tones of the renowned Salt Lake Tabernacle organ playing a familiar prelude. On the screen appeared one of the sweetest young boys I had ever seen. His countenance was radiant as he sang the words, 'I wonder, when he comes again.' I could do nothing but weep— so touched—so humbled." President McKay said in his talk that day that the sister who wrote this song was very ill, and he blessed her that she would have her health restored. Miraculously, her operation was successful.

There are six four-measure phrases in the song. The first part of the first phrase is repeated in the second phrase and again in the beginning of the fifth phrase. Some other melody patterns are also repeated, and there are many large interval jumps upward and downward. The rhythm alternates between measures of even and uneven beats. The leader should help the children understand the message and sing with expression and appropriate dynamics.

Teaching Suggestions:

1. Show the children a picture depicting the second coming of Jesus and discuss what is happening in the picture and what they think might happen when Jesus comes again: Will angels sing? What season of the year might he come? Will a special star shine in the heavens? Ask them to sing the first phrase, "I wonder when he comes again," as you sing the entire song.

2. Show pictures of Jesus as he gathered the children around him in the Holy Land and in America. Ask the children to imagine what it might have been like to be with Jesus at those times. Sing the song again, and ask them to find what Jesus said "in days gone by." After their responses, have them join in singing the last phrase. Ask a child to read Matthew 19:14 to the group.

3. Continue teaching the words by asking questions, singing the song, accepting responses, and inviting the children to sing the phrases with you. Use pictures to illustrate important words. Have the children place the pictures in the correct order as they listen to the song. Teach it in eight-measure segments.

4. Have the children tap or clap the rhythm. Illustrate the four main beat patterns of the measures and help them distinguish which words are sung to each. Make line drawings of the direction of the melody of some of the phrases and have the children determine which words belong to which melodies.

5. Help the children sing with expression and thoughtfulness, noting the fermatas and the slower tempo at the end.

When I Am Baptized 103

Words and Music: Nita Dale Milner
First Line: I like to look for rainbows
Topics Indexed: Baptism, Commitment, Morality

Nita Milner says, "Matthew [her son] was baptized two years before [this song] was written, but I will always remember how his face shone that day, and the simple sincerity of his testimony when he was confirmed. A discussion with him about repentance reminded me that no matter what our age, each of us needs to keep trying to be the best we can be. . . . One of my Primary teachers taught me as a child that the great flood of Noah's time was the earth's baptism by water. I think of that story when I see a rainbow. I think it is important to teach that baptism is a wonderful gift from our Heavenly Father—an opportunity to become clean again and, through repentance, keep our lives that way."

The song has two verses and a chorus. The two phrases of the verse are the same musically, and in the chorus the rhythm of the phrases is almost identical though the melody is different. The interval of F to high C is repeated in several places, particularly in the chorus. The melody moves smoothly on even beats throughout. The climax, and point of greatest expression, is in the third-to-last measure, when the melody rises to its highest pitch, D, followed by a fermata on F.

Teaching Suggestions:

1. Ask the children to describe what the earth smells and looks like after a rainstorm. Briefly tell the story of Noah, emphasizing that the earth was cleansed by the flood and no unclean thing was left on the earth. Show a picture of a rainbow and tell of God's promise about it. (Genesis 9:8–17.) Show pictures of rain and of Noah and the ark.

2. Sing the first verse and ask the children to discover what it is that I want to be as clean as the earth right after rain (my life). Sing the second verse and ask them what I must do to have my wrongs washed away.

3. Display a rainbow made of five curved strips of color, wide enough to place words on them, to represent the phrase lines. (Each phrase is four measures long except the last two, which are two measures.) As you sing the phrases of the song, move your hand across each strip of color. Have the children trace the phrases in the air.

4. Ask questions, sing the song, accept answers, have the children repeat that part of the song, and place important words on the colored strips where they occur in the phrases. Make the word strips in the shape of raindrops or small clouds. Ask questions such as these: "What do I like to look for?" "What do I ponder on?" "What do I want my life to be as clean as?" "What else do I want to be?" "Why do I want to be the best I can?" Help the children find which words are sung at the top of the rainbow phrases and which are sung at the beginning or end of the phrases.

5. Invite a child who has recently been baptized to express the feelings he or she had at that time. Share your testimony about the importance of baptism.

When I Go to Church 157

Words and Music: Faye Glover Petersen
First Line: I always have a happy feeling when I go to church
Topics Indexed: Chapel, Happiness, Quiet, Reverence, Sabbath

This song expresses the happy feelings children have when they go to church and participate in the activities there. It is frequently used as a reverence song.

The piano begins with a four-measure, chimelike introduction, which sets the mood for the song. There are three four-measure phrases, none of which are the same, except for the beginning of the first and third phrases. The rhythm is even and constant, with mostly eighth notes. There are opportunities for expression and dynamics in this little song, and the children will enjoy the louds and softs, along with the changes in tempo that the music seems to demand.

Teaching Suggestions:

1. Show pictures of a baseball game, a picnic, a circus, or other recreational activities, and one of a church house. Tell the children that going to all these places gives us a happy feeling, but that you want them to listen to some music and tell which of these places it makes them think of. Have the pianist play the chimelike introduction. After the children have responded, tell them that when we go to church we have a reverent, spiritual kind of a happy feeling. Invite them to listen to the song and join you in singing the words "When I go to church."

2. Make a picture of a church house with doors and windows. Behind each opening, put a picture of one of the words in the song (organ, seat, teachers, friends, and so on). (Find ideas for this illustration in the *Friend,* June 1991.) Help the children learn the lyrics by opening the windows to find the pictures that represent the words as they are sung.

3. For variety, invite the children to sing the phrases, getting louder and softer as the melody moves up and down the scale, then "whisper-singing" the phrases "When I go to church."

When Jesus Christ Was Baptized 102

Words and Music: Jeanne P. Lawler
First Line: When Jesus Christ was baptized
Topics Indexed: Jesus Christ—Baptism, Jesus Christ—
Example

Jeanne Lawler says, "Often I would wonder what it was like when Jesus Christ was baptized . . . and I wish I had been there and heard the voice from heaven and saw what others saw, and felt what they felt at that great event. That is why I wrote this song, and I wanted to put those feelings in the hearts of children who are going to be baptized or are reflecting on the time they were baptized." The song is beautiful and simple, yet it carries much information for children to learn relative to baptism. There is some revision of the lyrics for the *Children's Songbook* to relate the message to the child's own baptism, to the Savior's example, and to the presence of the three members of the Godhead at Jesus' baptism. The song can be sung at a baptismal service or in any gathering where there is a discussion of the purpose and meaning of this ordinance.

There are some interesting melodic sequences in this song. The first two-measure melody is repeated on different steps of the scale throughout the piece, sometimes with variation. The melody of the last four measures is the same as that in measures five through eight, so that the song form is A B C B. The two-measure rhythm pattern with the pickup beat introduced at the beginning is also restated throughout the song.

Teaching Suggestions:

1. Ask the children to share experiences about their baptism and what made it special for them. Tell the story of Jesus' baptism, show a picture of it, and have a child read Matthew 3:13–17.

2. Sing the song to the children and ask them who the song says were present there (the Godhead). Ask them to listen to it again and discover who the three members of the Godhead are that were present there. As the children identify them, write the names, or place a picture, on each of three cards. Do not use a picture of Jesus to represent Heavenly Father. Explain that the dove was only a symbol of the Holy Ghost, and not what the Holy Ghost looks like.

3. Continue to teach the words by asking questions, singing the song, accepting answers, and inviting the children to sing the parts that they learn.

4. Help the children feel the sequence and movement of the melody by illustrating melody patterns and leading the song with pitch-level conducting. Invite them to move their arms up and down to match the direction of the notes. Draw a picture of the recurring rhythm pattern and suggest that they clap the beats as they sing, accenting the first beat of every other measure which occurs on the dotted-quarter note.

5. Conclude the song presentation by expressing your testimony of the importance of baptism or your feelings about Jesus' baptism.

When Joseph Went to Bethlehem 38

Words: Bessie Saunders Spencer
Music: I. Reed Payne
First Line: When Joseph went to Bethlehem
Topics Indexed: Christmas

When Bessie Saunders Spencer's poem was published in the *Children's Friend,* December 1960, the Reed Payne family cut it out and had their children learn it for talks over the years. Some years later they decided it should be set to music to have its important message preserved. Brother Payne said, "In an hour's time the music was written. The poem seemed to call for a simple, flowing melody to match the beautiful and sacred words of that first Christmas. . . . 'When Joseph Went to Bethlehem' is a song that helps us picture the events surrounding the birth of Jesus more clearly from a father's perspective. Joseph was not just an observer or an onlooker, but very involved as a new father and guardian of baby Jesus. We can easily imagine Joseph's special combinations of strength and gentleness, of wisdom and humility, and of practical effort and spiritual awe as he assisted Mary in this most wondrous of all births."

The song has three verses. The first two are written together in the first sixteen measures. The third is written separately, with the same musical score as the last half of the other verses, making it eight measures long. The song form of verses one and two is A B A B: the first and third phrases are the same and the second and fourth phrases are the same, with some variation in the last two measures. The music flows effortlessly with repeated tones, by steps, and with some small interval skips. The rhythm is even with quarter notes throughout, except for the dotted-half notes at the ends of the phrases.

Teaching Suggestions:

1. Show the children some carpentry tools and ask them if they have ever seen a carpenter at work. Tell them that you are thinking of a carpenter who lived long ago whose name you would like them to guess. Give them hints to help them name Joseph, Mary's husband. Tell them that you know a beautiful song that tells some things about Joseph. Then sing the first verse.

2. Ask the children to think of the ways Joseph helped on the

journey to Bethlehem and when the baby Jesus was born. As they mention ideas from the song, show pictures or actual items to illustrate them.

3. Teaching one verse at a time, help the children learn the words through questions, pictures, objects, and word strips of keywords.

4. Make a chart that illustrates the four-measure melody phrases of the song with colored circles placed up and down as the melody indicates. (Use a different color to represent each of the seven notes of the scale in the song.) Use cutout pictures of Joseph, Mary, and the donkey to move above the notes as you sing, as if they were on a journey to Bethlehem. Have the children identify which of the phrases are the same and move their hands up and down in the direction of the melody as they sing.

When We're Helping   198

Words: Wallace F. Bennett
Music: German folk song
First Line: When we're helping, we're happy
Topics Indexed: Fathers, Grandparents, Happiness, Mothers,
  Service, Singing, Work

This little song is presented in the four- and five-year-old Primary class manuals to accompany some of the lessons and is a valuable teaching tool in the home. It is easy for the little ones to learn, and they love to repeat it again and again. For the *Children's Songbook* the key has been lowered from G to F, and the accompaniment has been lightened.

The melody and rhythm of lines one and two are almost the same. Each of the four phrases begins with two eighth notes, but all the rest of the notes are quarter notes (except for the final half note). Children can dramatize how to help mother as the "tra-la-la" of verse two is sung. The song can be varied by substituting "father," "grandpa," "grandma," "teacher," and so on, in place of "mother."

Teaching Suggestions:
1. Young children will learn to sing "When We're Helping" after they hear it sung several times. They learn more quickly as they participate in acting out how they can help, or as they clap to the beat of the song.

2. Ask the children how they can help mother or father, then have them sing the song, dramatizing the suggested helping activity as they sing the "tra-la-la's." The children can all dramatize the same activity, or one child can choose what he or she wants to portray, and the others can guess what this child is acting out.

3. Invite the children to participate in other activities as they sing the song, such as skipping around the room, joining hands and swinging them, or clapping the three beats to the measure, accenting the first beat of each measure.

Whenever I Think about Pioneers   222

Words: Della Dalby Provost
Music: A. Laurence Lyon
First Line: Whenever I think about pioneers
Topics Indexed: Pioneers, Singing, Two-part Songs

Laurence Lyon's father, noted LDS historian T. Edgar Lyon, suggested that to most children crossing the plains was a great adventure, an extended campout or picnic. They were seldom aware of the dangers or hardships of the trip. "Whenever I Think about Pioneers" expresses the joy that they felt during the journey and helps children of today identify with them through song. In the *Children's Songbook* the accompaniment has been simplified, with the melody now being carried in the piano part. Some word modifications have also been made so that the words match the notation more exactly.

The melody for verses one and three is distinctly different from the melody for verses two and four. However, they have similarities, including the same wide note range of almost an octave and a half—from B flat (below middle C) up to high E flat. The rhythm contains a mingling of eighth and quarter notes arranged in several beat patterns. The excitement of the song is achieved as the two melodies (verses three and four) are sung as a duet. The children should learn the verses well before they sing them together. The accompanist plays verse three for the duet.

Teaching Suggestions:
1. Ask the children to close their eyes and think about the pioneers and describe the pictures that come to their minds. Sing the first verse and display figures of pioneers.

2. Draw two lines on a chart, representing the melodies of the

song, and use it as a map. Use a cutout of a covered wagon to travel along the melody lines. Where the melody line goes up, draw it as mountains, draw an even melody line as the plains, and draw smaller ups and downs as bushes, canyons, or rivers. Teach the words to the verses by helping the children discover which are sung at different places along the pioneer map and placing word strips of keywords where they occur. Color code the key-words — one color for the girls' verses and another for the boys'.

3. Ask questions, sing the song, accept answers, and invite the children to sing the phrases as they learn them. You might ask: "What would I like to have been?" "What do I like to remember?" "What word is sung on the highest note?" "Who came besides the children?" "When did the pioneers sleep?" "Where did they sleep?" "What word rhymes with 'done'?" Use pictures to represent some of the word phrases, such as children playing games and a starry sky.

4. Demonstrate or tell about some of the games pioneer children played, such as races, jumping ditches, button on a string, carrying peanuts, pulling sticks, hide and seek, and so on. (See the Primary Sharing Time Resource Manual, p. 97.)

5. Ask the children to tap the rhythm of verse two, noticing that the last half of the verse uses the same short-short-long pattern several times. Invite them to count how many times it occurs.

6. Help the children notice that the words are almost the same for verses three and four so that they can be sung together. After the children learn the song thoroughly, divide them into two groups and have them sing verses three and four together. Help them become more secure in singing the duet by recording verse three and having them sing verse four with the recording.

Where Love Is 138

Words: Joanne Bushman Doxey and Norma B. Smith
Music: Joanne Bushman Doxey and Marjorie Castleton
   Kjar
First Line: Where love is, there God is also
Topics Indexed: Eternal Life, God's Love, Guidance, Love,
   Obedience, Prayer, Service, Teachers

"Where Love Is" was written for a presentation for the general conference of Primary leaders in 1970 or 1971. Some four hundred children's voices, thirty members of the Tabernacle choir, fifty child violinists, and the Tabernacle organist all combined to perform this most remarkable number. It enjoyed immediate success and popularity. Since that time it has been sung in many languages, at weddings, at funerals, in sacrament meetings, at general conference, and at stake conferences. One report came from a school of autistic children in Pennsylvania who could not communicate by talking, but they could by singing this song. For the *Children's Songbook* the previous seven pages of music have been simplified and condensed into two. All but one of the original verses are included and some word changes have been made, with the original writers participating in the revision. The song should be sung reverently and not too fast, expressing the message of the Savior's love for all of us.

There are three sixteen-measure segments in the song. The first and second segments begin with the same words and melody and have similar musical patterns. The third part introduces a new melody, beginning with the words "The comfort of loving arms around us," which feels like an interlude between verses. Then the music returns to the second segment for the final verse. The melody moves smoothly, with connected tones, and is contained mostly within the octave from middle C to high C.

Teaching Suggestions:

1. Introduce the song by showing pictures of people doing loving things, such as helping someone, singing a song, tucking a child into bed, and so on. Include a picture of Jesus in the Garden of Gethsemane and talk about the great love that he has for all of us. Sing the song for the children or play a recording of it.

2. You will probably want to teach this song in segments. Use pictures, word strips, illustrations of melody phrases, and questions to teach each part. Sing the song and ask the children to count how many times they hear the phrase "Where love is." Invite them to sing this with you each time it comes in the song.

3. Emphasize the action words of the song (guide, help, think, teach, talk, know, guide) by writing them on word strips, mixing them up on the chalkboard, and, as you sing the song, having a few children arrange them in the proper order.

4. Encourage the children to sing the song reverently and with expression, thinking of the Savior's love for each one of us.

Who Is the Child? 46

Words: Mabel Jones Gabbott
Music: Michael Finlinson Moody
First Line: Who is the child in the swaddling clothes
Topics Indexed: Christmas

This carol would make a wonderful addition to any Christmas program, and, though it is easy to learn and simple in structure, children of all ages will appreciate its beauty. The simplicity, artistic harmony, and lilting rhythm of the music enhance the message of the song.

The range of "Who Is the Child?" is ideal for children (middle C to high D). The melody of each of the four phrases is different, but there are several repeated notes to begin each of the first three phrases. The melody of the final phrase descends down the scale from high D to D. The rhythm is lilting throughout, and the beat pattern of each phrase is different. The words dictate that the song should be sung softly, yet as the melody rises there can be a slight crescendo, and as it descends it can become softer again.

Teaching Suggestions:

1. Ask the children if they have ever wished that they could go back in time and be present at some important events in history. Name one or two events and invite them to name some. Tell them that you are going to sing about a very special event that took place in Bethlehem many years ago. Tell them that perhaps many people who were there on that special night did not understand what was taking place, and they might have asked some questions. Ask the children to listen to discover two questions that the people could have asked. Sing the first verse, accept the children's answers, and invite them to join in singing the two questions as you sing the verse again.

2. Teach the other words of the first verse by asking the children: "Where is the child?" "Who is watching nearby?" After they listen to the song several times and respond to the questions, have them join you in singing the phrases. Use pictures or cutout figures to illustrate the words.

3. In teaching the words to the second verse, ask the children to listen to the song to find two names mentioned for the child (Son of God and Jesus). Teach the other words by asking: "What

is Jesus doing?" "Who have come to worship him?" "Who is keeping watch over the baby?" Each time you ask a question, have the children listen to find the answer and then join in singing that part of the song.

4. Ask the younger children to dramatize the song by pretending to rock the baby Jesus. They could dress in simple costumes.

5. Bear your testimony of the reality that Jesus is truly the Son of God. Encourage the children to sing the song reverently and sweetly in recognition of this sacred event.

Your Happy Birthday   283

Words and Music: Charlene Anderson Newell
First Line: This month is such a special one
Topics Indexed: Birthdays

Children all over the Church have learned to sing this happy and spirited birthday song. Of special interest for the children are the "fun" words, "zip-a-dee-ay and heigh-dee-ho," in the third line, and the fermata on the word "know" in the last line before "Happy birthday to you" is sung.

The song form of "Your Happy Birthday" is A B A C—the first and third phrases are almost the same and the second and fourth are different. The melody of the last phrase moves down the scale from high D to D, with one skip from F to D, and the final "Happy birthday to you" is reminiscent of the familiar happy birthday song. The rhythm carries an almost constant repetition of eighth notes, except for the variation in the final measure.

Teaching Suggestions:

1. Ask the children to name some of the words they might say when they are really happy. (Wow! Yippee! Great!) Ask them to find two words that mean that you are really happy in the song you will sing. After they discover them, have them practice saying "zip-a-dee-ay and heigh-dee-ho" several times. Sing the song again and ask the children to join in singing these words when you come to them.

2. Have the children move their bodies up and down to the pitches of the music while they sing.

3. To help with the sequence of the words, make word strips showing the rhyming phrase endings ("for you," "with you," "can

do," and "to you") and have four children hold them and arrange themselves in the order in which they occur as the song is sung.

4. Print keywords on colored paper candles and place the candles on a cake drawn on a chart. Remove the candles as the children become secure with the words.

You've Had a Birthday 285

Words and Music: Barbara McConochie
First Line: You've had a birthday; shout "Hooray!"
Topics Indexed: Birthdays, Rounds

While serving on a Primary stake board, Barbara McConochie was asked by a ward chorister for a new birthday song for the children. She felt they needed more variety, since birthdays are celebrated in Primary each week. Sister McConochie responded by writing this simple birthday song that can be sung in a variety of ways. It can be sung as a round or just as written. An alto part, sung one third below the melody, can be added to phrases two and three. Or it can be sung as an echo song, with a group of children softly singing phrases one, two, and four two measures behind the others. This echo could be played by an instrument. An ostinato can be added by singing the words "happy birthday" on even notes, F, F, C, C, (high C's) repeated through every measure of the song. No matter how it is sung, this lively song with a syncopated beat will prove to be an enjoyable number for any birthday celebration.

The melody of each of the four phrases is different. However, the second phrase imitates the first phrase, three steps higher. The unusual characteristic of the song is the syncopated rhythm established in the first measure. The children can tap or clap the rhythm or the straight beat to help them feel the pulse.

Teaching Suggestions:

1. Ask the children to stand who are being honored for their birthdays, and shake their hands as you sing the song.

2. Invite the children to keep the beat by slapping their hands on their laps three times and then clicking their fingers, for each measure of the song. Divide the children into two groups and have one group clap the even four beats to each measure, and the other group clap the rhythm of the melody. Help them feel the syncopation in the last measure by having them sing the "happy birthday"

in the next-to-last measure, clap the first beat of the last measure for the rest, and sing the final "to you."

3. After the children learn the song, have them try some of the variations described above—a round, an alto part, an echo, or an ostinato.

Authors and Composers

Adams, Lonnie Dobson

LDS. 1942–   . Lonnie Dobson Adams, born in Salt Lake City, holds a Master of Music degree from the University of Utah. She has played for dance classes and taught private piano for many years, and has taken part in many musical programs, as both soloist and accompanist. She and her husband, Bernard W. Adams, are the parents of three daughters.

I Want to Give the Lord My Tenth, page 150 (Words and Music)

Adams, Marilyn Price

LDS. 1926–   . Born in Long Beach, California, Marilyn Adams lived most of her younger life in Arizona. She has had a life of service in the Church organizations, having been a member of the Young Women's General Board, a Lambda Delta Sigma national officer, and an associate member of the Relief Society General Board.

The Adams family has a farm in Layton, Utah, where they enjoy special times with their children and grandchildren. Sister Adams loves to cook, write songs and scripts for the Church, paint with oils, do many handicrafts, and read. She especially likes to study and read about the gospel and our Church leaders. She married Beecher Adams and they are the parents of four children. She says she hopes that the children who sing her songs enjoy them as much as she loved the music in Primary when she was a little girl.

Hum Your Favorite Hymn, page 152 (Words)

Alexander, Cecil Frances

1818–1895. Mrs. Alexander, who was born in County Wicklow, Ireland, was a great religious teacher of children as a young girl, and later she helped establish a school for the deaf. When she became the wife of the Reverend Wm. Alexander, who later was the archbishop of Ireland for the Church of England, she became more zealous than ever in the education of children. Her errands of charity and helpfulness among the poor of the parish were numerous. Her *Hymns for Little Children* went through at least seventy editions, and the proceeds from its publication went to an Irish school for the handicapped. She wrote the text to three of our Latter-day Saint hymns, "There Is a Green Hill Far Away," "He Is Risen!," and "Once in Royal David's City."

All Things Bright and Beautiful, page 231 (Words)

Andersen, Dorothy S.

LDS. 1927–   . Dorothy Andersen was born in Brigham City, Utah. She was a Sunday School organist at age ten, playing an old-fashioned bellows organ (the type that requires the organist to force air through it by pumping the foot pedals very rapidly). She holds B.A. and M.A. degrees in English, a secondary education certificate, and an M.M. degree in musical composition from the University of Utah. She has taught at the University of Utah, in Bountiful and Salt Lake City public schools, at Westminster College, and at Salt Lake Community College, and has been employed as a paralegal for several years. She is married to Cyril Andersen, and they are the parents of two sons.

Sister Andersen has written instrumental and choral works and musical skits, and has had several of her songs published. Her song "The Spirit of Our Father" won first place in the Relief Society's musical composition competition in 1975. She says, "The most important things about music are, first, to enjoy it, and second, to share it with others. Music seems to be the most direct and natural expression of the heart about the things that matter most, so it is not surprising that we express our love for the Lord, our reverence for him, and our gratitude and praises to him, through music."

Oh, What Do You Do in the Summertime?, page 245 (Words and Music)

Anderson, Thelma McKinnon

LDS. 1913–   . Thelma Anderson, who was born and still lives in Price, Utah, is the mother of Charlene Anderson Newell, who composed the music to many of her mother's texts. She graduated from Brigham Young University and taught elementary school in Price. She directed operas and musical programs in the school district, and as a talented poet has written the words to many songs. She married Gerald J. Anderson, and they have two daughters. She enjoys temple work and missionary service and has helped to convert many to the gospel of Jesus Christ.

He Died That We Might Live Again, page 65 (Words)

Bach, Johann Sebastian

1685–1750. Johann Sebastian Bach was born in Eisenach, Germany, in a family of greatly gifted musicians, but he excelled them all. Bach acquired most of his musical knowledge from family members or through independent study. He was the father of seven children by his first wife and of thirteen more by his second. A skilled performer on both organ and violin, he wrote some three hundred church cantatas and many volumes of instrumental music. Though Bach was largely unrecognized as a composer during his life, he is now established as one of the musical giants of all time. The depth and feeling of his religious music have never been surpassed.

My Heart Ever Faithful, page 293 (Music)

Ballantyne, Dawn Hughes

LDS. 1932–   . Dawn Ballantyne was born in Salt Lake City and has lived most of her life in Bountiful, Utah. She graduated from Davis High School, attended Brigham Young University, and served a mission to the Gulf States. She has performed and been affiliated with several musical and dramatic groups.

Sister Ballantyne says, "I have loved to sing since I was very young. My mother was a song writer and used to write songs for me to sing. My father was a singer and one of my fondest memories is of sitting on his knee and singing songs with him. I especially loved Primary songs." She married W. James Ballantyne, and they are the parents of two boys and two girls.

Fathers, page 209 (Words)

Ballantyne, Joseph

LDS. 1868–1944. Joseph Ballantyne was born in Eden, Ogden Valley, Utah, the son of Richard Ballantyne, who was the founder of the Sunday School of the Church. He studied at the National Conservatory of Music in New York and with musicians from Chicago, New York, London, and Paris. He spent many years as the director of the Ogden Tabernacle Choir, and chaired the music committee of the Deseret Sunday School Board. During this period he composed and published children's songs, several of which appeared in the *Deseret Sunday School Songbook,* including "Little Purple Pansies," "Shine On," and "Christmas Cradle Song."

Joseph Ballantyne married Rosanna A. Brown, and they were the parents of three children. In 1933 he moved to Long Beach, California, where he became the director of the choir at St. Anthony's Church. At the same time he directed the Los Angeles Stake choir. His choirs performed on many important occasions, including at the San Diego World's Fair in 1935. He also taught private voice lessons, developing many fine musicians.

Jesus Once Was a Little Child, page 55 (Music)
Little Purple Pansies, page 244 (Music)
Oh, Hush Thee, My Baby, page 48 (Words and Music)
Shine On, page 144 (Words and Music)
Stand for the Right, page 159 (Words and Music)

Bassford, W. K.

1839–1902. William Kipp Bassford was born in New York City. He was a pianist and church organist and gave piano concerts in many locations. He composed church music, piano pieces, songs, and finished composing Vincent Wallace's unfinished opera, "Estrella."

Can a Little Child like Me?, page 9 (Music)

Bates, Elizabeth Fetzer

LDS. 1909–   . Born in Salt Lake City, Utah, Elizabeth Fetzer Bates graduated from LDS High School and received B.S., B.A., and M.A. degrees from the University of Utah. She served a mission to the Northern States as a young woman and later to Washington with her husband. At the age of forty-two she became totally blind, yet accepted this as a challenge and decided she would learn to do everything, including performing household tasks through touch, and reading and writing in Braille. Some of her experiences in learning to cope with blindness are told in *Stories that Strengthen* by Lucy Gertsch Thomson.

For many years Elizabeth Bates taught piano, and after she became blind, she decided to also compose since she could not read new music. She received a first-place award for one of her compositions from the Utah Composer's Guild. She has said, "The gospel of Jesus Christ is the plan for happiness. Happiness is a 'do-it-yourself-project,' and we cannot expect others to make us happy." She married Lucian H. Bates, and they have six children.

Book of Mormon Stories, page 118 (Words and Music)
Pioneer Children Sang As They Walked, page 214 (Words and Music)

Battishill, J.

1738–1801. Jonathan Battishill, one of the most eminent London musicians of his time, was born in London and died there. He was an organist and theater musician and composer for church, stage, and glee clubs. He wrote an opera and many popular anthems, glees, and songs. In his early years he was a choir boy in St. Paul's. He was recognized at this young age for his superior understanding of music and became a popular principal tenor soloist for many of the churches in England. It was said of him that he was as good a cathedral organist as any person in London at that time. J. Battishill became a harpsichord player at Covent Garden Theatre, organist of St. Clement, and a teacher of organ for many upcoming musicians. His addiction to alcohol handicapped him so that he never reached the success that could have been possible with his great musical talents. He was buried in St. Paul's Cathedral.

A Song of Thanks, page 20 (Music)

Beesley, Alvin A.

LDS. 1873–1940. Alvin Beesley, a son of pioneer musician Ebenezer Beesley, was born in Salt Lake City and studied music under the best teachers in Utah. He served a mission to the Indian Territory and Kansas and was president and general manager of the Beesley Music Company for thirty-four years, a twenty-five-year veteran Boy Scouter, and a member of the Executive Council of the Boy Scouts of America. Many of his compositions were included in the early children's songbooks. He was a bishop for seventeen years and was well known in Salt Lake for his creative role as leader of music in Sunday School. In this capacity he organized string and woodwind orchestras and taught religious songs by rote. He traditionally took his orchestra to the Utah State Prison to hold Sunday School for the inmates. He married Ruby Ross Pratt, daughter of apostle Orson Pratt, and they had eight children.

Heavenly Father, Now I Pray, page 19 (Words and Music)

Beesley, Wilford A., Jr.

LDS. 1927–   . Wilford (Bill) Beesley was born and educated in Salt Lake City, a son of Wilford A. and Evangeline Thomas Beesley and grandson of pioneer musician Ebenezer Beesley. He served a mission to Denmark and later graduated from the University of Utah law school. He is a practicing attorney in Salt Lake City and has participated in competitive sports, excelling as a skier and a golfer. He enjoys playing the piano, composing songs for special occasions, and singing with his family. He is married to the former Jane Pettigrew, and they are the parents of four children.

Thank Thee for Everything, page 10 (Music)

Bello, Georgia W.

LDS. 1924–   . Georgia Bello was born in Los Angeles, California, but spent her childhood in Magna, Utah. She is a Church-trained musician, taking courses in conducting and organ from local musicians. She graduated from Cyprus High School and attended Marin Jr. College in California and the Utah State Agricultural College in Logan, Utah. While in Logan she met her future husband, Clair L. Bello. They are the parents of five children. Sister Bello has received service awards from the Music Educators of Utah and the Mormon Youth Symphony and Chorus.

Popcorn Popping, page 242 (Words and Music)

Bennett, Wallace F.

LDS. 1898–   . Wallace F. Bennett, a native of Salt Lake City, graduated from the University of Utah and holds honorary degrees from the University of Utah, Brigham Young University, Southern Utah State College, and Northeastern University. He became the president of Bennett Glass and Paint Company, a firm organized by his father. He served on the General Church Music Committee and the Sunday School General Board. When his wife was serving on the Primary General Board, he was asked to write the text for several songs for children. He and his wife have performed together on many occasions, he as bass soloist and she as accompanist.

Brother Bennett served as a United States Senator from Utah from 1950 to 1974 and has written several books, including *Why I Am a Mormon.* He feels that "music is essential to the building of an emotional element in service in the Church." He married Frances Grant, the youngest daughter of President Heber J. Grant, and they have five children and many grandchildren and great-grandchildren.

I Like My Birthdays, page 104 (Words)
When We're Helping, page 198 (Words)

Berg, Richard C.

Lutheran. 1911–   . Richard Berg, who was born in Hoquiam, Washington, has spent much of his life promoting musical education. He graduated from the University of Washington (Seattle) with B.A. and M.A. degrees and received his doctorate degree from Columbia University. Subsequently he served as director of music education for public schools in Maryland, Massachusetts, New York, and Missouri. He also has been professor of music at the University of Missouri at Kansas City and Western Oregon State College. Several other universities have profited from his services as a visiting professor of music.

Lift Up Your Voice and Sing, page 252 (Words and Music)

Black, Carol Baker

LDS. 1951–   . Carol Baker Black was born in Logan, Utah, attended Southern Utah State College, and worked for several years as a legal secretary. She has enjoyed lifelong Church service, beginning at the age of twelve as the Primary pianist. As soon as the bell rang dismissing her from school, she would run to the Church a few blocks away and begin playing prelude music while the other children entered the chapel. She says, "My parents provided me with the opportunity of taking piano lessons, but I have had no formal training in music theory or composition. I do, however, possess a great love for good music and a testimony of its influence in our lives." At the request of Jaclyn Milne she began composing music in 1985 and together they have published seven songs, four of which have been winners in the *Ensign* music contests. She married Rod Black, and they are the parents of four children.

How Dear to God Are Little Children, page 180 (Music)
Search, Ponder, and Pray, page 109 (Music)

Bourgeous, Polly

LDS. 1937–   . Eva Pauline Bourgeous, born in Navasota, Texas, was a member of the Baptist Church until the age of nineteen. Since her conversion to the LDS Church, she has contributed much time and talent in all of the Church organizations, particularly in the area of music. She graduated from New Mexico State University and has been a teacher of piano since 1960. She married Aulvie Bourgeous, and they are the parents of five children and now live in Monrovia, California.

Our Chapel Is a Sacred Place, page 30 (Words)

Bradbury, William B.

1816–1868. William Bradbury, a popular conductor of musical festivals, was born in the state of Maine, attended the Boston Academy of Music, and later studied in New York and in Leipzig, Germany. He gave lessons in voice and piano and obtained a position as organist at the Baptist Temple in New York, where he offered free singing classes for children. During the last decade of his life he manufactured and sold pianos. He wrote the music for four of the hymns in our current LDS hymnbook: "Come, All Ye Saints Who Dwell on Earth," "Sweet Hour of Prayer," "We Are All Enlisted," and "God Moves in a Mysterious Way."

"Give," Said the Little Stream, page 236 (Music)

Bradshaw, Merrill

LDS. 1929–   . Merrill Bradshaw was born in Lyman, Wyoming. He received his B.A. and M.A. degrees from Brigham Young University and his doctorate degree from the University of Illinois. He is the John R. Halliday Professor of Music and composer-in-residence at Brigham Young University, where he has taught for thirty-three years. During that time he has composed over two hundred musical works, ranging from simple piano pieces and songs to symphonies, concertos, oratorios, and pageants. His works have been performed by the Utah Symphony and other symphonic groups in this country and in Mexico, Australia, and New Zealand.

Brother Bradshaw was one of the first recipients of the Karl G. Maeser Research and Creativity Award, was named BYU Distinguished Faculty Lecturer, and has served as a member of the General Church Music Committee. He took an active part in the initial work on the 1985 Church hymnbook and wrote the words and music to the hymn "We Will Sing of Zion." He has said, "Music gives us a way to communicate our testimony to God, especially those things that we feel too deeply to say in words. We worship not only when we are quiet and reverent, but also when we are joyful and happy and recognize the hand of the Lord in all things." He and his wife are the parents of seven children.

Listen, Listen, page 107 (Words and Music)
The Still Small Voice, page 106 (Words and Music)

Brady, Janeen Jacobs

LDS. 1934–   . Janeen Brady was born in Salt Lake City and attended Brigham Young University. She is a talented composer of children's music and has written several books of songs that center on teaching gospel principles and good moral values. She and her husband own and operate Brite Music, Inc., which publishes and sells her music throughout the United States and Canada. She has received national honors, is listed in the Congressional Record, and has performed in the White House for the Reagans. She says, "If we can fill our minds with good music and thoughts, we won't have room for evil thoughts. And when evil thoughts try to come in, we can sing the happy songs we know, and they will go away. Everyone should learn many happy songs . . . so they will have a lot of ammunition to fight evil." She and her husband, Ted Brady, are the parents of nine children and have several grandchildren.

I Lived in Heaven, page 4 (Words and Music)

Bray, Jo Marie Borgeson

LDS. 1925–   . Jo Marie Borgeson Bray, who was born in Salt Lake City and grew up in Santaquin, Utah, attended Payson High School and Brigham Young University. She married Lynn Bray, and they moved to Antioch, California, where they resided for thirty-five years and raised four children. They now live in Orem, Utah. Her first introduction to music was at age four when her father, Andrew A. Borgeson, started her on the violin and piano. She learned to play the violin, piano, trumpet, alto horn, baritone, oboe, flute, piccolo, sousaphone, and snare drums. She was music copyist for the Oakland Temple Pageant when it was first produced and later served as speech director and actress in this same pageant.

Love One Another, page 136 (Arrangement)

Brown, Newel Kay

LDS. 1932–   . Newel Kay Brown, a native of Salt Lake City, studied musical composition at the University of Utah and performed graduate studies there and at the University of California at Berkeley. While on his mission, he conducted a missionary chorus that performed throughout West Germany. Upon his return, he married Myrna Weeks of Provo, and they moved to New York where he studied with many notable musicians, receiving his doctorate at Eastman School of Music. He has taught on campuses in New Jersey, Arkansas, and Texas and is presently professor of music at the University of North Texas.

Brother Brown has received many awards for his musical compositions, which reflect a variety of styles and instrumental combinations. He wrote the music to the new hymn "With Songs of Praise." (*Hymns*, no. 71.) The Browns have five musically gifted children and several grandchildren.

I Hope They Call Me on a Mission, page 169 (Words and Music)
My Country, page 224 (Music)

Brown, Olga Carlson

LDS. 1894–1987. Olga Carlson Brown, who was born in Logan, Utah, received her early education there, graduated from the University of Utah, and taught for many years in elementary schools and at Utah State University. She married Nephi James Brown in 1938. Sister Brown was the executive secretary and director for the Girl Scouts in Salt Lake City for four years and served on their national staff for eight years. She was a member of the Primary General Board from 1940 to 1964.

Oh, How We Love to Stand, page 279 (Words and Music)

Bucher, Lester

No information available.

For Thy Bounteous Blessings, page 21 (Words)

Bunker, Wilma Boyle

LDS. 1910–   . Wilma Bunker was born in Provo, Utah, and received her B.A. degree from Brigham Young University. She was a teacher at Jordan High School for several years and taught piano lessons for sixty-three years. For over eight years she was a member of the Primary General Board, serving on the music committee. She was a national president of the National League of American Pen Women and received a Distinguished Service Award from the BYU Alumni Association in 1962. At present she is a member of the Emeritus Club and Board of BYU. She married S. Bertell Bunker, and they are the parents of three sons.

Hello, Friends!, page 254 (Words and Music)

I Will Try to Be Reverent, page 28 (Words and Music)

Cahoon, Matilda Watts

LDS. 1881–1973. Matilda Cahoon, born in Murray, Utah, attended the University of Utah for four years and the University of Chicago for additional musical study. She taught in the Salt Lake public schools, and elsewhere in Utah and Nevada, for thirty-nine years. She was the first woman delegate to the state legislature from Salt Lake County. She resumed her education at the University of Utah in her later years, graduating with honors at age sixty-five.

Sister Cahoon began her musical and Church service as a song leader in Primary at the early age of four. She served as chorister of the Primary General Board from 1913 to 1939, during which time she contributed to the musical heritage of the children in the Church, writing the lyrics to many songs. In a meeting in the Assembly Hall on Temple Square on September 3, 1985, President Gordon B. Hinckley paid tribute to Sister Cahoon, who, he said, "somehow coaxed a tune out of me as a part of the boy's chorus in junior high school. She was a great and delightful and lovely teacher." Matilda Watts Cahoon also created the text to the beautiful children's song "The Light Divine," composed by her dear friend Mildred Pettit and included in the LDS hymnbook (no. 305). She married Leonard Cahoon, and they had two daughters.

Beauty Everywhere, page 232 (Words)

Cameron, John C.

1951–   . No information available.

Every Star Is Different, page 142 (Words)

Campbell, Hal K.

LDS. 1927–   . Hal K. Campbell was born in Idaho Falls, Idaho, attended schools in Idaho and Utah, received his bachelor's and Master of Fine Arts degrees in music composition at the University of Utah, and was awarded his doctorate from Brigham Young University. He has taught music history, theory, composition, and piano at Southern Utah State College at Cedar City, where he was named Educator of the Year and Teacher of the Year by the faculty, staff, and students. He has blessed the community with his talents in preparing choirs for special programs and conducting the Orchestra of Southern Utah, a nonprofit group of about fifty members. He says, "There is an important place for uplifting music on earth and in heaven. Primary music has the potential to reinforce gospel subjects and children's testimonies." Brother Campbell and his wife, Joan, are the parents of four children.

The Priesthood Is Restored, page 89 (Music)
The Sacred Grove, page 87 (Music)

Campbell, Joan D.

LDS. 1929–   . Born in Yorkshire, England, Joan D. Campbell started school at age three, graduated at fourteen, and worked in the woolen mills as a weaver for over seven years before coming to America at age twenty-one. She is chairman of the Cedar City Music Arts Guild, a group of women who visit grade schools to prepare the children to attend musical concerts. She has also served as a local leader for her political party. Sister Campbell says, "Hal and I sang to our children when they were very tiny. We sing to our grandchildren and teach them all kinds of activity songs. Children learn very quickly and love to listen and participate." She and her husband are the parents of four children.

The Priesthood Is Restored, page 89 (Words)
The Sacred Grove, page 87 (Words)

Cannon, Tracy Y.

LDS. 1879–1961. Tracy Y. Cannon, an adopted son of George Q. and Caroline Young Cannon, exhibited a great musical talent at an early age. At fifteen he was invited by Evan Stephens to join the Tabernacle Choir. He was appointed choir leader of Cannon Ward at sixteen and shortly thereafter began studying piano, organ, and composition locally and with teachers in Ann Arbor, Berlin, Paris, New York, and Chicago. He was awarded the honorary degree of Master of Music by the Chicago Musical College. In 1909 Tracy Y. Cannon was appointed assistant organist of the Tabernacle Choir, serving in this capacity for twenty-one years, during which time the choir began its national broadcasts. When the General Church Music Committee was organized in 1920, he was called as one of the members. Under his chairmanship the committee compiled and published the 1950 edition of the LDS hymnbook, as well as *Recreational Songs* and *The Children Sing.*

Brother Cannon was a member of the Utah Institute of Fine Arts and director of McCune School of Music and Art for twenty-five years. He inaugurated a program that trained thousands of Church conductors and organists. Included in the current Church hymnbook are seven of his compositions, including "Come, Rejoice," and "Praise the Lord with Heart and Voice." Tracy Y. Cannon is the father of seven children.

I Like My Birthdays, page 104 (Music)

Careless, George

LDS. 1839–1932. George Edward Percy Careless was born in London. As a young boy he showed great musical ability and so was sent to the Royal Academy of London where he studied violin, piano, conducting, voice, and musical theory. He graduated in three years instead of the usual four. As a young convert to Mormonism, George Careless did valuable service for the Church as leader of the choir in London. In 1864 he immigrated to Salt Lake City and immediately became involved in musical pursuits as Brigham Young asked him to direct the Salt Lake Theatre Orchestra and, in 1869, the Tabernacle Choir. Because of his great talent and initiative, he received an offer to go to Virginia City at a high salary, but refused because, in his words, "I came here for my religion, and I am going to stay."

At least seventy of Brother Careless's hymn tunes have appeared in LDS hymn collections; nine are included in the 1985 edition of *Hymns,* including "The Morning Breaks" (which he composed on the boat that first took him to America), "Though Deepening Trials," and "Prayer Is the Soul's Sincere Desire."

I Thank Thee, Dear Father, page 7 (Music)

Carter, Daniel Lyman

LDS. 1955–   . As a young boy in Caldwell, Idaho, Dan Carter was listening to the Tabernacle Choir at conference time when he found himself crying because the music was so beautiful. He said,

"I always yearned to be able to share my testimony and feelings of the gospel through music." He attended Brigham Young University and graduated with a degree in musical composition in 1985. He has served as a member of the General Church Music Committee and has had several compositions published, including "As Now We Take the Sacrament." (*Hymns*, no. 169.) He works in the Church Music Editing and Publishing division, where he edits and reviews music to be printed in Church publications.

A *Young Man Prepared*, page 166 (Words and Music)
The Shepherd's Carol, page 40 (Words and Music)

Carter, Nancy K. Daines

LDS. 1935–   . Born in Murray, Utah, Nancy Daines Carter now resides in Waco, Texas. She received a B.S. degree from Brigham Young University, an M.A. from Columbia, and a Ph.D. from Florida State, all in the field of education. She taught grade school and education and statistics classes at the university level. Combining two families, she and her husband, Michael S. Carter, have nine children. Sister Carter says, "If you want to learn something, sing it! Children will better understand the Book of Mormon if they can sing its stories."

Book of Mormon Stories, page 118 (Optional Words)

Chadwick, Ruth H.

LDS. 1900–1973. Ruth H. Chadwick was born in Brigham City, Utah, attended Utah State University, and received a B.S. degree from the University of Utah. She married LeRoi C. Chadwick, and they are the parents of three children.

A talented writer, Sister Chadwick took an active part in the National League of American Pen Women and was a member of the Utah Poetry Society. She served on the Primary General Board for ten years.

Reverence, page 27 (Words)

Challinor, F. A.

1866–1952. Frederic Arthur Challinor was born in Longston, Staffordshire, England. He worked as a laborer in a brickyard, as a coal miner, and in a china factory during his early years. Later he pursued a musical education, gaining a diploma from the Royal College of Music and additional degrees in music from an English university. Challinor published over 1,000 compositions and wrote his own verses to many hymns and songs. He had hymns published in a Methodist hymnal and in the *Sunday School Hymnary,* 1905. He died in Paignton, England.

Tell Me the Stories of Jesus, page 57 (Music)

Cleator, Alice Jean

No information available.

Be Happy!, page 265 (Words)

Clinger, Richard

LDS. 1946–   . Born in Salt Lake City, Utah, Richard Wallace Clinger attended Brigham Young University before serving a mission in Florida. Subsequently he married, moved to Sacramento, California (where he has lived ever since), and received a B.S. degree in musical performance from the University of California at Sacramento. His natural musical talent was apparent at an early age, and he composed his first piano piece, "The Bear," at age three, after a trip to Yellowstone Park. At four and a half, he played his first recital—piano selections his mother taught him by rote and others he taught himself from listening to his sisters practice the piano—for the University of Utah music faculty.

Brother Clinger and his wife, Jerilynn, are the organizers and directors of a musical performing group, Galena Street East, the official convention performing group for the city of Sacramento. They have also organized an International Children's Chorus. Besides his private piano students, Brother Clinger teaches piano at Sacramento City College, conducts the music department at a private school (along with his wife), and is involved with the Sacramento Music Circus as assistant conductor, accompanist, and arranger. He and his wife are the parents of two children.

The Family, page 194 (Music)

Coleman, Satis N.

1878–1961. Satis Narrona Coleman, born in Tyler, Texas, was a music educator, author, and editor, known for her keen understanding of what children can appreciate in music. She studied privately, was a student at Texas State Normal School, and earned her B.S., M.A., degrees from Columbia University. She became a teacher of music in New York City and a music investigator at Lincoln School Teacher's College, also in New York City. Her experiments in music education involved training based on dancing, singing, poetry, and the making and playing of instruments. Her *Singing Time, Songs for Nursery and School,* and *Creative Music for Children,* published in 1922, have had a wide influence in the field of music education. She served as national chairman for the music committee for the Association for Childhood Education and was a life member of the National Educational Association. She married Walter Moore Coleman, and they had three children.

We're All Together Again, page 259 (Music)

Conant, Grace Wilbur

Grace Wilbur Conant, composer and musical editor, was born in Boston, Massachusetts. She studied piano, harmony, and composition under notable teachers in Boston and Paris and contributed to magazines and periodicals with a specialty in part songs, school, and kindergarten songs. Ms. Conant was the editor and compiler of *Songs for Little People,* published first in 1905, a songbook from which several songs were taken for the children's music resources of the LDS Church. She was the editor for the musical department of *Kindergarten Review* for many years.

God's Love, page 97 (Music)

Cooney, Betty Lou

LDS. 1924–   . Betty Lou Packard Cooney was born in Salt Lake City and lived there until she moved to Bellevue, Washington, in 1965. She graduated from the University of Utah with a B.S. degree in secondary education, taught music in secondary schools, and directed seminars in singing and conducting. This talented and energetic musician has taken an active part in the presentation of ward and stake musicals and roadshows. She married Lloyd E. Cooney, and they have four children.

Popcorn Popping, page 242 (Arrangement)

Cornwall, J. Spencer

LDS. 1888–1983. J. Spencer Cornwall was born in Salt Lake City. When only four years old, he learned to play on a pump organ and was so eager to advance musically that he would have a piano lesson in the morning, practice in the afternoon, and then go running back the next morning for another lesson. He studied music at the University of Utah, Northwestern University, and the Chicago Conservatory of Music, after which he spent twenty-three years in the school system, becoming supervisor of music for the Salt Lake City public schools. In this position he developed instrumental and vocal music programs and initiated city-wide music festivals. President Heber J. Grant called him to be the director of the Tabernacle Choir in 1935, a position he maintained for twenty-three years. During this time Brother Cornwall expanded the choir's repertoire and worked to improve its standards to become a well-known performing group. He was a member of the YMMIA General Board and of the General Church Music Committee. In this capacity he took part in the compilation of *The Children Sing.* He was a popular teacher and conductor and directed choral festivals throughout the country until he was in his nineties. Brother Cornwall said, "The first instrument was the voice. It was a gift from God. . . . My greatest pleasure was in teaching children to learn to sing and to discover the joy of making their own music through singing." He and his wife, Mary Alice Haigh, were the parents of seven children who have carried on their musical heritage.

The Golden Plates, page 86 (Music)

Crosby, Fanny J.

1820–1915. Born in a little cottage in Putnam County, New York, Fanny J. Crosby was permanently blinded when six years old. At the age of eight she wrote her first poem, which has become a classic in children's literature:

O What a happy soul am I!
Although I cannot see;
I am resolved that in this world
Contented I will be.
How many blessings I enjoy
That other people don't.
To weep and sigh because I'm blind,
I cannot and I won't.

Before her death at age ninety-five, Fanny Crosby had written more hymns, songs, and poems than anyone else since the beginning of the Christian era. She wrote her first hymn at age forty-four and had written 5,000 more before her death, including the text to "Behold! A Royal Army," which appears in the LDS hymnbook. Her favorite saying was, "I think that life is not too long and therefore I determine that many people read a song who will not read a sermon." She married a blind musician, Alexander Van Alstyne.

"Give," Said the Little Stream, page 236 (Words)

Cundick, Robert

LDS. 1926–   . Robert Cundick, born in Salt Lake City, was the first Mormon musician of note to receive his entire musical training, including a doctorate degree from the University of Utah, in the Salt Lake Valley. He worked his way through school playing jazz piano in dance bands. Brother Cundick taught at Brigham Young University for several years until his call by President David O. McKay to serve as the organist for the Hyde Park Chapel in London, England. After this two-year assignment, he returned to Utah and was called as Tabernacle organist, in which position he served for more than twenty-five years. More recently he was called as organist in the BYU Jerusalem center. He has received awards from the

American Guild of Organists and holds associate and fellowship certificates from the Guild. He married Charlotte Clark, and they have five children. Two of his compositions appear in the 1985 LDS hymnbook: "That Easter Morn" and "Thy Holy Word."

To Think about Jesus, page 71 (Music)

Darley, Roy M.

LDS. 1918–   . Roy M. Darley was born in Wellsville, Utah, a descendant of a long list of pioneers — seven of his ancestors pushed handcarts across the plains. He received his B.A. degree from Utah State University in Logan, studied at the Associate Royal College of Music in London, and was awarded his M.A. degree in music at the University of Utah. Brother Darley was a chaplain in World War II. He also served a mission in the Eastern States, was assigned as organist and chapel director in the Washington, D.C., chapel, and became the organist in the Hyde Park Chapel in London. For thirty-seven years he performed as Tabernacle organist and in this capacity gave over 6,000 organ recitals. Other Church assignments include a mission to New Zealand with his wife, twenty-five years on the YMMIA General Board, and ten years as a temple worker. He has published six volumes of hymn arrangements. Brother Darley and his wife, the former Kathleen Latham, have five children and many grandchildren.

I Want to Live the Gospel, page 148 (Music)

Davidson, Marcia

No information available.

Westward Ho!, page 217 (Music)

Davis, D. Evan

LDS. 1923–1979. D. Evan Davis was born and educated in Los Angeles and received a B.A. degree at UCLA, Master of Music at Northwestern University, and Doctor of Music Education from the University of Oregon. He taught at the University of Northern Arizona in Flagstaff, at Oregon State in Corvallis, Oregon, at the

University of British Columbia, and at Brigham Young University, where he headed the Music Education Department. While serving on the Sunday School General Board, Brother Davis wrote numerous articles for the *Era* and a monthly column in the *Instructor* from 1968 to 1970 titled "Our Worshipful Hymn Practice." He composed several hymns, a cantata, and at least three children's songs. Brother Davis died at the age of fifty-six from a brain tumor. He and his wife, C. Janice Davis, have five children who carry on the tradition of music and service.

Help Us, O God, to Understand, page 73 (Words and Music)

Davis, Mary Jane McAllister

LDS. 1925–1988. Mary Jane McAllister Davis, of Salt Lake City, Utah, was a gifted poet and composer. She attended schools in Salt Lake — East High School and the University of Utah — and served in many capacities in the Church including writing and directing programs and musicals. She married Kent L. Davis, and they were the parents of two sons. She suffered for many years with crippling rheumatoid arthritis and died at the age of sixty-two.

The Prophet Said to Plant a Garden, page 237 (Words and Music)

Dayley, K. Newell

LDS. 1939–   . K. Newell Dayley, born in Twin Falls, Idaho, has had a prominent role in the composition and production of musical programs for the Church, including the soundtrack of the show at the Polynesian Cultural Center. He has acted as director of bands, director of the entertainment division, and chairman of the Music Department at Brigham Young University and was a member of the General Music Committee of the Church for eight years. He has said, "I have a deep love for children's music and feel that some of our most important work ought to be focused in that direction." Brother Dayley and his wife, Diane, live in Provo and are the parents of eight children.

Every Star Is Different, page 142 (Music)
Home, page 192 (Music)
Hum Your Favorite Hymn, page 152 (Music)
I Feel My Savior's Love, page 74 (Words and Music)

The World Is So Big, page 235 (Music)

Dodge, Mary M.

1831–1905. Mary Elizabeth Mapes Dodge, who was born in New York City into a wealthy family, was educated at home by tutors and enjoyed the company of many literary and scientific people. She married William Dodge in 1851, and he died just seven years later, leaving her with two sons to raise alone. Moving her family to Newark, New Jersey, she began writing as a means of support. She wrote with brilliance, originality, and love for fun and was recognized as a leader in juvenile literature for almost a third of a century.

Mrs. Dodge became associate editor of Harriet Beecher Stowe's *Hearth and Home* magazine before founding *St. Nicholas* children's magazine, of which she was the editor for some thirty-two years. *Irvington Stories* and *Hans Brinker or the Silver Skates* are perhaps her best known works. The latter was inspired by stories she heard from Dutch emigrants. Mary Dodge died in Onteora Park, New York, after a long illness. She was honored by a funeral procession of children.

Can a Little Child like Me?, page 9 (Words)

Doxey, Joanne Bushman

LDS. 1932–   . Joanne Doxey was born and educated in Salt Lake City, receiving her B.S. degree in Interior Design and Child Development at the University of Utah, where she served as a student-body officer. Graduate work took her to Brigham Young University, where she studied Family Sciences. She has been active in Church affairs, serving as a national officer of Lambda Delta Sigma, a member of the Primary General Board, and a counselor in the general Relief Society presidency. Joanne married David W. Doxey, and they are the parents of eight children. She accompanied him when he was called to preside over the Barcelona Spain Mission. She has said, "The most important of all activities and honors, the most time-consuming and most rewarding, has been the rearing of a righteous family."

Seek the Lord Early, page 108 (Words and Music)

Where Love Is, page 138 (Words and Music)

Excell, Edwin O.

1851–1921. Edwin O. Excell, born in Uniontown, Pennsylvania, was a composer of gospel songs and an excellent singer. From his father, a minister of the German Reformed Church, he learned to appreciate music, especially as it relates to religion. At the age of twenty he moved to the West Coast and took up work as a brick mason, studying piano in his spare hours. He became a chorister for an evangelist and was recognized as one of the great song leaders of the day. Two of his spirited hymns appear in the LDS hymnbook: "Scatter Sunshine" and "Count Your Blessings."

Jesus Wants Me for a Sunbeam, page 60 (Music)

Fisher, Aileen

Aileen Lucia Fisher was born in Iron River, Michigan. When she was five years old her father was advised by his doctor to give up his business in town and move to the country where life would be less strenuous. This provided an environment that Aileen dearly loved and created a background for her writings. She studied at the University of Chicago and the University of Missouri, after which she served as the director of the Women's National Journalistic Register in Chicago, research assistant for the Labor Bureau of the Middle West, and since 1932 as a free-lance writer. She has had published many works of poetry, plays, and prose for children. In an article written for *Highlights for Children,* she says: "Ideas for poems lie all around us, in the everyday things we see and do and think and feel and remember, as well as in unusual sights and happenings. In the city as well as in the country, poems are waiting to be discovered, yours for the taking. Who knows . . . perhaps you are living a poem right now which some day you will put down on paper."

Hinges, page 277 (Words)

Fox, Luacine Clark

LDS. 1914–   . Luacine Clark Fox is the daughter of J. Reuben Clark, an apostle who served as a counselor to President David O. McKay, and Luacine Annette Savage. She was born in Washington, D.C., and has also lived in Mexico City and Salt Lake City. She attended the University of Utah and McCune School of Music and Art and has served on the MIA General Board. In 1936 she married Orval C. Fox, and they have three children. They served as missionaries in Nauvoo, Illinois. Sister Fox wrote and appeared on a children's radio program, "Story-telling Time," for many years and is active in presenting plays that she writes and directs. Other creative endeavors include award-winning media productions, Book of Mormon dramas, and two cantatas.

Love One Another, page 136 (Words and Music)

Franklin, Benjamin

1706–1790. Benjamin Franklin, born in Boston, Massachusetts, was a printer, author, publisher, inventor, scientist, public servant, and diplomat. Young people remember him for his role in the discovery of electricity and for the part he played in framing the Constitution. He was recognized for his profound statements of wisdom, many of which have survived many decades of repetition. Beyond question he was one of the best known and most admired men in the world during the last half of the 18th century.

Healthy, Wealthy, and Wise, page 280 (Words)

Gabbott, Mabel Jones

LDS. 1910–   . Mabel Jones Gabbott, who was born in Malad, Idaho, is one of the most prolific writers in the Church; many of her texts have been set to music by prominent Church composers. She received her advanced education at the University of Idaho and the University of Utah, and served a mission to the Northwestern States under President Preston Nibley, who encouraged her in her writing. She and her husband, John Donald Gabbott, have five children and now live in Bountiful, Utah.

Sister Gabbott has worked on the staffs of the *Friend, Improvement Era,* and *Ensign* magazines. Many of her poems have been included in these publications. She was also a member of the YWMIA General Board and the General Church Music Committee, and chaired the Hymnbook Text Committee when the 1985 edition of *Hymns* was being prepared. Four of her hymn texts appear in that edition, including "In Humility, Our Savior." She exceeds all other authors or composers in the *Children's Songbook,* with credit lines for sixteen songs.

Baptism, page 100 (Words)
Before I Take the Sacrament, page 73 (Words)
Did Jesus Really Live Again?, page 64 (Words)
Father Up Above, page 23 (Words)
Had I Been a Child, page 80 (Words)
Have a Very Happy Birthday!, page 284 (Words)
Have a Very Merry Christmas!, page 51 (Words)
He Sent His Son, page 34 (Words)
My Country, page 224 (Words)
Samuel Tells of the Baby Jesus, page 36 (Words)
Sleep, Little Jesus, page 47 (Words)
The Family, page 194 (Words)
There Was Starlight on the Hillside, page 40 (Words)
To Think about Jesus, page 71 (Words)
We Are Reverent, page 27 (Words)
Who Is the Child?, page 46 (Words)

Gardner, Lyall J.

LDS. 1926–   . Born in Salt Lake City, Lyall J. Gardner grew up in Oregon and received his B.A. degree from the University of Oregon. He continued his studies at the Eastman School of Music in New York, and received an M.A. degree in musicology and organ at Brigham Young University, the University of Utah, and at the University of Michigan. He is manager of the Church Consultation Center and also president of Gardner Micro-Systems, Inc., a software development company. He has served as a member of the General Music Committee of the Church. He is married to Ruth Muir, who has joined him in the composition of hymns and songs, including "Go Forth with Faith." (*Hymns,* no. 263.) They are the parents of four children.

I Believe in Being Honest, page 149 (Music)

Gardner, Marvin K.

LDS. 1952–   . As a young boy, Marvin K. Gardner of Morenci, Arizona, rode the school bus to piano lessons every Wednesday after school. His first calling in the Church was as Primary pianist when he was just eleven years old. He received his B.A. and M.A. degrees in English from Brigham Young University, where he also studied music and taught English composition. Subsequently he worked as a free-lance writer and editor for the LDS Church Missionary Department and for Deseret Book Company. He has been a member of the General Church Music Committee and of the Hymnbook Executive Committee responsible for editing much of the text for the 1985 hymnbook. He is married to Mary Catherine Hoyt, and they have five children who love to sing.

This Is My Beloved Son, page 76 (Words)

Gardner, Ruth Muir

LDS. 1927–   . Ruth Muir Gardner was born and raised in Salt Lake City and graduated from the University of Utah. She worked as an accountant, secretary, and teacher of English and business subjects on a high-school level. For many years she has taught music lessons in her home, training young musicians to appreciate and love good music. For fourteen years she served on the Primary General Board, particularly contributing her expertise to the music committee. She wrote the words to two hymns that appear in the 1985 hymnbook: "Go Forth with Faith" and "Families Can Be Together Forever." She is married to Lyall Gardner, and they have four children.

Families Can Be Together Forever, page 188 (Words)
Go the Second Mile, page 167 (Words and Music)
I Believe in Being Honest, page 149 (Words)
To Be a Pioneer, page 218 (Words and Music)
We Welcome You, page 256 (Words)

Gates, Crawford

LDS. 1921–   . A noted composer and musical director, Crawford Gates was born in San Francisco, California, and received his B.A. degree from San Jose State College, his M.A. degree from Brigham Young University, and Ph.D. from Eastman School of Music. He was a member of the BYU music faculty for sixteen years and is music director of the Beloit Janesville Symphony Orchestra, a position he has held since 1966; concurrently he was the music director of the Rockford Symphony for sixteen years. Dr. Gates's music has been performed by many major U.S. orchestras; two of his orchestral/choral works have been recorded by the combined Utah Symphony Orchestra and Mormon Tabernacle Choir. He has received a Grammy award for his album "The Lord's Prayer," and the ASCAP (American Society of Composers, Authors, and Publishers) award each year since 1967. Members of the LDS Church are familiar with his *Promised Valley*, created for the Utah centennial celebration; he also composed music for the Hill Cumorah Pageant. Brother Gates has served as a missionary in the Eastern States and on the MIA General Board and the General Church Music Committee. He and his wife, Georgia Lauper, are the parents of four children.

Baptism, page 100 (Music)
On a Golden Springtime, page 88 (Music)

Gluck, Christoph W. von

1714–1787. Gluck was a German composer and reformer of music drama (opera) during the second half of the 18th century. His father probably wanted him to continue in the family employment of forestry, but he showed a strong inclination toward music. In order to escape from disagreements with his father, the young Gluck finally left home. Supporting himself by his music, he made his way to Prague, where he played in several churches and completed his musical studies. He is best known for his operas.

Air from Orpheus, page 296 (Music)

Gordon, Glenn

LDS. 1956–   . Glenn Howard Gordon was born in Newcastle, Australia, and was baptized a member of the LDS Church with his parents in 1969. He began almost immediately in Church service as the Jr. Sunday School pianist; at age fifteen he was called as ward organist and as assistant stake organist at sixteen. He served in the Australia Perth Mission. His education includes an honor certificate from Ricks College and a B.A. degree in Fine Arts and Semitic Studies from the University of Sydney. He has also completed graduate work in Jewish Education at the University of Judaism in Los Angeles, California, and is working towards a Master's degree in Australian Jewish History at the University of Sydney. He is married to Kathryn Pamela Andrews Gordon, and they have two children.

Friends Are Fun, page 262 (Words and Music)

Gordon, Grace

Grace Gordon, a writer of children's poetry, had her works published in several magazines, including the *Youth's Companion.* Several of her poems, set to music, were included in *The Primary Songbook,* 1927 and 1939.

Called to Serve, page 174 (Words)

Gordon, Ingrid Sawatzki

LDS. 1949–   . Ingrid Gordon was born in Koln, Germany, and immigrated with her parents to Utah when she was two years old. At an early age she showed a love for music, and learned how to lead it from her Primary music director. She graduated from Granite High School and later received training at a college of beauty. Her favorite Church calling was as the director of a children's choir. She is married to Donald C. Gordon, and they are the parents of seven children.

Sing a Song, page 253 (Words and Music)

Gottschalk, Louis

1829–1869. Louis Gottschalk, born in New Orleans, was among the first American pianists to achieve international reputation. He was sent to Paris at age thirteen for musical training. Hector Berlioz was one of his teachers and Frederic Chopin prophesied that Gottschalk would become "a king of pianists." When Gottschalk performed in concert, he usually played his own works and often conducted his own orchestral compositions. He died in Rio de Janeiro, Brazil.

Loving Shepherd, page 292 (Music)

Graham, Patricia Kelsey

LDS. 1940–   . Pat Graham, who was born in Hollywood, California, received a B.S. degree in elementary education from Brigham Young University and a Master of Education with emphasis in music from the University of Utah. Her studies also included a major in commercial art. She was called to the Primary General Board in 1980 and served there for eight years, much of this time as chairman of the music committee and, as such, overseeing the preparation and production of the *Children's Songbook*. She has had articles published in the *Friend* and has published two songbooks of her own music. She has been an officer in the Utah Composers Guild and Children's Literature Club, twice receiving first-place awards in the children's division of the Utah Composer's Guild Contest.

Sister Graham has been a teacher and consultant for the Granite School District and an instructor at BYU Church Music workshops. A piano teacher for many years, she has inspired many young musicians to unusual accomplishment. She herself is a proficient accompanist. She married G. Robert Graham, and they are the parents of six children.

I Am like a Star, page 163 (Words and Music)
Picture a Christmas, page 50 (Words and Music)
The Hearts of the Children, page 92 (Words and Music)
The Nativity Song, page 52 (Words and Music)
We Are Different, page 263 (Words and Music)

Graham, Rose Thomas

LDS. 1876–1967. Rose Thomas Graham was born in Salt Lake City. Her poems for children appeared in local and national publications, and she published a collection of original children's poetry. She was a member of the National League of American Pen Women, the Art Barn Poets, and other writers' groups. She married Samuel T. Graham and lived with him in Los Angeles until his death in 1923. They had one son who died as a young boy.

The Golden Plates, page 86 (Words)

Gunn, Carol Graff

LDS. 1929–   . Carol Graff Gunn was born in Minersville, Utah, and moved to Salt Lake City when she was ten years old. She played piano "by ear" even before she started school. Right after she graduated from Primary, she was called to be the Primary organist; she was sustained as ward organist at age sixteen, after having had just three formal lessons. She has composed songs for her family and has had some compositions printed in the *Friend.* She married Jack W. Gunn, and they have five children.

Family Night, page 195 (Words and Music)
My Dad, page 211 (Words and Music)

Hansen, Bill N., Jr.

LDS. 1952–   . Born in Ames, Iowa, Bill Hansen grew up in Utah and southern California. He served a mission to Brazil and attended Brigham Young University, receiving his B.S. degree and a J.D. from the J. Reuben Clark Law School. He and his wife, Lisa Tensmeyer Hansen, are the parents of five children. He is an attorney in Payson, Utah, and has been a leader in this community through service in the Kiwanis Club and the Chamber of Commerce, motivating the area's economic development. He has said, "I especially enjoy missionary work and serving with other members of the Church. I believe that living the gospel can be fun as we develop our many talents in the service of others."

Nephi's Courage, page 120 (Words and Music)

Hansen, Lisa T.

LDS. 1958–   . Lisa Hansen, who was born in Logan, Utah, and grew up in Indianapolis, Indiana, began composing songs at the age of thirteen. She attended Brigham Young University as a Kimball scholar, completing course work for graduation while raising her five children in Payson, Utah. Her husband is Bill N. Hansen, Jr. She says that when she was Primary age, she was the only member of the Church in her school, so Primary became a good place to take her friends to show them why she loved being a member of Christ's church. She testifies, "I know the gospel of Jesus Christ is true. I felt the Spirit reveal this to me when I was eleven years old. Every child who is worthy to receive the Holy Ghost can learn things by faith."

Nephi's Courage, page 120 (Words and Music)

Hanson, William Frederick

LDS. 1887–1969. William Frederick Hanson, composer, conductor, and singer, was born in Vernal, Utah. He was an outstanding musician from a very early age, playing at dances with his father's nine-piece orchestra by the age of ten. He graduated from LDS High School in Vernal, where he was class president, and served a mission for the Church in the Northern States. During this time he was assigned to edit, select, and proofread songs for a new songbook called *The Songs of Zion,* which was used by all Church missions in the United States and in many stakes and wards. He taught school at the Uintah Academy for fifteen years, along with teaching forty private music students and performing community service. He collaborated with a full-blooded Indian woman, Gertrude Bonnin, on an opera, "The Sundance," which was based on Indian lore.

After attending the Chicago Musical College and studying public school music, music composition, and piano with many masters, William Hanson accepted a position at Brigham Young University in its music department, where he remained until retirement. He wrote the music for the BYU school song and "Utah, We Love Thee," among many others. He and his wife, Afton Pack, were the parents of seven children.

I Have Two Little Hands, page 272 (Music)

Harrison, Thelma J.

LDS. 1906–1991. Born in Pocatello, Idaho, Thelma Jones Harrison lived in Bountiful and Ogden, Utah, and several California communities. She was educated at Weber State College, Utah State University, University of California, Fresno State, and San Francisco State Teacher's College, and subsequently taught elementary school, nursery school, and kindergarten in several localities. She served on the Primary General Board for some sixteen years, much of that time as a curriculum writer for the younger age groups. She wrote a series of "Bobby Stories" for the *Children's Friend* and was gifted in writing, teaching, and telling stories to the little ones. She was a member of the National League of American Pen Women. She said, "Music is one of the lovely gifts with which our Heavenly Father has blessed us. . . . The healing words of hymns slip into our minds to bless us in times of sorrow or to guide us in our actions." She married J. Melvin Harrison, and they had three children.

Quickly I'll Obey, page 197 (Words)

Haydn, Franz Joseph

1732–1809. Franz Joseph Haydn was one of the world's great composers. He perfected the early symphonic form, invented the modern string quartet, and was the principal founder of the Viennese classical school. Concerning his early years, Haydn wrote, "My father was a wheelwright, and he served at a country castle of a Count, a great lover of music. My father played the harp without knowing a note of music, and I sang all his simple little pieces correctly. I was sent to St. Stephens cathedral in Vienna where I learned the art of singing, the harpsichord, and the violin. Finally I lost my voice, and my zeal for composition came forth. My first attempts were not correctly done, and I, then, had the good fortune to learn true composition."

Thanks to Our Father, page 20 (Music)

Hiatt, Duane E.

LDS. 1937–   . Duane E. Hiatt was born in Payson, Utah, and attended Brigham Young University, where he received a B.A. degree in journalism and an M.A. in communications. He is producer-director of Media Productions for the Division of Continuing Education at BYU, in which position he produces and directs television and other learning programs. He also works and has won awards as a free-lance radio and television scriptwriter and magazine feature writer. For sixteen years he was a professional entertainer, performing throughout the United States and abroad in the musical comedy group "The Three D's," which recorded songs for Capitol Records. Brother Hiatt married Diane Robertson, and they are the parents of fifteen children. She died in 1987, and he subsequently married Sharon Lee Johnson.

Follow the Prophet, page 110 (Words and Music)

Hill, Chester W.

LDS. 1912–   . Chester W. Hill, born in Fayette, Utah, loved to play the piano from the age of three. He took lessons at age six and played for priesthood meeting at age ten. In his early teens, he composed many songs and went on to study music at Snow College, the University of Utah, Brigham Young University, Juilliard School of Music, and Teacher's College, Columbia. He taught for nineteen years at Ricks College and taught private piano at BYU. He has served as director of the Bureau of Information and Concerts at the Washington, D.C., Chapel and recently filled a Northern Washington, D.C., mission with his wife, Helen. They are the parents of eight children.

Hosanna, page 66 (Arrangement)
Saturday, page 196 (Arrangement)

Hill, Mildred

Mildred Hill was involved in kindergarten work and in teaching Sunday School. She and her sister, Patty Hill, wrote a book called *Song Stories for the Sunday School,* which was copyrighted in 1893.

They were believers in the rich learning experience music can provide. Mildred wrote the music to the well-known "Happy Birthday to You," and Patty wrote the words. (See the information about Mildred Hill's sister, Patty Smith Hill, below.)

Once within a Lowly Stable, page 41 (Words and Music)

Hill, Patty Smith

1868–1946. Patty Smith Hill was born in Anchorage, a suburb of Louisville, Kentucky. She and her brothers and sisters spent their early childhood in the atmosphere of a college for young women of which their father, the Reverend William Wallace Hill, was president. While she was still very young, she announced that she intended to spend her life caring for little children. After finishing high school in a private school, she attended a training school for young ladies who wished to become kindergarten teachers, which led her to a lifelong pursuit as a pioneer in early childhood education. She became the director of a model kindergarten in Louisville, which educators from all over the country came to observe. Later she became the director of the department of primary education at Columbia Teacher's College. She contributed articles on her philosophy of education to periodicals and was the joint author of *Kindergarten and Song Stories for the Kindergarten.* She, with her sister, Mildred, is most famous for the song "Happy Birthday to You," for which the present copyright owner still collects royalties. Patty Smith Hill died at her home in New York City.

Once within a Lowly Stable, page 41 (Words and Music)

Holbrook, Glenna Tate

LDS. 1925–   . Glenna Holbrook was born in Logan, Utah, one of eight children. She served a mission to the Southern States where her first poem was written, and she has continued to write song lyrics, poems, roadshow scripts, and even a children's operetta. While serving as Jr. Sunday School chorister in the Ensign Ward, she became acquainted with Marjorie Kjar, who was the pianist. They decided to write some children's songs together, and the result was a songbook, *Songs to Sing for Latter-day Saint Children.* Two of the songs from this collection are included in the *Children's Songbook.* Glenna and her husband, Fred Holbrook, have seven children.

Birds in the Tree, page 241 (Words)
Stand Up, page 278 (Words)

Huffman, Laurie

LDS. 1948– . Laurie Huffman was born in Salt Lake City and lived primarily in Utah until 1985, when she moved to New Hampshire. She attended Brigham Young University and married Kenneth Lee Huffman. They have three children, whom they have educated in their home. Her talents in writing poetry and lyrics were recognized, and she was asked to assist in this way for the Young Women's organization, working with composer Newell Dayley. She continues to write poetry and teaches personal and family history writing.

I Feel My Savior's Love, page 74 (Words)

Hunter, Donnell

LDS. 1930– . Born in Rigby, Idaho, Donnell Hunter has lived in Idaho most of his life. He holds a Master of Fine Arts degree from the University of Montana. Most of his professional life has been as a teacher at Ricks College, with short teaching assignments at Brigham Young University and BYU—Hawaii. He has been a sealer in the Idaho Falls Temple and has served nearly twenty years in the temples in Idaho Falls and Hawaii. He has published more than 250 poems in more than 100 different magazines in 43 states. He and his wife are the parents of eight children.

The Lord Gave Me a Temple, page 153 (Words)

Jack, Mary R.

LDS. 1896–1985. Associate editor of the *Children's Friend,* secretary-treasurer of the Primary Children's Hospital board, and secretary-librarian of the Tabernacle Choir, Mary Jack has a long record of devoted and efficient Church service. She served on the Primary General Board from 1920 through 1939 under Louie B. Felt and

May Anderson. She had an extended association with the *Children's Friend*, joining the staff as a typist in 1913 and working in various capacities, primarily as managing editor, until her retirement in 1970. Adele Cannon Howells, general president of the Primary, said that Mary Jack had a great devotion to her labors, an ability to accomplish her assigned task, and a record of showing a constant interest in the welfare of children.

Thanks to Thee, page 6 (Words)

Jackson, Beatrice Goff

LDS. 1943– . Beatrice Goff Jackson was born in San Francisco, California, but grew up in Salt Lake City. She graduated from Granite High School, attended Brigham Young University where she had a composite major in elementary education, arts, and sciences, and taught school in the Granite and Murray School Districts. She plays piano, violin, string bass, and alto recorder, and has played with the Granite Youth Symphony, BYU Symphony Orchestra, Fairbanks (Alaska) Community Orchestra, Murray Symphony, and American West Symphony and Chorus. She married Samuel Wallace Jackson, and they have two children. Sister Jackson says, "I know the Lord accomplishes his work by using ordinary people who are willing and obedient. If we trust him and keep his commandments, he will direct our paths so that all things will work together for our good."

Faith, page 96 (Words)

Jensen, Joyce Mills

LDS. 1936– . Joyce Mills Jensen was born in Nephi, Utah, but grew up in Salt Lake City and Bountiful, Utah. When she was nine years old, she decided she had to choose one thing and do it well, though she enjoyed many creative things, including drawing, writing poetry, and composing music. She chose to compose music. She read every book she could find on music composition and harmony and took many music classes in college. She graduated from Brigham Young University and subsequently taught music to troubled adolescents and used music as therapy in nursing homes.

Sister Jensen has won many musical awards, including first place in the National Mu Phi Epsilon Music Composition Contest; first place in the Utah Academy of Arts, Sciences, and Letters Contest; first place in the Relief Society Song Contest; and three first-place awards in the Utah Composers Guild Competition. She married Vernon Y. Jensen, and they have six children.

Fathers, page 209 (Words and Music)

Johns, Cecilia

No information available.

Fun to Do, page 253 (Music)

Johnson, Anna

LDS. 1892–1979. Anna Johnson, who was born in Logan, Utah, but lived most of her life in Salt Lake City, found it easy to express her reaction to life, people, and countries in poetic form. She worked in the office of the YWMIA for many years, besides writing a popular children's column, "Hopscotch Valley," for the *Deseret News.* Alexander Schreiner, the well-known Tabernacle organist, composed some 100 melodies for her poems. Her collection of dolls, which she accumulated during her extensive travels, was presented to the Primary Children's Hospital in Salt Lake City.

A Smile Is like the Sunshine, page 267 (Words)
An Angel Came to Joseph Smith, page 86 (Words)
I Think the World Is Glorious, page 230 (Words)
Jesus Is Our Loving Friend, page 58 (Words)
My Flag, My Flag, page 225 (Words)
We Bow Our Heads, page 25 (Words)

Jolley, Mary Ellen Jex

LDS. 1926–   . Mary Ellen Jex Jolley was born in Provo, Utah, to a family that made music the center of their home. She attended elementary school at the BYU Training School and received her college training at Brigham Young University. For three years she was on the editorial board of the *Children's Friend.* She served for over eight years on the child committee of the Sunday School General Board, during which time she felt a need for some short activity songs and verses to help children express themselves about gospel principles. She wrote some songs to fulfill this need. Sister Jolley was also a writer for a missionary tract writing committee. She and her husband, Joel M. Jolley, are the parents of seven children.

I Have a Family Tree, page 199 (Words)

Kaelin, Anne

Lutheran. 1917–   . "Anne Kaelin" is a pseudonym used by Doris R. Fisher, who was born in Brooklyn, New York, and grew up in Queens. She moved to Massachusetts when she married William Fisher, a music educator. She received both B.A. and M.A. degrees in mathematics from her studies at Hunter College, New York, and Columbia University, and taught high school mathematics for many years. Doris Fisher wrote the lyrics for many of the children's songs that her husband composed. They have four children.

Covered Wagons, page 221 (Words)

Kaillmark, George

1781–1835. George Kaillmark was an Englishman, though he was born in Germany. He was a violist, teacher, and composer of popular music. His well-known hymn "Do What Is Right" has been included in the LDS hymnbooks since 1863.

The Books in the Old Testament, page 114 (Music adaptation)

Kammeyer, Virginia Maughan

LDS. 1925–   . Born in Cedar City, Utah, Virginia Maughan Kammeyer lived in Logan during her early years and later attended Brigham Young University, receiving a B.A. degree in English and Speech. After her marriage to Fred T. Kammeyer, she moved to the Seattle area, where the family has remained. They are the parents of six children. Sister Kammeyer says, "The songs sung in

Primary are among the most beautiful in the Church. They tell of our love for Jesus and his church. A song to Jesus is like a prayer set to music."

On a Golden Springtime, page 88 (Words)
Pioneer Children Were Quick to Obey, page 215 (Words)

Kimball, Maud Belnap

LDS. 1889–1971. Maud Belnap Kimball was born and raised in Ogden, Utah, and taught school there. She was an accomplished singer and had lead parts in many concerts and operas in the Salt Lake area. An active civic and political leader, she served on the Salt Lake Women's Legislative Council, was reader in the Utah House of Representatives, and was at one time one of four women in the United States to serve as mortgage credit examiner for the Federal Housing Administration. She was the social service director of the former Salt Lake General Hospital and served as a clerk in the county recorder's office. She married Stanley Fielding Kimball, and they were the parents of three children.

Mother Dear, page 206 (Words)

Kirkell, Miriam H.

Miriam H. Kirkell was an American poetess who was commissioned by the publishers of *Childcraft* to write the lyrics to "Westward Ho!" in 1937 for their publication.

Westward Ho!, page 217 (Words)

Kjar, Marjorie Castleton

LDS. 1927–   . Marjorie Kjar was born in Salt Lake City. She has composed music, accompanied and conducted choirs and musical programs, and for forty years has taught piano lessons. Her hope in teaching music to young people is that she can instill in them the desire to serve by preparing them to play the hymns and songs of the Church. She studied piano for ten years and graduated from the University of Utah with a degree in music. She and her husband, Morris Ashton Kjar, have six children. She accompanied him as he presided over a mission in New Zealand. As a member of the Primary General Board for five years, she contributed in preparing musical presentations and composing music for the children. She urges, "I would like all music directors and pianists throughout the Church to prepare ahead by learning the gospel messages of the songs. I strongly feel that the music director is her [own] best visual aid."

Birds in the Tree, page 241 (Music)
Come with Me to Primary, page 255 (Words and Music)
Stand Up, page 278 (Music)
We Welcome You, page 256 (Music)
Where Love Is, page 138 (Music)

Kleinman, Bertha A.

LDS. 1877–1971. Bertha Kleinman was born and lived for thirty-five years in Salt Lake City. Mesa, Arizona, became her home for the remainder of her life. At an early age she showed a talent for writing, had her first poem published at age twelve, and has since written hundreds of poems, hymns, short stories, dramas, and pageants. Her work has been published in many periodicals, including *Ladies Home Journal* and *Harper's Bazaar,* and she had a book of poetry, *Through the Years,* published in 1953. Sister Kleinman attended Brigham Young University, where she earned a degree to teach kindergarten. She also obtained a secretarial degree from LDS Business College and became the first female secretary to the Presiding Bishopric of the Church. President Heber J. Grant commissioned her to write pageants celebrating the one-hundredth anniversary of the founding of the Church and the one-hundredth anniversary of the pioneers entering the Salt Lake Valley.

Sister Kleinman received many awards and recognitions: the Rotary Award for outstanding citizenship, the first David O. McKay Humanities Award from BYU, Poet Laureate of the state of Arizona, and Club Artist of the year for the Fine Arts committee of the Mesa writers club. The governor of Arizona designated 1953 as "Bertha Kleinman" year. In her later life she worked in the Arizona Temple as assistant recorder and served as the secretary to several temple presidents. Until her death at age ninety-three, she continued to write and participate in various activities. She and her husband, Orson C. Kleinman, had six children.

I Have Two Little Hands, page 272 (Words)

Lawler, Jeanne P.

LDS. 1924– . Jeanne Lawler was born in Minneapolis, Minnesota. She graduated from Minnehaha Academy in Minneapolis and entered the U.S. Coast Guard in 1944. After military service, she received an associate degree in music from Glendale College in California and began writing children's music for Gospel Light Publishing Company, having many songs published in their church materials. She married, had a daughter, and moved to Colorado, where she came in contact with the LDS missionaries. She accepted the gospel after three weeks of discussion, and she and her daughter were baptized in Vernal, Utah. About this time she was divorced and moved to Provo, Utah, where she became head resident in a Brigham Young University dormitory. Subsequently she married Frederick Lawler—who was also a new convert and the branch president in Farmington, Maine—and in so doing acquired four teenaged children. While living in Maine, Sister Lawler enrolled in the BYU Independent Study Program and graduated at the age of fifty-seven. As part of the requirements for this degree she wrote and produced a musical called "Sing Unto the Lord," based on the book of Isaiah. Brother and Sister Lawler served a proselyting mission in Ohio, and, after his death, she was called on a mission to the Swedish Temple. She now lives in Salt Lake City and plans to continue her musical interests and her family research. She tells music leaders to "teach with enthusiasm and sing more and talk less. Children will remember thoughts set to music longer than conversation."

Genealogy—I Am Doing It, page 94 (Words and Music)
Hinges, page 277 (Music)
I Often Go Walking, page 202 (Music)
The Holy Ghost, page 105 (Words and Music)
When Jesus Christ Was Baptized, page 102 (Words and Music)

LeeMaster, Vernon J.

LDS. 1904– . Vernon J. LeeMaster was born in Moab, Utah, where his father dry-farmed. He was called as the ward organist at age eleven, and received his advanced musical training at McCune School of Music, Brigham Young University, and the University of Southern California, where he was awarded Bachelor of Arts, Bachelor of Music, and Master of Music degrees. A teacher of music in the Carbon, Jordan, and Salt Lake City schools for several years, he was asked to become the supervisor of music for the Salt Lake City schools, a position he held for twenty-one years. He says, "Directing the all-city festivals in the Tabernacle with hundreds of angelic voices ... is not soon forgotten. The sweet voices of children singing [create] a beauty unsurpassed." He feels that those who teach children to sing should understand that children have natural, pure, sweet voices, and they should cultivate this natural sweetness instead of encouraging harsh, loud sounds. Brother LeeMaster was a member of the Sunday School General Board for twenty-two years and also sang with the Tabernacle Choir for a number of years. He and his wife, the former Helen Palfreyman, are the parents of one daughter.

Dearest Mother, I Love You, page 206 (Words and Music)

Lehenbauer, Ruth Benson

LDS. 1933–   . The daughter of Serge and Elizabeth Benson, Ruth Lehenbauer was born in Washington, D.C., when her father worked for the United States Senate. She was raised in Silver Springs, Maryland, where she studied piano and found a great love and interest in composing music. Coming to Utah for her college training, she attended Utah State University and Brigham Young University, graduating with a master's degree in French. She earned her spending money by accompanying dance classes, where she learned to improvise at the piano. She served a mission in Germany and returned to Utah to teach French and German at Utah State University. She married and moved to Dearborn, Michigan; the Lehenbauers raised their six children there. She now lives in Logan, Utah, continues to write songs, poetry, and prose, and has published two books.

I'm Glad to Pay a Tithing, page 150 (Words and Music)

Likes, L. Clair

LDS. 1908–   . L. Clair Likes was born in Teton, Idaho, and lived near Rexburg, Idaho, for the first twenty-one years of his life. His father was a dry farmer and their land was isolated, so he lived too far from the meetinghouse to attend "religion class" (Primary) very often, yet his memories of Primary are pleasant. He attended six different grade schools, two high schools, and the University of Utah, where he received his bachelor's degree and a high school teaching certificate. He went on to get a master's degree in theater and accepted positions in the welfare, education, and drama fields. He has written, directed, and produced skits, roadshows, pageants, and plays for the Salt Lake Area Boy Scouts, the Sons of Utah Pioneers, The Days of '47, the Ogden Pioneer Days, and for the organizations of the Church (he served twenty-one years on the drama committee for the YMMIA). He married Eula Waldram, and they had three children. She died in 1964, and Brother Likes later married Margaret Davis Ball.

The Things I Do, page 170 (Words)

Lloyd, Leah Ashton

LDS. 1894–1965. Leah Lloyd was born in Salt Lake City, Utah. At the age of fourteen she was the Primary organist, and later became the ward choir organist. She was a member of the Primary General Board for twenty years, and in this position wrote over thirty songs for children and was instrumental in the preparation of *The Children Sing.* For many years she taught music to children at the Primary Children's Hospital, and in her early years of marriage she taught music lessons while her husband served a mission. She was also a member of the National League of American Pen Women. She married her childhood sweetheart, George C. Lloyd, and they had one son.

I Think When I Read That Sweet Story, page 56 (Music)
Reverence, page 27 (Music)

Lloyd, Sylvia Knight

LDS. 1933–   . Sylvia Knight Lloyd was born and raised in Salt Lake City, graduated from East High School, and received a B.S. degree in elementary education and an early childhood education certificate from the University of Utah. For a short time she taught in the Salt Lake City schools and was a flight attendant for United Airlines. She served as a tour guide on Temple Square in Salt Lake

City, and for twelve years she has been the office manager of Lloyd Design Group, an architectural firm. She is a daughter-in-law of Leah Ashton Lloyd (see above), having married Glen Ashton Lloyd. They are the parents of five children.

Repentance, page 98 (Words)

Lowden, C. Harold

?-1963. C. Harold Lowden lived in Camden, New Jersey, and was organist at the Linden Baptist Church there from 1920 to 1954, except for a period when he was organist at the First Methodist/ Episcopal Church in Camden. He also played and directed his own choir. Many of the songs he wrote were used in songbooks for the less formal services of the Methodist and Baptist Churches; the most popular among these was "Living for Jesus." He wrote a Christmas program called "God's Gracious Gift," which was published by Heidelberg Press in 1919.

Tell Me, Dear Lord, page 176 (Music)

Luch, Phyllis

LDS. 1937–   . Phyllis Luch, a convert to the Church, was born in Allentown, Pennsylvania. When her first child was five months old, missionaries taught the family the gospel. She is a self-taught artist with no advanced schooling, yet has taught illustration at Brigham Young University. Her first published work was for the *Improvement Era,* and since then she has illustrated covers for all the Church publications and has created thousands of art pieces for the Church. For four years she was a designer for the *Friend* and was one of four artists chosen to illustrate the *Children's Songbook.* She has her own art business and has won local, state, and national awards. Her husband, Warren, is also an artist, employed by the Church in the graphics design department. They have two daughters. Sister Luch has said, "Music has great power to lift the spirit. I'm sure great composers were inspired by God and numbers of people have been drawn closer to heaven through music."

I Often Go Walking, page 202 (Words)

Luke, Jemima

1813–1906. Jemima Luke was an English hymn writer. She was a contributor to *Poems for the Children's Hour,* compiled by Josephine Bouton, 1845. "That Sweet Story," a poem by Jemima Luke which uses the same words as her song, appeared in 1874 in *Sunday At Home,* a family magazine published by Piccadilly.

I Think When I Read That Sweet Story, page 56 (Words)

Lundberg, Joy Saunders

LDS. 1936–   . Joy Saunders Lundberg, who was born in Ogden, Utah, and grew up in Vale, Oregon, has made music, art, and writing an important part of her life. She recalls that as a child, on cold winter evenings, she used to lie on the floor by the stove in the family's farmhouse and draw pictures and write poems as country music played on the radio. Her education included a year at Brigham Young University, one year at a private art school in Germany, a commercial art correspondence course, and various writing workshops. In 1978 she was called as a writer for the Church curriculum department, where she served for four years; the final year she was chairman of a committee writing Primary lessons. She and her cousin, Janice Kapp Perry, have worked together to create some significant music for the Church. They have produced cantatas, songbooks, individual songs, and an LDS musical play titled "It's a Miracle," which has been presented in stakes throughout the Church. Sister Lundberg has also published her writings and poetry, which encourage children and families to live the gospel. She is married to Gary Lundberg, and they have five children.

I'm Thankful to Be Me, page 11 (Words)

Lyon, A. Laurence

LDS. 1934–   . A. Laurence Lyon was born in Rotterdam, Holland, while his father, T. Edgar Lyon, was serving as president of the Netherlands Mission. His mother reports that before he was three he said, "Mommie, someday I want to 'piano' in the Sunday

313

School." He played the piano at age seven and the violin and viola at ten. He returned to Holland as a missionary and, while there, conducted the Netherlands Choir for the dedication of the Swiss Temple in 1955. He received his B.S. and M.A. degrees from the University of Utah and a doctorate in composition from the Eastman School of Music. Dr. Lyon now teaches musical composition, theory, piano, violin, and music history at a four-year college in Oregon. He is composer of over a hundred published works, which have been performed by symphony orchestras and by the Tabernacle Choir. Two of his hymns appear in the 1985 LDS hymnbook: "Saints, Behold How Great Jehovah" and "Each Life That Touches Ours for Good." He has been a member of the Sunday School General Board and of the General Church Music Committee. He and his wife, Donna, have four children.

An Angel Came to Joseph Smith, page 86 (Music)
Christmas Bells, page 54 (Words and Music)
How Will They Know?, page 182 (Arrangement)
I Have Two Ears, page 269 (Music)
Little Pioneer Children, page 216 (Words and Music)
We Are Reverent, page 27 (Music)
Whenever I Think about Pioneers, page 222 (Music)

McAllister, John Daniel Thompson

LDS. 1827–1910. John Daniel Thompson McAllister, born in Lewes, Sussex County, Delaware, joined the Church at the age of seventeen. His father was so bitter against the Church that young John left home. He married Ellen Handley in Philadelphia, and they joined the Saints in Iowa in 1848. With a large wagon and five yoke of cattle, the McAllisters arrived in Salt Lake City in October 1851. Later he was called to serve a mission in Scotland and Wales and, upon his return, was in charge of the ship *Manchester,* bringing 376 souls to America. The family located in St. George where John McAllister was stake president for many years and was the second president of the St. George Temple; later he served as president of the Manti Temple. He was a carpenter and worked on the Salt Lake Tabernacle, he belonged to a brass band that played at the Salt Lake Temple ground-breaking ceremony, and he acted as the chief of the Salt Lake City fire department for a time.

The Handcart Song, page 220 (Words and Music)

McConochie, Barbara A.

LDS. 1940–   . Barbara McConochie, who was born in Ogden, Utah, and raised in Salt Lake City, started studying music at the age of five. She began teaching piano at thirteen and was called to be ward organist at that time. She attended Brigham Young University and the University of Utah, graduating with a Phi Kappa Phi scholastic recognition. After teaching high-school English for two years, she moved with her husband to Glendale, California. She and her husband, Douglas McConochie, have a combined family of nine children. Sister McConochie says to children, "If we strive to keep the commandments, life will be sweet to us even in our most dire trials. True peace will come to each individual, family, and nation only as we learn obedience to the laws of our Heavenly Father. . . . Keeping the commandments is the anchor for our safety amidst the storm."

Keep the Commandments, page 146 (Words, Music, and Obbligato)
You've Had a Birthday, page 285 (Words and Music)

MacDowell, Edward

1861–1908. Edward Alexander MacDowell was born in New York City and became known as one of the foremost American composers and pianists. At age fifteen he went to France to study, having won a scholarship to the Paris Conservatory. He was appointed head of the piano department at Darmstadt Conservatory in Germany when just twenty years of age. Later he returned to the United States where he received wide acclaim for his musical excellence and was appointed head of the newly formed music department at Columbia University in 1896. At an early age MacDowell suffered a nervous breakdown and began to lose his health, and so settled in a log house in New Hampshire where he resided the last years of his life. He loved nature and wrote the popular *Woodland Sketches* for piano, which included ten parts.

To a Wild Rose, page 289 (Music)

McMaster, Clara W.

LDS. 1904– . The eleventh child of her family, Clara McMaster was born in Beaver Dam, Utah, and raised in Brigham City. She attended Utah State College in Logan and taught school for a time. For twenty-two years she sang with the Tabernacle Choir. For their great musical contributions to the Church and community, she and her husband, J. Stuart McMaster, received the Franklin S. Harris Fine Arts Award from Brigham Young University in 1978.

Sister McMaster was a member of the Primary General Board for fourteen years, serving on the Primary music committee most of this time. One of her songs is included in the LDS hymnbook: "Teach Me to Walk in the Light." For three years she and her husband lived in Independence, Missouri, while he served as mission president. They are the parents of four children.

Choose the Right Way, page 160 (Words and Music)
Kindness Begins with Me, page 145 (Words and Music)
My Heavenly Father Loves Me, page 228 (Words and Music)
Remember the Sabbath Day, page 155 (Words and Music)
Reverently, Quietly, page 26 (Words and Music)
Teach Me to Walk in the Light, page 177 (Words and Music)

Maeser, Georgia

LDS. 1893–1972. Georgia Maeser was born in Beaver, Utah, and lived there and in Provo most of her life. She was stricken with a serious illness the day before her third birthday, which caused permanent injury to her spine. Though physically handicapped, she never let her affliction deter her from accomplishments. She had a quest for learning and was always at the top of her class. She attended Brigham Young University, earning a degree in elementary education and later a Bachelor of Science degree. Further education took her to the University of California and Columbia University, where she was awarded a Master of Arts degree. She was an active member of the National Education Association and the International Association for Childhood Education and taught at the Brigham Young University Training School for twenty-six years. Sister Maeser filled a mission to the Southern States. She was greatly loved by her family, especially her nieces and nephews.

I Have Two Ears, page 269 (Words)

Major, Marian

1899–1985. "Marian Major" is the pseudonym used by Lorrain E. Watters, music composer, arranger, director, and teacher. He was born in Springfield, Illinois, attended the University of Missouri, received a bachelor's degree from Drake University and master's degree from Columbia University, and studied at the Juilliard Institute in New York City. Mr. Watters moved to Des Moines, Iowa, and served as director and teacher of music education in the public schools for many years. He was the editor of two well-known music series, *Our Singing World* and *The Magic Of Music,* published by Ginn and Co. He was founder and president of the Civic Music Association and participated in Iowa and national music organizations. He won the Freedom Foundation Award in 1967 for the choral setting with band accompaniment of "American Heritage," based on the famous John F. Kennedy quotation, "Ask not what your country can do for you, but ask what you can do for your country." He was married to Ellen Jane Watters.

(Information about Lorrain Watters [Marian Major] was obtained from his wife, who lives in Des Moines, Iowa.)

When Grandpa Comes, page 201 (Words and Music)

Mangum, Marzelle

LDS. 1914–   . Marzelle Jesperson Mangum was born in Tucson, Arizona, and has lived in Arizona most of her life. She attended Brigham Young University and then left to help support her family, since she was the oldest of seven children and her father was out of work during the depression years. She has been a teacher of piano and music theory for thirty years and has served in the American Red Cross, Matinee Music Club, Community Concert Association, State Music Teachers Association, and other community groups. She and her husband, Eugene K. Mangum, have three children.

Our Primary Colors, page 258 (Words and Music)

Mann, Margaret

No information available.

I Pledge Myself to Love the Right, page 161 (Words)

Manookin, Robert P.

LDS. 1918–   . Robert Park Manookin was born in Salt Lake City, received his early education in Utah and California, and began studying music at the age of eight. He attended Brigham Young University, the University of Illinois, and the University of Utah, earning B.A., M.A., and doctoral degrees in music theory, composition, and conducting. He has held various teaching and administrative positions at BYU and the University of Utah and was named Professor Emeritus of Music at BYU. He has composed and published numerous works, some of which have been performed by the Tabernacle Choir. Dr. Manookin has served in the Church as a bishop, a member of the General Church Music Committee, and as a patriarch. As a young man he served a mission in Germany, and in recent years, with his wife, has been a missionary in the New Zealand Temple, the Manila Philippines Temple, and the Sydney Australia Temple. He composed the music for the New Zealand Temple pageant, as well as that used in the dedication of the Orson Hyde Memorial Gardens in Jerusalem in 1979. Brother Manookin has contributed six hymns to the 1985 LDS hymnbook. He married Edna Burningham, and, after her death, married Helene Haugan. He is the father of nine children from these two marriages.

A Prayer Song, page 22 (Words and Music)
Our Bishop, page 135 (Words and Music)
Repentance, page 98 (Music)

Matthews, Daphne

LDS. 1917–   . Daphne Matthews's grandparents were Mormon pioneers sent from Utah to colonize Arizona, and she was born in Thatcher, Arizona. She attended schools there and worked for an electric company for many years. She is married to Harold

I. Matthews, and they have six children and many grandchildren and great-grandchildren.

The Books in the Book of Mormon, page 119 (Words)

Maughan, Patricia Critchlow

LDS. 1926–1980. Patricia Critchlow Maughan was born in Ogden, Utah, attended Weber College, and received a B.A. degree in music from Brigham Young University. She earned a teaching certificate from the University of Utah and did graduate study there. She taught in the Salt Lake and Davis School Districts and gave private voice instruction. She was a soloist for the former Utah Opera Theater and for the University Civic Chorale. She was a member of the Tabernacle Choir and of the Primary General Board. During this last calling she served on the Primary music committee and directed a large Primary children's chorus in the Tabernacle. She was a member of the Association for Childhood Education and the National Association of Teachers of Singing. She married Datus H. Maughan, and they are the parents of three children.

Come with Me to Primary, page 255 (Words and Music)

Mendelssohn, Felix

1809–1847. Mendelssohn was born into a culturally refined home in Germany. At the age of nine he appeared in public in Berlin as a pianist, and when he was thirteen, he began to compose. He became a great conductor, giving concerts with choirs and orchestras at his father's home for family members and friends. His many compositions have become his famous musical heritage. He conducted his great oratorio "Elijah" many times, both in England and on the Continent. In 1840 Mendelssohn founded the Academy of Fine Arts in Berlin and a conservatory in Leipzig. With many unfinished plans, he was taken ill and died a few weeks later at the age of thirty-eight.

If with All Your Hearts, page 15 (Words and Music)
O Rest in the Lord, page 295 (Music)

M. E. P.

No information available.

Tell Me, Dear Lord, page 176 (Words)

Meredith, Joleen Grant

LDS. 1935–   . Joleen Meredith was born in American Fork, Utah, where her grandfather, William Grant, had been asked to settle and take music to the people many years before. She began writing music when eight years of age and would come home from grade school to work on her compositions at lunchtime. One of her treasures is that early book of musical manuscripts. Sister Meredith encourages children who might like to write music to seek help from parents or teachers and put it down on paper. She has published several musical numbers including piano solos, choral works, and children's songs; she also wrote the music for "Where Can I Turn for Peace?" (*Hymns,* no. 129.) She has served in the Church in many capacities, including as a member of the Young Women's General Board. She is married to Gary Meredith, and they are the parents of four children.

Because God Loves Me, page 234 (Words and Music)

Metz, Lois Lunt

LDS. 1906–   . Lois Lunt Metz was born in Nephi, Utah. She graduated from Utah State Agricultural College with a B.S. in education and did graduate work at Utah State Agricultural College, Brigham Young University, the University of Utah, and San Diego State. She taught in elementary school, junior high, and high school in Utah, Nevada, Idaho, and California, where she presented operettas, programs, and plays with her students. She has written and published five books of children's songs and rhythms and has had songs, articles, and poems published in children's magazines. She has received honors and recognition for her achievements. She is married to Leroy Metz.

Falling Snow, page 248 (Words and Music)

Millett, Mildred E.

LDS. 1925–   . Mildred E. Millet, who was born in Mesa, Arizona, displayed a great love of music at an early age, but her father died when she was seven, and there was no money for music lessons. A grade-school teacher intervened and generously gave of her time and talents to teach her to play the piano. In her youth she was an accompanist in church and school; she was also busy in the high-school dance program and taught ballet for several years. She married Howard F. Millett, and they moved to California where she established a private dance studio. While her children were still young, she was asked to be the Primary chorister, which gave her the incentive to compose children's songs and helped her realize the power Primary songs have on the lives of the children. Her husband became very ill, so she changed from composing to teaching piano lessons, which she continues to do today. He died in 1968, after which she and her four sons moved to Orem, Utah. She later married George Emerson NcNees. She says, "I'm grateful for the beautiful gift of music that God has given us to uplift and edify us in numerous ways."

Happy, Happy Birthday, page 284 (Words and Music)

Milne, Jaclyn Thomas

LDS. 1949–   . Born in Riverside, California, Jaclyn Milne has lived the majority of her life in the St. George, Utah, area. Her father was tragically killed when she was two years old, leaving her mother to raise three daughters. Many times, as a young child, she became very ill, and her mother would call the elders into their home to administer to her. She remembers how almost immediately after each blessing she was made well, and she learned that her Heavenly Father loves her and is always near. She attended Dixie Jr. College and Weber State College. Sister Milne has always enjoyed writing as a hobby and has received recognition in the *Ensign* writing and music contests. She and Carol Black have published several compositions, one of which, "The Miracle of America," was performed at the Kennedy Center in Washington, D. C., at the nation's bicentennial celebration. She is married to Claude Gary Milne, and they are the parents of six children.

How Dear to God Are Little Children, page 180 (Words)
Search, Ponder, and Pray, page 109 (Words)

Milner, Nita Dale

LDS. 1952–   . Nita Dale Milner was born in Salt Lake City to a family where music was as important as eating three meals a day. Her parents, at great sacrifice, made certain that their five children studied piano and other instruments. As a young woman Nita became seriously ill with kidney disease, which hampered her desire to study music more seriously. She tried some composing but was unable to do much for many years. In 1985 a kidney transplant (the kidney was provided by her mother) restored her to better health than she had known since being a teenager. She feels that she can best express her gratitude to her Heavenly Father through music. She has taught piano since she was fourteen and continues teaching at the present time. She is married to Scott Milner, and they have one son. She has said, "The music you store inside of you is something no one can take away and can help you go through times in your life that may be difficult. I believe that music is a gift from our Heavenly Father to comfort us, teach us, and make our lives happier."

When I Am Baptized, page 103 (Words and Music)

Miner, Caroline Eyring

LDS. 1907–   . Caroline Miner was born and lived her younger years in Colonial Juarez, Mexico. She also lived in Pima, Arizona, and in Logan, Utah, before locating in Salt Lake City. She is a sister of Camilla Eyring Kimball. Sister Miner graduated from Brigham Young University and was awarded a master's degree from Utah State University. For thirty years she taught high-school English in Arizona and Salt Lake City. She is the author of thirteen books of poetry and prose, including *Building a Home to Last Forever, To Everything a Season,* and *Camilla.* She has served as a hostess at the Church Office Building and a member of the YWMIA General Board for almost twenty years. She and her husband have eight children and many grandchildren. She has said, "I want to emphasize the loving influence gentle music and words can impart in the home and for our Heavenly Father."

Home, page 192 (Words)

Moody, Michael Finlinson

LDS. 1941–   . Born in Payson and raised in Spanish Fork, Utah, Michael Moody has spent his life in the world of music. He was called to serve a mission in France and France East missions, 1960–63. He received his B.A. in music theory and M.A. in music theory and composition from Brigham Young University and a doctorate in church music from the University of Southern California. Upon completion of his schooling, he accepted employment as executive secretary of the General Church Music Committee from 1972 to 1977, and subsequently became the chairman of that committee and director of the music division of the Church, a position he still retains. He was chairman of the 1985 Hymnbook Executive Committee. "Music is a tool for building families in good ways," he says. "It can bring a sweet spirit into the home. We sing before scripture reading, before meals, and on our way in the car. It keeps gospel messages in the minds of the children." He wrote the music to the hymn "Testimony," included in the LDS hymnbook. He and his wife, the former Maria Toronto, have seven children and one foster child.

Faith, page 96 (Music)
Have a Very Happy Birthday!, page 284 (Music)
Have a Very Merry Christmas!, page 51 (Music)
He Sent His Son, page 34 (Music)
Sleep, Little Jesus, page 47 (Music)
Teacher, Do You Love Me?, page 178 (Words and Music)
There Was Starlight on the Hillside, page 40 (Music)
Who Is the Child?, page 46 (Music)

Mozart, Wolfgang Amadeus

1756–1791. Wolfgang Amadeus Mozart, noted composer and pianist, was born in Salzburg, Austria. When just four years old he began studying piano from his father, and within a year was taking daily lessons that were an hour long. At age five he was composing short pieces, and at six he went on a concert tour. After his return, the Archbishop of Salzburg demanded that Mozart write an oratorio to prove he was not a fraud. The Archbishop had him locked in a room for a week by himself to accomplish the task, which he was able to do. He composed and conducted an opera for the Archbishop at age twelve. Mozart was a prolific composer, completing over 600 works including symphonies, operas, concertos, sonatas, and choral and chamber works. He led a sad life and died at age thirty-five.

I Pledge Myself to Love the Right, page 161 (Music)
Prelude in F, page 298 (Music)

Murray, James R.

1841–1905. James R. Murray was born in Andover, Massachusetts, to recently arrived Scottish immigrant parents, and studied music under fine musicians in the East. From 1856 to 1859 he was educated at the Musical Institute in North Reading, Massachusetts. After the Civil War, during which he served as a Union soldier, he alternated between teaching music in the public schools and working for music publishing houses such as Root and Cady, where he edited a monthly periodical, the *Song Messenger.* The Chicago fire of 1871 destroyed the publishing firm, and he returned to Andover to teach music. From 1881 until his death he was employed by a Cincinnati publisher, the John Church Company, heading their publishing department and editing the monthly magazine, the *Musical Visitor.* James Murray composed many Sunday School songs, gospel songs, and anthems, and compiled and edited many collections. He died in Cincinnati, Ohio.

Jesus Once Was a Little Child, page 55 (Words)

Newell, Charlene Anderson

LDS. 1938–   . Charlene Newell, who was born and raised in Price, Utah, has a great love for the arts, spiritual education, children, and family. She graduated with honors from Brigham Young University and continued studies at the University of Utah, BYU — Hawaii, and the New England Conservatory of Music. She teaches music in the Granite School District and has taught private voice and organ lessons for twenty-five years. Her music has been published in the *Friend* and other publications, and in 1977 she won the Relief Society song contest for her composition "A Woman's

Prayer," which was performed at the dedication of the Nauvoo Monument to Women and at an LDS women's conference in the Tabernacle. She wrote the music to the hymn "A Key Was Turned in Latter Days." (*Hymns,* no. 310.) She and her husband, Robert R. Newell, are the parents of twelve children.

He Died That We Might Live Again, page 65 (Music)
Little Jesus, page 39 (Music)
The Commandments, page 112 (Music)
Your Happy Birthday, page 283 (Words and Music)

Newell, Mark

LDS. 1961–   . Mark Newell was born in Price, Utah, the oldest of twelve children. His mother is Charlene Newell, who is the composer of several songs in the *Children's Songbook.* He is creative and loves music, playing drums, piano, and trumpet. By trade he is a carpenter and auto mechanic, and enjoys playing basketball and football. He says, "Music is an eternal gift and is enjoyed at home, church, and work. Melodies and lyrics that make you feel good are constructive to the soul."

Little Jesus, page 39 (Music)

Nibley, Reid N.

LDS. 1923–   . Reid Nibley was born in Santa Monica, California, where he spent his younger years. He received his advanced education at the University of Utah (B.F.A. and M.A.) and at the University of Michigan (D.M.A.). He has performed as a concert pianist for some fifty years; he started piano lessons when six years old, played his first concert at thirteen, and soloed with the Los Angeles Philharmonic at seventeen years of age. Reid Nibley has been a Professor of Music at the University of Utah, University of Michigan, National Music Camp at Interlaken, Michigan, and at Brigham Young University for sixteen years. He was the official pianist for the Utah Symphony Orchestra for ten years. Dr. Nibley has published several LDS hymn arrangements for piano, choral pieces, and a beginning piano method series. His Church service has been wide and varied, including Temple Square guide and a member of the General Church Music Committee. He reports that he especially enjoys writing music for children. His children's song "I Know My Father Lives" also appears in the LDS hymnbook. Reid Nibley is married to the former Marjorie McBride, and they have six children.

I Know My Father Lives, page 5 (Words and Music)
I'll Walk with You, page 140 (Music)

Nielsen, Patricia Haglund

LDS. 1936–   . Patricia Nielsen, born and raised in Los Angeles, has been involved in music education since she received her B.A. in music at UCLA and her M.A. in music education at Teachers College, Columbia University. She taught in Los Angeles City Schools, at the Lab School at UCLA, at Mills College of Education in New York City, and for twenty years at Brigham Young University. She has given music workshops all over the United States and Canada. She has served as the elementary vice president for the Utah Music Educators Association and was honored by them in 1988 as the Elementary Music Educator of the Year. Her publications include *Mockingbird Flight,* songs and teaching suggestions for children, and *Sing with Me in Harmony,* LDS Primary songs with harmony. She provided teaching suggestions for two volumes of *Songs for Little Angels with Dirty Faces,* folk songs for children. Pat filled a mission in Germany, where she and her companions started nonmember Primaries, with music being the initial drawing card. She is married to F. Kent Nielsen, and they have seven children and several grandchildren.

Oh, Hush Thee, My Baby, page 48 (Ostinato)
Quickly, I'll Obey, page 197 (Ostinato)

Obray, Barbara Boyer

LDS. 1927–   . Barbara Boyer Obray, a homemaker, secretary, piano teacher, and composer, was born and grew up in Monrovia, California, but has lived for the past thirty-two years in the Phoenix, Arizona, area. After high school she attended Brigham Young University, majoring in music. Now, as a grandmother, she is working toward her B.A. degree in fine arts at Arizona State University. She is a member of the Arizona Mormon Songwriters Association and has had several songs published. Her present projects are a book of songs for beginning pianists and music for a children's video. She married Bryce W. Obray, and they have six children.

Two Happy Feet, page 270 (Music)

Oglevee, Louise M.

Presbyterian. Abt. 1866–1954. Louise McAroy Oglevee was born in the Chicago area and lived for the last fifty years of her life in Rock Island, Illinois. She was a lively, talented girl who was a perfect match for her preacher husband, William G. Oglevee. She served not only the usual functions of a minister's wife, but worked tirelessly with Sunday School and youth groups, developing what became widely used nursery school and Sunday School materials when she found no suitable ones available. She also wrote words for many of her husband's songs. Louise Oglevee continued as a "pillar" of the church that her husband had developed, for the fifteen years she lived after his death. They had two children. (This information and spelling of the name was obtained from a granddaughter, Mary Louise Oglevee Rack.)

This Is God's House, page 30 (Words)

Oglevee, William G.

Presbyterian. 1865–1939. William G. Oglevee was born in Liberty, Pennsylvania. He began his musical training at an early age on an old reed organ in his home, where his father led singing for the church. He studied piano, organ, and the cornet at Lincoln College in Illinois, and graduated from McCormick Theological Seminary in Chicago, Illinois. He was the first pastor at the Home-mission Church, now the First Presbyterian Church, in Ponca City, Oklahoma, where his first song was written about 1900. He moved to Mediapolis, Iowa, and soon after to Rock Island, Illinois, where he was first the assistant pastor at Broadway Presbyterian Church and then took over the mission in the south of town, which he built up to the current South Park Presbyterian Church. He remained there until illness forced his retirement. William Oglevee collaborated with his wife, Louise M. Oglevee, in writing songs for church and Sunday School; his music was published in many volumes. The Oglevees had two children. (This information and the spelling of the name was obtained from a granddaughter, Mary Louise Oglevee Rack.)

This Is God's House, page 30 (Music)

Olauson, Maggie

LDS. 1949–   . Margaret Louise Olauson was born in Cedar City, Utah, grew up in Provo, and has lived in various East coast states since her marriage. She attended Brigham Young University, graduating in interior design. She loves music and teaches piano in her home, which is currently in the Washington, D.C., area. She is married to Douglas J. Olauson, a Navy Chaplain, and they are the parents of three sons and three daughters.

Reverence Is Love, page 31 (Words and Music)

Olsen, Rita Mae

LDS. 1932–   . Born and raised in Richmond, Utah, Rita Mae Olsen recently retired from twenty-seven years of school teaching; she also taught private organ and piano lessons for many years. She has been honored on several occasions for her achievements in the teaching profession. At present she enjoys playing the organ in the chapel at the Ogden Temple, and writing children's music has become one of her favorite hobbies. She is married to Sherman F. Olsen, and they have two children. She has said, "Beautiful music is inspirational, uplifting, and delightful. Whenever I am depressed or down, it lifts my spirit and brings joy back into my life. . . . Music is an international language; even though many different languages are sung . . . it seems to be understood by all."

It's Autumntime, page 246 (Words and Music)

Ozment, Maurine Benson

LDS. 1932–   . A musician of much accomplishment, Maurine Benson Ozment was born in Logan, Utah, and has lived in California, Colorado, Arizona, and currently in Georgia. She received her B.A. degree from Brigham Young University and her Master of Music Education from Utah State University. She co-authored and taught music classes, "Petite World of Music," for preschool children in Orange County, California; taught elementary school for ten years; taught private piano for thirty years; and taught piano at the university level. She toured for the University of Wyoming's Cultural Outreach program, conducted the Ogden City Elementary School Chorus, and was the accompanist for the Ogden and Weber College Community Chorale and the Anaheim Pops Chorale. She and her husband, Arnold D. Ozment, have eight children. Sister Ozment says, "In our international church, music is one of the things that remains the same from one culture to the next, building bonds of unity among the members. One can travel the world over and not understand the language at church in a faraway land, but the familiar music of a beloved song can immediately bring feelings of security and belonging to one's heart. Oh, how I love our wonderful Primary songs and the joy they bring to people everywhere!"

Feliz Cumpleaños, page 282 (Words and Music)
Hello Song, page 260 (Words and Music)

Pace, Cynthia Lord

LDS. 1955–   . Cynthia Lord Pace was born in Salt Lake City, one of ten children in a musical family. Her father, who is a singer, wanted to have a "built-in" accompanist, so he started her on the piano at age seven, and she became his constant accompanist. She attended Brigham Young University for two years and then married. Early in her marriage Sister Pace was diagnosed as having cancer of the lymph system. The following years were difficult, but she feels she has had rich spiritual blessings and has enjoyed a full recovery. Her five children are her greatest source of joy and inspiration. She says, "I think music is a deeper form of communication than talking, and it makes me feel wonderful things."

Latter-day Prophets, page 134 (Words)

Parker, Judith Wirthlin

LDS. 1919–   . Judith Wirthlin Parker, born in Salt Lake City, Utah, is a musician and educator, having received her B.A., M.A., and Ph.D. degrees at the University of Utah. She served on the

Primary General Board for fifteen years, much of that time as a member of the music committee. She directed children's choruses in the Tabernacle for Primary conferences and was chairman of the committee that produced *Sing with Me* in 1969. Since 1986 she has spent considerable time in Egypt, teaching professionally and researching the music and culture. This interest was heightened when she and her husband were called by the Church as special representatives to Egypt. She has been an adjunct professor of ancient studies at BYU since 1982 and has written two books: *Goha — Egyptian Folktales for Children* and *The Music of Egypt*, as well as articles for the *Ensign* and the *Friend*. Sister Parker is married to Thomas O. Parker, and they have six children.

I Need My Heavenly Father, page 18 (Words and Music)

Parker, W. H.

Baptist. 1845–1929. William Henry Parker, a composer of hymns, was born in New Basford, England. He was apprenticed in the machine- construction department of a New Basford lace-making plant and later headed an insurance company. He was a member of the Chelsea Street Baptist Church in Nottingham and was active in Sunday School work. Most of Parker's hymns were written for Sunday School anniversaries. Fifteen appear in the National Sunday School Union's *Sunday School Hymnary*, 1905. He died in Nottingham, England, at the age of eighty-four.

Tell Me the Stories of Jesus, page 57 (Words)

Payne, I. Reed

LDS. 1930–   . I. Reed Payne was born in Duncan, Arizona, and moved to Idaho as a child. He attended Ricks College for two years, received his B.S. degree from Brigham Young University, then went to Penn State, earning his master's and Ph.D. in psychology. He filled a mission in Eastern Canada.

Brother Payne studied music beginning as a small child; as a young man, he played for dance bands to earn a little extra money. Music has always been part of the gospel in his life. He states, "Music carries the message of a song, stirs our feelings, and strengthens our testimony. Music helps us worship with meaning and expression." Brother Payne teaches psychology at Brigham Young University, including a psychology of music course. He is married to Ruth Goodson Payne, and they have one daughter and five sons.

When Joseph Went to Bethlehem, page 38 (Music)

Pearson, Carol Lynn

LDS. 1939–   . Carol Lynn Pearson was born in Salt Lake City. Many of her ancestors were pioneers who came to Utah before the railroad. She earned B.A. and M.A. degrees in theater from Brigham Young University, has taught drama and English at a college level, and has traveled extensively both as an actress and as a speaker. She has written many books of poetry and prose and numerous plays, including "It's My Life" and "My Turn on Earth." She is also the author of several educational motion pictures, including "Cipher in the Snow," an eight-time international award-winning film. Now living in Walnut Creek, California, she considers her ward to be a "larger family" for her and her four children.

I'll Walk with You, page 140 (Words)

Perry, Janice Kapp

LDS. 1938–   . Born in Ogden, Utah, and raised in Vale, Oregon, Janice Kapp Perry now lives in Provo, Utah. She received her musical training at Brigham Young University and has contributed immensely to the music of the Church. She has been writing music on Church themes for over twelve years and has produced sixteen albums and songbooks of original music, five sacred cantatas (two of which have been performed in the Salt Lake Tabernacle), and numerous musical presentations for the auxiliaries of the Church. She composed the music for the popular LDS musical "It's a Miracle." Many of her songs have been published in the Church magazines, and she composed the music for "As Sisters in Zion," included in the 1985 LDS hymnbook. Until she and her husband can serve a full-time mission, she feels that writing music is the best way she can strengthen members' testimonies and introduce the gospel to nonmembers. She and her husband, Douglas C. Perry, are the parents of five children and several foster children.

A Child's Prayer, page 12 (Words and Music)
I Love to See the Temple, page 95 (Words and Music)
I Pray in Faith, page 14 (Words and Music)
I'm Thankful to Be Me, page 11 (Music)
I'm Trying to Be Like Jesus, page 78 (Words and Music)
Love Is Spoken Here, page 190 (Words and Music)
Mother, Tell Me the Story, page 204 (Words and Music)
The Church of Jesus Christ, page 77 (Words and Music)
The Word of Wisdom, page 154 (Words and Music)
We'll Bring the World His Truth, page 172 (Words and Music)

Petersen, Faye Glover

1914–   . Born in Midvale, Utah, Faye Glover Petersen grew up on a farm. She was a tomboy who loved to climb trees and play outdoors, yet she studied piano and voice and took several classes at a college level, spending one year in New York. She worked at the State School Board Office in youth corrections and for nineteen years at Zions Bank. An enthusiastic traveler with a great interest in various cultures, she has visited India, China, Tibet, Kenya, Turkey, Greece, and South America. She is married to LaMar Petersen, and they have six children.

Because It's Spring, page 239 (Words and Music)
When I Go to Church, page 157 (Words and Music)

Peterson, DeVota Mifflin

LDS. 1910–   . DeVota Mifflin Peterson, who was born and reared in Malad, Idaho, began taking piano lessons at an early age and remembers her father paying Professor Powell, from Wales, one dollar a lesson. She became the ward Primary pianist at fourteen and in high school earned extra money by playing the piano in a dance band. She studied at the McCune School of Music, specializing in piano. Attending college at Utah State, the University of Utah, and the University of Idaho, she received a teacher's diploma and a bachelor's degree and taught for a number of years in Malad and in Salt Lake City. She says, "Our Heavenly Father blesses us when we serve Him and do what is right.... Good music is a noble and inspiring gift from God. A child will long remember the hours spent singing in Primary, and with parents, brothers, and sisters in the warmth of the family circle." DeVota Peterson married Phil L. Peterson, and they are the parents of two daughters.

Family Prayer, page 189 (Words and Music)

Pettit, Mildred Tanner

LDS. 1895–1977. Mildred Tanner Pettit, a descendant of the Mayflower pilgrims and of the original Utah pioneers, was born in Salt Lake City, Utah, and lived in California and Michigan as a child. She attended LDS High School in Salt Lake, and later the University of Utah. She studied music—piano, pipe organ, harmony, counterpoint, and advanced composition—for ten years at the McCune School of Music. She also spent a year at Azchwer Hahn Musical Academy at Philadelphia. After teaching school for several years in Salt Lake City, she married William A. Pettit, a medical school graduate. She served in the Primary for thirty-five years, including four years on the Primary General Board. During this time she collaborated with Matilda Watts Cahoon on many programs and songs for the children of the Church. Altogether she authored 145 musical selections, two of which are included in the 1985 LDS hymnbook: "I Am a Child of God" and "The Light Divine."

Beauty Everywhere, page 232 (Music)
Father, I Will Reverent Be, page 29 (Words and Music)
I Am a Child of God, page 2 (Music)
Mother Dear, page 206 (Music)

Pheatt, Fanny Giralda

Her song "Springtime Is Coming" was published in *Sing a Song* of *The World of Music,* 1936, by Ginn and Company. No further information is available.

Springtime Is Coming, page 238 (Words)

Phelps, W. W.

LDS. 1792–1872. William Wines Phelps, who was born in Hanover, New Jersey, became interested in Mormonism through reading the Book of Mormon. The Lord's instruction for him to be baptized and take part in the early Church is noted in the Doctrine and Covenants, section 55. He became active in preaching the gospel and assisting the Prophet. He was a member of the presidency of the Church in Missouri and one of the scribes for the Prophet in translating the Book of Abraham from papyrus. He was appointed to revise the hymns selected by Emma Smith and to prepare them for publication; he contributed many hymns to that volume. For a time he became separated from the Church, but he later rejoined and fulfilled a mission to the Eastern States. He crossed the plains to Salt Lake City and became one of the first regents of the University of Deseret and a member of the Utah legislature. He contributed the text to fifteen of the hymns in the 1985 LDS hymnbook, including "The Spirit of God," "Now Let Us Rejoice," "Redeemer of Israel," and "Praise to the Man."

The Books in the New Testament, page 116 (Arrangement)

Pinborough, Jan Underwood

LDS. 1954–   . Jan Underwood Pinborough was born and raised in Midland, Texas. She attended Brigham Young University, where she received a B.A. in English and an M.A. in linguistics. She became an editor in the curriculum department of the Church and subsequently an assistant editor of the *Ensign* and an associate editor of the Church's international magazines. She has had a number of articles published in the *Ensign* and other Church publications and has served on Church writing committees responsible for the Family Home Evening Resource Book and for Relief Society lessons. She is married to Thomas Vince Pinborough, and they have two daughters.

Mary's Lullaby, page 44 (Words)

Ponsonby, A. B.

This writer and composer had several songs published in *Songs for Little Children,* 1905, by the Pilgrim Press. These songs were also included in a songbook published by the Congregational Sunday School and Publishing Society in the early 1900s. No other information is available.

Autumn Day, page 247 (Words and Music)

Poorman, Nellie

Her song "God Is Watching Over All" (formerly "Loving Care") was published in *Tuning Up* of *The World of Music,* 1936, by Ginn and Company. No other information is available.

God Is Watching Over All, page 229 (Words)

Provost, Della Dalby

LDS. 1910–1973. Della Dalby Provost was born in Rexburg, Idaho, and attended the University of Utah, receiving a B.S. degree in education. She taught kindergarten and high school art for some fifteen years, then left teaching for a time to attend Brigham Young University, where she received a masters degree in elementary education at the age of fifty. After this she taught in the BYU education department, supervising student teachers. She served on the Primary General Board for three years and at the time of her death was serving on the Church Correlation Committee. Sister Provost wrote many stories for the *Children's Friend* and lessons for Family Home Evening manuals. She married Emery Orval Provost, and they were the parents of two children.

Whenever I Think about Pioneers, page 222 (Words)

Randall, Naomi Ward

LDS. 1908–   . Born in North Ogden, Utah, Naomi Ward Randall was an imaginative child, beginning to tell her own stories and making up her own rhymes and jingles from the time she could talk. She graduated from Ogden High School and took courses from Utah State, Weber State, and Brigham Young University. She served for twenty-eight years on the Primary General Board, four of them as a counselor to President LaVern W. Parmley. She served on the editorial board for the *Children's Friend* for over thirteen years and wrote articles, poems, stories, and lessons, including the "Barnabee Bumbleberry" series, a children's picture story, and a series of children's Bible stories. She traveled to many areas of the world, including all fifty states, conducting and speaking at Primary conventions. Following the death of her husband, Sister

Randall served a full-time mission in Washington, D.C. She and her husband, Earl A. Randall, have one daughter.

I Am a Child of God, page 2 (Words)
I Want to Live the Gospel, page 148 (Words)

Randolph, Richard

1911–1969. "Richard Randolph" is a pseudonym used by William R. Fisher, a music educator and composer of music for children. He was born in New York City and received his education at New York University and Boston University. He became a professor of music at Lowell State College (later Lowell University) near Boston, where he was appointed head of the music department and was the assistant dean of the graduate school for the two years before his death. He compiled the third-grade book for the *This Is Music for Today* series, published by Allyn and Bacon. Many of the songs in this book are his own compositions, including "Covered Wagons." His wife, Doris Fisher, was the lyricist for most of his children's songs. The recital hall at Lowell University is named the William Fisher Hall after this respected and loved music educator. William and Doris Fisher had four children.

Covered Wagons, page 221 (Music)

Read, Dorothy Little

LDS. 1920–   . Dorothy Little Read was born in Ogden, Utah. At thirteen she became the pianist for Jr. Sunday School, and at sixteen the organist for Sunday School, pianist for Primary, teacher, and counselor. She says of her Primary callings: "It was in Primary that I learned about planning ahead, scheduling time, children's characteristics at a given age, gospel principles at a child's level of understanding, the importance of music as a teaching tool in Church, dedication, punctuality, and much more. I loved serving in the Primary." She has written many songs, poems, and programs for wards and stakes and has taught piano and organ to students and church groups for over forty-two years. Recently she wrote and published a series of music study books. She and her husband, Keith J. Read, have served a mission to the Oakland California Temple Visitor's Center. They are the parents of two children.

The Chapel Doors, page 156 (Words and Music)

Reading, Lucile Cardon

LDS. 1909–1982. Lucile C. Reading, a talented writer and educator, was born in Logan, Utah, attended Utah State University, and taught school for a time. During her lifetime she was the owner of an infants and children's wear shop, secretary of the Utah division of the American Cancer Society, secretary of the Berkeley-Contra area council of the Boy Scouts of America, executive secretary of the South Davis Chamber of Commerce, and a member of the Davis County school board. She was called to the Primary General Board in 1962 and a year later became a counselor to President LaVern Parmley, a position she held for seven years. She served as the managing editor of the *Friend* magazine until her death. She was married to Keith E. Reading, and they had two sons.

The Handcart Song, page 220 (Words)

Remsen, F.

No information available.

Thank Thee, Father, page 24 (Music)

Renstrom, Moiselle

LDS. 1889–1956. Born in Huntsville, Utah, Moiselle Renstrom was a well-known writer of music for little children. She taught school for many years in Salt Lake City and in Weber and Davis Counties. She had the gift of "becoming as a little child"; perhaps her greatest talent was the ability to be simple in her approach to music and to learning. Her songs and rhythms help children pretend as they move with and feel the music. Her songbooks, *Rhythm Fun, Merrily We Sing,* and *Musical Adventures,* have been used in primary-grade classrooms throughout the world. During the year before her death, she was asked by the General Church Music Committee to write a number of little songs and sermons for Jr. Sunday School children. Her name is attached to thirteen songs in the *Children's Songbook.*

A Happy Family, page 198 (Words and Music)

A Happy Helper, page 197 (Words and Music)
A Prayer, page 22 (Words and Music)
I Am Glad for Many Things, page 151 (Words and Music)
I Love to Pray, page 25 (Words and Music)
Jesus Loved the Little Children, page 59 (Words and Music)
Jesus Said Love Everyone, page 61 (Words and Music)
Little Seeds Lie Fast Asleep, page 243 (Words and Music)
Once There Was a Snowman, page 249 (Words and Music)
Rain Is Falling All Around, page 241 (Words and Music)
The World Is So Lovely, page 233 (Words and Music)
To Get Quiet, page 275 (Words and Music)
Two Little Eyes, page 268 (Words and Music)

Reynolds, Becky-Lee Hill

LDS. 1944–   . Becky-Lee Hill Reynolds was born in Abilene, Texas, but has lived in Utah since she was three months old. She attended the University of Utah for four years. At an early age she was recognized for her ability in writing and composing, which was considered a family gift. (Her grandmother, Maryhale Woolsey, wrote the words to an American favorite, "Springtime in the Rockies," and some Primary songs, including "I Have a Garden.") Sister Reynolds served as a missionary in France for two years. She married Don Wilson Conover Reynolds, and they have five children.

Heavenly Father, While I Pray, page 23 (Words and Music)
My Mother Dear, page 203 (Words and Music)

Riley, Alice C. D.

1867–1955. Alice Cushing Donaldson Riley was an American poetess, born in Morrison, Illinois. She was educated at Park Institute in Chicago and also studied abroad. She wrote plays, pageants, poems, song verses, and other works for children. Mrs. Riley belonged to writing and drama clubs and had her works published in a number of books and periodicals. She and her husband, Harrison B. Riley, lived much of their lives in Pasadena, California.

Thank Thee, Father, page 24 (Words)

Robinson, Rita S.

LDS. 1920–   . Rita S. Robinson was born in Salt Lake City. Her father died when she was three years old, and her mother, though she did not have a testimony of the gospel, sent Rita to LDS meetings because the gospel had meant so much to him. Rita graduated cum laude from the University of Utah and taught school in Milford and Salt Lake City. During World War II she worked for the Navy in Long Beach, California, as a welder, was recognized as a Master Welder, and took part in a film prepared to train others. Her natural musical talent lead her to write music for many occasions. She wrote the words and music for twenty-seven children's songs that were published in 1962 by Deseret Book Company in a collection called *I Like to Sing*. She was married to Oscar Robinson, and they had three children. After her husband's death she served a mission in California, and she now lives in Salt Lake City.

Hosanna, page 66 (Words and Music)
Saturday, page 196 (Words and Music)

Rodgers, Ralph, Jr.

LDS. 1936–   . Ralph G. Rodgers, who was born in Salt Lake City, earned a B.S. in music from the University of Utah, where he also did graduate studies in educational administration. He has written, performed in, and directed various productions on gospel subjects and has served on the General Church Music Committee, the Young Men's General Board, as a missionary and mission president to Samoa, and as a Regional Representative. For six years he was associated with the Polynesian Cultural Center in Hawaii as president/general manager and technical consultant. He was general manager and director of Promised Valley Playhouse as well as starring in, producing, or directing over fifty professional productions. He has said, "I believe that God gave us talents to be used in his service and not just for our own enjoyment. As long as we use those talents in that way, he will continue to bless and magnify those talents." He and his wife, Joan Mary Williams, have six children.

I Feel My Savior's Love, page 74 (Words)

Rowley, Grietje Terburg

LDS. 1927–   . Grietje (pronounced GREE-chuh) Terburg Rowley is a convert to the LDS Church born in Homestead, Florida. She attended the Oberlin Conservatory of Music and received a bachelor of music education degree from the University of Miami in Florida. She joined the Church while teaching school in Hawaii, and subsequently moved to Salt Lake City. She has written children's songs, prize-winning Relief Society songs, piano preludes, choir songs, vocal solos, hymn arrangements, and a mini-cantata for Christmas. When she is working on a song, she always prays that the words will say what Heavenly Father wants them to say. She tries to make the music sound pretty, to make it easy to sing and to play and, above all, easy to remember. She is a member of the Composers Guild, the Association of Latter-day Media Artists, and the National League of American Pen Women.

Sister Rowley assisted in the preparation of the *Children's Songbook*, editing, proofreading, transposing, and arranging. She composed the text and music to "Be Thou Humble," (*Hymns*, no. 130), and is a member of the General Church Music Committee. She is married to Grant Rowley, and they have three children.

A Smile Is like the Sunshine, page 267 (Music)
Distant Bells, page 299 (Music)
Each Sunday Morning, page 290 (Music)
Father, We Thank Thee for the Night, page 8 (Music)
I Want to Be a Missionary Now, page 168 (Words and Music)
Roll Your Hands, page 274 (Arrangement)
Samuel Tells of the Baby Jesus, page 36 (Music)

Ryser, Thelma Johnson

LDS. 1898–1984. Thelma Johnson Ryser was born in Salt Lake City, Utah. She served in many capacities in the Church, including as a member of the Primary General Board for ten years. For over forty years she played the organ for the Larkin Mortuary. She was a member and patroness of Mu Phi Epsilon, Honorary Musicians Sorority, a member of the Federation of Music Clubs, member and president of the Opera Appreciation Club, and member and director of the Art Barn. She married Jonas T. Ryser.

Jesus Has Risen, page 70 (Words and Music)

Ryskamp, Peggy Hill

LDS. 1949– . Peggy Hill Ryskamp was born in Seattle, Washington, and raised in Fresno, California, the oldest of seven children. She attended Brigham Young University, receiving a B.A. in English and French. She served a mission in France from 1970 to 1972 and, upon returning, taught high school in Idaho Falls, Idaho. She has served in many Church callings and recently had the opportunity to serve in the Riverside, California, DeAnza Spanish Branch (where her husband served as branch president) as Primary first counselor, Spiritual Living teacher, Young Women first counselor, and Primary president and chorister. She is married to George Ryskamp, and they have four children. She says, "I know that when the children in Primary try their hardest to sing, our Father in heaven really is proud of them."

Children All Over the World, page 16 (Words)

Schreiner, Alexander

LDS. 1901–1987. Alexander Schreiner was born in Nurnberg, Germany, and immigrated to Salt Lake City as a boy of eleven. He began playing the piano at the age of five and at age eight became the church organist. He also became proficient on the violin. By the time he was seven, he had memorized most of the music in the LDS hymnbook. He served a mission in California, after which he returned to Europe to study with celebrated organists. He majored in composition and earned the first Ph.D. in music given at the University of Utah. He played his first recitals at the Tabernacle before he was twenty-one years old and soon after was appointed Tabernacle organist. Millions of people all over the world have heard Dr. Schreiner's magnificent organ broadcasts from the Tabernacle, as he maintained this position some fifty-three years. Not only did he excel as an organist, but he also made great contributions as a composer, arranger, writer, and concert artist. He composed the music for nine hymns in the 1985 LDS hymnbook, including "While of These Emblems We Partake," "God Loved Us, So He Sent His Son," and "In Memory of the Crucified." He married Margaret Lyman, and they are the parents of four children.

I Think the World Is Glorious, page 230 (Music)
Jesus Is Our Loving Friend, page 58 (Music)
My Flag, My Flag, page 225 (Music)
We Bow Our Heads, page 25 (Music)

Schubert, Franz

1797–1828. Franz Schubert was born in Vienna, Austria, to a musical family who cultivated string-quartet playing in the home, the boy Schubert playing the viola. He studied organ and musical theory and, in 1808, at age eleven, won a scholarship to the Imperial Court Chapel Choir. He also entered a teachers' training college and became assistant in his father's school. Schubert was inclined to be shy and was reluctant to show his first compositions to his school friends. Their interest and encouragement helped him overcome his shyness. In his thirty-one years of life, Schubert composed more than 600 beautiful songs and 1200 compositions in all. Few people of his time recognized his genius.

Andante, page 294 (Music)
God Is Watching Over All, page 229 (Music)
Impromptu, page 288 (Music)

Scott, Louise B.

1914–   . Louise Binder Scott was born and grew up on an Iowa farm, her pioneer ancestors coming from Kentucky. She received her B.A. degree from Emerson College and an M.A. in education from Boston University. Further studies took her to Yale and the University of Southern California. She was an audiologist and speech pathologist with the San Marino School District for eight years and associate professor of speech at Cal State (Los Angeles) University for twelve years before resigning to write full-time. In 1986 she was given the Outstanding Achievement Award by the California Speech-Language-Hearing Association. While teaching in Los Angeles, she collaborated with her friend and colleague Lucille F. Wood in writing and composing *Singing Fun* and *More Singing Fun,* which are still in print. Her *Time for Phonics,* four children's expendable books K-3, sold five million copies before revision. She is a member of the prestigious group of poets, essayists, playwrights and novelists, International P.E.N.

I Wiggle, page 271 (Words)
My Hands, page 273 (Words)

Seely, Gladys Ericksen

LDS. 1899–1985. Gladys Ericksen Seely was born in Mt. Pleasant, Utah, the ninth of ten children, five of whom died in infancy. Gladys's mother prayed for a daughter who could play the piano, and she was an answer to these prayers, showing a natural talent at a very young age. She could play any piece she heard by memory in any key. By age twelve she was playing for the silent movies in the local movie theater, and later she played for dancing schools and taught private piano lessons. Through playing the piano, she felt she expressed her belief and love for the gospel. She married Chesley P. Seely, and they were the parents of three children.

Before I Take the Sacrament, page 73 (Music)
Father Up Above, page 23 (Music)

Shurtleff, Lynn R.

LDS. 1939–   . Born in Vallejo, California, Lynn Richard Shurtleff received his B.A. and M.A. in music theory from Brigham Young University. Graduate studies took him to Indiana University and Vienna, Austria. He began his teaching at the Moapa Valley High School in Overton, Nevada, and then joined the music faculty of Santa Clara University, where he is currently chairman of the music department. He has toured many foreign countries on concert tours, principally as the musical director and conductor of the Santa Clara Chorale. He founded the Prune Hollow Choral Society, a choir composed of students from all high schools of the Santa Clara Valley; they toured Romania, Mexico, Hawaii, and Europe under his directorship. Many musical compositions are attributed to Dr. Shurtleff, including a symphony, music for chamber orchestra, choral works, and pageants. He has received the Ferdinand Grossman Fellowship for study in Europe, the Thomas Terry Grant for composition, and the Santa Clara University Distinguished Faculty Award. He served a mission in Uruguay, Paraguay, Argentina, and Brazil and has served for four years as a member of the General Music Committee of the Church. His hymn "Father, This Hour Has Been One of Joy" is included in the LDS hymnbook. He is married to Alma Don McArthur, and they have five children.

Pioneer Children Were Quick to Obey, page 215 (Music)

Sleeth, Natalie W.

Protestant. 1930–   . Natalie Sleeth was born in Evanston, Illinois, and is a graduate of Wellesley College, where she majored in music theory. She married Dr. Ronald Sleeth, now deceased, a distinguished Methodist teacher, preacher, and writer, and they have two children. She began composing about 1969 after taking a course in the choral department of Southern Methodist University, and since then has composed over 180 songs, words and music, both sacred and secular. She has been a member of ASCAP for over fifteen years and has received annual awards from them since 1975. She was awarded an honorary doctorate by West Virginia Wesleyan College in December 1989. Natalie Sleeth has written a book about music, *Adventures for the Soul,* and collaborated with Marvin Payne to produce a work about Old Testament stories called *The Wonderful Story of Old,* which includes sixty songs connected by dialogue. She has said, "I want to write something worth singing and something worth singing about." The Mormon Tabernacle Choir has sung several of her works.

How Will They Know?, page 182 (Words, Music, and Arrangement)

Smith, Joseph

LDS. 1805–1844. Founder, prophet, and first president of The Church of Jesus Christ of Latter-day Saints, Joseph Smith was born in Sharon, Vermont. Through his earnest searching for the truth regarding religion, he was blessed to be visited and instructed by the Father and the Son. Joseph Smith translated, with heavenly guidance, the ancient record on gold plates that was ultimately published as the Book of Mormon. Under his direction, The Church of Jesus Christ of Latter-day Saints was organized in 1830. Priesthood authority was restored and the keys to the kingdom of God were given to the Prophet and his associates. Joseph Smith was martyred by an angry mob in Carthage, Illinois, in 1844, but the church he founded has continued to flourish and move across the earth, as he prophesied.

The Articles of Faith, page 122–132 (Words)

Smith, Norma B.

LDS. 1923–   . Norma Broadbent Smith was born in Heber City, Utah, and attended Wasatch High School and the University of Utah. Through her talents in writing, public speaking, and music, she has contributed to the community and to the Church. She sang with the Carlson Singers of Preston, Idaho, and the Celeste Singers of Ogden and was a member of the Ogden School Foundation and the Citizens Advisory Board of the University of Utah College of Nursing. She was chosen the Ogden Mother of the Year in 1985. Her service in the Church has included member of the Primary General Board, writer of manuals for the Church instructional development department, and counselor in the Young Women General Presidency. She and her husband, Lowell D. Smith, have eight children and many grandchildren.

Where Love Is, page 138 (Words)

Smyth, A. C.

LDS. 1840–1909. Adam Craik Smyth was born in Manchester, England, and was a pupil of Sir Isaac Pitman, the originator of the shorthand system. He was converted to the gospel in Utah, having immigrated in 1864, not knowing of the Mormons until he arrived. He taught school and music in Cache County and in Salt Lake City and became prominent in musical affairs as a choir leader and choral instructor. He composed many beautiful hymn tunes and anthems which have been included in LDS publications. Four of his hymns, including his musical adaptation of "Joseph Smith's First Prayer," appear in the LDS hymnbook. Brother Smyth organized a Juvenile Opera Company and organized and produced musical performances in the Salt Lake Theatre including the operettas of Gilbert and Sullivan. Later he moved to Manti, where he directed the local choir and became a recorder and singing conductor for the Manti Temple. He married Emily Brown, Rhoda Waeson, and Frances Harriet Townsden and had several children.

Dare to Do Right, page 158 (Arrangement)

Sorensen, Nonie Nelson

LDS. 1925–   . Leonora Nelson Sorensen, who was born in Salt Lake City, graduated from the University of Utah with a B.A. degree and taught modern dance at the University for several years. Her mother taught her to play the piano at an early age, and, though she is an accomplished pianist and composer, she took few formal lessons until college age. Her major musical interest has been in creating historical dramas about persons in Mormon history. She has written over a dozen such presentations. She has served as a member of the Young Women's General Board and, with her husband, Maynard Sorensen, has completed several short missions to Nauvoo where she was called to create and produce LDS musicals for the summer season. She and her husband have eleven children and many grandchildren. She has said, "I grew up listening to great music in my home and still find a most delicious experience is to watch a magnificent sunset or another of God's great wonders while listening to great music. I love to sing fun songs, too; and I love to hear my grandchildren sing to me."

Grandmother, page 200 (Words and Music)

Spencer, Bessie Saunders

Methodist. 1898–1989. Bessie Saunders Spencer was born in Pueblo, Colorado, and was a free-lance poet and writer. Her poetry appeared in many religious and popular magazines, including the *Friend.* She contributed to anthologies, including "This Is America," and was the recipient of numerous awards in national and local poetry contests between 1944 and 1959. She was a member of the National League of American Pen Women, American Poetry League, Poetry Society of Colorado, and Daughters of American Colonists. She married Walter Grant Spencer, and they had one son.

When Joseph Went to Bethlehem, page 38 (Words)

Spencer, Beverly Searle

LDS. 1921–   . Beverly Searle Spencer was born in Salt Lake City and graduated from the University of Utah with a degree in secondary education, majoring in physical education and speech. She taught in junior high schools in Salt Lake City and in California for several years, but further study took her into the field of early childhood education, and subsequently she taught in the Head Start program. She has assisted the Sunday School and Primary General Boards by writing and participating in presentations. She and her husband, Harold M. Spencer, are the parents of five sons.

The World Is So Big, page 235 (Words)

Sprunt, Lois Coombs

LDS. 1930–   . Lois Coombs Sprunt, who was born in Salt Lake City, Utah, attended Brigham Young University and the University of Utah where she received her B.A. degree in elementary education, after which she taught school for two years. She served a mission to the Eastern States. For several years she has been the writer and coordinator of the "Back to School Carnival" sponsored by the Salt Lake *Tribune* and the downtown merchants. She served on the Primary General Board for five years and as a member of the Child Correlation Review Committee. She has been a contributor to the *Friend* magazine. She and her husband, William John Sprunt, are the parents of nine children.

We Welcome You, page 256 (Words)

Steed, Sharon

LDS. 1935–   . Sharon Mann Steed was born in Salt Lake City, Utah, but spent her most impressionable years in Flowell, Utah, where her father was a farmer. Her mother was very musical, and taught Sharon how to sing and perform at an early age. She studied voice and piano and has continued to involve herself in musical pursuits. She attended Weber State College and graduated from Excelsis Beauty School. While her children were in the home, she taught piano and voice lessons, but later was employed as secretary of the Ogden City Schools, a position she held for sixteen years. She has sung with the Weber State College Symphonic Choir for twenty-two years. She has composed a number of children's songs that her friends and family have sung over the years. She is married to Dale J. Steed, and they have three children.

A Special Gift Is Kindness, page 145 (Words and Music)

Stevens, Rebecca

No information available.

Fun to Do, page 253 (Words)

Stevenson, Robert Louis

1850–1894. Robert Louis Stevenson was born in Edinburgh, Scotland. He wrote some of the most celebrated poems, essays, and fiction of his time, and his works remain popular for young and old alike. His enduring works include *Treasure Island, Dr. Jekyll and Mr. Hyde, Kidnapped,* and a collection of poems, *A Child's Garden of Verses.* He was a master of description and had the ability to put life into his works. In search of a place where he could receive some relief from his lifelong health problems, he traveled to Samoa in 1888, where he remained until his death.

Thanks to Our Father, page 20 (Words)

Stratton, Beth Groberg

LDS. 1944–   . Beth Groberg Stratton was born in Idaho Falls, Idaho. She graduated from Brigham Young University with a B.A. in music and taught private piano for over fifteen years. She is a certified music teacher from the American College of Musicians. She is married to Barry Stratton, and they are the parents of four boys. The family resides in Auburn, Washington.

Children All Over the World, page 16 (Music)

Talbot, Nellie

No information available.

Jesus Wants Me for a Sunbeam, page 60 (Words)

Taylor, Daniel

No information available.

Smiles, page 267 (Words)

Taylor, Elizabeth Cushing

Elizabeth Taylor was a writer of children's poetry who published a number of her works. One of these was *Happiness to Share,* 1939, in which "God's Love" was included as a poem. This poem was also printed in *Picture Story Paper,* copyrighted by Stone and Pierce. No other information is available.

God's Love, page 97 (Words)

Taylor, Frances K.

LDS. 1870–1952. Frances Kingsbury Thomassen Taylor, born in Salt Lake City, was prominent in the Salt Lake Valley as an early childhood educator and songwriter. She attended the University of Utah and Columbia University to receive her musical education in piano, organ, harmony, and counterpoint. She became a member and secretary of the General Primary Association, where she served for eight years. She was the chairman of the educational committee of the Salt Lake Council of Women, member of the Women's Medical Auxiliary, and the treasurer of the Ladies Literary Club. Her songbook, *Kindergarten and Primary Songs,* was published by the Deseret Sunday School Union and used in many Jr. Sunday Schools of the Church. She married Olaf Thomassen, who was killed in an automobile accident, and later married Dr. Alfred H. Taylor.

Daddy's Homecoming, page 210 (Music)

Help Me, Dear Father, page 99 (Words and Music)
The Dearest Names, page 208 (Words and Music)

Tchaikovsky, Peter Ilich

1840–1890. Peter Ilich Tchaikovsky was born in Russia and has become known as one of Russia's greatest symphonic composers. As a young man, Tchaikovsky studied law in St. Petersburg and then worked for three years as a clerk in the Department of Justice. In 1866 he became professor of harmony at the Moscow Conservatory. He was greatly discouraged when his first compositions were not well received. A brief unhappy marriage in 1877 discouraged him even more, and he had a nervous breakdown. Later he was able to give up his teaching and concentrate on composing. In 1880 he wrote the *1812 Overture* celebrating the defeat of Napoleon in Russia and the completion of the Temple of Christ in Moscow. In the year before his death, Tchaikovsky composed the popular *Nutcracker Suite.*

Morning Prayer, page 292 (Music)

Thayne, Mirla Greenwood

LDS. 1907–   . Mirla Greenwood Thayne was born in Midvale, Utah. As a young girl she expressed a great love of music and was able to sit at the piano and create melodies and harmonies. She began composing songs as she was asked to prepare music and programs. She has had a number of songs and books published and has won state and national awards for her articles, music, books, stories, and poetry. She was elected to the Writer's Hall of Fame of the League of Utah Writers and is a member of several literary and music groups, including the National League of American Pen Women, ASCAP, League of Utah Writers, Utah State Poetry Society, National Federation of State Poetry Societies, American Poetry Society, and Composer's Guild. She has said to children, "Do you know that in your wonderful brain is a tiny recorder that records and holds tight to the music you hear? Beautiful music comes from our Heavenly Father and is given to you to inspire you and lead you closer to Him." Sister Thayne and her husband have four children and many grandchildren and great-grandchildren.

When He Comes Again, page 82 (Words and Music)

Thomas, Norma Madsen

LDS. 1908–1988. Born in Lakeview, Utah, Norma Madsen Thomas was recognized as a talented poet from age ten. She wrote more than 200 poems during her lifetime, centered on faith, family, and love of life. Though her life was filled with difficulties, she was hard-working, determined, and able to persevere to accomplish much. Most of all she loved children and enjoyed writing poems and songs for them. She and her husband, Myron Thomas, served a mission to San Antonio, Texas. She raised six children of her own and a son from her husband's first marriage.

Two Happy Feet, page 270 (Words)

Turner, Nancy Byrd

Episcopalian. 1880–   . Nancy Byrd was a writer, editor, and lecturer who was born in Boydton, Virginia, the daughter of an Episcopalian pastor. She was educated at Hannah Moore Academy in Maryland. She was the editor of the children's page of the *Youth's Companion* for many years and wrote several children's books, including *Zodiac Town, Adventures of Ray Coon,* and *Magpie Lane.* She contributed to magazines in America and England and was a member of the New England Poetry Society and the Boston Authors Club. She worked on the editorial staff of the *Boston Independent,* and later on that of Houghton-Mifflin Co. Miss Turner was never married but showed great understanding and love for children through her writings.

Stars Were Gleaming, page 37 (Words)

Twitchell, Royce Campbell

LDS. 1939–   . Royce Campbell Twitchell was born in San Jose, California, lived in Utah from 1960 to 1987, and has since resided in New York City. At the age of eleven she decided that she was going to be a professional accompanist and worked to make this a reality. She took every piano assignment offered to her, first playing for Primary at age twelve. She has been an accompanist for the Sacramento Music Circus, for the Valley Music Hall in North Salt Lake, at Brigham Young University, and at the University of Utah, and has been the musical director at Promised Valley Playhouse and the Triad Theatre in Salt Lake City. She was a coach-accompanist for the Utah Opera Company for a number of years, accompanist for the Utah Oratorio Society, and now is pianist and accompanist on Broadway. She married Noel Twitchell, and they are the parents of three adopted daughters.

Did Jesus Really Live Again?, page 64 (Music)

Tyler, Walter G.

1855–1933. The *American Literary Yearbook*, 1919, indicates that "Walter G. Taylor (Tyler)" was the pen name used by Adam Geibel. Adam Geibel was a composer and organist born near Frankfort-on-Main, Germany. As an infant he lost his sight through the application of an eyewash prescribed by mistake. At an early age he displayed musical inclinations, playing tunes on the piano that he had heard itinerant musicians play in his little town. He immigrated to Philadelphia with his parents when seven years old and lived in that area most of his life. He studied harmony, counterpoint, orchestration, and composition and became a musical director at Temple University. He founded the Adam Geibel Music Company, a music publishing house. Dr. Geibel composed hundreds of cantatas and part songs for men and women, as well as Sunday School songs. These include "Stand Up, Stand Up for Jesus," "Let the Gospel Light Shine Out," and the popular ballad "Kentucky Babe." At the time of his death in 1933 he had composed about 3,000 works. Several of his compositions for children appeared in the early editions of the *Primary Songbook*. Adam Geibel wrote the music to "Behold! a Royal Army," which is included in the 1985 LDS hymnbook; "Called to Serve" also appears in the hymnbook.

Called to Serve, page 174 (Music)

Watkins, Vanja Y.

LDS. 1938–   . Vanja Yorgason Watkins, who was born in Ogden, Utah, was introduced to the joy of music as a child — her family loved to sing songs and hymns in harmony without accompaniment. She graduated from Brigham Young University with B.A. and M.A. degrees in music education and became television teacher and music coordinator in the primary grades for the Ogden City schools. She served as a member of the Primary General Board from 1963 to 1970, on the General Church Music Committee, and as director of several children's choruses in the Salt Lake Tabernacle. She served on the Hymnbook Executive Committee for the 1985 hymnbook and as a musical consultant in the early preparation for the *Children's Songbook.* Two of her hymns, "Press Forward, Saints" and "Families Can Be Together Forever," appear in the LDS hymnbook. She has taught music education at Brigham Young University and conducted workshops on teaching music to children. She is serving as a music specialist in the Salt Lake public schools. She married Jack B. Watkins, and they are the parents of five children.

Easter Hosanna, page 68 (Words and Music)
Families Can Be Together Forever, page 188 (Music)
For Thy Bounteous Blessings, page 21 (Arrangement)
I Want to Be Reverent, page 28 (Music)
I Will Be Valiant, page 162 (Words and Music)
I Will Follow God's Plan, page 164 (Words and Music)
It's Autumntime, page 246 (Arrangement)
Latter-day Prophets, page 134 (Music)
Thank Thee for Everything, page 10 (Words)
The Articles of Faith, pages 122–132 (Music)
The Sacrament, page 72 (Words and Music)
The Things I Do, page 170 (Music)
This Is My Beloved Son, page 76 (Music)
To Be a Pioneer, page 218 (Arrangement)
Truth from Elijah, page 90 (Words and Music)

Weston, Rebecca

Rebecca Weston has written children's poetry that appears in several collections. The poem "Father, We Thank Thee for the Night" was printed in *My Little Book of Prayers and Graces,* London, 1964, a Rutledge Book. Some of her poems have been set to music. No other information is available.

Father, We Thank Thee for the Night, page 8 (Words)

Wheelwright, Lorin F.

LDS. 1909–1987. Lorin F. Wheelwright, who was born in Ogden, Utah, took piano lessons as a small boy, and at about age ten he became pianist for the Jr. Sunday School. He earned a B.A. degree in music from the University of Utah, an M.A. in educational psychology at the University of Chicago, and a doctorate from Columbia University, financing his education largely by playing piano and organ. His first teaching positions were in Sandy and Cedar City, Utah, and at Oswego State Teacher's College in New York, but he returned to Utah in 1937 to be music supervisor for the Salt Lake City schools. Brother Wheelwright was a member of the Sunday School General Board for thirteen years, and chairman and associate editor of the *Instructor* magazine. He was a member of the Utah Symphony Board and the Utah Legislative Council. In 1967 he was named dean of the College of Fine Arts and Communication at Brigham Young University and served for three years as assistant to President Dallin Oaks. He directed the University's centennial celebration and was presented the BYU Alumni Association's Distinguished Service Award in 1975. He was president of Wheelwright Lithography Co., Wheelwright Press, and Pioneer Music Press. Lorin Wheelwright wrote three hymns, words and music, that appear in the LDS hymnbook. He and his wife, Ila Spilsbury, are the parents of four children.

Mother, I Love You, page 207 (Words and Music)

White, Marilyn Curtis

LDS. 1941–   . Marilyn Curtis White, who was born in Washington, D.C., and has lived in Hawaii, California, and Utah, is a freelance writer of essays, short stories, poetry, and articles. She received a B.S. in journalism and an M.A. in American history at Brigham Young University. She was editor for the magazine *Asia Pacific Defense Forum* and has had an essay published in *Mormon Women Speak.* She is a resource chairperson for the American Association of Women. She is married to Weston J. White, and they have eight children.

Little Jesus, page 39 (Words)

Wilton, Arthur

Arthur Wilton's song "Be Happy!" was copyrighted in 1914 by Hall-Mack Company. No other information is available.

Be Happy!, page 265 (Music)

Wolford, Darwin

LDS. 1936–   . Darwin Wolford, who was born and raised in Logan, Utah, is one of the most widely published composers in the Church. He did undergraduate work at the University of Utah and at Utah State University and graduated from USU with a B.A., a Master of Music, and a Ph.D. in organ and composition. Between 1956 and 1967 Darwin Wolford served as a field representative for the General Church Music Committee and taught classes in beginning conducting and organ playing in stakes throughout the western United States. He has taught in the music department at Ricks College, where he is currently Director for Organ Studies and Coordinator of Theory. His compositions include works for chorus, orchestra, piano, and organ, and have been performed by the Utah Symphony and the Mormon Tabernacle Choir. His organ method book, *Organ Studies for the Beginner,* is published in Japanese as well as English. He is listed in the *International Who's Who in Music.* Brother Wolford served on the 1985 Hymnbook Executive Committee and also made an enormous contribution to the *Children's Songbook* as he reviewed, edited, and arranged music for this publication. He and his wife, Julie Lofgren, are the parents of five children.

Beautiful Savior, page 62 (Arrangement)
Had I Been a Child, page 80 (Music)
I Am a Child of God, page 2 (Arrangement)
I Have a Family Tree, page 199 (Music)
In Quietude, page 291 (Music)
Keep the Commandments, page 146 (Arrangement)
Mary's Lullaby, page 44 (Arrangement)
Our Chapel Is a Sacred Place, page 30 (Music)
Stars Were Gleaming, page 37 (Arrangement)
Supplication, page 297 (Music)

Wood, Lucile F.

Methodist. 1915–1986. Lucile F. Wood, a noted music educator and composer of children's music, was born in Deep River, Iowa. Her musical interest surfaced early, when she was barely old enough to reach the keys of the family's old pump organ. She took piano lessons, played for church services, and at fifteen played at the silent movies in her small town. She moved to California and graduated from UCLA. Her contributions to music education are significant: as editor, lecturer, author, and composer, and as associate professor of music at California State College in Los Angeles. She created over 150 multimedia aids to education, which were adopted as basic materials in schools throughout the United States, Canada, and some foreign countries. Among her published books are *The Bowman Orchestral Library, Meet the Instruments, The Small Musician Series, Symphonic Fantasies,* and *Rhythms to Reading. Singing Fun,* published by McGraw-Hill, has been a successful songbook for young children.

Appendix: A Brief History of Children's Music in the Church

On Sunday, August 25, 1878, Latter-day Saint children in Farmington, Utah, were gathered together for the first time in their own meeting of the newly organized Primary. Aurelia Rogers had been set apart two weeks earlier as the president of that first Primary. According to her journal, music was part of that gathering. She says, "At first the children were very timid about singing; Brother Joseph E. Robinson came in a few times and assisted in starting them. Finally their voices rang out sweet and clear, and in some cases much talent was displayed."

Two years later Eliza R. Snow compiled *Hymns and Songs: Selected from various authors, for the Primary Associations of the children of Zion*, published by Deseret News Printing and Publishing, 1880. This little songbook contained 121 pages of songs with words only. Many of them were identified only by number, but some titles were included. Some of the early hymns of the Church were incorporated into this publication, such as "In Our Lovely Deseret," "Do What Is Right," "O My Father," "The Spirit of God," and "Joseph Smith's First Prayer." Also included were a number of children's songs, some of which have survived to be part of the *Children's Songbook*: "I Thank Thee, Dear Father," "Child's Desire" ("I Think When I Read That Sweet Story"), "All Things Bright and Beautiful," "Dare to Do Right," and "Christmas Cradle Song." The melodies suggested to go with these verses, however, are not the ones that are sung today. This book of songs was republished in at least two further editions.

Also prepared by Eliza R. Snow was the *Tune Book for the Primary Associations of the Children of Zion* (Salt Lake City: Juvenile Instructor Office, 1880). Aurelia Rogers reports of this publication, "She (Eliza R. Snow) engaged Mrs. Doctor Ferguson to arrange the music for the songs, which was called the *Tune Book*." This book contained forty pages of songs with words and music; a cross-reference list in the front indicated which melodies could also be sung with the verses in *Hymns and Songs*. Sometimes several verses were recommended for the same tune.

Within a few years Primary organizations had sprung up in many wards of the Church. A general Primary president, Louie B. Felt, was called in 1880, and a Primary General Board was organized. As this group of women devoted their thoughts and energies to the children, more consideration was given to music for the little ones. Under the board's direction, *The Primary Song Book* (Salt Lake City: The General Board of the Primary Associations, 1905) was produced with words and music together. It contained ninety-three songs, some new and some from *Hymns and Songs.*

The Primary General Board continued over the years to update their songbook. Editions of *The Primary Song Book,* including marches and voluntaries, were published with dates of 1920, 1924, 1927, 1935, 1939, 1941, 1946, and 1948. With each new edition some songs were added and some deleted, and organizational changes were made. However, each of these songbooks had the same general appearance, except for color changes on the cover.

Of course, in those days the Primary was not the only Church organization that dealt with children. In the early 1900s, the *Deseret Sunday School Song Book* was published by the Deseret Sunday School Union. This book of songs was intended to be used primarily for the Sunday School, but was also suitable for Primary. A few of the songs now in the *Children's Songbook* first appeared in this book. It was reprinted several times and was used into the 1930s.

In 1940 the Deseret Sunday School Union prepared and published a collection of songs for younger children titled *Little Stories in Song.* Moiselle Renstrom and Frances K. Taylor, Latter-day Saint musicians and educators for early childhood, were major contributors to this volume, and many of their pieces that appear now in the *Children's Songbook* were first printed here. Also included in *Little Stories in Song* were these *Children's Songbook* pieces: "All Things Bright and Beautiful" (titled "God's Work" and accompanied by a different tune), "Once Within a Lowly Stable" (titled "Christmas Night"), "Father, We Thank Thee for the Night" (different tune), and "Little Lambs So White and Fair."

The next major revision in the songbooks for children of the Church came with the printing of *The Children Sing* in 1951. This book was published by Deseret Book Company and copyrighted by the LDS Church. It was "designed for children everywhere, but primarily prepared for use of children of the Junior Sunday School and Primary organizations." In the Preface it states that "The book has been prepared under the direction of the First Presidency by a joint committee from the Deseret Sunday School and Primary Association general boards, in cooperation with the General Music Committee." One hundred ninety-nine songs were included, along with thirteen musical selections under the heading "Instrumental Devotional Music."

Eighteen years later, in 1969, *Sing with Me* was published by Deseret Book Company. The possibility of a new songbook for children had been discussed by the Primary leaders for more than ten years, since several new favorite songs had been composed and were available only in sheet-music form. In 1967 the work of preparing the new songbook began in earnest. The Primary music committee selected, as a nucleus, worthy and appropriate songs from *The Children Sing*, the *Children's Friend*, Primary music kits, Primary programs, old Primary songbooks, school music texts, and books of children's songs. The committee conducted a survey of 150 stakes to determine the children's favorite songs, using the results as a guide in the selection process.

At this time the General Church Music Committee recommended that the proposed songbook be correlated to include the needs of the Jr. Sunday School. A correlation committee was organized with representatives from the General Music Committee, the Sunday School, and the Primary.

Through the *Church News* an invitation was issued to all who were interested in submitting songs. Hundreds were received from all over the world, including South Africa, Scotland, England, and many states in the United States. Several of these were included in the final printing. In addition, since there were few songs available on some gospel subjects, about fifteen well-known LDS composers were invited to write songs on assigned topics, such as baptism, the Word of Wisdom, temples, and the priesthood. Many responded with not just one song but several.

Sing with Me was planned, organized, and constructed with the intention of updating it periodically. However, this did not happen. Instead, additions to the music for the children were made with the printing of supplemental songbooks: *Activity Songs and Verses* in 1977, *More Songs for Children* in 1978, and *Supplement to More Songs for Children* in 1982. These did not replace *Sing with Me* but were used as companions to it.

How the *Children's Songbook* Came to Be

Dwan J. Young was called as the general Primary president in 1980. The consolidated meeting schedule was implemented about this time, with an extended time for Primary on Sunday; children no longer attended Jr. Sunday School. Under President Young's direction, new lesson manuals (which had been commenced while Naomi M. Shumway was president) were completed for all of the Primary classes. Several new class songs were also written, so the Primary presidency requested the publication of a music supplement to include the Primary class songs and a few other well-known children's songs. General priesthood advisors to the Primary gave permission for this project, with the admonition that the Primary should begin to prepare a consolidated music book of the songs from all the resources that were then being used: *Sing with Me* and its three supplements, song pages in the *Friend,* and songs that had been published in Primary programs. Since the purpose of the new songbook was primarily to bring together all the existing resources under one cover, a general invitation for new music was not extended to the members of the Church.

A survey was carried out for the Primary by the Correlation Evaluation Committee of the Church and completed in the early part of 1983. In this survey, all the children's songs were evaluated by Primary presidencies and music leaders in many sections of the United States and a few other countries. The songs were rated as to (1) those most frequently sung, (2) those most familiar to the children, and (3) the children's favorites. The results of the survey helped determine, along with other important criteria, the songs to be retained and those to be dropped.

A tracking form was prepared for each song. On this form the accumulated comments from the general Primary presidency, the Primary music committee, the General Church Music Committee, and from an ad hoc committee were entered. These people represented a wide range of expertise and understanding of children's music, from the Church Music Committee who had a deep understanding of quality music, to the ad hoc committee who worked directly with children in teaching the songs. All these people sang through, analyzed, noted suggested changes, and rated every song. From their evaluations and from the results of the songbook survey, lists of songs were made. A song was included when:

1. It received a high rating on the songbook survey and from the committees who evaluated the songs.

2. There was a need for the subject of the text in the children's resources. (Most sacramental songs, for example, were deleted, since the sacrament was no longer served in the children's meetings.)

3. Music was of high quality and melodically and harmonically correct.

4. The message or text was doctrinely accurate, poetically sound, and meaningful to the children.

5. The words and music were unified in mood and purpose.

It was determined that the songbook should contain a few songs for parents, teachers, or leaders to sing relating to their responsibility to teach children. Also, there was a need to provide a section of easy-to-play prelude music that carried a spiritual quality into the children's meetings.

The songs that were selected to be included in the *Children's Songbook* were carefully analyzed and critiqued by musical and lyrical specialists. Some changes in words or music were made for the following reasons:

1. To present a message that was doctrinely accurate. For example, some words were changed and some verses deleted that seemed to indicate that we pray to the Lord Jesus Christ. The Correlation Review Committee of the Church examined all the lyrics for accuracy.

2. To strengthen the music in harmonic or melodic structure.

3. To match the natural word emphasis with the strong beats of the music.

4. To simplify the accompaniment for less experienced pianists, without destroying the essential and desirable harmony.

5. To include changes that composers or authors wanted to make in their music or words.

6. To place the melody in a more singable range for the children. Several songs were transposed down a note or two and a few were raised in pitch.

7. To identify songs by an appropriate title. A title change might have been made to provide an easier identification for the song, or because there were other songs with similar or identical titles.

Some new melodies or lyrics were written when the copyrights were expensive or difficult to obtain. For example, new words were written to the melody of "Mary's Lullaby" since the former lyrics were under copyright that required a heavy price. The music was in public domain.

The committees responsible for the songbook studied many possibilities for organizing and dividing the songs into sections. The suggestion was made that the first section of the book be titled "My Heavenly Father" and include a number of songs previously grouped with prayer songs and songs of the gospel. This section title felt right and seemed to dictate a natural flow of section titles that followed. This also made it possible to have the first song in the book be the favorite "I Am a Child of God."

The second section, appropriately the one about the Savior, begins with "He Sent His Son," which introduces the important mission of Jesus Christ. The section continues with songs about his birth, his life on the earth, his death and resurrection, why we want to be like him, and ends with the song "When He Comes Again."

The third and largest section, "The Gospel," includes songs about many gospel subjects. They are arranged in a logical sequence, with like topics together. The section begins with songs about the restoration of the gospel, then songs of the priesthood, genealogy and temple work, first principles of the gospel, scriptures, Church leaders, the commandments, missionary work, and a few songs appropriate for leaders.

The other five sections — Home and Family, Heritage (including some universal patriotic songs), Nature and Seasons, Fun and Activity, and Prelude Music — are also presented in a logical order by subject. The prelude section consists of thirteen simple but beautiful pieces, several from the masters, grouped according to key signature to allow the pianist to play continuously from one piece to another. Each section has its own color of border and begins with a beautiful two-page art piece.

The typesetting and printing of the music for the songbook were notable for the new achievements in musical typesetting that had been developed by this department of the Church. Many new and time-efficient procedures had evolved during the production of the 1985 edition of *Hymns*, and this experience proved most valuable in preparing the *Children's Songbook* with skill and proficiency.

Most of the people who worked on the songbook project did so on a "Church-service" basis, giving their time and efforts without remuneration. Also instrumental in producing the *Children's Songbook* were full-time employees of the departments of copyrights and permissions, graphics design, editing, musical typesetting, printing services, and those associated with the production coordination and distribution departments. Most of the composers and authors of the songs gave their words and music without charge. A few songs were taken from other publications that required a copyright charge, but many of the songs were written specifically for the children of the LDS Church and were given with no strings attached.

The value of children's music in the Church is summarized well by this quotation from one of the contributing authors to the

Children's Songbook, Ruth Muir Gardner: "Some of my closest friends are the songs I have learned in Primary. These songs have helped me to understand the gospel and to remember to live the way my Heavenly Father wants me to live. They cheer me up when I am sad, they prepare me for prayer, they even help me to rest when I feel restless. I hope these songs are your best friends, too. If we memorize the songs, we will be able to sing them for the rest of our lives, and they will help us to always do the right thing."

Children's Songs in the 1985 LDS Hymnbook

Several well-known children's songs were chosen to be printed in the 1985 edition of *Hymns*. It was determined that, since the hymnbook was readily available to Primary music leaders, only those songs that could be presented with a different musical arrangement would be repeated in the *Children's Songbook*. Primary music leaders can choose which arrangement they will teach the children for songs that are presented in both these sources. The following songs appear in the 1985 LDS hymnbook; those that are also printed in the *Children's Songbook* are noted.

Title	Hymn No.	Children's Songbook Page No.
Called to Serve	249	174
Families Can Be Together Forever	300	188
God's Daily Care	306	—
I Am a Child of God	301	2
I Know My Father Lives	302	5
In Our Lovely Deseret	307	—
Keep the Commandments	303	146
Love One Another	308	136
Teach Me to Walk in the Light	304	177
The Light Divine	305	—

New Songs in the *Children's Songbook*

Most of the 255 songs in the *Children's Songbook* were taken from the previous children's songbooks, from past issues of the *Friend* magazine, and from Primary programs printed by the Church. The following songs in the *Children's Songbook* are new additions to LDS children's music, some of which were written specifically for the new songbook.

*Printed in the *Friend* after being selected for the *Children's Songbook*

Songs with Title Changes

Like Sunshine in the Morning	203	My Mother Dear
Loving Care	229	God Is Watching Over All
Lord, We Thank Thee	24	Thank Thee, Father
My Heavenly Father Wants Me to Be Happy	18	I Need My Heavenly Father
My Prayer	23	Heavenly Father, While I Pray
Our Easter Song	65	He Died That We Might Live Again
Our Savior's Love	73	Help Us, O God, to Understand
Pioneer Children	214	Pioneer Children Sang as They Walked
Quiet Song	27	We Are Reverent
Thanks for Our World	10	Thank Thee for Everything
Thanksgiving Round	21	For Health and Strength
The Family Tree	199	I Have a Family Tree

Previous Printings of Songs

Songs appearing in the *Children's Songbook* that were printed in early editions of *The Primary Song Book* are as follows:

Title	First Year Printed
Autumn Day	1939
All Things Bright and Beautiful	1905 (music different)
Be Happy	1920
Beauty Everywhere	1927
Called to Serve	1920
Can a Little Child Like Me?	1920
Child's Desire (I Think When I Read That Sweet Story)	1905 (music different until 1939 edition)
*Christmas Cradle Song (Oh, Hush Thee, My Baby)	1905
Dare to Do Right	1905
"Give," Said the Little Stream	1920
Hand Exercise Song (Roll Your Hands)	1905
How Do You Do (In the Leafy Treetops)	1939
I'll Be a Sunbeam (Jesus Wants Me for a Sunbeam)	1927

I Thank Thee, Dear Father	1905
*Jesus Once Was a Little Child	1905
Jesus, Unto Thee I Pray (Heavenly Father, Now I Pray)	1905
Lord, We Thank Thee (Thank Thee, Father)	1920
*Shine On	1905
Smiles	1939
*Stand for the Right	1939
Tell Me, Dear Lord	1920
Two Little Hands (I Have Two Little Hands)	1920
When We're Helping	1939

*Also in the *Deseret Sunday School Songbook*

Top-rated Songs in the 1983 Music Survey

Familiar Songs

1. I Am a Child of God
2. Book of Mormon Stories
3. Popcorn Popping
4. The Golden Plates
5. Smiles
6. Jesus Wants Me for a Sunbeam
7. Reverently, Quietly
8. Happy, Happy Birthday
9. "Give," Said the Little Stream
10. A Happy Family
11. Families Can Be Together Forever
12. Jesus Said Love Everyone

Favorite Songs

1. Popcorn Popping
2. I Am a Child of God
3. Book of Mormon Stories
4. The Golden Plates
5. Smiles
6. Families Can Be Together Forever
7. Do As I'm Doing
8. Jesus Wants Me for a Sunbeam
9. I Hope They Call Me on a Mission

10. The Chapel Doors
11. "Give," Said the Little Stream
12. A Happy Family

Frequently Sung Songs

1. I Am a Child of God
2. Book of Mormon Stories
3. Popcorn Popping
4. Reverently, Quietly
5. The Golden Plates
6. Happy, Happy Birthday
7. Families Can Be Together Forever
8. Jesus Said Love Everyone
9. The Chapel Doors
10. Kindness Begins with Me
11. "Give," Said the Little Stream
12. Smiles

Index to Titles and First Lines

This index lists the title of each song in bold print. When the first line of a song differs substantially from its title, it too is included in this index, in lighter type.